C. B. Segel

THE

Toscanini Legacy

ARTURO TOSCANINI

Born Parma, 25 March, 1867; died Riverdale, New York, 16 January, 1957

THE
Toscanini Legacy

A critical study of Arturo Toscanini's performances of

Beethoven, Verdi and other composers

by SPIKE HUGHES

SECOND ENLARGED EDITION

WITH 199 MUSICAL

ILLUSTRATIONS

Dover Publications, Inc., New York

Published in Canada by General Publishing Company, Ltd., 30 Lesmill Road, Don Mills, Toronto, Ontario.
Published in the United Kingdom by Constable and Company, Ltd., 10 Orange Street, London WC 2.

This Dover edition, first published in 1969, is an unabridged, corrected and enlarged republication of the work first published in 1959 by Putnam & Company Ltd., London. A new *Preface, Supplement, Table of Original and Current Record Numbers,* and *Index* have been added.

Standard Book Number: 486-22100-8
Library of Congress Catalog Card Number: 79-81300

Manufactured in the United States of America
Dover Publications, Inc.
180 Varick Street
New York, N.Y. 10014

In Memoriam

HYAM GREENBAUM

(1901–1942)

Musician

❧CONTENTS❧

❧PREFACE TO THE SECOND EDITION❧

IT is now over ten years since Toscanini died, and my desire to preserve for posterity his unparalleled legacy of recorded performances continues. This desire was what first prompted me to write this book and I wish I could say, in looking at the record catalogues, that the situation was really satisfactory. It isn't. Nothing like the same number of recordings is available in today's RCA-Victor English catalogue, for instance, as there was on the HMV label in 1958. Far too much has disappeared—Verdi's *La Traviata*, *Un ballo in maschera*, and *Te Deum*; Puccini's *La Bohème*; Cherubini's Symphony and Requiem; the two Mendelssohn symphonies. (A recording of the *Midsummer Night's Dream* scherzo has at last re-appeared in the English lists and Beethoven's *Fidelio* is promised soon.)

There are signs, nevertheless, that things are improving a little; not only have we been getting records that have never been issued before, such as Berlioz's *Romeo and Juliet*, the Beethoven Fourth Piano Concerto with Rudolf Serkin, and the famous Philadelphia performance of the Schubert C major Symphony (though, alas, no new Verdi), but classic performances long out of the catalogues have been transferred to LP and issued on a low-priced label without loss of status. Having discovered that there is nothing to lose and everything to gain by making Toscanini's unique recorded performances more accessible, even without the benefit of stereo and other electronic conceits, the authorities are beginning to see that it could be to everybody's advantage to explore the possibilities of the Victrola label. In Italy, the seven records of Toscanini's complete Beethoven symphonies have been issued in a Victrola album by RCA-Italiana. A similar procedure has been followed in England, where I believe it is planned to use the same label for the re-issuing of records which have been missing since the switch to HMV, as well as for the preservation of those expensive classic recordings which will eventually have to be marked down in price. In the United States, an eight-record set of the nine symphonies and other selections is available.

I do not profess to understand the economics of the gramophone industry or the mentality of those thousands of its customers who are known to ask quite seriously why they should buy Toscanini's monaural *Falstaff* when they can get Mr Bernstein's in stereo for the same price, but if Toscanini's recordings are available at a lower price then what could be better? What is important here is not price so much as availability, and as far as this is concerned the European situation would be fairly desperate without the current RCA-Italiana list. This catalogue is remarkably comprehensive, lacking only very few of the important items that were available in Europe in 1958 (the Mendelssohn "Reformation" Symphony, Strauss' *Don Quixote*, some Wagner and a handful of recordings released posthumously in the last two or three years are missing). It does, on the other hand, contain three gems never yet issued in England—the 1953 Eroica broadcast, Tchaikovsky No 6 (listed under "C" for Ciaikovski, if you want to find it), and a transfer of the enchanting 78 rpm performance of Haydn's Symphony No 88.

Our local RCA list in England, as I have indicated, is not nearly so full as this, but in spite of our currency-restricted circumstances we have not as yet been prevented from ordering the Italian records through the many specialist gramophone shops. (The Italian catalogue numbers are the same as those in the United States, which is a welcome convenience to collectors.)

One great change has occurred in the past decade and that is that Toscanini's recordings are more and more officially presented, and instinctively accepted, as "Historic Performances". This has saved the industry the embarrassment of having to excuse any technical shortcomings of the actual recording and has made the critics concentrate on the records as musical performances and not as marvels of science. There has also, because of this changed attitude, been far less reference to the stop-watch in deciding whether a Toscanini performance of a certain symphony is necessarily worse than another Toscanini performance of the same work because it happens to be half a minute faster.

There is still a tendency to take it for granted that all Toscanini's later performances were much faster and, therefore,
musically less satisfying than his earlier ones. A glance at the
wonderfully detailed *Discography* of his father's records compiled
by Walter Toscanini in 1965, which includes the timing of every
single piece Toscanini recorded from the 1 minute 13 seconds
of *The Star Spangled Banner* to the 2 hours 14 minutes 47 seconds
of *Aida*, shows some surprising contradictions to this commonly
held theory. The classic recording of the Mendelssohn *Midsummer Night's Dream* scherzo made on a single side of a 78 with
the New York Philharmonic Orchestra in 1929 was a whole
quarter of a minute shorter than the record made in 1946—
4:05 against 4:20. The overture to *The Magic Flute* recorded
in 1938 was 6:35; in 1949 it was 6:50. The Schubert C major
Symphony of 1953 was 45:38; in 1947 it was 44:09—a difference of nearly a minute and a half. The first *Traviata* Prelude
in 1929 was 25 seconds shorter than in 1941—3:35 against
4:00.

Some of the Rossini overtures also offer interesting comparisons. The 1953 *William Tell* was 21 seconds longer than the
1939 recording, whereas there was a difference of only 2 seconds
between the 1936 (7:25) and 1950 (7:23) recordings of *L'Italiana
in Algeri*. The Brahms Tragic Overture in 1953 (13:45) was
1 minute and 20 seconds longer than in 1937 (12:25). But
perhaps the most unexpected examples are among the Mozart,
Haydn and Beethoven symphonies. The Mozart G minor was
22:42 in 1939—1:13 shorter than in 1950 when it was greatly
improved by being extended to 23:55; the Haydn "Clock"
Symphony, almost incredibly, was 48 seconds longer in 1947
than in 1929. But it is in Beethoven that the most spectacular
differences are to be noted. The Fourth Symphony of 1939,
with 30:08, was a modest 25 seconds slower than in 1951
(30:33); the Eighth improved on this with being 1:35 faster
in 1939 (23:53) than in 1952 (25:28). The prize, however,
goes to the Sixth Symphony, with a 1937 total of 37:52—no
less than 2:44 faster than the 40:36 of 1952. This was such a
remarkable difference that I wondered whether, in the later
version, Toscanini uncharacteristically made the repeat in the
first movement; he did not. It was just 2:44 longer, and that
was all. The most significant point of the whole thing was that

neither performance was a whit less convincing or enjoyable for being longer or shorter than the other. Both were still Beethoven's Sixth Symphony conducted by Toscanini.

I have referred to these timings in Walter Toscanini's *Discography* for no other reason than that they are a healthy reminder of the dangers of generalization. Music is not a matter of metronomes and stop-watches as so many would have us believe. Toscanini was as relaxed with the tempos of the 1937 Pastoral as he was with those of the slower 1952 performance. Significantly, the earlier, faster Beethoven Fourth and Sixth Symphonies, *The Magic Flute* overture and Tragic Overture, which I have mentioned, were all recorded with the BBC Symphony Orchestra—an orchestra with whom he was more noticeably and exceptionally at ease than with almost any other.

In the new Supplement, I have continued to follow the format of the first part of this book—namely, to make it a deliberately selective, critical study of what I consider the most important of Toscanini's performances. As before, my personal taste in music has inevitably influenced my selection, though omission does not necessarily indicate dislike, as is the case with *The Skaters Waltz*, *Stars and Stripes Forever*, and the overtures to *Zampa* and *Poet and Peasant*. It is just that they are, by their very nature, slightly irrelevant, particularly if they take the place of *La Traviata*, *Un ballo in maschera* and *La Bohème* in the catalogues.

RCA-Victor, as a tribute to the centenary of Toscanini's birth, has recently released an album of five records entitled *A Toscanini Treasury of Historic Broadcasts* (LM 6711). The set consists of ten works performed between 1940 and 1944, not all of which, however, are included in this study. The recordings of Toscanini's numberless broadcasts are, I imagine, likely to provide us with new material for some time to come, though, again, I hope it will not be at the expense of the unique, earlier masterpieces.

Perhaps what most needs organizing now is the publication of records of some of the Toscanini rehearsals, a service to posterity the gramophone is uniquely able to perform. Apart from those known to be in the BBC's Archives (an excerpt from a rehearsal of Beethoven's Seventh Symphony was broadcast during the 1967 centenary programmes), official tapes and acetates were made by NBC, among them the complete series of *Otello* rehearsals. The one record of this kind issued so far—the *Memorial Tribute to Arturo Toscanini*, sold to aid the Musicians Foundation—was a transfer of a broadcast narrated by Miss Marcia Davenport in 1959 and included bits of rehearsals of *The Magic Flute* overture, the last movement of the Ninth Symphony and *La Traviata*. I have been able to prepare a tape of this record without the commentary which, while I am sure it was necessary for the radio programme, is a sheer waste of the intelligent musician's time on a disk.

If any Toscanini rehearsal needs explaining, a printed transcript of what he says is all that is needed to accompany the record. My bootleg dubbing of a dubbing of an almost inaudible dubbing of a three-minute orchestral rehearsal of *Otello* told me more about Toscanini's methods, and the reasons for his rages (with first-class examples), than all Miss Davenport's well-meaning remarks on the extremely docile, almost genteel collection of rehearsal excerpts which made up her broadcast.

The publication of recordings of Toscanini's rehearsals is the one sphere in which it cannot be said that posterity is being properly served. Rehearsals by Bruno Walter and Pierre Monteux—long, generous sequences followed by a "take" of the music they were rehearsing—have been issued *commercially*. The only Toscanini rehearsal record was issued semi-privately —for the benefit of a worthy cause, certainly—but one couldn't go into a gramophone shop and buy a copy of it along with the Philadelphia Orchestra's recording of the Schubert C major Symphony. I have heard it suggested that it is Toscanini's children and grandchildren who refuse to allow the rehearsal records to be issued because the conductor is heard cursing and swearing. But that *was* Toscanini, who cursed and swore in the greatest and noblest of causes: the cause of the composers to whom he dedicated his whole prodigious, cursing and swearing musical life. His *furie*, just as much as his *carezze*, belong to posterity.

I would like to express my warmest thanks to Toscanini's son Walter for his help in the preparation of this additional section of *The Toscanini Legacy*. Mr Toscanini, who has been a regular and stimulating correspondent since he first read the original edition of this book and borrowed its title for his Thursday night programmes on WNYC, has been endlessly helpful in supplying me with new issues and acetate pressings of records not yet released. He has also kept me well posted about his own tireless propaganda for his father's records adding, from time to time, colourful little by-products like the prettily produced Toscanini catalogue in Japanese (I think I can now recognize the Japanese for "Toscanini", though it may well be "NBC Symphony Orchestra").

I would also like to thank Mr Michel J. Vermette, Manager, Artists Promotion of RCA-Victor in New York, and Mr Robert Angles, Manager of RCA-Victor Records in London whose co-operation entirely spared me the necessity of engaging in acrimonious arguments with Her Majesty's Customs.

One final note is necessary in reference to the record numbers in the text. The numbers which appeared in the first edition have not been changed; however, a Table of Original and Current Record Numbers has been prepared by Walter Toscanini, Arthur M. Fierro and Mel Schwartz to cast some light on the now complicated story of Toscanini's discography. With many of the original recordings being re-issued on various labels, it has grown increasingly difficult to pinpoint a specific recording. The Table lists all the recordings discussed in this book with the corresponding original and current British and American numbers. The complete discography of Toscanini's recordings in the U.S., compiled by Walter Toscanini, has been published by Radio Corporation of America (1966).

Ringmer,
Sussex
1969

⚜PREFACE TO THE FIRST EDITION⚜

FEAR is not one of the emotions commonly known to inspire the writing of a book; nevertheless it played a very real part in the writing of this one. My fear was—and still is—that in an age when it seems recording engineers have usurped the position of the impresarios of gramophone companies as arbiters of what the public shall and shall not be allowed to hear in the home, there might come a time when some trivial offence against the canons of the new and priest-ridden religion of High Fidelity would deprive us, on technical grounds the layman could not care less about, of irreplaceable musical experience.

This is particularly my fear for what I have called "The Toscanini Legacy". For some years past Toscanini recordings have been quietly disappearing from the catalogues, performances originally recorded at 78 rpm, and they have shown little sign of being transferred to LP. In addition to this we have, in England, just experienced the transfer of the rights of the Toscanini catalogue from one gramophone company to another, a commercial operation which may or may not prejudice our chances, and—more important—those of the next generation, of continuing to enjoy something unique in the history of music.

If my worst fears are ungrounded, so much the better; nonetheless, this book has been written to meet one or other of two possible eventualities: the survival of the Toscanini recordings or their complete disappearance. In the first eventuality this study is intended as a kind of companion to the recordings which have been saved from the scrap heap and a plea that something be done to make them permanently available to posterity—if necessary by passing an Act of Parliament or adding another Amendment to the American Constitution. In the second eventuality, I hope this book will do something to explain to an under-privileged posterity exactly what it was that made the art of Toscanini a unique and unforgettable experience.

For there is no doubt that Toscanini's contribution to music was unique. The gramophone has preserved the singing of Caruso and the violin playing of Kreisler, two artists of incomparable genius; but their greatness was to a large extent dependent on the exploitation of purely physical gifts with which ordinary singers and violinists are not always endowed. There is not much to be "learnt" from Caruso, and what Kreisler has to teach us about the interpretation of the classic concertos is a lesson only half-learned if we do not possess the physical means to put it into practice. But with Toscanini it is another matter. By its very nature the art of conducting is incomparably wider in its scope than singing or playing the violin (for good measure, of course, Toscanini's art threw in a little singing as well from time to time, for in some of his finest recordings the conductor may be heard singing as loud, if not quite so in tune, as Caruso), and with Toscanini it is also an art from which a great deal can be learnt by all but the most obstinately conceited of conductors and unimaginative of critics. Not the least of Toscanini's qualities, of course, was his artistic humility; but that is not a very infectious virtue at any time in any branch of music.

What can be more easily learnt from Toscanini, however, is his almost fanatical insistence on the importance of tempo, which was the keystone of his whole musical outlook, and his recognition, for instance, that Beethoven uses the instruction "Allegro vivace e con brio" at the beginning of the Eighth Symphony to mean what it says and not to suggest that the movement should be taken at the speed of a minuet. Perhaps Toscanini's interpretation of five common words in his mother tongue is simple and obvious, but it is surprising how difficult the simple and obvious are to achieve, and how more difficult still it is to perceive that the simple and obvious are, in fact, what was originally intended by the composer. Toscanini himself once remarked: "The oddest thing about conductors, even the best of them, is the way they will hold the score up to the light or turn it back to front. They're always looking for something which isn't there and never see what is." Unfortunately, being able to see what is in a score will not automatically make a Toscanini of anybody; but at least it may help a little towards it.

Now while this study does not aim to be a do-it-yourself manual of conducting I hope that the significance of some of the points I have drawn attention to in the course of it will not be altogether lost on the student. Although I can suggest something of the care of detail taken by Toscanini in his conducting, and in terms of simple metronomics perhaps indicate the tempo at which he took a movement, nobody on earth can show the would-be or even long-established conductor how to translate Toscanini's all-important tempo into *rhythm*. In conducting, the difference between an acceptable tempo and a rhythm which corresponds to the natural pulse coming from the heart of all great music is the difference between talent and genius; it is a gift of alchemy which, like Caruso's voice, is something you are born with. Nevertheless, if Toscanini's maxim that one should see what is there in a score and not look for what isn't, and his observation that "it is easy to play *a piacere*—the thing is to play *a tempo*" are properly respected we shall be a little nearer to raising the general standard of performance in whatever surroundings and circumstances music is made and whatever its nature.

It is a standard of performance which is perhaps the most valuable single item in Toscanini's legacy: a standard created partly by his own peculiar experience and education as a conductor, partly by the indefinable quality of genius—two factors which together combined to give an unparalleled authority and authenticity to his performances. Conductors of genius will doubtless occur again, but we in our generation will have enjoyed our own unique experience which no other conductor will ever be able to give us again: namely, the personal link provided by Toscanini's association with Verdi.

This association was not the kind of slender tie which inspired a delightful revue number many years ago about a girl who'd danced with a man who'd danced with a girl who'd danced with the Prince of Wales. Toscanini's association with Verdi was first-hand and dated from the time when, as a boy of nineteen, he filled the interval between seasons conducting at the Teatro Carignano in Turin, by applying for, and getting, the post of second violoncellist in the orchestra at La Scala in order to be able to play at the first performance there of Verdi's *Otello* in February, 1887. Thus, it is not just a sentimental thrill one may have, in listening to Toscanini's recording of *Otello*, to realize that in the famous seven bars for four solo violoncellos which introduce the love duet at the end of Act I, the second violoncello part was first played by Toscanini. To play in the orchestra at any Verdi première was to come directly under the musical influence of a composer who supervised, and indeed dominated, the pre-production period of his work far more than any conductor ever did. The young musician who had come to pay tribute to the ageing composer did not waste the opportunities for personal contact which the occasion provided, and so long as the composer lived Toscanini was permitted a peculiar and privileged access to Verdi which had a lasting effect on the conductor's understanding of his music.

If, at nineteen years of age, we find Toscanini sitting at the feet of the Master, it is less than ten years later, in 1896, that he is encountered in a position of tremendous authority conducting the first performance of a work which has proved one of the most universally popular in the whole operatic repertoire—*La Bohème*, by Puccini, which Toscanini lived to conduct and record on the fiftieth anniversary of its première in 1946.

To have played in the first performance of Verdi's greatest opera, *Otello*, to have conducted not only *La Bohème*, but also the first performance in 1926 of *Turandot*, Puccini's last and greatest opera too, and to have continued conducting for almost another thirty years after that, is a span of musical activity surely without equal; certainly nothing comparable to the fruit of this vast experience of nearly seventy years has so far been preserved for posterity as the music-making of Toscanini has been preserved by the gramophone.

Toscanini's recording career covered the years 1920 to 1954, and in that time he recorded some 180 works ranging from Beethoven's Mass in D to Sousa's *Stars and Stripes*. As this volume was never conceived as a "discography" of Toscanini the reader will not, I hope, expect reference to much more than a third of this stupendous repertoire. The remainder is either completely inaccessible, irrelevant to what I have called a "critical study", or both. For this study is selective and critical insofar as it is very much the result of a critic's prejudices. It is a study of the music Toscanini recorded in his lifetime which I personally think justifies and repays analysis and criticism and contributes most to the wealth of a remarkable musical testament. Music is unique among the arts in its power to inflict literally physical pain on the consumer, and there are limits, I find, to the extent to which critical objectivity can remain uninfluenced by personal taste. Those who admire the music of Brahms, Richard Strauss and Wagner will, I fear, find my short chapters dealing with Toscanini's performances of these composers' music unsympathetic and inadequate. But what is one to do when faced by a dish which one is sure is composed of the highest-grade ingredients, created and immortally christened "Pêche Melba" by the great Escoffier himself if one doesn't happen to like peaches with ice cream and raspberry sauce? All one can do is admire the artistry of the whole thing, and admit regretfully that owing to a palate beyond one's control one just doesn't like Pêche Melba.

And so it is with music. To have excluded Brahms, Strauss and Wagner altogether from this study merely because I dislike their music would have been dishonest, for my experience of Toscanini's performances certainly added to my knowledge of scores which he approached and illumined in a highly characteristic way. But not even Toscanini could stimulate in me an affection for music where none had existed before, or transform musical Pêche Melba into a food my palate could relish or my stomach retain.

If I am not concerned with "discography" still less am I concerned with Arturo for Arturo's sake. No doubt there was a public for Toscanini's recording of Gershwin's *American in Paris* and Ferdie Grofé's *Grand Canyon Suite*; but to me, who have a catholic taste in music which has become almost notorious and embarrassing, there have been few things in the history of recorded music a more criminal waste of time than the couple of days Toscanini spent in recording these two pieces of inflated salon music.

It is not just a question of what he might more profitably have recorded in the time, as of letting the side down with an unnecessarily jarring bump. Posterity, brought up like us to believe in Toscanini's unassailable "artistic integrity", will not want to know *how* he performed the works of Gershwin and Grofé; it will want to know *why*. There will be no answer.

The question of the mechanical quality and technical niceties of Toscanini's recordings is one which I propose to ignore, for the simple reason that I am not qualified to discuss it, and which, on the whole, I find is something irrelevant to the object of this book. Throughout all the years I have known Toscanini's recordings I have always been less anxious that the recorded sound of the oboe at the beginning of Beethoven's Seventh Symphony should be indistinguishable from a real live oboe than that the phrasing and tempo and whole musical significance of the passage should be indistinguishable from what Beethoven intended.

This is undoubtedly a heretical attitude to adopt in this electronic age, but it remains that whereas "High Fidelity" does not in itself make a performance worth listening to its absence does not necessarily mar it either. Thus not even the notoriously bad recording made by Toscanini of the Eroica in 1939, with its wooden acoustics, infuriating change-overs and coughing audience, could ever disguise the unapproachable "class" of the performance. "Class", in fact, will always come through, as it came through the acoustic records of Caruso and will continue to come through the records of Toscanini when they are eventually compared with whatever miracles of recording the future may offer. Consequently I shall not hesitate from time to time in this study to refer to Toscanini recordings made as long ago as 1929. My generation learned from them when they were first issued, and anybody may continue to learn from them today, tomorrow and the next day—if not from the long-deleted records themselves, at least, I hope, from my analysis of them. But with any luck, as a counterpart of the three Caruso LP records issued in the series, "The Golden Treasury of Immortal Performances", it will sooner or later be seen fit to issue a collection of no less immortal performances of the pre-hi-fi Toscanini—even if, once again, it needs an Act of Parliament or an Amendment of the Constitution to get it done.

From time to time in the course of this study I have recalled one or two incidents in Toscanini's working life inasmuch as they bear some relation to the music he has left behind him. These incidents occurred many years ago during his orchestral rehearsals at the Queen's Hall in London, when I made notes in an old exercise book of what I heard and saw. On the face of things it may appear that to recall near-anecdotal events which happened so long ago can have little bearing on music that Toscanini recorded some time afterwards. But one of

Toscanini's greatest qualities was always his consistency, his repeated striving to make each performance of a work more convincing and "right" than the previous one. As a result I have found that the effect of the concentrated attention Toscanini gave to two particular phrases in Beethoven's Ninth Symphony which I remember at a 1939 rehearsal is as powerful and noticeable as ever in the recording of the work, although more than fifteen years separated the two occasions.

We cannot tell, and in any case it serves no purpose to contemplate whether or not Toscanini can rank as the "greatest" conductor who ever lived. He did a number of things superbly, uniquely well; he did a surprising number of things quite remarkably badly, and there were still other things in which he never began to rival his great contemporary, Bruno Walter (whom the gramophone has unaccountably not treated very generously, for there is no such thing, so far as I know, as a Walter recording of a complete Mozart opera). What is certain, however, is that the history of the gramophone can point to no greater conductor to whom it has done comparable justice.

The Toscanini Legacy, as I have suggested, is something without parallel in the history of music. Those things which the conductor did well, particularly his Beethoven and his Verdi, have set a standard of what can only be described as "re-creation" of great music which should be an inspiration and a yardstick for generations to come. The things he did badly will serve a purpose no less, for they are almost cautionary tales of how far some music can be so misunderstood as to be apparently not understood at all. Perhaps it is one of the signs of greatness in an artist that we can learn from his mistakes and failures as well as from his masterpieces. There is certainly no doubt that from time to time in his phenomenal career, Toscanini gave some superbly instructive lessons in How Not To Do It. I have deliberately cited one or two instances of his misunderstanding of music in this book, because they are typical and important facets of the total musical character revealed in his recordings. They prove, too, that in spite of the unthinking *toscaniniani* whose adulation of the Maestro can be so damagingly, indiscriminately whole-hearted, Toscanini was as human in his weaknesses as the great composers to whom he devoted his life.

That Toscanini will prove to be one of the immortals of

music I think there is little doubt. He became a legend in his lifetime; his legacy of recordings at least will substantiate most of what was said in praise of him. It is up to us now to see that what we have inherited from him is recognized and preserved as a tremendous manifestation of a spirit of passionate devotion to music and untiring pursuit of perfection in its execution which must not be lost to posterity.

There will never be another Arturo Toscanini.

Ringmer,
Sussex
1958

The author wishes to thank

THE GRAMOPHONE COMPANY for their help and co-operation for nearly a quarter of a century in making available to me so many of the recordings which are the subject of this study; MESSRS. G. RICORDI AND CO., LTD., for permission to quote from the scores of *Otello*, *Falstaff*, *La Bohème* and Verdi's *Requiem*; HAROLD C. SCHONBERG, American Correspondent of *The Gramophone*, for his advice and assistance; JERRY THORPE, of RCA-VICTOR, for sending me many Toscanini recordings which were unobtainable in England while I was writing this book.

JOHANN SEBASTIAN BACH

✠[1685–1750]✠

IT may appear a little eccentric to begin this study of Toscanini's performances with a composer whose music— with the exception of the so-called *Air on the G String*—he apparently never recorded and which he did not greatly care for. But while comparatively few people ever heard Toscanini conduct Bach (I must have been one of a very small company which ever heard him conduct both the only two Brandenburg Concertos he ever performed), there was nevertheless something in the experience worth recording.

The last time I heard Toscanini conduct Bach made so little impression on me that I have had to consult the archives to remember the work and the occasion. It proves to have been a performance of the second Brandenburg Concerto in F which was included in the programme of the London Music Festival of 1938. Five years earlier, in 1933 in New York, however, I heard Toscanini conduct a Brandenburg Concerto which has remained a memorable experience. I will not pretend that it was an experience of tremendous elation; but it was something unexpected, very much more satisfying than I had ever heard before and very characteristic of Toscanini. Also, the two performances I heard Toscanini give seem to have been the only two performances he ever gave in his life of Bach's Sixth Brandenburg.

Perhaps of all the six Brandenburgs the last, in B flat, is the one most suited to Toscanini's temperament and which I wish the performers of Bach in this country—who alternate between an unintelligible gabbling on the one hand and a dry pedestrianism on the other—could have heard him play. Two aspects of this Concerto clearly had a strong appeal for Toscanini. First, the instrumentation for violas, violoncellos and basses, which is "different" and colourful, and in itself was something to intrigue Toscanini's highly developed feeling for orchestral colouring. The instrumentation also set a problem which I think appealed to Toscanini's mentality: the problem of making such an uncompromisingly "dark" collection of instruments give clarity to complicated six-part counterpoint.

The second aspect of the Sixth Brandenburg Concerto which I feel must have attracted Toscanini to the work was also purely physical: the delight in the rhythms of the first and third movements. The insistent eight-in-a-bar of the first Allegro became so infectious in Toscanini's performance that if the audience didn't start actually rocking in the aisles of Carnegie Hall, it indulged in a lot of automatically reflexed foot-tapping just the same.

The second movement, Adagio, curiously enough seems to have left no memory. On the other hand, the thoroughly relaxed graciousness of the lilting last movement came as the pleasantest surprise of the whole performance. The experience of Toscanini playing Bach was entirely novel to me, and after the sunlit overtones and superbly rhythmic attack of the first movement, somehow the last thing one expected to encounter was the ease and charm with which the gigue-like character of the 12/8 finale was endowed.

In spite of that memorable way with the Sixth Brandenburg, however, J. S. Bach was unfortunately never Toscanini's cup of tea, although he may have thought he was paying the composer tribute by frequently performing Respighi's earsplitting transcription of the C minor organ Passacaglia. It was a pity that particular Brandenburg performance of Toscanini's was never heard in England or recorded at all, for it displayed principles of Bach playing which are far too seldom accepted. It was music with great vitality, rhythm, colour and charm. And it was never dull.

BEETHOVEN
❧[1771–1827]❧

IF, looking back on my experience of Toscanini, I have
found that his performances of Verdi provided me with
the greatest revelation of a composer, I think that perhaps
his performances of Beethoven, when I first encountered
them, provided me with the greatest revelation of Toscanini
himself.

It was a revelation of Toscanini because, frankly, I had never
expected an Italian who was a superb conductor of opera to be
able to interest me more in the concert hall than Weingartner
and Bruno Walter, from whom I had had my early practical
education in the symphonies of Beethoven. An Italian's place
was in the orchestra pit, not on the rostrum. That, at least, is
how I felt when Toscanini first came to London with the New
York Philharmonic-Symphony Orchestra in 1930, and I made
no great effort to try to hear his performance of the Eroica at
Queen's Hall—a performance which incidentally elicited from
a well-known and since beknighted British conductor the
opinion that Toscanini "lacked technique", whatever that
might mean. I did, however, go to one of Toscanini's concerts,
but I will not pretend that I number it among the major musical
experiences of my life. It was a quite abnormally undistinguished programme—Moussorgsky's *Pictures at an Exhibition*,
César Franck's *Les Éolides*, Eugène Goossens's Sinfonietta and
Richard Strauss's *Tod und Verklärung*. The din Toscanini
evoked in the Strauss was monumental and a thoroughly
exciting physical experience, but on the whole it was not a very
uplifting evening's music.

A little less than three years later I went to New York for
some months, and having in the meantime become more
closely acquainted with Toscanini's work through his gramophone records, I found that on my arrival in America I was
disposed to take a more friendly view of his conducting in the

concert hall. Unfortunately, when I studied the programme at Carnegie Hall it appeared that Toscanini was just about to embark on a Beethoven cycle—all the symphonies except the Ninth, together with a concerto or two and some overtures. I say "unfortunately" because while I had been persuaded over the years by my friend Hyam Greenbaum, who had first made me listen to him at all in the concert hall, that even though Toscanini was an Italian his Beethoven was nevertheless remarkable, I was just at that time going through a phase when Beethoven did not greatly interest me. However, out of curiosity I listened to the broadcast of Toscanini's first concert of the cycle and early the following morning hurried up-town to book seats for the remaining four concerts. Toscanini, I decided, had given a good account of himself in the concert hall and was clearly a man to be reckoned with.

This first experience of Toscanini as a conductor of Beethoven (he had at that time not yet made any gramophone records of his music) was what can only be called a prodigious ear-opener. By approaching music in the concert hall in the same in-stinctive manner as he had always approached it in the theatre, by remaining basically what he had always been and always remained—namely, the greatest of opera conductors— he revealed Beethoven in a light that was not only unfamiliar but quite blinding in its clarity and intensity. In other words, the very quality which had originally prejudiced me against the acceptance of Toscanini in the concert hall proved to be pre-cisely the quality which made him so remarkable in what I had considered unnatural surroundings.

My prejudice had not been altogether unjustifiable. Although Toscanini was by no means inexperienced in the conducting of concerts, he was nevertheless more than sixty years old before he first became an almost full-time conductor of a symphony orchestra. It seemed altogether unlikely that a mature, elderly man could suddenly and successfully change direction like that and not until what we had every reason to suppose would be the final (and probably not very long) phase of his career. In fact, as I have suggested, it was the experience of over forty years of opera that made Toscanini the phenomenon he proved to be in the concert hall. Those long years of experience had developed Toscanini's two most striking qualities: his sense of drama and his accentuation of the lyrical aspects of the music he conducted. He took a long-term view of a Beethoven symphony, so that his performance was never just a performance of four movements, played one after the other, but the realization of the conception of the work as a whole that built up to its climax as logically, inevitably and dramatically as a Verdi opera. Toscanini's preoccupation with the lyrical element whenever it occurred in music was also the outcome of his nature and education. It was no mere coincidence that Toscanini fanatically implored his orchestras to *sing*, that he cried "Cantare! Cantare!" so often at rehearsal; he instinctively thought of all music in terms of the human voice, because that was what he was brought up on and he knew that the human voice, as a medium of lyrical expression, was the greatest instrument ever given to mankind. The nearer to the human voice he could get his orchestra to sound, the nearer he felt he was to the attainment of his ideal: the interpretation of the composer's melody as the composer himself conceived it.

Exactly what it was that Toscanini brought to the first two Beethoven symphonies which made me hurry to Carnegie Hall to book seats for the rest of the series (and for every other concert Toscanini was due to conduct that season) is something which I hope to show in the course of the study which follows.

There is one final and characteristic Toscanini touch to be mentioned: whenever he performed a cycle of these symphonies he did not keep to the strict chronological order of their composition. As those who heard the London Music Festival of 1939 will remember, Toscanini paired them off in this order: First and Second, Fourth and Third, Sixth and Fifth, Eighth and Seventh, with the Ninth occupying the major part of the fifth programme. This habit, I am convinced, was an unconscious throw-back to Toscanini the opera conductor; it is generally accepted that after the first two Beethoven symphonies the odd-numbered works—Third, Fifth, Seventh—are more intense than those which followed them, and that the even-numbered symphonies show the composer in a comparatively relaxed frame of mind.

In Toscanini's view to have played the Fifth Symphony in a

concert and ended the programme with the Sixth would have left the listener with an inevitable feeling of anticlimax. It would have been dramatically wrong.

SYMPHONY No 1 in C, Opus 21
[1800]

NBC Symphony Orchestra

GREAT BRITAIN: HMV ALP 1040
RCA RB–16101
U.S.A.: Victor LM 6009
1951

1. *Adagio molto – Allegro con brio*

Toscanini always gave one the impression that he had never heard of Beethoven until the moment he had begun rehearsing for the concert you were listening to. There was a unique quality of wide-eyed innocence, of deliberate refusal to be wise about Beethoven's symphonies after the event—that is, to adopt any musico-historical attitude towards Beethoven by suggesting that there was any such thing as "early" or "middle period" or "late" Beethoven. Toscanini did not know that Beethoven was going to write another eight symphonies, for the simple reason that there was absolutely nothing in the score of Opus 21 to tell him so; all he knew was that this was the first utterance in this particular medium of a vital, vigorous and revolutionary young composer. Toscanini did not observe any "tradition" in the performance of this or any other Beethoven symphony, because he could not. What "tradition" could there possibly be attached to a brand-new work? It was his ability to regard every Beethoven symphony he ever performed as "a brand-new work" which made Toscanini's performances so uniquely illuminating—and with his Beethoven particularly it was, as Constant Lambert once wrote, "as though Beethoven himself had become endowed with conducting technique".

Constant Lambert was writing in this context of a performance of Beethoven's First Symphony, which in its way was one of the subtlest of Toscanini's performances because it was one of the most unexpected. To the casual radio listener the immediate effect of hearing Toscanini and the New York Philharmonic in that first Beethoven broadcast was to wonder: "if he can do that to the First Symphony, which is a comparatively minor work, what on earth is he going to do to the Eroica and the rest?"

The gramophone has fortunately provided us with an immortal answer to the question.

Toscanini's recorded performance of Beethoven's First Symphony is a lesson for conductors from the very first bar, though I fear they will have to discover for themselves the secret of the peculiar "singing" tone Toscanini managed to draw from a string pizzicato, not only in this symphony but everywhere else it occurred in the music he conducted. Equally they will have to discover how he succeeded in making the miraculously instantaneous transition from the Adagio molto of the Introduction to the vigorous Allegro con brio.

In their way these twelve opening bars of this first movement are worth endless study, not only for the wonderfully balanced "voicing" of the wind parts which Toscanini always blended so superbly, but for the full value given to the *tenuto* marked in the dialogue between strings and wind—

Ex. 1

—and, above all, for the first instance I can quote in this study of what I call Toscanini's sense of "matching dynamics". One of Beethoven's favourite tricks in his symphonies was the echo, or imitation, of a phrase in one section of the orchestra by another. In the quotation above there is a typical example—the *forte* of the strings alone echoed by a *forte* in the wind alone. Toscanini always matched the dynamics in such cases so carefully that while the *colour* of the sound changed with the instrumentation its volume did not. I will not swear that the number of decibels registered by the strings is exactly the same as that registered by the wind instruments; the main thing is that to the non-electronic ear the two sounds are perfectly balanced.

The vigour of the Allegro con brio owed nothing to any eccentricity of tempo; it was taken at the indicated $\srightarrow = 112$, as the Introduction conformed to its prescribed $\sright = 88$. Its strength came from the typical, almost pedantic insistence by Toscanini on strict note-values which gave the opening theme a compelling rhythmic vitality:

Ex. 2

The fact that the second and third notes in the first two bars are marked to be played in one bow by the violins did not in any way alter the value of the notes played in that bow. The dotted quaver and the semi-quaver are given full value—a pretty obvious thing to do, one would have thought, until you listen to other conductors and realize how often what they play sounds more like:

Ex. 3

Toscanini, by accepting what was written, underlined the characteristic gruffness of this Beethoven first subject, which is no less gruff for being played *piano* on its first statement.

Whether he was right to do it or not I do not know, but Toscanini had one habit which disconcerted me whenever I encountered it and that was a curious "pressure" he seemed to put on a certain kind of phrase found in the classics. I have shown an instance of this in the chapter on Mozart.* In Beethoven it occurs twice—in the Ninth Symphony † and in the first movement of the First when the second subject, which

* See page 161.   † See page 87.

is written simply to be played *piano* without either crescendo or
diminuendo, is made to sound:

Ex. 4

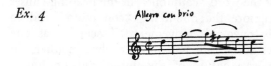

I do not know what precedent there is for this unless it is
the purely retrospective precedent provided by the first subject
of the first movement of Brahms' Fourth Symphony, where a
phrase very much like it is marked to be played as I have
shown Toscanini played the tune in Beethoven's First. It was
a strange departure from the text and I am far from convinced that it is a desirable one. It had a momentary effect
on the style of the music but though it occurred no fewer than
twenty-four times it did no lasting damage and within a
moment one was absorbed by the superb rhythmic precision of
what followed and Toscanini's characteristic dovetailing as the
music goes from *ff* to a new subject played *pp* without a perceptible "join" of any kind in the transition.

Toscanini observed the repeat, and on proceeding with the
development section demonstrated his unmatched mastery of
the art of syncopation with which he always created the
necessary sense of urgency without having to disturb the basic
tempo by the faintest hint of a *stringendo* unless it was definitely
authorized by the composer. For the rest, apart from an
effective but unmarked diminuendo in the unison string
passage which leads to the return of the second subject (Ex. 4)
at bar 205* the movement went its wonderfully smooth and
inevitable way, the chords spread across the strings of the
violins with that peculiar combination of crispness, richness
and musicalness Toscanini always evoked from any *ff* chord,
and the repetitive C major of the final bars of the coda endowed with the natural impetus which enabled a passage of
twenty-one bars of the same chord to sound exactly right and
not to outstay its welcome.

* Beethoven doubles the solo flute part with one clarinet an octave lower for the
first phrase of this C major reprise, but unaccountably leaves the flute to play its
next phrase alone. Toscanini added the clarinet and so restored logic and symmetry
to the instrumentation of this four-bar passage.

2. *Andante cantabile con moto*

The inclusion of the word "cantabile" in the heading causes many people to ignore the qualifying "con moto" and so dawdle intolerably over this movement. Toscanini, as one might expect, certainly did not dawdle, but neither, in observing the *con moto* nature of the music, did he hurry. The metronome marking printed in most scores is ♪ = 120, which is ridiculously fast if we are to have anything at all *cantabile*; Toscanini in consequence adopted a tempo between 104 and 108 which allowed the tune time to breathe without becoming sentimental. Only at one point did he introduce a slightly unexpected flourish when he permitted the suggestion of a *ritenuto* and breath-pause between the bars:

Ex. 5

The same thing naturally occurred again—the movement being in sonata form—when the phrase is heard again in the tonic key in the second half, and there was also an understandable *espansione* in the course of the coda at the passage in the strings:

Ex. 6

These, and the rallentando in its last two bars, however, were the only moments in the whole movement where anything resembling eighteenth-century graciousness was suggested in any way. Beethoven's own intensely characteristic rough-hewn charm is there, of course, but it is only on the occasions I have noted that we are aware that if the composer did not still have one foot in the eighteenth century (he started composing this symphony in the late 1790's), he nevertheless still had one ear in the slow movements of Mozart and Haydn. Perhaps in any other symphony of Beethoven's this would be "out of character"; I don't think it is wholly so in this one where, after all, the slow movement starts off with more than a coincidental resemblance to the beginning of the slow movement of Mozart's G minor symphony.

3. Menuetto: Allegro molto e vivace

The term "Menuetto" being, of course, only a courtesy title for as vivacious a scherzo as anybody had ever heard in 1800, Toscanini understandably translated "Allegro molto e vivace" literally into terms of something like ♩. = 112 (or four bars a minute more than the printed score of this remarkable Minuet allows for). Toscanini's was an irresistible performance, filled with the vitality of a composer who has suddenly discovered that he has happened on a musical form of which nobody else had really realized the significance and possibilities, and is bursting to tell us all about it.

In a remarkable way Toscanini communicated something of Beethoven's breathless excitement and bursting energy, by convincing us that we had never heard anything quite like it before. It is a scherzo in everything but name, and in the best sense, for it is full of wit and fun in the way of unexpected dynamic contrasts, syncopation and "wrong-footed" rhythms which Toscanini's wonderful rhythmic sense gave a peculiar virility and exuberance.

The Trio, since the score suggests nothing to the contrary, Toscanini took at the same tempo as the "Minuet", and by doing so somehow added to the effect of the whispered inter-jections from the violins in their p octave passages. In fact, the "whispered" quality of these string figures was purely illusory; they were merely further admirable examples of "matching dynamics", for they echoed not the literal musical line of the wind passages but their dynamic character with remarkable fidelity—decrescendo was echoed by decrescendo, pp by pp, with uncanny certainty. If some of the string playing sounded "whispered" then it was because Toscanini had the inimitable ability to make a string *pianissimo* sound as quiet as if mutes were being used; and yet it never sounded as though it was being played with mutes, because mutes produce an entirely different tone-colour. In some extraordinary way a Toscanini *pianissimo* was music played more quietly; it was never music

that sounded *fainter,* and it never in any circumstances lost any
of its essentially musical quality.

One other noteworthy and refreshing touch in his performance of the Trio was Toscanini's characteristic observance of
what was written at the climax of the section when the first
fortissimo tutti occurs. In order to make the crescendo from *p* to
ff in bars 122–125,

Ex. 7

he never had to hold the tempo back in a dragging *ritenuto* in order
to make sure we didn't miss the crescendo. In a strange way
Toscanini never considered we were such fools as other Beethoven
conductors did, and that was a maxim he mercifully maintained
throughout his entire career. In this way we were spared many
of the irritating mannerisms of "interpretation" affected by
ninety-nine per cent of his less gifted colleagues, whose mannerisms without exception included the deadening *ritenuto* at the
point I have indicated.

Perhaps in fairness, however, it may be said that for a
moment they were interpreting at least one aspect of Beethoven's movement literally: by introducing the *ritenuto* the
music *did* sound like a minuet for one fleeting, horrible instant.

4. *Adagio – Allegro molto e vivace*

I think the easiest way to begin any study of this last movement as Toscanini played it is to reproduce the introductory
Adagio and the first phrase of the Rondo proper to enable the
listener to compare what is written with what can be heard in
Toscanini's recording:

Ex. 8

It will be noted that what is written for the first violins and what they played for Toscanini are two rather different things. For instance, there is a definite moment of silence between the *ff* and the *piano* in the first bar (or would be if, in my copy, there were not a definite pre-echo), and a noticeable rallentando in the fourth to give extra point to the *piano* which follows the crescendo. And so on. It is a fascinating little study in the interpretation of one of the most difficult of all orchestral passages to make sense of. So often it can sound like an exercise which one is surprised to think anybody would want to perform in public. With Toscanini it was the deliberate creation of a tension to be relaxed, a few moments not so much of the violins "trying their wings", as Rosa Newmarch described it, as of a baseball pitcher waving his arm about to loosen up before he actually pitches the ball and the game gets under way again.

The release by Toscanini from the tension of the Adagio was a breath-taking moment of such ease and apparent simplicity that it was hard to realize that the little scale leading into the theme of the Rondo is one of the most difficult problems a conductor has to face in the entire repertoire. Few conductors will admit this, of course, but comparison with the smooth, effortless effect Toscanini always achieved leaves little doubt that they find it so nevertheless.

The Rondo itself had that peculiar air of inevitability, of running effortlessly at its natural speed, which Toscanini brought to all Beethoven finales. The irresistible rhythm, the "matching dynamics", the sheer musical fascination of those passages which on paper look, and in practice so often sound, merely like scales, all combined to give this last movement a vigour and logic which brought the symphony to its good-tempered and playful end at precisely the right moment: when the conductor had given it all he had, and all that the work needed.

It was a performance which has lost none of its force or conviction as a novel and refreshing experience in its perpetuation on record.

SYMPHONY No 2 in D, Opus 36
[1802]

NBC Symphony Orchestra

GREAT BRITAIN: HMV ALP 1145
RCA RB–16101
U.S.A.: Victor LM 1723
1949/51

1. Adagio molto – Allegro con brio

To the listener who had heard Toscanini conduct the First
Symphony of Beethoven, the Second did not come as a surprise
so much as a confirmation of the status of a composer whose
debut had been arresting and whose future would certainly
command attention and respect.

In the Introduction to this Second Symphony Toscanini
stressed particularly that element of drama which Beethoven
was beginning to bring to the symphony; and for all that we
have been brought up to regard Beethoven's even-numbered
symphonies as "relaxed" compared with the violence and
intensity of the odd-numbered works, for Toscanini to have
regarded the Second Symphony as anything but the extremely
vigorous and urgent piece it is would have been entirely out of
character. Once again, there was nothing in the score to tell
Toscanini that this would eventually be regarded as one of the
"even-numbered" symphonies.

Certainly, the Second Symphony includes elements that we
have come to regard as typical of the "even-numbered" works.
There is a certain tenderness, for instance, in the very first
phrase of the Adagio introduction, but Toscanini did not in
any way emphasize this lyrical passage at the expense of the
dramatic sequence that follows it on the grounds that this was
an "even-numbered" symphony. As always, while he saw
"what is there", he saw a great deal more besides, including
how to make Beethoven's reiterated scale-passages sound like
music instead of technical exercises. Toscanini's ability to get
all the orchestral players under him to do exactly the same
thing, in the same way, at the same time, and so breathe musical

life into every detail of the score, however unpromising the music might look on paper, is not something on which I can hope to throw any light; all I can do is to draw attention to his fantastic achievements in this direction and trust that it will remain an inspiration for the generation of conductors who will follow. Just as I hope, too, that these same successors will unravel for themselves the secret of Toscanini's remarkable transition from the Adagio to the main Allegro con brio which just "happens" so imperceptibly, effortlessly and perfectly.

When I heard this for the first time in this recording I thought that perhaps the metronome might provide a clue. But all I learnt was that the ♪ of the Introduction was played at about 69, and the 𝅗𝅥 of the Allegro at about 96–100. It was not, as I had thought from the whole feel of the music's pulse, a result of the Allegro being taken at twice the speed of the slow introduction—a common enough practice in eighteenth-century music which the young Beethoven might well have followed. It was just a wonderfully spontaneous transformation which in some miraculous way Toscanini made to sound like the logical continuation and development of a tempo and rhythm to which, in fact, the new episode is entirely unrelated.

Once the Allegro con brio was under way there was no doubt that we were in for another fierce first movement—an impression Toscanini always made by his tremendously powerful rhythm, the careful observance of note-values, and by the electric incisiveness of a dynamic marking which, until one heard this symphony performed by Toscanini, one did not realize Beethoven used so often, so effectively, or in so revolutionary a manner—namely, the sudden *sf* in which this movement abounds.

Toscanini's insistence on full note-values was heard once more when, in a case similar to the one quoted in the First Symphony (Ex. 2 on p. 26), he did not detract from the character of the second subject by demanding that the *rhythm* should be strict, even though the woodwind or violins are expected to play the two-note groups *legato* in the phrase:

Ex. 9   Allegro con brio

("Legato", it cannot be stated too often, was never synonymous in Toscanini's mind with "unrhythmical".)

The repeat marked in the first movement was not made in this recording, and though I cannot remember if Toscanini always omitted it, it was obviously logical to have done so in the present case, since he reached the end of the exposition section with the listener desperately keen to know what happened next. (On the other hand, it would be interesting to consider whether Toscanini, if he *had* made the repeat, would in fact have stimulated the listener's curiosity so much by the end of the "first-time-through" that the repeat would have come as an anticlimax; or whether he would have held something in reserve for the repeat and so embarked on the following development section only when the listener was ready for it. In short, it is all rather a question of the chicken and the egg: did Toscanini go straight on without the repeat because he had done what he did, or did he do what he did because he was going straight on without the repeat?)

There was very little of the typical "even-numbered" mildness to be heard in the way Toscanini continued with the development section of the first movement, a wonderfully intense and dramatic performance which derived its prodigious vitality from the energy and strength of Toscanini's rhythm. Drama, indeed, was the keynote of the whole conception and when the second subject (Ex. 9) was heard again in this section, echoed *piano* by the violins, the effect of the *piano* was not one of charm but of dramatic tension deliberately built up to be relaxed when the recapitulation begins.

2. Larghetto

The eternal paradox of Toscanini's conducting was that while he insisted so forcefully on the Sacrosanctity of Tempo, in practice the strict, unyielding relentlessness of the legendary Human Metronome was entirely illusionary. Toscanini himself, when reproached for boasting that he kept an unwaveringly strict tempo whereas he and a metronome showed considerable difference of opinion, retorted: "Man is not a machine!" The truth is that Toscanini was an unequalled master of the difficult and dangerous art of Rubato. His obsession with the

importance of tempo and the maintenance of a firm, unshakable
rhythm, was in effect a means of establishing a rule so
thoroughly that he had the authority to break it—and to know
exactly how and when to break it.

To try to match a metronome to the slow movement of this
Second Symphony as Toscanini played it is a hopeless task: his
beat varied between 80 and 100. Perhaps if you set the metronome at the prescribed ♪ = 80 at the first bar of the movement
the music will be found to be ticking away quite happily at 80
when the last bar arrives; personally, I abandoned all hope of
finding the mean tempo of this movement long before the
second subject was reached on the recording. It was only an
academic question anyway. . . .

On examination, Toscanini's performance of this slow movement was founded on a fascinating series of unorthodox, unauthorized, but musically entirely justified deviations from the
text of Beethoven's score. But not one of these deviations was
anything but a superb example of an exception proving a rule,
and of Toscanini's genius for what one might describe as
"freedom of expression within the limits of tempo".

In the very first bars of this slow movement Toscanini introduced an effective digression from the strait and narrow path
of rigid tempo by making a noticeable "breath-pause" between
the sixth and seventh bars in the string phrase:

Ex. 10

The same thing happened when the tune is echoed immediately
afterwards by clarinets and bassoons. In neither case, however,
was this little nuance exaggerated; it was just hinted at and
was gone, a perfect instance of Toscanini's sense of timing.
The "breath-pause" was a natural feature of this slow movement, for the whole of Toscanini's phrasing of it was typically
conceived in terms of the human voice—a well-disciplined
human voice, needless to say, for Toscanini did not allow his
cantilena all that much freedom to ramble at will. But there was
still time to stand and stare, as it were; an effective *ritenuto*

was permitted to lead in the recapitulation, for instance, and the players were encouraged to draw a new breath and a new bow after the *ff* bars of the phrase:

Ex. 11

Since the movement is written in sonata form the features I have quoted in Examples 10 and 11 occurred more than once, of course, as did the characteristic cases of wonderful "matching dynamics" and the purely illusory *stringendo* which was the result of the powerful crescendo Toscanini inspired in the urgent syncopated phrase for violins which first occurs as

Ex. 12

More actual than illusory, however, was the slightly faster tempo Toscanini adopted towards the climax of the development section, when he created a dramatic tension which more than justified the relaxing *ritenuto* I have mentioned leading to the recapitulation.

The final relaxation came in the coda to which Toscanini gave a peculiar charm by spotlighting the tender little arpeggio figures of the solo flute. This was a most captivating moment.

3. *Scherzo: Allegro*

This Scherzo, which Toscanini took at about ♩. = 112 (and the Trio at about 100), was an outstanding model for even the most advanced of post-graduate conductors of the practice of perfect "matching dynamics". The main part of the movement consists of a series of instrumental statements-and-echoes, questions-and-answers which were performed with all that meticulous attention Toscanini paid to detail and which, in the end, must surely have been the secret of his fabulous control of orchestral texture. The balance between

one instrumental section and another, the synchronized gradation of instrumental tone were things which Toscanini achieved
almost as though he had taken not merely each single group of
instruments through the score separately, but each member of
each group, so that the junior member of the back desk of the
second violins applied exactly the same required length of bow,
intensity of vibrato and tone as every other violinist in the
orchestra, who, like himself, had been individually coached
by the Maestro and could claim to be Pupil of Toscanini.
This movement, which is more carefully provided by the composer with expression marks than most conductors would have
us know, is not a madly fascinating piece of music; but it is a
wonderful test-piece for the application of what is known as
Style. Toscanini's answers to all the questions posed by the
score should enable future examinees at least to make the right
kind of noise with this Scherzo. With the best will in the world
I cannot see them making much more of it than an essay in
rhythm and dynamics—although, heaven knows, those are two
elements any Beethoven scherzo can always do with, even a
comparatively uninteresting one like this.

4. Allegro molto

Always, when he came to the Finale of a Beethoven symphony, Toscanini seemed automatically to think back for a
quick moment to the musical situation in which he had left us
at the end of the first movement. The first movements of his
Beethoven symphonies were almost without exception of a
quite prodigious dramatic intensity, of such intensity indeed
that on first experience it seemed impossible that the Finale
could be anything but an anticlimax to what one had heard.

That no Finale did ever prove to be an anticlimax was
largely due, I believe, to Toscanini's upbringing in the theatre.
As he always had the final curtain in mind from the first bar of
the overture, so in finding drama in a Beethoven first movement
he never failed to find the drama to cap it in a Beethoven
Finale. It was not that he ever played down the drama of
the first movement, for he always played it for all it was
worth. But he was a living proof that there was always plenty
more where that came from; he could draw on seemingly

inexhaustible reserves of physical and intellectual energy which he unleashed with the sense of timing of a great athlete who holds back his final burst until the last critical moment.

Toscanini interpreted the Allegro molto of this last movement with admirable literalness, for it is indeed "very cheerful", a model of the kind of "crackle" Toscanini so often drew from an orchestra and which was quite unlike the sound made by any other orchestra under any other conductor. In this performance of the Finale Toscanini made no exorbitant demands of tempo; he took it at the officially indicated $\downarrow$ = 152. But while the fast passages sounded properly fast, the tempo did not prevent the adequate presentation of the warm *dolce* of the second subject. There was always room for the music to move, as it were, however confined the framework formed by the tempo promised to be.

The last movement of this Second Symphony was the sort of music Toscanini always revelled in; he refused to recognize that he was performing a "classic" and enjoyed every opportunity provided by Beethoven to emphasize the general playfulness of the music, and though "charm" was not a quality Toscanini was generally credited with being able to evoke from music there was a liberal quota of it in this performance. It came from the conductor's typical approach to Beethoven's dynamics and his peculiar ability to make such effortless links between extremes of loudness and softness, between the *ff* followed immediately by a *pp* without a moment's interruption of the rhythm of the movement, and to bring a remarkable clarity to the orchestral texture of the development, or "working-out", section.

In the end the "even-numberedness" of this Second Symphony was not specially noticeable from Toscanini's way with it. There was a fierce vitality in this Finale particularly, which can compare with that of the odd-numbered and (one is led to suppose) consequently more "significant" Seventh. But as I have said, Toscanini was not very impressed by how history categorized Beethoven's symphonies. To him Opus 36 was not the second of nine symphonies by Beethoven. It was the second of two.

SYMPHONY No 3 in E flat, Opus 55
("Eroica")
[1804]

NBC Symphony Orchestra

GREAT BRITAIN: HMV ALP 1008
RCA RB–16102
U.S.A.: Victor LM 1042
1949

1. Allegro con brio

If I had not already known what to expect from my experience in New York I would have known how Toscanini was going to approach the Eroica after the first few moments of his rehearsal at Queen's Hall, London, in 1937. He stopped the orchestra and shouted, in that mixture of three languages which he fondly imagined to be English: "No! No! Nein! Is-a not Napoleon! Is-a not 'Itler! Is-a not Mussolini! Is Allegro con brio! From the beginning—Bitte! *Da—caaaaa-po!*" And "Allegro con brio" was indeed the quality which dominated an electrifying performance from the first crunching chords of the first movement to the exclusion of all extramusical images.

Toscanini, so faithful to Beethoven's score in other respects, systematically ignored the composer's instructions which appeared in the first violin part of the original edition of the Eroica: "This Symphony, being purposely written at greater length than usual, should be played nearer the beginning than the end of a concert, and shortly after an Overture, an Air, or a Concerto; lest if it is heard too late, when the listener is fatigued by the previous pieces it should lose its proper and intended effect." Anybody who ever heard Toscanini conduct this symphony or who even has heard this recording will readily understand why. What on earth *could* he have played after it in a programme? In a Beethoven Series, as I have said, he would play the Eroica after the Fourth Symphony for what one must regard as reasons of dramatic logic. But when he included the Eroica in an ordinary mixed concert programme he still always ended with it. I doubt if even the Fifth Symphony would have avoided the suggestion of anticlimax after the Eroica; there was nothing except the Ninth that could possibly have followed it, and that was mercifully never proposed. It would have been an intolerably exhausting experience.

The "brio" was put into this first movement by the sheer force of Toscanini's rhythmic attack. The tempo itself was roughly ♩ = 160, which is not nearly so unreasonable as the tempo optimistically recommended by the editor of my full score, who hopes for something approaching 180 (he suggests ♩. as 60). But, as one soon learned by experience, whatever the tempo adopted by Toscanini there was always time for the display of tenderness in the music. This occurred early on in the movement when in contrast to the fierce incisiveness of the frequent *sf*, the admonition "dolce" in the little phrase passed from one instrument to another—

Ex. 13

inspired a wonderful smoothness of phrasing so that the passage split up between clarinet, flute, violins, oboe and bassoon sounded in a remarkable way as though it was all being played by a single player in one breath, marked *piano*. Once again a great part in this easy-flowing smoothness of phrasing was played by the perfectly matched dynamics.

One admirable break with tradition—or rather, one admirable modification of tradition—was made by Toscanini when he came to the episode beginning:

Ex. 14

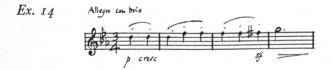

It has been apparently universal practice at this point to change gear down to a much slower tempo, picking up the original Allegro con brio again some twenty-odd bars later.

Toscanini's modification consisted of not slowing down quite so much as other conductors do. He "changed down" so gently that one was aware less of a change of tempo than of a change of mood and tone of voice. My memory of the first Eroica I heard by Toscanini is that he did not vary the tempo at all; this, as the recording suggests, may well have been an illusion. But compared with, say, Weingartner's tempo at this point, Toscanini sounded almost as though he had made no change whatever; playing his recording again after Toscanini's I found that Weingartner makes the episode sound ridiculously exaggerated by comparison and it seems improbable, as each phrase is played slower than the last, that the original tempo will ever be regained. It was not that Toscanini was brusque with the passage; he just did not dawdle over it. He considered that by making a slight ritardando at the end of the four-bar phrase in Ex. 14 (and in analogous instances during the passage) sufficient contrast had been suggested.

Personally I am not convinced that the original tradition of taking this episode at any speed lower than the original Allegro con brio is in any way a good one. I do not see that it is at all necessary, provided the dynamic markings are observed which give the episode its character. And my belief is strengthened by the impression I have retained since 1933 that Toscanini *did*, on one occasion at least, take it *a tempo*.

In accordance with Beethoven's own custom Toscanini did not make the repeat of the exposition but continued with the development section. This part of the movement always showed Toscanini at his greatest and most inimitable, clarifying the orchestral texture so that neither a single detail of the figures developed by woodwind or strings was lost, nor—in the course of creating this phenomenal clarity—any of the tremendous dramatic intensity of the music sacrificed either. The control and realization of Beethoven's dynamics, the remarkable smoothness of transition from $f\!f$ to p, the balance of the sudden $s\!f\!p$ in the string parts, which was clearly heard but never obscured the detail of the instruments playing behind it, were features of a performance which have been preserved in this Toscanini recording and are clearly perceptible by all but the most unmusical hi-fi addicts. If anything was lost in the recording it was certainly nothing that ever occurred in any Toscanini performance of the Eroica I ever heard, least of all was it the great hammering dissonances, the mixed chords of A minor and F major together which Beethoven is so reluctant to resolve after eight *forte* reiterations.

Toscanini relaxed the tension of this phrase not, as some do, by making a rallentendo towards a slower tempo in the E minor episode which follows—

Ex. 15

—but by introducing for the first time (at the *same* tempo) a strongly lyrical note which characterized not only this theme but any tune that resembles it or is any way related to it.

As an object lesson in "matching dynamics" there was little in Toscanini's performance of this symphony to compare with the gradual descent from the near-climax of this episode to the recapitulation. Strings answered wind dynamic-for-dynamic, *f* was matched by *f*, *p* by *p*, *decrescendo* by *decrescendo*, *pp* by *pp* pizzicato and *pp* tremolo in an uncanny manner.

The recapitulation presented no noticeable surprises; everything was as before so far as detail was concerned, but in a peculiar way, which was not achieved by any change of tempo or forcing of dynamics, the music grew in intensity and urgency. Toscanini's control and command of the sheer physical potentialities of an orchestra were amazing, of course, and as this movement of the Eroica neared its end one was constantly aware of his masterly sense of timing, which always held something in reserve so that the false climax could never be mistaken for the real thing.

When he came to the genuine dynamic peak of this movement Toscanini conformed to common usage and added the trumpets which have reinforced the final triumphant *ff* statement of the first theme since the days of Wagner, and have been endorsed by Weingartner's edition of Beethoven's symphonies —an edition which, on the whole, Toscanini followed fairly closely and always to the extent of multiplying the number of woodwind instruments by two in the louder *tutti* passages.

2. Marcia funebre: Adagio assai

Toscanini's Eroica on a gramophone record enables one to enjoy what one was inevitably denied by Toscanini's Eroica in the concert hall: the opportunity to relax after the extremely exhausting experience of the first movement before continuing with the second. To be sure, when one does eventually listen to this slow movement one finds that one has merely exchanged one kind of tension for another perhaps even more powerful and concentrated, but a few minutes' rest between the two parts enables the listener to get his second wind.

To talk of tension in connection with Toscanini's performances is not to suggest that lyrical warmth was absent when it was called for. As one has been able to see already in this particular Eroica there was no disregard of the phrases marked "dolce" in the first movement in spite of the general hurly-burly of an Allegro with lots of *brio*. So in this slow movement there were passages of quite beautiful *cantilena* super-imposed, as it were, on the unceasing rhythm of what is, after all, a funeral march. It was the funeral-march element of this movement that Toscanini stressed most strongly. He took it a comfortable ♪ = 69 or thereabouts and maintained that as the basic speed throughout. There was no slowing-up for the C major Trio, though there was a slight retard on the last two notes of the first bar in the phrase leading back to the recapitulation of the main minor theme:

Ex. 16

But there was no quickening of the pace at the great sequence of dissonant suspensions on the pedal D which forms the climax of the *fugato* passage. The tension, in fact, was heightened by the immensely tight rein on which Toscanini held the tempo; there was nothing *dolce* about the singing of the strings in this episode, for Toscanini made of it a quite remarkable expression of grief too deep for tears. In the course of building the climax of this passage Toscanini added three extremely effective notes

to Beethoven's orchestration—an addition, I may say, that
was no more than the doubling of the clarinets' part by the
third horn (with the customary Weingartner extra horn or two
in unison with it) in the tune which otherwise tends to fade
away if the horn gives up in the last bar. In Toscanini's logical
and effectively carpentered version the horns play in unison
with the clarinets through the whole of the phrase:

Ex. 17

The last three notes—A natural, B natural and C—were not a
very good risk on the horn in Beethoven's day; if they had been
there is little doubt that, having thought of the tune as a horn
tune for the first four bars of the phrase, Beethoven would have
finished it off as Toscanini did. (Whether the final C in the last
bar is sustained in the recording for longer than I have suggested I cannot tell for certain. Whatever the horn plays at
that point is obliterated by the entry of *ff* C's by the trumpets
and the other horns.)

While Toscanini maintained the steady march rhythm of the
slow movement there were one or two other instances of
rubato to be heard besides the emphatic but unindicated
ritenuto I have already cited in Ex. 16. For example, in the bar
before the sonorous G-string second subject returns in the
strings he made what was an unusual departure from common
procedure by making a *ritenuto* in the first half of the bar and
resuming strict tempo in the second:

Ex. 18

Most conductors reverse the process and make the rallentando
on the triplet lead-in, playing the first half of the bar *a tempo*.

The very few hints of breath-pauses, of near-rallentandos,
but perhaps, most of all, the moments when Toscanini care-

fully avoided any such nuances, are things which the student
can best recognize and appreciate by following this recording
with a score. There is, however, one detail worth drawing
attention to for the way in which it illustrates the virtually
instinctive logic of Toscanini's preoccupation with the instrumental texture of a work. There occurs at the beginning of the
coda of this slow movement a string phrase which was played in
Toscanini's recording, but not written in Beethoven's score as:

Ex. 19

The crescendo–diminuendo shown in the quotation was Toscanini's own contribution to the score. Beethoven marked the
passage to be played *pp*. Toscanini, on the other hand, allowed
the strings to be influenced in their dynamics by the marking
of the solo oboe part in which an A flat is sustained for two bars
and a quarter with the expression marks I have indicated in the
musical example above. This looks on paper as though it were
a doubtful form of theatricalism; in practice—since the last
thing Toscanini could be considered was theatrical—it sounds
absolutely right and proper.

In the last moments of the Coda it was Beethoven, by his dis-
jointing of the theme, rather than Toscanini, who created the
effect of the march slowing down until it finally stops. Toscanini did, in fact, take these bars at a slightly slower tempo,
but he underplayed them in such a way that the final emotional
impact of the movement acquired an added poignancy. The
melancholy closing chords in the wind sounded indeed what
Verdi so often called "come un lamento".

3. Scherzo: Allegro vivace

It is difficult to decide whether it was what Toscanini did or
what he did not do that was the most important feature of his
performance of this movement. As usual, I think, it was a bit
of both. His mastery of "matching dynamics" was never more

apparent than in this Scherzo which abounds in phrases thrown about from one part of the orchestra to another, changing the colour but not the volume of the sound. What Toscanini did not do, on the other hand, was to add dynamic flourishes where none was shown in the score. In his faithful adherence to the principle of seeing "what is there" Toscanini was almost alone among conductors in *not* making a crescendo at the passage for wind:

Ex. 20

Even Weingartner, in so many ways "correct" and honest in his Beethoven, could never resist a crescendo at that point.

Mention of Weingartner leads me to observe that while Toscanini was almost universally believed to take music so much faster than anybody else, in fact Weingartner took this Scherzo at the same speed as Toscanini—namely, at about ♩. = 126. Indeed, at times he took it even faster, for Weingartner never had quite the superhuman control of tempo and rhythm that Toscanini had and, as they did with Bruno Walter too, things were occasionally allowed to run away with him.

Toscanini's tempo for the Trio of this Scherzo seems to exasperate many people, some of whom go so far as to insist that "everyone else slows down for it". It is just simply not true to say this, of course. Weingartner's recorded performance of the Eroica with the Vienna Philharmonic, for instance, shows quite clearly that the conductor carried straight on with the tempo without the slightest hesitation.

Like Weingartner, Toscanini did not agree with "everyone else" and took the Trio at the tempo marked—or rather, *not* marked by the composer, since it is obvious that it is to be played at the same speed as the rest of the Scherzo.

There was one final touch in the Trio to be noticed which was the result of the combination of Toscanini's remarkable gift for phrasing a melodic line almost to eternity, and his technique of "matching dynamics", which made the passage which begins in the woodwind with this phrase

Ex. 21

sound as if it was still being played in the same breath when it is carried on by the strings in various groupings—first violins and violas, the second violins, violoncellos and basses. The episode was a wonderful realization of Beethoven's instruction—*dolce sempre legato*—played without a moment's interruption of the powerful, inexorable rhythm of the movement.

4. Finale: Allegro molto – Poco andante – Presto

If ever there was proof that the exception proves the rule it was surely provided by this Finale as Toscanini recorded it. So far as tempo is concerned it was, to say the least, an elastic performance. There are frequent variations of speed to be noted which are by no means indicated in the score—instances of rubato, of slowing up, of whole sequences being played faster before returning to the basic ♩ = 132. And so on. But listened to all in one piece, as it were, one is barely conscious of any of this. It is only on examination, on checking closely with the score one discovers that Toscanini, the Human Metronome, permitted himself a great deal of latitude one way and another. In a curious way, however, the predominant impression is one of a strict, relentless tempo building up with immense excitement; the clarity of the detail in the counterpoint, the scrupulous observance of Beethoven's meticulously indicated dynamics, the insistence on full note-values (which gave the vigorous ♪♩ figure of the G minor section such bounce and bite)—these were the important factors in the performance, for while some of the changes of tempo may be regarded as "traditional" the quality of the sound and the forcefulness of the musical thinking used in the course of them are, alas, far from traditional. It will not be the fault of Toscanini or the gramophone if they do not become so.

SYMPHONY No 4 in B flat, Opus 60
[1806]

NBC Symphony Orchestra

GREAT BRITAIN: HMV ALP 1145
RCA RB–16103
U.S.A.: Victor LM 1723
1951

1. Adagio – Allegro vivace

The idea that Beethoven's "even-numbered" can in any way be automatically regarded as of a more docile nature than his "odd-numbered" symphonies was never more strongly dispelled by Toscanini than in the slow introduction to this Fourth Symphony. The sinisterly dramatic, *misterioso* atmosphere of this whole remarkable passage was created not by any exaggeration of what Beethoven wrote but, on the contrary, by Toscanini's strictest possible, literal observance of note-values, the production of wonderfully balanced "matching dynamics" and an unvarying rhythm in a slow, dead-right tempo. The result was that an uncanny sense of tension, of apprehensive understatement was finally dispelled only by the outburst of the Allegro vivace.

As he did with the fast movements which follow the slow introductions to the First and Second Symphonies of Beethoven, Toscanini achieved a miraculously imperceptible transition from the Adagio to the Allegro of this Fourth Symphony—a transition so smooth and logical, indeed, that one believed it must be a simple matter of *doppio tempo* and no more. Consultation with the metronome, however, shows that in this, as in the earlier 1939 recording made by Toscanini, there was no question of the slow four-in-a-bar of the introduction dissolving conveniently into the two-in-a-bar of an Allegro in *lo stesso movimento*; the opening section was played at roughly $\flat = 50$, while the rest was something like $\flat = 144$.

While the mood of the Fourth Symphony, once the first Allegro has begun, is not so obviously intense as that of the Eroica, Toscanini never considered for a moment that its performance should be any less vigorous. He never made the mistake, made by so many conductors and encouraged by so many critics, of taking what is loosely called a "relaxed" view of this work because it is an "even-numbered" symphony. Toscanini saw the instruction "Allegro vivace" and observed it; and in doing so he avoided that miserably soft, emasculate performance which is generally tolerated as being "relaxed" and appropriate to Symphonies Nos. 2, 4, 6 and 8. Toscanini perceived what few conductors seem to realize: that Beethoven's laugh was a full-throated bellow; it was not a snigger, and for sheer volume and intensity it was every bit as vigorous and commanding as the rage and fierce anguish of the more "serious" Beethoven.

Toscanini did not "relax" in the Allegro vivace of this Fourth Symphony; there was the same powerful, irresistible rhythm which characterized passages of syncopation whenever he encountered them and gave them such an intense urgency,* the familiar refusal to be tempted to change gear into a slower tempo merely because Beethoven had changed the character of his music when he introduced his second subject. In the case of this particular second subject

Ex. 22

adherence to the original tempo adds to the effect of angularity and melodic awkwardness of the tune which Beethoven emphasizes with his playful treatment of it as a rather naive canon. It is not a "lyrical interlude" or anything like it.

The great emotional contrast in this movement does not occur until the development section when, after a beautiful all-in-one-breath passage of phrasing for strings which Toscanini made to sound as though it were played by one instrument with a compass ranging from the E string of the violin to

---

* Toscanini's superb rhythmic control of syncopated passages in Beethoven's symphonies and in Verdi's operas was an object lesson in the dramatic effect of a strict tempo. He understood, as so few performers do, that to allow the slightest hint of accelerando can kill the whole point of the syncopation stone dead. Urgency needs the restraint of a firm tempo to bring it into relief. What can a passage syncopate *against* if the tempo is allowed to get out of hand?

the C string of the violoncello, the long episode in the extremely foreign key of B major at last modulates and the movement returns to the parent key of B flat. The modulation itself
is achieved in a couple of bars and in the second of them Toscanini made an unindicated but breath-takingly dramatic
ritenuto at the flute's solo in

Ex. 23

To describe what Toscanini did as a "ritenuto" is to give an
exaggerated idea of what was in practice no more than a
hesitation lasting the fraction of a moment. It was something
which could not be measured or analysed; all one can do is to
draw attention to it in the recording and hope that one day a
conductor will arise who will have something like Toscanini's
sense of timing and be able to repeat the experience for us.

2. Adagio

The word "cantabile" appears in the first violin part as soon
as the tune starts in the second bar of this movement; it provides
the listener with an immediate clue to the kind of performance
he might expect to hear from Toscanini. The *cantabile* quality
of Toscanini's playing of a movement like this was always to be
expected, of course, but one never realized exactly how beautiful
it could sound, nor how superbly phrased it could be until one
heard it again. The memory inevitably mislaid one or two of
the details between one hearing and another.

Perhaps even more remarkable than the "singing" which
Toscanini drew from his orchestra was the extraordinary feeling he created of breadth, of phrases effortlessly stretching
apparently to eternity, so that a Beethoven slow movement had
the majesty of some great and noble river. It was an impression which grew increasingly stronger as one heard him
conduct each successive Beethoven symphony, until in the slow

movement of the Ninth one was presented with a conception of oceanic expansiveness.

The great generalizers among Toscanini's critics have always, if rather grudgingly, admitted that he could do justice to *cantilena* (though how they reconciled this reluctant tribute with their familiar complaint that he was an inhuman metronome they were careful not to tell us). The *cantilena* was something which I must admit I always took for granted with Toscanini. What was less obviously to be expected, and was always such a stimulating revelation, was the remarkable detail of what was after all little more than the orchestral accompaniment to the main tune of something, for instance, like the slow movement of the Fourth Symphony.

The precision of the rhythmic figure which dominates this Adagio from the first bar onwards was what provided the easy natural pulse of an Adagio of ♪ = 72; and it was a precision never obscured or unbalanced by the loudest *ff* tutti, nor lost in the *pp* of the hushed solo timpani of the movement's coda.

A Beethoven slow movement played by Toscanini as he played this one, was an experience of unending enchantment, where every single bar offered some novel and intriguing aspect of what one had been brought up to regard as a fairly well-worn and familiar piece of music. I am thinking particularly of the uncannily *legato* and *cantabile* quality of such otherwise untie-able and unsingable passages as the pizzicato sequences which accompany the subsidiary section immediately following the astonishingly powerful, unhurried, two-bar crescendo–diminuendo that ends the first episode of the movement. (The movement being in rondo form these details are to be noted more than once in the recording, of course.)

The typical Toscanini "matching dynamics" were again in evidence in this performance, though perhaps less obviously so than usual because they were found in the far subtler matching of the dynamics of groups of the same family of instruments—in this case most noticeably the descant, responses, echoes and imitations of violins, violas and violoncellos which combine to produce an instrumental texture, in addition to dynamic unity, which I can only describe as "cross-phrasing". A more acute ear than mine may be able to distinguish the first violins from the smaller number of second violins when the passages

occur in this recording, but to me it is just another instance of
that remarkable and fabulous string instrument with its range
from the E string of the violin to the C string of the violoncello
which Toscanini unearthed in the first movement.

3. Scherzo: Allegro vivace

The Scherzo, as performed by Toscanini in this recording,
will hold no surprises for the pedant. The conductor took the
Trio slower than the Scherzo (as the composer told him to)
and the performance was deprived neither of vigour nor of the
playful charm characteristic of a Beethoven scherzo.

The opportunities for "matching dynamics" abound, of
course, and Toscanini made the most of them as he did in any
Beethoven movement of this kind; but in this particular
Scherzo there emerged from them a quite charming little tune
which is nearly always lost by conductors who allow the
phrase to be "thrown about" between first and second violins
so wantonly that its line is broken up into unconnected fragments. Toscanini put a wide phrase-mark over the whole
thing so that it sounded:

Ex. 24

It made an unexpected "extra" in the way of a tune out of an
episode one had otherwise always tended to regard as "thematic
development" or the like.

4. Allegro ma non troppo

Just to prove that the Human Metronome was just as fallible
as the next conductor the first tutti phrase in the recording of
this Finale—third and fourth bars—is distinguished by a most
refreshing outbreak of ragged orchestral disunity. It was a
lapse that lasted less than three bars; and it did not occur
again when, in the due course of sonata form, the passage was
repeated. But it is thoroughly noticeable, and having re-

assured us that such things could happen (and that if they did, they were not really so monumentally disastrous that everything had to stop and be started all over again), Toscanini returned to the matter in hand with renewed enthusiasm to present a wonderfully stimulating Finale.

Toscanini had a particularly tender spot in his heart for this Fourth Symphony, and he inclined to include it in his concert programmes—that is, in non-Beethoven-cycle programmes—more often than one would expect. The Eroica, the Fifth, the Sixth, the Seventh—these were regularly heard in ordinary programmes as natural "high spots". But the Fourth would be comparatively tucked away, usually to end the first half of a programme that finished with something spectacular like *Ibéria*, *La Mer* or *Daphnis and Chloë*. Or, at least, so it seems to me, looking back over twenty-five years of Toscanini's programmes. What was important, however, was that one remembered hearing Toscanini's performance of Beethoven's Fourth Symphony as an outstanding item in any company—even when it was coupled with the Eroica (which invariably followed it) in a Beethoven series. And this, I think, is a remarkable tribute to a work which one is expected to regard as an "even-numbered" symphony of minor quality.

Toscanini, as I have said, recognized no such thing as "even-numberedness" and brought just as fierce an attack to bear on the Fourth as on any other Beethoven symphony that demanded it. This was particularly true of the Finale which is Beethoven at his most gruffly playful, enjoying the fun of false climaxes, long, tremendous crescendos and an incessant "busyness" of figures which Toscanini treated to a crystalline clarity which lacked nothing in rhythmic vigour and robustness of tone.

Toscanini brought moments of great charm to this Finale too, making, for instance, a *stringendo* in the passage which starts the development after the second-time-bar of the first section (the repeat was naturally made), then suddenly relaxing with a fractionally slower tempo when we come again to the phrase,

Ex. 25   Allegro ma non troppo

and reverting to the original tempo as the development of the original semi-quaver theme gets under way once more.

Toscanini's ability to influence the whole style of an individual instrumentalist to such a degree that it sounded almost as though Toscanini himself were playing the instrument was shown to great effect in the famous solo bassoon entry in this last movement when (there are no phrasings in the score) he phrased the passage to sound:

Ex. 26

and the same phrasing is reflected by the strings when they take up the tune again after the bassoon solo and, again, there are no markings in the score.

This little touch was typical of Toscanini's attention to a detail which made all the difference between a pedestrian and an inspired performance, and his Finale of the Fourth Symphony of Beethoven was an inspired performance which always stood out as a model of characteristic Beethoven vitality and good humour.

SYMPHONY No 5 in C minor, Opus 67
[1807]

NBC Symphony Orchestra

GREAT BRITAIN: HMV ALP 1108
RCA RB–16103
U.S.A.: Victor LM 1757
1952

1. Allegro con brio

I don't think anything I heard Toscanini do ever had quite the startling effect of his performance of the five opening bars of this symphony. With one powerful down-beat he swept

away the cobwebs of a long and bad tradition: the tradition
based on the false belief that if Fate knocked at Beethoven's
door it necessarily did so in the deliberate tempo of the
Commendatore knocking at Don Giovanni's. Toscanini saw
that the movement was marked "Allegro con brio" (one can
almost hear him saying: "Is-a not Fate! Is-a not a door!
Is Allegro con brio! *Da-caaaaa-po!*") and that there was no
hint in the score that the opening phrase of the symphony
should be played in any way except that in which it was
written:

Ex. 27

Toscanini's belief in the importance of tempo was never more
clearly proclaimed than in this first movement of the Fifth,
nor more obviously justified; the too-often-performed, tired
old hack of a work that should long ago have been put out to
grass was suddenly revealed as a dazzling, thoroughbred
masterpiece once more. Drama there was in plenty; but it
was not a melodramatic performance; all the "ham" was
ruthlessly removed and in its place emerged a tremendous
ferocity and force, which drove the music relentlessly, irresistibly forward with all the vitality and excitement Toscanini
understood by the term "con brio".

None of this, however, meant that the lyrical element was
disregarded; Toscanini took good care that the second subject,
for instance, which is marked "dolce" should sound like it.
Although Toscanini was popularly regarded as having grown
less "relaxed" as he grew older and increasingly insensitive to
the finer shades of music (all of them sacrificed, of course, on
the insatiable altar of Tempo) it is interesting to note that in
the case of Beethoven's Fifth Symphony exactly the opposite
seems to have happened. I recall having been uneasily
dubious in the 1930's about the way he approached the whole
question of the phrasing of the second subject of this movement. I was well aware that he was playing the whole
sequence as it was written in the score. I was not convinced
that the literal way was the natural way. In the course of

the statement of the second subject there occurs the passage for strings,

Ex. 28

which Toscanini phrased as it is phrased above, namely in two-bar phrases. This certainly gave the passage a breathless kind of urgency which maintained the tense atmosphere that Toscanini deliberately created in this first movement. But the sequence, after all, *is* meant as a contrast as the very word "dolce" suggests, and Toscanini, it seemed to me, did not make the contrast which I am sure the composer must have intended. Now, however, in this recording, I notice that Toscanini has modified his conception and extended the phrasing so that it was played in groups of four bars at a time instead of two, and with such a smooth link between the two groups that two 4-bar phrases sounded almost like one 8-bar phrase. This not only sounds right to my mind, but it is also, I believe, the logical, symmetrical way of doing it. A study of the part played by the basses in Beethoven's score shows that they play every third and fourth bar during this whole 20-bar episode of the second subject and in doing so neatly round off what is obviously intended as a 4-bar melodic pattern.

Once having decided on this broader conception of the whole sequence beginning with the statement of the second subject, Toscanini shaped it so that its *legato* quality gave extra point to the ferocious *ff* of the *legato–staccato* string figure which brings this first section of the movement to a close.

While the spirit of this first movement may be regarded as unrelenting there were nevertheless typical deviations from the rigid enforcement of strict tempo—as, indeed, there were to be found in all Toscanini's performances of Beethoven. If his reputation for insistence on a metronomic adherence to tempo with singers seemed not to apply quite so consistently and firmly to a purely orchestral performance, I think it was largely because Toscanini knew he could trust himself, but not his singers, with an elastic tempo. He would not give them the inch to take an ell out of.

So it happens that we hear in this recording the occasional, very slight hint of "meno mosso" as, for instance, in the long diminuendo sequence of dialogue between wind and strings which leads eventually to the *ff* tutti of the recapitulation, and in a scarcely perceptible *ritenuto* at the three-quaver hammer blow of the return of the opening theme itself at this same recapitulation. Like so many of Toscanini's deviations from rigidly strict tempo this *ritenuto* was little more than a drawing-in of breath before making an important statement. It certainly defies measurement by any metronome that I can manipulate, for it was the result of a sense of timing that was essentially human; no machine could ever have matched it.

These barely noticeable pauses for breath, however, naturally did nothing to impede the inexorable progress of a tremendously powerful dramatic performance. The secret of its force lay primarily in Toscanini's revolutionary view of the tempo at which this first movement should be played, and particularly of the precise moment when that tempo was considered to begin (which was in the very first bar—not in the seventh or eighth). Once one heard that opening statement of Beethoven's theme it was obvious that one was in for a thoroughly unusual musical experience. It was a "different" performance only in the sense that for the first time one had the feeling that this was the genuine Beethoven: the sheer emotional impact of the music was so powerful and unfamiliar that one could truthfully say that this must have been how the Fifth Symphony sounded the day it was born in the composer's brain. It was an emotional experience that was physically exhausting for the listener too; it left me personally limp enough to wish that there could have been an interval in which to recover from a punishing spiritual battering (an interval which the gramophone now enables me to enjoy).

Certainly, no slow movement ever came as so welcome a relief from dramatic tension as the one which follows in this symphony.

2. *Andante con moto*

This slow movement could always be pointed to as a model demonstration of three aspects of Toscanini's technical genius: his evocation of *cantabile* from an orchestra, his understanding and interpretation of the words "Andante con moto", and his wonderful sense of instrumental balance. The first of these aspects was clear from the warm, singing "dolce" of the opening passage for violas and violoncellos, the second from the easy, inevitable flow of the music which never stopped to admire itself in the looking-glass, as it were, and the third from the superbly clean and dynamically balanced voicing of the wood-wind in such little passages as their communal contribution to the statement of the main theme. (As an aside: Toscanini took this Andante at roughly $\flat = 84$. My score suggests it should be 92, though on whose editorial authority it does not state. And yet people still say Toscanini played things too fast. . . .)

A close analysis of Toscanini's performance of this movement would in the end resemble an academic programme note: he did no more than the composer asked of him in the score, but did it in his own inimitable way. It would be pointless to pretend that there was nothing idiosyncratic about the way his ear could balance the "matching dynamics" of the echoes, imitations and responses between woodwind and strings, the translucent quality of the detail of the inner parts of the orchestral texture, or the wonderfully apt *sotto voce* excitement of the hushed *pp* of the short "più mosso" sequence—which Toscanini never allowed to increase its initial speed and permitted to grow louder only when the score demanded it. But these were things which are still there for the playing by any conductors who have the imagination and the patience to observe that Beethoven's instructions are magnificently unequivocal. There were few movements Toscanini ever performed in Beethoven's symphonies which were treated so literally as this slow movement of the Fifth Symphony. It was the supreme example of seeing "what is there".

3. *Scherzo: Allegro*

leading to

4. Finale: Allegro

When I first heard Toscanini conduct the Fifth Symphony I
was in New York and separated from my scores by 3000 miles
of the Atlantic. When he came to the opening phrase of the
Scherzo he did something which I had never heard before,
and which so impressed me that one of the first things I did on
returning to England some months later was to go to my
score to see what was in it that I had not noticed before, or
whether what Toscanini had done was in it at all. On consulting
the printed note I had my first experience of Toscanini's
habit of doing something exactly as the composer asked that it
should be done and thereby making the most familiar music
suddenly sound startlingly new. It was no more than the
performance of a single bar that had led me to check what I
had heard with the score, the bar marked "poco rit." in the
phrase:

Ex. 29

It may seem remarkable that anybody could possibly need to
consult a score to check up on such a familiar moment in such a
familiar symphony; I did so because Toscanini had made it
sound so different that I could not believe my ears. It was
different because he *underplayed* it by comparison with the
performances of other conductors to which I had been accustomed. The operative word in Beethoven's instructions
Toscanini considered to be "poco". Instead, as so many others
had done, of stretching the *poco rit.* to such a point that it sounded
several bars long (and with a crescendo thrown in for good
measure), Toscanini had brought his supremely vocal view of
music to bear on the phrase to make it sound as though it were
not being bowed but *breathed* (which, of course, it is later on by
the wind instruments). Its timing and effect were as subtle and
uncommunicable on paper as the typical anticipation of the
second beat and the delaying of the third in the "chuck-
chucks" of a Viennese waltz played by the Vienna Philharmonic. Mostly, I think, it was the result of Toscanini's

greatest, most imponderable gift: the gift of timing, which dominated his entire musical being whether he was concerned with the detail of a single bar of "poco rit." or the four acts of *Otello*.

The drama Toscanini brought to the Scherzo of the Fifth Symphony was tremendous, and it was a drama that was by no means out of place. Regarded quite objectively this Scherzo is perhaps the most thoroughly, queerly odd that was ever conceived. Its whole mood is one of conspiratorial stealth. The principal subject is never played louder than *piano*, and for the most part it is *pianissimo*; it lacks the broad playfulness of Beethoven's other scherzos, and there is scarcely an instance of the characteristic tossing backwards-and-forwards of a theme between one section of the orchestra and another. "Matching dynamics" there certainly were for Toscanini to demonstrate, but they were less obviously notice-able than in the Scherzo of the Eroica, for instance. By making the "poco rit." bars sound as though they were expertly inserted moments of rubato (it has been said that Toscanini was uniquely able to do more in the way of expression, phrasing and rubato "within the beat" than anybody who ever lived) the basic rhythm of this deliberate-paced Scherzo had a sinister determination and inexorability which became more intense without for a moment quickening during the *fugato* of the C major Trio.

The uncanniest episode of all, however, was what Toscanini made of the recapitulation. Here the *sempre pp* of the whole passage assumed a quality of what I can only describe as com-parable to the "audible silence" which Verdi created at such moments as the beginning of the last act of *La Traviata* and the entrance of Otello into Desdemona's room. The orchestral detail is mercifully clear in this recording of Toscanini's and untold generations of conductors will, I hope, marvel how he managed to get a pizzicato passage to sound *cantabile* and how he induced the feather-weight brushing of the strings in the bowed passages by the first violins and violas. Perhaps one day a conductor will discover the secret of these details again. I hope so—for Beethoven's sake.

The link between this peculiar Scherzo and the Finale was another tour de force by Toscanini. He seemed to start the long *ppp* passage with its throbbing drum beat if anything one *p* quieter than it is shown in the score. The degree of "pianis- simo-ness" was purely relative, of course; and the main thing, as with any Toscanini *pianissimo*, was that it was always *audible* because it was music, not a conjuring trick to make music somehow disappear before our very ears. The most important feature of his performance of this bridge passage was not that when he encountered the instruction "sempre pp" he took that as an invitation to keep the music as quiet as it had always been ("sempre" could hardly mean anything else to an Italian musician), but that he refrained from beginning any kind of crescendo until Beethoven asked for it—eight bars before the Finale proper bursts out with its C major Allegro. In these final bars Beethoven adds instruments to reinforce his crescendo and it was not until the bassoons came in with their first notes that there was the first hint of the sudden emergence of light from the darkness of a Scherzo which has no counterpart in any of Beethoven's symphonies.

The first impression of Toscanini's lifting of the curtain on the Finale of the Fifth Symphony was always one of brilliant sunlight, of music which automatically created a tremendously powerful visual image such as one really did not expect to experience in the context of a performance so mercifully devoid of romantic nonsense about Fate Knocking at the Door. The impression was inescapable, however, whether one approved of it or not. The second impression was made as immediately as the first: the impression that in spite of the prodigious intensity and dramatic force of the first movement this Finale was not going to be an anticlimax or anything like it. As usual Tos- canini had held something in reserve; his prodigious energy and powerful rhythmic control had not been squandered entirely on the dramatic tenseness of the first movement; and yet it hardly seemed possible, listening to that movement, that he was not devoting to it all the vitality he possessed. Perhaps of all the unfathomable secrets of Toscanini's genius one of the most mysterious of all was his incredible reserve of physical, nervous and plain, simple musical energy which permitted no slackening of concentration or dedication, either by himself or by the orchestra he was conducting.

So it was that in the Finale of the Fifth Symphony there was

always that sense of what one can only regard as inevitability
created by an irresistible rhythmic force which gave every
note its full value and kept the tempo going like the beat of
some gigantic heart. This control of tempo and rhythm was
particularly noticeable at those points where the majority of
conductors allow the music to run away with them and the
rhythm to lose its tautness. One example of Toscanini's characteristic "bounce" was always heard in the incisiveness of the
detached notes in the phrase:

Ex. 30

While there was no slowing up of the tempo for the second
subject or of any of the other themes which it is fashionable
to treat as exempt from the basic tempo of this movement,
there was equally no lack of *dolcezza* where it was marked nor
interruption of the long rapid *legato* lines which play such an
important part in the development section. The sheer physical
marvel of Toscanini's building up to the typical *ff* half-climax
found in Beethoven's finales, was another peculiar mystery,
of course—the mystery being how he could possibly ever sur-
pass the intensity of that half-climax (apparently played as *ff*
as was humanly possible) when the final true climax of the
work came to be faced. But he could, and did.

The force of the half-climax automatically intensified the
contrast of the echo of the Scherzo which follows, to which
Toscanini's infallible sense of tempo and instrumental balance
brought all the conspiratorial stealth of the earlier movement
together with an added sinisterness created by the difference
in orchestration between this quotation and the Scherzo
proper.

With the recapitulation Toscanini returned to the business of
building towards his final climax; the Coda found him, like
some superb athlete, timing his effort perfectly (how often and
instinctively one uses the term "timing" in studying Toscanini's
greatness!) and bringing the Finale to its end at the psy-
chological moment of maximum impetus. The finishing spurt

(I use the term to describe intensity of effort, not increase of tempo, for Toscanini naturally did not quicken the pace once he had made the authorized "sempre più allegro" and reached the final Presto) succeeded in making sense of Beethoven where it seemed none had existed before: namely, in the last four pages of the score, with their repeated tonic and dominant chords and—so often—unending reiteration of the chord of C major which ends the symphony. Until I heard Toscanini's performance the final pages had invariably seemed to last too long; just when one thought Beethoven had said all there was to say, he said it again. But that, I now realize, was not Beethoven's fault; it was the fault of the average conductor, who had never conceived this last movement in such a way that it led inevitably, logically and unanswerably to those famous last words. Toscanini, on the other hand, *timed* his climax and so brought out the musical significance of those last twenty-four bars of C major; they ceased to be meaningless, curtain-lowering chords, as it were, but in a miraculous way became a tune, an essential part of the pattern of the whole work.

In those words "part of the pattern of the whole work" we find what is perhaps the keystone of Toscanini's greatness. When he began the Allegro con brio of the first movement of the Fifth Symphony where Beethoven had put it—over the very first bar—he knew that with the inevitability of a Verdi opera Beethoven's music had embarked on a course of organic growth which reached its final maturity only at the final *ff* of the last bar of the symphony, three movements later. I have frequently referred in this study to what I call "matching dynamics". There was also in Toscanini's performances of Beethoven's symphonies an equally important quality that one might call "matching tempi". His famous maxim that "it is easy to play *a piacere*—the thing is to play *a tempo*" did not, on the face of it, explain how tempo could be converted into rhythm, but perhaps in making that observation he did in fact say all there was to be said in the matter. For in the end didn't the secret of Toscanini's great rhythmic control and energy lie, in fact, in his choice of exactly the right tempo which once it was adopted, automatically created an irresistible and natural rhythm?

SYMPHONY No 6 in F, Opus 68
("Pastoral")
[1808]

NBC Symphony Orchestra

GREAT BRITAIN: HMV ALP 1129
RCA RB–16104
U.S.A.: Victor LM 1755
1952

1. Allegro ma non troppo
("Cheerful impressions received on arriving in the country")

The French version of Beethoven's heading to this first movement reads: "Sensations agréables qui s'éveillent à l'arrivée a
la campagne", and I think the word "agréable" is what most
closely described Toscanini's way with it. It was a performance
of great charm and warmth with the more peaceful aspects of
the countryside expressed in a lovely easy-flowing *cantilena*.
As always, Toscanini showed what manner of performance it
was going to be by his handling of the opening phrase. He
gave great grace to the first theme by making a slight rallentando in the third bar before settling on the pause in the
fourth:

Ex. 31

The easy tempo of this fragment and the string episode
which follows quickened considerably into a faster movement
when the oboe takes over the theme—an unorthodox process
which gave an unexpectedly cheerful and perky touch to the
section in which the theme is heard complete for the first time.
　　Perhaps because of its very *agréable* expansiveness and sense
of relaxed good humour, Toscanini allowed himself many
intriguing little moments of deviation from the printed note of
the Pastoral, as well as some illuminating demonstrations of
literal interpretation; and the symphony seemed to me to offer

more obvious examples of close attention to detail than one encountered in Toscanini's performances of some of the other symphonies. Many of these details were in their way so peculiar to Toscanini and sounded so right that one tended to take them for granted. There was nothing, for instance, more deceptively simple, nor more easily overlooked, than the little figure for two clarinets, two bassoons and two horns which first occurs just after the statement of the principal theme:

Ex. 32

Toscanini used to take endless trouble at rehearsal to achieve the right balance of this phrase between the six instruments— two with a single reed, two with a double reed and two brass instruments. The finished result sounded as smooth as velvet; but there were often long periods of blood, tears, toil and sweat in the process of reaching this result. (The same wonderful balance was achieved when, in the recapitulation, the phrase is scored with violas in thirds added, and the sound lost none of its original clarity or extraordinary lightness of touch.)

Another typical detail, very shortly after the passage in Ex. 32, which was gone almost before one noticed it (though being a movement in sonata form with a repeat of the exposition—which Toscanini observed—it could be heard at least three times in one key or another) was the tiniest suggestion of a *ritenuto* which was no more than a hesitation in the first bar of the phrase:

Ex. 33

Whether or not one should draw attention to these things is a matter that it is not easy to decide. While one of the reasons I

embarked on this book at all was to study Toscanini's performances in the hope that their analysis might prove instructive
to later generations of conductors, there is obviously a danger
that the unconsidered imitation of the details of these performances might be regarded as sufficient to make an interpretation of a Beethoven symphony "different", and therefore of
some musical value. "Difference", however, is not in itself a
virtue in music, whether we are concerned with its composition or performance, and it is pointless for the mediocrely
gifted conductor to set about apeing Toscanini's subtle application of rubato unless he possesses Toscanini's instinctive sense
of the timing of these nuances. On the other hand, one cannot
let details like the hinted-at *ritenuto* in Ex. 33 pass without
comment. To be able to introduce a *ritenuto* of that kind, with
the effect and stylistic justification that Toscanini could,
should be the ambition of every conductor, and I hope they
will regard it as something worth emulating; just as I hope that
pointing out Toscanini's vigorous attack on the opening bars
of the Fifth Symphony will do something to make conductors
in general revise their views of a masterpiece that has become
hackneyed, not because it has been played too often, but too
seldom—too seldom, that is, as its composer wrote it.

The *ritenuto* in the Pastoral is for the advanced student, of
course; the tempo of the first bars of the Fifth is a question of
broad principle which should be a compulsory subject of
study for all. At least, I feel that the young conductor who
accepts the basic fact of Toscanini's tempo of the Fifth as an
article of musical faith starts with an advantage over his
colleague who does not. It is a step in the right direction that
cannot do any harm and might—if it is backed up by talent,
humility, integrity and fierce determination—perhaps even
do a little good.

The basic principles demonstrated by Toscanini were not
always defined with such spectacular clarity as some of the
details of his performances; but they were present nevertheless.
The little theme which is first heard in the violoncellos under
the figure starting in the second bar of Ex. 33, a slow-starting
8-bar theme which is taken up by first violins, flute, basses and
violoncellos together, and finally by horns, was given *equal*
prominence by Toscanini with the more clearly noticeable

quaver figure which runs through the whole sequence, and which most conductors allow to dominate and obscure the slower-moving counter-subject.

While the predominant note of Toscanini's performance of this first movement was one of a gentle and supple lyricism, there were moments of strongly contrasted vigour and tension. One of these moments, indeed, was something which has stood out in the memory over the years: the tautness and electric incisiveness of the sudden *f* of the strings' entry with the theme:

Ex. 34

The "crackle" of these few bars introduced a completely new colour to the general orchestral picture; it was not just a matter of the strings playing loudly at this point. They made an entirely different noise which was gone as quickly and un-expectedly as it had come, as though on Beethoven's country walk somebody, in opening the window of a farmhouse, had suddenly reflected the sun in the window pane. It was a queer moment, this unanticipated brilliance in a movement of characteristically "soft" orchestration which ended, in Tos-canini's hands, in two final bars of the most exquisitely *piano* chords of F major.

2. *Andante molto mosso*
("By the brook")

To say that Toscanini understood and observed Beethoven's tempo indication at the start of this movement is almost enough to convey to those familiar with his performances what manner of music they are likely to hear in this recording. He made of it a supremely easy-flowing movement of long, warm, "singing" phrases, played *dolcissimo* and giving a phenomenal sense of breadth and gentle perpetual motion. It was a wonderfully peaceful and evocative interpretation of one of Beethoven's most endearing slow movements.

As usual there were characteristic instances of Toscanini's

flexibility, of variation of tempo "within the beat". One of the most effective of these was the *ritenuto* in the two notes preceeding the trill whenever this phrase (or its counterpart) appears:

Ex. 35

The clarity of the detail which Toscanini revealed in this particular slow movement was more than usually remarkable, for with its constant onomatopœic burbling by the strings (including two solo violoncellos) it is a thicker orchestral texture than one encounters elsewhere in Beethoven's scores, the blue-print of much of the "thickening-up" of orchestral sound which reached its densest in the scores of Wagner and Richard Strauss. With the Pastoral, however, Toscanini was still able to bring a chamber-music quality to the playing— as, indeed, he succeeded in doing with Wagner, too, when it came to it.

To show that his eternal admonition "Cantare! Cantare!" was not meant only for those instruments with the top-line melody to play, Toscanini's concern that the inner parts should "sing" just as much as the others was especially well demonstrated from the first bar of this very *agréable* scene. He induced in the purely subsidiary accompanying parts of second violins, violas and the two solo violoncellos not merely a "singing" tone, but gave what can so often sound nothing but a series of dull, repetitive figures an interesting melodic life of their own. It was Toscanini's preoccupation with the quality of every single strand of the orchestral texture which made him the unique figure he was in music.

3. Scherzo: Allegro
("Peasants' Merrymaking")

The gentleness which had prevailed through the two preceeding movements still lingered on at the beginning of the

Scherzo with Toscanini. There was a superb lightness of touch both in the opening unison *pp* passage for the strings and in the *dolce* and *legato* passage that succeeds it. But though the first episode is marked *pp* until the quick crescendo to the loud (*ff*) tutti, there was no question of one section having more or less rhythmic vitality than the other—an obvious enough observation, perhaps, but it is surprising how many conductors and even people who ought to know better, like jazz-band leaders, confuse noise with rhythmic vitality. It was one of Toscanini's most exciting and stimulating beliefs that a rhythm had to be strict, in tempo and convincing, whether it was to be presented *pp* or *ff*.

In this Scherzo, in spite of the promise of rustic revelry in the movement's sub-title, the music is paradoxically light on its feet. It is the angular simplicity of the melody played by the peasants' wind band which creates a pastoral atmosphere; there are no heavy dynamics to suggest the galumphing of peasant feet. No suggestion, that is, until the 2/4 Trio brings on as robust and hearty a dancing troupe of rustics as Toscanini knew how to describe on the composer's behalf. This short Trio, with its gruffness and primitive vigour, provided another instance of Toscanini's remarkable ability to produce music from no matter how loud or coarse an instrumental texture. It may all have been marked *ff*; but he still had time to let us hear the detail of the precisely played "snap" of phrases like:

Ex. 36

This same outstanding command of instrumental tone and dynamics which always produced music from the most ear-splitting *ff* was particularly apparent in the storm sequence of the Pastoral Symphony. When Toscanini reached the interlude which is formally presented in the score as

4. Allegro
("Tempest and Storm")

there was music to be heard in every flash of lightning, in every menacing roll of distant thunder, in the very opening of the heavens themselves that Beethoven depicted in this fantasy.

Beethoven, so many conductors forget, was not making a "sound picture" of his Tempest and Storm. He was not a composer of film music; he was writing in essentially musical terms about a thunderstorm and it was the music that Toscanini gave us in this episode, with its modulations and figures, its fascinatingly dramatic variety of dynamics and—as so few other conductors have ever done—its tunes as well. It took a true musician, in other words, to find where the music lay.

Purists, students and others may be interested in what sound like Toscanini's personal additions to the timpani part in the score of this sequence. He prolonged the first *ff* timpani roll for a further four bars, added timpani to the first beats of bars 53 and 54, and introduced, in addition to Beethoven's timpani in C and F, a third drum in G at Letter E in the score (bar 78). In no case did these adornments do anything but add appropriate colour to Beethoven's score.

There remains to be mentioned Toscanini's typically gracious phrasing of the flute's two *dolce* bars leading to:

5. Allegretto
("The Shepherd's Hymn—Thanksgiving after the Storm")

Compared with the Finales of the other five Beethoven symphonies considered so far in this study, the last movement of the Pastoral conducted by Toscanini was remarkably straightforward—or, in other words, faithful to the letter as well as to the spirit of the score. It was a case of an easy-flowing tempo and a performance as characteristically *sempre cantando* as the slow movement had been—a movement which it greatly resembles, of course, in its use of almost incessantly burbling quaver figures. It was a conception of immense warmth and charm, in which there were neither frills nor rallentandos (not even in the last two bars of all), but a tremendous breadth and atmosphere of serenity about music which seemed to play itself. Tovey's saying that the Pastoral Symphony "has the enormous strength of someone who knows how to relax" applied as much to its performance by Toscanini, of course, as to its composition by Beethoven; and I think this recording, at any rate, shows that Toscanini's reputation for inflexibility and relentless driving was more than ever unjustified.

The Finale of the Pastoral was one of Beethoven's most gentle conceptions. Toscanini treated it as such and made of it a thing of rare beauty.

SYMPHONY No 7 in A, Opus 92
[1812]

NBC Symphony Orchestra

GREAT BRITAIN: HMV ALP 1119
RCA RB–16105
U.S.A.: Victor LM 1756
1951

1. Poco sostenuto – Vivace

Except that one could say it about almost any performance of any Beethoven symphony by Toscanini, one is tempted to consider that perhaps his performance of the Seventh Symphony was his supreme rhythmic tour de force. Whereas in the other symphonies he seemed to create rhythm, or at least draw attention to rhythm which we had not realized was so strong a feature of the music as he saw it to be, by the application of his own unique sense of rhythm to the Seventh Symphony Toscanini made a work, already nicknamed by Wagner "The Apotheosis of the Dance", a tremendous and compelling experience without parallel in his time. The young Guido Cantelli came nearest in my experience to Toscanini's essentially rhythmic conception of the work; he perceived the primarily rhythmic nature of the music, but fell down on the matter of tempo. He kept an admirably strict tempo and there was no doubt that the rhythm was precise; but the tempo was just too fast for the natural pulse of the music. To use a term readily understood and accepted as a cardinal virtue in another sphere of music: it did not "swing".

Toscanini's Seventh Symphony always "swung" in the sense that the conductor had an infallible sense of the natural pulse of the music from the very first bar. The slow introduction to the first movement was an exemplary demonstration of the importance of an unbroken, unforced rhythm in making *musical* sense of one of the most difficult problems encountered in Beethoven's music: the scale-passages which play so powerful a part in the gradual building up of the climax of this introduction. Weingartner, in his study of Beethoven's symphonies, always stressed the danger of allowing these scales to degenerate into such musical insignificance that they sounded merely like exercises. Toscanini was Weingartner's prize pupil in this respect, for he gave these particular passages an unusual dramatic intensity comparable, indeed, to the famous scales associated with the Commendatore's music in Mozart's *Don Giovanni*.

Toscanini's typical concern for instrumental balance was also demonstrated in this introduction where the *dolce* passages for the woodwind had the same almost pastel quality which was found in the beautifully balanced figures in the Pastoral Symphony referred to on page 65 (Ex. 32). There was, too, a fine example of "matching dynamics" to be noted in the echo by violins of the flute and oboe unison in the six bars leading to the Vivace.

The transition from the slow introduction to the principal section of this first movement was a fascinating exhibition of Toscanini's ability to establish a change of tempo and rhythm without a trace of a "join". It was a transition made with such superb ease, indeed, that there was time for the faintest suspicion of a breath-pause before the sudden *piano* with which the flute states the first 6/8 theme.

From this point onwards Toscanini produced a remarkable "bounce" in the rhythm, and the secret of it, I believe, was that throughout this whole 6/8 movement there was what one might call "rhythmic equality" between such figures as

Ex. 37

and

Ex. 38

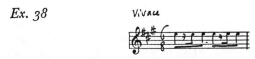

The notes were given their full time-value and there was no suggestion that the first example shown above was in any way less rhythmically pregnant than the second. The precision with which Toscanini demanded these figures should be played also had the salutory effect of making Beethoven's more difficult rhythms sound as if they were meant, instead of making us feel that the orchestra was getting out of the conductor's control. This was particularly apparent, I remember, in passages where the figure in Ex. 38 is played by the strings while the wind have a figure based on

Ex. 39

Toscanini created a remarkable tension in this first movement, but within that apparently rigid beat there was always time for the unexpected and intriguing suggestion of a *ritenuto* in the " lead-in" to the *ff* recapitulation which matched the little breath-pause made, as I have already remarked, when the flute first gave out the theme at the beginning of the Vivace.

The building up of the climax of this movement, beginning with the reiterated phrase in the basses, was an object lesson by Toscanini in the dramatic force of an increase in volume which is not accompanied by an increase in tempo. So often one has heard this relentless, menacing sequence deprived of its whole "bite" by conductors who try to raise our pulses by the artificial introduction of a stepped-up tempo. Toscanini never allowed the drama of this great crescendo to lose its grip on us by losing his grip on it.

2. Allegretto

Toscanini took longer over perfecting the opening and closing chords of this movement than over any detail I ever heard him concentrate on at rehearsal. These chords of A minor played by eight wind instruments also provided a very rare instance of Toscanini's description of what he wanted in non-musical terms. Usually he was sternly insistent in thinking of music in terms of music, as we know from his description of the first movement of the Eroica. But when he came to this second movement of the Seventh Symphony, he described the sound he wanted as "like a mirror". Listening to the effect of the chord when it was finally played to his satisfaction it is clear what Toscanini had in mind; but how the first oboist, for instance, set about playing his instrument to create a sound "like a mirror" I can't quite imagine. There was nevertheless a strange quality of remoteness about the sound Toscanini created, a sound which might have been the audible counterpart of an image seen smokily in an old mirror. Whether or not the simile will immediately strike the listener who has heard no mention of Toscanini and his effect of sound "like a mirror", is another matter; but the 2-bar diminuendo from f to pp was certainly a superb display of Toscanini's control over instrumental dynamics. Each of the eight players seemed to make the diminuendo at exactly the same moment and to exactly the same degree as the other seven. It was a wonderful testimony to the phenomenal acuteness of Toscanini's ear.

A colleague, reviewing this recording when it was first released in England, remarked with admiration and astonishment on a "sudden pp" Toscanini introduced into this Allegretto. As I had not yet heard the record I presumed Toscanini had in some way departed from his usual practice, or rather from the practice I was familiar with, for I could not see from the score where any "sudden pp" could possibly be made without wrecking the line and intentions of the whole movement. When, eventually, I came to compare Toscanini's

recording with the score, all I found was neither more nor less
than the conductor's characteristically strict adherence to
Beethoven's markings. The "sudden" *pianissimo* was the *pp*
which characterizes the repetition of the passage,

Ex. 40

when it is played by the second violins after the theme has been
stated by violas. Why my colleague should have noticed the
pp on this occasion and not when the music goes through the
identical procedure played by the violas an octave lower
twenty-four bars earlier, I do not know.

On the other hand, if the critic's surprise was not so much at
the occurrence of the "sudden *pp*" as its quality then the remark is understandable. This whole movement was a masterly
exhibition of Toscanini's command of dynamics and nowhere
was it better shown, I think, than in the crescendo which
begins soon after the "sudden *pp*" itself and, after the climax
of the *ff* tutti, in the gradual diminuendo which ends the first
section and leads into the second section in A major. The
quality of a Toscanini *pp*, sudden or otherwise, was something
which it is difficult to analyse. As I have suggested, it was as
though the music were in some way quieter without ever being
fainter, or less clearly audible. I think this was particularly
noticeable in the wind chords which top and tail the Allegretto,
where the diminuendo made by the players was so perfectly
graded and synchronized that it sounded just as if the chord
had been played *forte* for the whole couple of bars but a master-
hand at some control knob had slowly faded it down to *pp*.
This "grading-down" of volume, but never of tone or expression, was particularly remarkable in the short fugal
development by the strings in the recapitulation where, as
usual, there was a typical clarity and dynamic balance which
made wonderful contrapuntal sense of the part-writing.* This

* There is another characteristic and scarcely perceptible breath-pause at the
ff lead-in to the *p dolce* recapitulation section in the recording which is most beguiling
in its unexpectedness.

regard for polyphonic detail was noticeable throughout almost the entire movement, for once the long *legato* tune makes its appearance after the statement of the first theme, there is scarcely a moment when two themes are not being played simultaneously, for even in the interlude in the major the characteristic rhythm of the opening theme is heard in the basses.

Unlike some of his contemporaries, Toscanini did not look on "Allegretto" as suggesting that a funeral march had been in the composer's mind—even though this is the only slow movement in Beethoven's nine symphonies, with the exception of the Eroica, which is in a minor key. He took it at an easy-going ♩ = 76 or thereabouts.

3. *Scherzo: Presto – Trio: Assai meno presto*

To those who knew Toscanini's way with a Beethoven scherzo this was always one of his most characteristically vigorous performances. It abounded in "matching dynamics" of quite exquisite grading, and *sforzati* of ferocious incisiveness. By Toscanini's standards, indeed, it was an academic interpretation. There have been some who have quarrelled with the tempo of the Trio, but I have never been among them. "Assai meno presto" means "much less fast"; it does not mean "adagio assai", or "this must be taken at a snail's pace". To me, whatever the "correct" and traditional tempo for this Trio may be, Toscanini's dropping from ♩. = 132 for the Scherzo to between 76 and 80 for the Trio seemed to me *assai meno* and (which is what counts most in music, oddly enough) *sounded* absolutely right—in spite of the 84 recommended in my score.

So far as indicated tempo is concerned Toscanini made one change: the four bars of the sustained unison A which leads with a diminuendo from *ff* to *p* to the Assai meno presto of the Trio were not played—each time they occur in the movement —at the tempo of the Scherzo but used as a bridge passage in which the tempo as well as the key was changed, Toscanini making his rallentando from Presto to Assai meno presto in the course of them. How the rallentando was made, whether it began at the beginning of the 4-bar phrase, in the second or third bar, or whether the Scherzo tempo was sustained but a pause made in the fourth bar, I do not remember. Probably only those orchestral musicians who played under Toscanini will be able to say; the young conductor who wishes to emulate an effective gesture will have to make up his own mind how to do it.

The Trio itself was another occasion which delighted that same colleague of mine writing, I believe, in *The Gramophone*, who was intrigued by what he called the "flick" given by Toscanini at the end of the phrase:

Ex. 41

As in the case of the "sudden *pp*" all Toscanini was doing was to play the phrase as Beethoven wrote it—four notes *legato*, the fifth with the staccato mark shown in the score. When this passage is heard for the last time in the tutti at second hearing of the Trio (before the last recapitulation of the Scherzo) Toscanini made no alteration in the actual phrasing of the passage, but held the tempo back for a split second in the second bar to give the tune a momentary deliberateness. It was one of those typical Toscanini touches of pure timing which are best disregarded by the student conductor. Far better ignore the whole affair than make a mess of it by exaggeration.

4. *Allegro con brio*

A symphony which Toscanini began with such a vigorous and exciting first movement ended with an even more vigorous and exciting view of the meaning of the term "con brio". Like the Finale of the Fifth, the last movement of the Seventh Symphony was a prodigious climax to a work which, hearing Toscanini conduct it for the first time, it seemed impossible that even he could prevent being a slight anticlimax. But, as always, Toscanini had power in reserve for his last lap, and the phenomenal energy expended on this Finale, the tremendous rhythmic tension and seemingly inexhaustible power of lifting the orchestra to ever greater dynamic heights, was an emotional experience which left the listener as physically exhausted as the conductor should have been but uniquely never was.

The tautness of Toscanini's rhythm in this Finale to the Apotheosis of the Dance was astonishing, and his performance had a "bounce" which was perhaps most noticeable in those passages where the whole of the string section of the orchestra played in this rhythm:

Ex. 42

These bars I think provide the final and supreme test of any conductor's feeling for rhythm. A huge majority of conductors let this passage run away with them. There is a difference, however, between allowing a tempo to run away with you and raising the "rate of striking" of a tempo. Toscanini never normally let a tempo run away with him, but he had an instinctive sense of when—and how much—to quicken a tempo. He did it with subtle and magnificent effect in this Finale when he came to the passage in the development section which builds up to a false climax with the sequence beginning:

Ex. 43

It is hard to decide exactly where, or how much in purely metronomic terms, Toscanini increased the tempo in this passage. It was an almost imperceptible quickening of the musical pulse, corresponding, one might say, to the quickening of the listener's own pulse as it was naturally affected by the tension of the music itself, with its dramatic and persistent building-up of the motif I have quoted.

In the case of the sequence leading to the climax proper, Toscanini maintained a rigid tempo which, by its very relentlessness, added to the drama of the grim *ostinato* of the basses, just as a similar rigidity of tempo had intensified the effect of the great *ostinato* passage on which the climax of the first movement was built. In this Finale it was clear that Beethoven expected the performers to pull out a little extra something, for he marked his climax to be played *fff*—a dynamic marking one does not encounter often in Beethoven's symphonies. Toscanini observed it with his whole heart and soul.

SYMPHONY No 8 in F, Opus 93
[1812]

NBC Symphony Orchestra

GREAT BRITAIN: HMV ALP 1108
RCA RB–16106
U.S.A.: Victor LM 1757
1952

1. Allegro vivace e con brio

Of all Beethoven's symphonies I am inclined to think that the Eighth is the most often badly performed. The reason for this is largely a carelessness of approach on the part of conductors who have heard a great deal about the nature of the "even-numbered" symphonies of Beethoven and not enough about seeing what the composer has to say for himself.

As a consequence the Eighth Symphony is more often than not treated in such an enervatingly "relaxed" and "even-numbered" manner that the music is scarcely able to get up off the floor, let alone speak up for itself. Beethoven has his gentler moments, but a caress from Beethoven is about as cozy as a hug from a friendly bear, and it seems to me to show a wilful disregard, or just plain ignorance, of Beethoven's intentions to carry the fetish of "even-numberedness" to such a length that the first movement is played as though it were a stately minuet. But that is how most conductors make it sound to me after experience of Toscanini's tempo for this first movement. Once again, it seemed, Toscanini saw "what is there" more clearly than others, though perhaps he was helped a little by the lucky chance that he happened to speak Italian and so understood what the composer meant by the words "Allegro vivace e con brio".

This enabled Toscanini to attack the Eighth Symphony at some 160 vigorous and rhythmic beats to the minute, and in so doing presented the listener hearing him conduct the work for the first time with what was yet another astonishing demonstration that the "even-numbered" Beethoven was in his way no less vital or dramatic than the composer of the "odd-numbered" symphonies.

The irresistible rhythm of Toscanini's performance, not only of this movement but of the whole symphony, was such that it made one think that the Eighth as well as the Seventh Symphony qualified to be regarded as the Apotheosis of the Dance. But perhaps the reason the Eighth has not been adapted as a ballet (so far as I know) is that the experience of would-be choreographers has been limited to those unfortunate pedestrian performances which have become more or less standard in the concert halls of the world, and which are as choreographically inspiring as the Good Friday Music in *Parsifal*.

Toscanini's establishment of a "natural-pulse tempo" and the precise observance of note-values were, as usual, the principal factors of the tremendous rhythmic impetus of this movement. The characteristic insistence on note-values was particularly noticeable in passages such as the sequence following the statement of the second subject, when the whole orchestra played those dotted-quaver-semi-quaver phrases which Toscanini always made to "bounce" so captivatingly:

Ex. 44

The second subject itself was kept free of all sentimentality by Toscanini's strict adherence to Beethoven's markings. He made a ritardando in the bar it is marked (and not before) and resumed the original tempo in the bar immediately following—which is where Beethoven put it, as the following quotation shows:

Ex. 45

This may seem a rather obvious thing to draw attention to, but it is always the obvious things that most need drawing attention to. Time and again one hears the ritardando beginning in the bar before it is marked (if not earlier), while the *a tempo* bar is used as a starting-point for a gradual accelerando which does not bring us back to the original tempo until two bars later, when the tune of the second subject is repeated by the woodwind. Toscanini did exactly what Beethoven asked and so preserved a unique continuity of musical thought. The ritardando did not interrupt the rhythmic progress of the movement, as it so often does; it acted as a wonderfully effective pause for breath, the more effective for being so brief.

Toscanini always made the repeat of the exposition section and then got down to the business of the development. How anybody could ever have regarded this section as mild, "even-numbered" Beethoven is incredible—at least, when it was played with the intensity and determination that Toscanini brought to it. Listening to Toscanini's performance of this part of the movement one did, ironically, hear a suggestion of a minuet. But it was no stately, charming minuet; it was the echo of the grim minuet of Mozart's G minor symphony.

The development leads to one of Beethoven's rare *fff* climaxes with the recapitulation. The building of the climax was something Toscanini put so much into that immediately after the *fff* repetition of the first theme of this movement at this point, he allowed the tempo to slacken for a few moments. The quiet *dolce* echo of the theme by the woodwind and horns at a slightly slower tempo came as a welcome and completely justified relaxation of a comparatively long period of tension. In this recapitulation, Toscanini did in fact introduce another element of that unmeasurable flexibility into his otherwise rigid tempo. After the little episode of *meno mosso* I have mentioned above, he returned gradually to the basic tempo but permitted a suggestion of ritardando when the subject is heard again—in the bar *before* it is marked by the composer; on the other hand, the tempo is resumed at once in the bar marked "a tempo".

In the final moments of the first movement—the last twelve bars—there was a ravishing and typical passage of "matching dynamics" in the short diminuendo passage of dialogue between pizzicato strings and the rest of the orchestra, trumpets, drums and all. It is a sequence that leads to a breath-taking "pay-off" (I can think of no other term to describe it) provided by the whispered, *pianissimo* quotation from the opening theme by the strings in the final cadence.

2. *Allegretto scherzando*

Paradoxically it is a more or less fruitless task to take a metronome to Toscanini's recorded performance of this movement: paradoxical, because for all the well-known association of this tick-tocking movement with Dr Mälzel, the inventor of the metronome, Toscanini's tempo was most refreshingly flexible—varying between 92 and 96 with a suggestion of a retard here and an accelerando there. But—and this was a further paradox—the overriding impression of Toscanini's performance of this movement was one of quite extraordinary precision of tempo allied to relentlessness of rhythm. So it seemed that the man who could so often make people believe that they were hearing something played faster than in fact it was, could also delude one into believing that there was no resilience or variation of tempo in a movement notoriously inspired by the invention of the metronome itself.

The barely perceptible fluctuations of tempo, however, were as nothing compared to the miraculous sense of instrumental balance that Toscanini always displayed in this movement. There was a lightness of touch and sparkle in the detail which suggested to me that so far as Toscanini was concerned it was on the whole not only Beethoven, but Rossini as well who was enjoying himself as a disciple of Mozart. And, with the exception of the *forte* theme played a couple of times by the strings in unison which is characteristic of the gruffness of the playful Beethoven, so it might well be; for nowhere is the Rossini touch more evident than in the comic crescendo and illusory accelerando which brings the movement to an end.*

This Allegretto scherzando was a masterpiece of Toscanini's purely orchestral technique—by which I mean that the sheer mechanics of the balance of the instruments, the gossamer quality of the tone he drew from the strings, the fantastic lightness and clarity of the staccato passages, the superb and inevitable "matching dynamics" and the typical "singing" sound he knew how to evoke from an apparently uninteresting pizzicato sequence in one of the inner string parts were things which, however much one may attempt to analyse them, were in the end too peculiar and personal to be imitated. All one can do is to draw attention to them as spectacular manifestations of Toscanini's genius and hope that later generations will be inspired by his example. It is when we consider the purely physical quality of the sound Toscanini got out of an orchestra that we have to admit that his ear, like Caruso's voice or Kreisler's tone, was never quite like anyone else's.

3. Tempo di Menuetto

After the *scherzando* quality of the previous movement, Toscanini did not try to make us believe, as so many would, that this Minuet is another pseudo-scherzo like the minuet in the First Symphony. He accepted it as a minuet pure and simple and took it at a moderate tempo in the region of $\downarrow$ = 120 and so provided the listener with a welcome feeling of relaxation, emphasizing Beethoven's simple sense of fun and giving the whole thing a sincere and quaint charm of its own in such passages as the exquisitely matched dynamics of the question-and-answer passage between wind and strings just before the solo bassoon recapitulates the theme in the second section of the Minuet.

The Trio Toscanini took a little slower than the Minuet but not much, and he permitted the first horn a slight *ritenuto* in his solo 3-note lead-in to the *dolce* passage for two horns; but to me

---

* The effect of an accelerando is created not by increasing the tempo but by increasing the number of notes to the beat.

the real joy of this episode was the wonderful richness of the tone Toscanini always inspired in the violoncello obbligato. Perhaps because he had played the instrument himself, it always seemed that the violoncellos in an orchestra conducted by Toscanini played better for him than for any other conductor. Toscanini clearly took a personal interest in the instrument in the Trio of this third movement.

4. Allegro vivace

With the Eighth Symphony Toscanini revealed more than any other conductor I ever heard an aspect of Beethoven which one would not normally associate with the composer— namely, his quite extraordinarily delicate orchestral touch. Beethoven's personality as an orchestrator was powerfully individual, of course, but one does not in the ordinary way look for more from him than a fierce dramatic intensity, a rough humour in the scherzos and a warm colouring for the *cantilena* of his slow movements. In the second and fourth movements of the Eighth Symphony Toscanini showed that Beethoven, for all his deafness, was capable of unusual, untypical, and in some cases singularly "forward-looking" orchestral effects. As, on the whole, the history of orchestration has been made by music that whispers rather than by music that shouts, so Beethoven's orchestral invention in this symphony is most noticeable where the orchestra is quietest. That Toscanini should have been virtually alone in perceiving the originality of these passages was not surprising. He did not, as others do, accept Beethoven's orchestration as "classical" and leave it at that; he saw "what is there" and with his unique sense of balance and feeling for orchestral texture, re-created an old and familiar score in such a way that it sounded as new and surprising to us as it must have done to Beethoven's contemporaries.

The last movement of the Eighth Symphony, like the Allegretto, is almost a virtuoso vehicle for the display of "matching dynamics" and subtle detail that demands the utmost clarity and meticulous balance of each individual thread in the orchestral texture in order to make its full effect. Toscanini brought all he knew to reveal the purely physical beauties of this Finale and its delicate figures and intricate cross-rhythms.

The very first bars, indeed, were a master-lesson in the articulation of the triplets which play such an important part in the design of the whole movement:

Ex. 46

Toscanini's basic tempo for the Finale was in the region of ♩ =152; I say "basic" for this tempo was by no means inelastic. He introduced moments of *espansione* whenever the broad *dolce* second subject occurred without, in some curious way, ever seeming to interrupt the flowing rhythmic continuity of the conception—even though, after these momentary breathers, he naturally had to quicken up again in order to resume his original "rate of striking".

That Beethoven did not automatically discard his natural ferocity even for an "even-numbered" symphony was demonstrated by Toscanini in the development section of this Finale, which was every bit as dramatic as its counterpart in the Seventh Symphony for example. But more than with most of Toscanini's Beethoven recordings the full extent of his performance of the Eighth is best understood by careful comparison of the recording with the full score, for in doing so the student, however well he may think he knows his Beethoven symphonies, will be able not only to "see what is there", but to know what it can sound like. From no other Beethoven symphony did Toscanini have the opportunity to evoke such purely sensuous beauty as from the Allegretto and Finale of the Eighth.

SYMPHONY No 9 in D minor, Opus 125 ("Choral")
[1823]

NBC Symphony Orchestra
Eileen Farrell (Soprano)
Nan Merriman (Contralto)
Jan Peerce (Tenor)
Norman Scott (Bass)
Robert Shaw Chorale

GREAT BRITAIN: HMV ALP 1039/40
RCA RB–16106/7
U.S.A.: Victor LM 6009
1952

1. Allegro ma non troppo, un poco maestoso

Like the first movement of Beethoven's Fifth Symphony, the first movement of the Ninth was propelled (there is no other word) by Toscanini with tremendous power. Tension and drama dominated the whole conception, from the menacing *sotto voce* beginnings of the opening crescendo to the final *ff* unison cadence, with such force and relentlessness that it seemed impossible that Toscanini could possibly draw on any reserves of energy to prevent the rest of the symphony being something of an anticlimax. In his own peculiar, superhuman way, however, Toscanini never muffed a climax and there was no clearer pointer to the nature of the Finale to come than the ferocious intensity of the first movement.

Denis Matthews, in the course of an article in *The Gramophone*, described Toscanini's conception of the opening bars of the symphony as "a gigantic anacrusis to the unison theme, in which all the elements are unleashed". It is an apt description, for however well one knew Beethoven's score and what to expect, the tremendous impact of Toscanini's *ff* at this point was quite shattering in its unexpectedness and vigour.

When Toscanini conducted the Ninth Symphony in London in 1939, I went to the rehearsals at Queen's Hall. It was an

enlightening experience, as one may imagine; particularly the
first rehearsal, which ended abruptly with the conductor walking out at a point somewhere near letter G in the score of the
first movement—that is, after some 210 bars—and not returning until the next day. Not unnaturally what one might call
the vital Point of No Return proved to be one of the most
interesting features of Toscanini's whole conception of the
work, and something to which I will refer in a moment.
Before the rehearsal broke up, however, Toscanini spent a lot
of time on aspects of the music which are as noticeable in the
1952 recording, for instance, as they were in a performance
nearly fifteen years earlier, details which were typical of his
extraordinary consistency not only in what was superbly good,
but also in what could be disquietingly bad, or at best, puzzling.

Among the things he took infinite trouble over was the playing of the last three notes of the phrase,

Ex. 47

Toscanini's concern with this was that the dotted quavers
should be given their full value—so full, indeed, that it sounded
at first as though they were being unduly lingered over. As so
often happened with Toscanini, this turned out to be another
illusion; one had grown so used to other people *not* giving the
notes their full value that one scarcely recognized the literal
observance of "what is there" as anything but a rather doubtful
indulgence in rubato.

Less pleasing than Toscanini's treatment of this particular
detail, I always found his un-literal view of another phrase
early in the first movement—namely, his performance of a
passage which Beethoven marked simply "sempre pp" but
which Toscanini interpreted in this manner:

Ex. 48

I found this disquieting principally because I have never seen any point in giving a Beethoven phrase a dynamic treatment which would be more appropriate to Brahms; in fact, as I have already mentioned in the chapter on Beethoven's First Symphony, there is in the first movement of Brahms' Fourth Symphony a phrase which closely resembles the passage I have quoted above and which Brahms decorated with the crescendo–diminuendo Toscanini applied, for reasons best known to himself, to the Beethoven passage. Certainly this dynamic embellishment was only a momentary distraction (although in accordance with the formal construction of the movement, it naturally occurred not once but twice), but I have always found it disturbing because it seemed to me so unnecessary. Beethoven uses the figure as an important and repeated element in building up a crescendo from *sempre pp* to a *f* leading in the course of another six bars to a *ff*. I cannot see that it does anything but exaggerate and altogether over-romanticize the passage to introduce a foreign note of Storm and Stress with a crescendo–diminuendo of growing intensity as each bar goes by. But, as I have said, this was a consistent feature of Toscanini's performance of the Ninth Symphony; he did it as blatantly in 1939 as he did it in his 1952 recording.

It is also worth remarking, I think, that when he reached this B flat section which introduces the second subject Toscanini quickened the tempo slightly; but again it was one of those characteristic, scarcely perceptible increases which to describe as "un poco più mosso" would be an exaggeration; still less could one ever decide exactly how or when the original tempo was resumed.

The flash-point of the rehearsal Toscanini walked out of was the second occurrence of the motif:

Ex. 49

What it was that upset the conductor at this point nobody clearly remembers. There is a theory that on demanding a return to "Letter G" a Scottish or North Country member of the BBC Orchestra had acknowledged the instruction with "Ay", which Toscanini had misunderstood as a dissenting voice insisting that it should have been "Letter I". Whatever it was, the storm broke out in all its violence, with a downpour of pure Italian without a hint of the Anglo-Franco-German esperanto which Toscanini favoured in his more amicable moments of contact with foreign orchestras. Up to that point relations had been normal enough, with Toscanini beating out the rhythm with his baton on the closed leather-bound score which he held in his left hand, and crying "Tempo! Tempo!" The six bars were played again and again, until at the mysterious, critical moment, Toscanini walked off the platform. He had failed to make himself clear, and when that happened he almost invariably lost his temper—not so much with his players as with himself and the general frailty of mankind which had denied the composer his due. Toscanini came back next day and rehearsals of the Ninth Symphony were resumed as if nothing had happened.

Perhaps recalling the six bars which had so frustrated Toscanini made an understandably deep impression on me; on the other hand, they were clearly bars which Toscanini regarded as unusually important, for what he was striving for is as apparent in the recording as it had been at the performance of the work at Queen's Hall. In fact, all it really amounted to was a question of note-values once more—the maintenance of a strict tempo until the "rit." was reached, which was made to sound surprisingly broad by the strictness of the tempo of the preceding bars, and the full value given to the notes in the bars marked "a tempo". It was these last two bars which had a peculiar, incomparable magic and whose execution I suspect was the source of so much concern on Toscanini's part. The four notes played by clarinet and bassoons were made to sound as though they were played by strings, *piano* counterparts of the dotted notes in Ex. 49—but to such an extent that the wind instruments seemed to caress the notes like a violinist drawing a long bow *sul tasto*.

The effect of details such as these was something that has too often been ignored in considering Toscanini's performances which were accepted—or dismissed—according to personal prejudice, as characteristically tense and dramatic. In the course of making this study it has been quite extraordinary to discover how often he introduced a quality of gentleness and faithfully observed the composer's plea for a *dolce* approach when one somehow expected him—at least, from reading reviews of his recordings before hearing them—to drive on relentlessly without pausing for a moment to stare by the wayside.

This first movement, in fact, included moments of quite remarkable tenderness—notably when violins and violas play the first subject in octaves in G minor immediately following the first occasion the theme of Ex. 49 is heard (at letter F), and when, shortly before the final crescendo in the Coda, the theme of Ex. 49 is the subject of a duologue between wind and strings. In this last instance Toscanini made very free with the tempo to give the passage a strange unexpected pathos, by starting the little tune considerably *meno mosso* than the strictly-beaten tempo of the bars all the fuss had been about, and continuing the ritardando through the bars marked "a tempo" so that the basic tempo was not resumed until the long crescendo began, with its tremolando chromatic figure in the strings and the slowly building, repeated phrases of the wood-wind which Toscanini made sound superbly sinister.

Just as Toscanini was uniquely able to combine expressiveness with a rigid tempo so he seemed able to incorporate comparatively long sequences of rhythmic freedom and elasticity without for a moment weakening the tremendously firm and powerful rhythmic foundation on which the whole movement rested. The final three unison bars of this first movement of the Ninth, which Toscanini took without the faintest hint of a rallentando, epitomized the rhythmic force and intensity of a conception of fantastically extraordinary incisiveness and impetus. It was a conception which, like that of the other Beethoven symphonies, gave new life to a too-familiar work. Toscanini not only found powerful drama in this first movement, but he achieved something equally rare by his performance: he made it sound the right length. And this, let me assure those who have not experienced some of the performances of the Ninth Symphony that come a critic's way, is no trivial assertion. Toscanini timed this first movement as a great Shakespearean actor will time a long blank-verse speech: one was conscious of listening to poetry, but above all one was conscious that the sense of the poetry was as clear and easy to grasp as prose. Beethoven had something urgent to say; Toscanini ensured that it was said as directly and emphatically as possible.

For the purist there were two further divergencies from Beethoven's score to note in Toscanini's performance. The first occurred in the timpani part of the *ff* recapitulation. Though Beethoven marked the phrase *ff* throughout, Toscanini started *ff* and made a powerful crescendo so that the passage sounded

Ex. 50

and applied the crescendo to the timpani phrase shown in the fourth bar above, when it occurred again, four and six bars later respectively.

The other alteration to Beethoven's score was the playing an octave higher by the violins of the passage I have indicated as (a) in the phrase:

Ex. 51

Beethoven clearly had this in mind, for he wrote the flute part to sound as the string passage has now been arranged to sound; the only reason Beethoven did not write it that way himself was that he could not trust the orchestral violinists of his day to play an unprepared high A in the seventh position in tune. The high A which is heard in the first violin part four bars earlier was another matter: it came at the end of an ascending scale passage and was therefore "safe". I do not doubt this modification of Beethoven's score has been made many times; in

Toscanini's performance it sounded so particularly effective because of the intensity of the crescendo it precipitated, in a great cascade of sound.

2. Scherzo: Molto vivace

Just as the music itself is on a monumental scale which places it in a different class from the rest of Beethoven's scherzos, so Toscanini's performance of the Scherzo of the Ninth Symphony was a supremely exhilarating experience. It would not be true to say that in no other scherzo did he equal the dramatic excitement and tremendous rhythmic impetus of this movement nor achieve such perfectly balanced "matching dynamics"; he did. It was just that the Scherzo of the Ninth offered more and greater opportunities for the exhibition of these unique qualities.

"Molto vivace" Toscanini took to mean roughly $\downarrow$. = 126, and a *molto vivace* conception it was in which every detail of Beethoven's contrapuntal ingenuities—the *fugato* passages, the use of imitation and canon—was apparent to the meanest ear. Also apparent to the meanest ear, but less often appreciated, was Toscanini's amazing control over the volume as well as the quality of the sound coming from the orchestra. The first thirty-six bars of the main theme are marked *pp* with an occasional reminder in the form of "sempre pp". In the course of this passage one group of instruments after another is added; the opening oboe-and-second-violins phrase of four bars is augmented first by clarinet and violas, then by bassoon, horn and violoncello, flute and first violins, two horns and double basses, and finally, when the woodwind are playing in pairs, the trumpets join in—but all *sempre pp*. In spite of this progressive increase of the number of instruments playing, Toscanini in a miraculous way seemed to keep the total volume of the orchestral sound at the same *pp* level, so that while the colour changed the Scherzo was no louder in bar 40, when twelve wind instruments had been added to the strings, than it had been when a single oboe had supported the second violins thirty bars earlier. It was in the fantastic attention paid to details like this that Toscanini was unique, though one wondered not so much that he paid attention to detail as at his instinctive assessment of the importance, purpose and potentialities of these details in the first place.

Toscanini followed the Weingartner edition of Beethoven's symphonies closely in the matter of what are now accepted as the standard modifications and augmentations of Beethoven's instrumentation; but he also introduced one or two notions of his own, and when it came to the boisterous second subject of this Scherzo, Toscanini had horns reinforce the 16-bar phrase which begins,

Ex. 52

and it sounded so right and effectively in character that it was surprising to realize, when one looked at the score after hearing it for the first time, that it was something Toscanini had added on his own account. At any rate, I never noticed it in Weingartner's version.

The Trio Toscanini took at the tempo suggested to him by the *stringendo* which leads to the Presto—a brisk affair full of rough fun and allowing none of the coyness which so often afflicts conductors when they come, for instance, to the end of the phrase:

Ex. 53

The clarity of the detail, the beauty of the phrasing, and the easy, unelaborate matter-of-factness of Toscanini's whole conception of this Trio are something the student is best advised to study for himself, for what Toscanini did in the concert hall has been well preserved in the recording.

It also goes without saying, I hope, that Toscanini made all the repeats shown in Beethoven's score, including, of course, the *da capo* of the Scherzo. The omission of the *da capo* repeat is not so rare as some might think, and there have been several occasions in my life when I have known a conductor—with a modesty that was as welcome as it was unusual—decide that he was not capable of holding our interest with a reprise of the Scherzo and had proceeded mercifully from the Trio straight to the Coda. On the other hand, I have known far too many conductors who have not had the sense or humility to administer this *coup de grâce* and one has suffered a lingering agony in consequence.

3. Adagio e molto cantabile – Andante moderato – Adagio

Once more Beethoven's instructions at the head of this movement were a clear pointer to the class of performance one was to expect from Toscanini. My own memory of his Ninth Symphony with the BBC Orchestra is of a better performance of the slow movement than the one perpetuated on this recording; but then few orchestras in the world at that time could match the woodwind section of the British orchestra, and this movement depends a great deal on the warmth and quality of the woodwind playing. Consequently, the recording does not seem to me to give as worthy an account of Toscanini's conception of this slow movement as my recollection of the performance I heard in 1939. It has nothing to do with "hi-fi" or such conceits; it is just that the woodwind players of the NBC Symphony Orchestra were not capable of rising to such heights as those of the BBC Symphony Orchestra. That is nothing for the Americans to be ashamed of, of course; I doubt if there are many orchestras that could ever have set a quartet of woodwind principals in the field to compare with Messrs Murchie, MacDonough, Thurston and Camden.

In the course of this study of Beethoven's symphonies as they were performed by Toscanini, I have purposely made no mention of the musical quality of the latter-day recordings. The differences between what has been bequeathed to us and what those of us remember who heard Toscanini in person are not so great that the average listener cannot compensate automatically for comparatively trivial shortcomings of execution in the recordings, and in doing so get some idea of how the best Toscanini performances must have sounded. With this slow movement of the Ninth, however, it is only by asking the studious listener to the recording to ignore what he hears coming from the woodwind and supply in his own mind in its place what his experience of Toscanini's temperament and methods will tell him he should expect to hear, that anything approaching the true nature of much of this particular item in Toscanini's Legacy can be enjoyed. The spirit of Toscanini's contribution was naturally willing; the flesh of some of the musicians under him in this recording was a little weak.

Having warned the student that he must use his judgment and imagination in filling some of the gaps that are apparent in the purely physical details of the recording of this movement, he will need no reassurance of the tremendous breadth and dignity which characterized Toscanini's conception and so repeatedly proved the total sum to be greater than the parts. The total sum in this case was an unending musical line flowing in a smooth and effortless rhythm which not even the fanfare-like interruptions towards the end of the variations disturbed for a moment. Perhaps more than any other quality, Toscanini found and respected in this slow movement Beethoven's phenomenal simplicity. Toscanini allowed the composer to speak for himself; he exaggerated nothing; he dramatized nothing; the music just "sang" and was as *dolce* and *cantabile* as he could persuade his orchestra to make it. Even the pizzicato passages had a singing quality, a melodic life of their own which raised them above the level of mere mechanical devices to keep the accompanying harmonies going, while for sheer loveliness of sound there was little to compare with the feather-light brush strokes of the grace notes in the accompaniment played by the strings in the bars which immediately precede the two playings of the long *espressivo* tune of the second theme:

Ex. 54

Toscanini's conducting of this slow movement was a masterly demonstration of the perception of "what is there", the wisdom of restraint and the abjuration of any form of "expression" not clearly implicit in the composer's score. Only one nuance occurred which was not in the score: the suggestion of a rallentando in the final bar of the modulation leading to the Adagio section which follows the second playing of the theme quoted in Ex. 54; but even this was based on a certain logic for there is a pause marked in the final bar of the modulation leading to the Tempo I° variation which follows the first playing of the second theme.

4. *Presto – Allegro ma non troppo – Allegro assai – Presto – Allegro assai – Allegro assai vivace, alla marcia – Andante maestoso – Allegro energico, sempre ben marcato – Allegro ma non tanto – Poco adagio – Prestissimo*

Toscanini's handling of the instrumental recitatives at the beginning of this movement was one of the most interesting features of his performance of the Ninth Symphony. Once again, one hesitates to recommend his method to the student conductor, for so much of the effectiveness of Toscanini's unorthodox touches depend on his superb sense of timing, on the gauging of a *ritenuto* to the fraction of a split second that made the difference between its sounding natural and sounding laboured and affected. Nevertheless, I think it is worth while describing in some detail how Toscanini gave dramatic character and musical interest to those unaccompanied passages for violoncellos and basses which so many conductors plod through as though the whole idea was a tiresome formality. The first noticeable modification of Beethoven's text was in the third passage of recitative, immediately following the quotation from the first movement, when Toscanini began the diminuendo some three bars earlier than indicated in the score. The next modification was rather more drastic. It occurred in the fourth recitative (following the quotation from the Scherzo) where in place of Beethoven's simple dynamic markings— *forte* for five and a half bars and then a diminuendo—Toscanini introduced a breath-pause and a superbly dramatic *piano subito* to make the passage sound like this:

Ex. 55

The next recitative, after the quotation from the slow movement, ended not with the *ff* indicated but with the last note *piano* to match the *piano* of the woodwind chord that follows it. Finally, Toscanini ended the introduction with a lengthy pause before embarking on the main theme of the Finale at a vigorous Allegro assai of about ♩ = 80.

From this moment onwards this last movement had a quite incredible air of suppressed excitement, later to burst out with a dazzling brilliance and force as the first tutti was reached. The recording fortunately gives some idea of the remarkable contrapuntal clarity of this first statement of the theme and the warmth of the *dolce* quality that Toscanini brought to this lovely passage for strings and solo bassoon—a superb example of his gift of combining lyrical warmth and rhythmic vigour without ever allowing one element to detract from the other.

As the tutti ended Toscanini introduced another typical "breath-pause", this time where the general *forte* gives way to a sudden *piano* at the bar marked "poco ritenuto". It was an unexpected touch, but, once more, so carefully timed that it sounded absolutely natural.

After the vocal recitative Toscanini reverted to an Allegro assai that was slightly faster than the earlier tempo. A gradual increase in the tempo as the emotional intensity of the music grew stronger was one of the most remarkable features of Toscanini's interpretation of this Finale of the Ninth Symphony. Not only did he take the Allegro assai reprise of the theme faster than its original statement, but when he came to the Alla marcia—a wonderfully exhilarating and *assai vivace* episode—he quickened the tempo for the long fugal instrumental variation which follows the tenor solo, and quickened it yet again for the final choral outburst in the tune which brings this 6/8 section to a close. This process, of course, was quite contrary to all Toscanini's frequent proclamations of the inviolable Sanctity of Tempo; there is no indication in the score that any of the three sections of this Alla marcia episode should be played at anything but the initially prescribed Allegro assai vivace. But there is no doubt that in adopting a progressively quicker tempo as this movement-within-a-movement proceeded Toscanini increased that sense of excitement and jubilation which is, after all, the essence of this whole Finale. There was an air

of strangely appropriate recklessness about the long *sempre pp*
wind and percussion introduction to the tenor's solo and the
gradual crescendo leading to the vigorous instrumental interlude, which gave the music that refreshing Shakespearean
vulgarity and exuberance which was peculiar to Beethoven's
genius. Toscanini made this inspired street music vulgar in the
best and most universal sense. Lesser conductors, lacking Toscanini's infallible dramatic instinct, nearly always make it
sound commonplace; which is another matter altogether and
not at all what the composer had in mind.

The Alla marcia episode was, in its way, perhaps the most
fascinating sequence in the whole Finale as Toscanini conducted it. It showed, above all, his prodigious ability to make
the most complicated inner parts of instrumental polyphony
"speak" with the utmost clarity; in this respect the contrapuntal orchestral passage following the tenor-and-chorus
marching song was a remarkable model, particularly in view
of the brisk and exciting tempo at which Toscanini took it and
the superbly taut control he exercised over the breath-takingly
energetic rhythm.

That same polyphonic clarity was naturally also as apparent
in the subsequent sections, which are for the most part entirely
choral, as it had been in the purely instrumental episodes. No
detail, no subsidiary figure, whether in the most thunderous
fortissimo or in the magically eloquent *pianissimi* in the bars
leading to the Allegro energico, was obscured either in the
chorus or in the orchestra. Nor, in this concern for individual
detail, was the climax deprived of a single atom of its fullest
possible power, or the quiet B major interlude for the solo
quartet of any of its lyrical warmth.

The tremendous reserves of energy Toscanini could call on
as each stage of the final climax was reached, made this Finale
a stupendous and inspiring achievement. To me, at least, it
was the ultimate revelation of what Beethoven must have
heard in his inner ear, and a supremely fitting conclusion to a
personal experience which came all too rarely: Toscanini's
performance of the Nine Symphonies of Beethoven.

Until artistic values are sacrificed once and for all to the false
gods of some new electronic marvel of high fidelity and they

are finally deleted as out-moded, Toscanini's recordings of the
Beethoven symphonies will continue mercifully to give posterity
some idea of how he made this music sound and to jog the
memory of those of us who were fortunate enough to experience
the event of a lifetime in person. Whatever the technical
shortcomings of these records as a medium of reproduction,
nothing can obscure—except to the meanest imagination—the
greatness of the whole conception.

One was conscious of Toscanini, I believe, only when he was
doing things the wrong way; when he was doing things the
right way one was conscious only of the composer. This was
never more the case than in the unique panorama provided by
Toscanini of Beethoven's symphonies, each one of which in
some miraculous way appeared to us again in all its original
freshness to startle us with the novelty of its construction, its
harmonic and instrumental daring. For us in the twentieth
century, who have had fifty years of atonality, dissonance has
surely few terrors left; and yet there was never a time when I
heard them played by Toscanini that I was not physically
shocked by the dramatic violence of the discords in the first
movement of the Eroica and in the Presto passages at the
beginning of the Finale of the Ninth Symphony. We heard such
things not as slices of the familiar history of the symphony, but
as their composer's contemporaries heard them—the latest and
most daring stroke by a revolutionary and modern composer.

I confess that since first hearing Beethoven's symphonies conducted by Toscanini in New York in 1933 I have not willingly
listened to their performance by other conductors. Now and
then, for the sheer masochistic joy of it, I listen to some contemporary conductor on the radio to hear how he gets along
with something like the Fifth or the Eroica. I switch off and
reflect that it is incredible that the good gentleman should not
have learned at least *something* from Toscanini: after all, he left
quite respectable recordings of Beethoven's symphonies. Then I
realize that it is not Toscanini who seems to have lived in vain but
Beethoven, whose dynamic markings and descriptions of tempo,
whose note-values and phrase-marks, whose very language, it
seems, are not yet understood. Once more, I feel, a conductor
has stood between me and Beethoven. Toscanini never did:
he stood at Beethoven's side and humbly led him towards us.

FIDELIO

Opera in Two Acts, Opus 72 b
[1814]

Don Fernando	Nicola Moscona
Don Pizarro	Herbert Janssen
Florestan	Jan Peerce
Leonore	Rose Bampton
Rocco	Sidor Belarsky
Marzelline	Eleanor Steber
Jaquino	Joseph Laderoute

NBC Symphony Orchestra and Chorus

GREAT BRITAIN: HMV ALP 1304/5
U.S.A.: Victor LM 6025
1944

It happened that I came to hear Toscanini perform *Fidelio* at Salzburg after I had already heard him conduct eight of Beethoven's nine symphonies in New York. Quite accidentally it also happened that in writing this study I did not hear the recording of Beethoven's opera until I had heard and already written about the recordings of the symphonies. This experience ought, one thinks, to make a critic's task easier when he comes to study Toscanini's performance of *Fidelio*; he must surely know by now what to expect. Familiarity with Toscanini's methods, with his approach to Beethoven or any other composer, however, was in itself no guarantee whatsoever that the critic would know what to expect. He would certainly hear what he hoped to hear; but he was just as certain to hear for the first time in his life the most unexpected things which, to his astonishment, he would then discover had always been in the score.

In my own case, nevertheless, I found that the general principles which applied to Toscanini's performance of the symphonies applied to *Fidelio*, and that the student conductor who had learned, through his experience of the symphonies, the importance Toscanini attached to rhythm, to the ideal of a *cantabile* tone, the art of instrumental balance and the conception of "matching dynamics", and, above all, to the essentially dramatic character of Beethoven's music, would recognize that these familiar elements were all to be found in *Fidelio*.

Consequently, if this study of *Fidelio* seems to lack the examination of detail applied to the symphonies, it is because experience and understanding of Toscanini's performances of the nine symphonies will enable the student to take for granted those basic principles of Toscanini's Beethoven referred to above. These are the expected things. The unexpected things were the result of Toscanini's unique interpretation of the expected, or obvious, what-is-there things.

To those of us who heard Toscanini's Salzburg performances of *Fidelio* in 1935 the recording will serve as an incomparable aide-mémoire to an incomparable experience; to those who never heard Toscanini conduct the opera the recording will certainly give a pretty powerful idea of what they missed.

For the experienced and inexperienced alike, however, the recording has one great disadvantage which only the listener himself can combat. The performance—a broadcast—was given without the spoken dialogue, with the result that the musical numbers follow on, one after the other, with scarcely a moment's breathing space between them. Without the respite granted by the dialogue in a stage production it is my experience that the emotional intensity of the music is on too consistently high a plane. The absence of dialogue denies the listener the opportunity to relax. Beethoven made allowances in his music for the inclusion of dialogue to break up the sequence of numbers; if there had been no dialogue there would have been recitative to perform the same function, and if he had lived in a later operatic age he would just as certainly have introduced sequences of "conversation music" to lead from one high spot to another.

The trouble with *Fidelio* is that it is rather inclined to be full of high spots, anyway; to remove the listener's only chances to recover from one high spot before tackling the next does not altogether conduce to relaxed and easy listening. The remedy is certainly in the listener's own hands, of course. He can always get up as each number comes to an end, lift the tone-arm off the record and read the libretto to himself before continuing with the next number. The only drawback of this procedure is that it may well take twice as long to find the right place on the record again as it does to read the dialogue, and the dramatic continuity is infuriatingly interrupted in consequence. There is no doubt, however, that without the moments of respite provided by the dialogue in *Fidelio* the emotional and dramatic tension of the music is well-nigh overwhelming. It is certainly an exhausting experience the way Toscanini played it.

ACT I

One of the happiest features of *Fidelio* is the absence of any "traditions" associated with it. I do not regard the interpolation of the Leonore Overture No 3 as a "tradition": it is an expedient enjoyed, among others, by conductors who want to show off their ability to conduct "straight", instead of "musical" as it were, and by the more eccentric producers who, like a German gentleman at Covent Garden before the war, used the opening bars of the overture, with their *descending* scale, to match step by step Mme Lotte Lehmann's *ascent* of the stairs from the dungeon.

By "traditions" I mean the kind of messing-about with the score that is considered "time-honoured" and leads to the introduction of notes, tempi and "expression" which the composer never authorized. *Fidelio* has been spared such things because it has never been a popular opera, still less has it been a "singers' opera". On the other hand, it has in its time been made into a "conductor's opera", and almost automatically it has sounded monumentally dull as a result. Toscanini regarded *Fidelio* as he regarded *Aida* or *Otello*: as a "composer's opera", and it was in the revelation of Beethoven that the greatness of his performance lay.

In the very first bars of the Overture Toscanini indicated the nature of the performance we were to hear. The vigour of that arresting unison phrase was characteristic of the vigour and vitality which dominates the whole score of *Fidelio* and which Toscanini faithfully reproduced. The long Adagio which leads to the main Allegro section of the Overture was also a typical nutshell-example of the great expansiveness and breadth Toscanini invariably found in Beethoven's slow music. And there was particular drama, too, in the twice-a-bar crescendo sequence of drum beats. Toscanini somehow always made percussion instruments sound more musical than other conductors did and this timpani passage was unusually musical.

The opening number of the opera, the duet between Marzelline and Jaquino, was another typical indication of the quality and general features to come in Toscanini's performance of *Fidelio*—typical of the phenomenal clarity of all the orchestral detail, the unerringly "right" tempi, and those perfectly welded, imperceptible transitions from one tempo to another (there was a superb instance of this in the change from the Adagio to the main Allegro in the Overture).

Instrumental clarity was also what brought to Marzelline's aria just that touch of Beethoven's gruff charm which is nearly always missing from performances of *Fidelio*. Because Beethoven's charm was not so polished and aristocratic as Mozart's, many people presume that he had none at all. Toscanini recognized its existence in *Fidelio* as he recognized it in the symphonies, and he brought it to life by making every note in the score tell a story, as it were; so that for the first time in one's life there was a real and rare enchantment in the last dozen bars of Marzelline's aria. Toscanini gave this coda what Beethoven had obviously meant it to have: the charm, surprise and point of a good exit line.

The famous quartet in canon was remarkable for two typical Toscanini qualities: the ability to phrase a long slow movement so easily that it sounded as though the whole thing were being played in one breath or one bow, and the lovely "singing" tone of the pizzicato passages which double each statement of the theme by the voices.

Toscanini's control over instrumental tone was something which not even those who played under him have been able to explain or analyse satisfactorily. Two specific examples spring to my mind in this first scene of *Fidelio*: the brilliance and detail of the violin figures in Rocco's song about gold, and the wonderful *piano* of the two final chords of the trio which follows it, when the orchestra seemed to caress, instead of merely play, the notes. This was a moment of ravishing sound,

comparable to the final chords of the first movement of the
Pastoral Symphony—which, incidentally, is also in F major.

Toscanini's insistence on literal note-values made the not-
very-distinguished march tune which accompanies Pizarro's
entrance a little more interesting than one expected it to be.
It was Vivace and crisply rhythmical. There being no stage
business to justify it, Toscanini did not observe the repeat in the
recording.

The next episode in the recording—Pizarro's aria with the
chorus—seems to me more than most things to cry out for the
dialogue which precedes it in the opera. Obviously, Toscanini
was well aware of the dramatic situation at that point; the
music shows that. But the listener, I feel, would have been
helped to appreciate even more the shrill and fierce crescendo
of the 4-bar introduction to the aria if he had been able to hear
the sinister passage of dialogue which leads up to it. The
dramatic tension in this sequence was something Toscanini
made particularly powerful, largely by the understated
delivery of the chorus's first *piano* comments. By taking an
untheatrical view of this, Toscanini paradoxically created one
of the few theatrical moments in his recorded performance of
Fidelio. It is an opera full of drama, but not even Toscanini's
vast experience of the opera house could ever reproduce the
atmosphere of the theatre in *Fidelio* that he did in his studio
performances of Verdi's operas.

As I listen to this recording more frequently I begin to
wonder more and more whether it would not have been a good
idea to have slotted in the dialogue after the dialogue-less
broadcast performances of the music and so have given the
whole thing a more authentically theatrical atmosphere.
Toscanini, after all, never had much to do with the speaking of
the German dialogue of *Fidelio*, and even the listener who did
not understand German could scarcely have failed to benefit
from the introduction of non-musical moments which would
not only have enabled him to relax, but by their very sound and
mood would have conveyed something of the drama and so
heightened the contrast of words with the music either side of
them.

The duet between Pizarro and Rocco, in which the Prison
Governor propounds his plan to the jailer to kill Florestan, had

three superb moments in Toscanini's performance: a wonderful pathos in the *pp* passage in which Rocco asks Pizarro if he is talking about the man "who is barely alive, and who sways like a shadow", the unison passage for strings (also *pp*) which accompanied the Governor's description of how he plans to creep into the dungeon when Rocco has dug the grave for his victim, and the impact of the *ff* wind chord which follows it as the cue for Pizarro's declaration: "One stab . . . and he is silent" ("Ein Stoss . . .").

Leonore's great scene—"Abscheulicher!"—is one of the really satisfying dramatic moments in Toscanini's recording, for it re-created something of the dramatic effect of *Fidelio* heard in the theatre. The reason for this was very simple: "Abscheulicher!" follows directly on the Pizarro–Rocco duet; it is the immediate musical consequence of what has gone before and its impact is not delayed by explanatory dialogue.

The opening of Toscanini's grim Allegro agitato was an unforgettable moment. Contempt is not one of the emotions one expects to hear expressed in purely musical terms, but it seemed to me that the rapid, angry string figures which began the recitative had a quality of violence and bitterness that came very near to it. It was inevitable, of course, that from the most familiar number in the opera there should have emerged a typical example of Toscanini's genius for revealing aspects of music which one realized had apparently never been heard before. In this case he employed his miraculous sense of instrumental balance in the six bars of woodwind accompaniment to Leonore's reflection on the bright rainbow she can see shining against the black clouds. The effect was so obviously what Beethoven must have intended: a wonderfully ethereal sound to match Leonore's vision.

The aria itself was a model of Toscanini's infallible sense of the drama of Beethoven's music; his performance ranged from the most exquisite and moving *cantabile* accompaniment in the Adagio section to an exciting, fiery Allegro con brio in which everybody nevertheless seemed to have time to breathe—a most necessary concession for the three solo horns who play such an important part in this episode so quaintly scored for three horns, one bassoon and strings.

Once the Finale of the first act starts there is no more

dialogue, of course, and so we can enjoy Toscanini's recorded presentation of the drama without feeling that something is missing. And drama there is in abundance in this music, which Toscanini illumined with his remarkable mastery not only of the tempi, the rhythms, the "meaning" of the music, but of the purely physical quality of the instrumental sound. The Prisoners' Chorus was an incomparable display of this mastery which could produce the *pianissimo* (which was always audible because it was not exaggerated) of the prisoners' awe and wonder at their sight of the sun, the tense, secretive *piano* of the little woodwind figure heard when the prisoners echo the pleas of one of their number that they should speak softly in case they are overheard. The dynamics of this whole choral passage were astonishingly conceived, especially in the warmth and *dolce* phrasing of the woodwind.

This same easy-flowing "singing" of the woodwind parts characterized the Andante con moto duet between Leonore and Rocco a few pages after the Prisoners' Chorus. It was another sequence with all that immense breadth of phrasing and melodic line which one heard in Toscanini's performances of Beethoven's symphonies, flexible enough—"*espressivo* but *in tempo*"—to include the occasional unexpected rallentando as it included the unindicated accelerando in the last few bars leading to the Allegro molto of the breathless entrance of Marzelline and Jaquino with the news of Pizarro's approach.

The Finale, with all its excitement and tension, was indeed remarkable for Toscanini's very liberal approach to a great deal of it. The passage, for instance, in which Rocco excuses himself to Pizarro for having allowed the prisoners to come out into the spring sunshine, was suddenly and quite unexpectedly taken more slowly than the Allegro molto which, from the score, one thought had applied to the tempo ever since Marzelline's entrance.

The final moment of dynamic enchantment in this Finale came with Toscanini's bewitching treatment of the coda on which the curtain falls, and in which every detail of the *pp*-to-*ppp* "dying fall" is heard to emphasize what a superbly original end to an act this is.

ACT II

Scene 1

Toscanini brought to the long orchestral introduction to Florestan's aria a remarkable atmosphere of nobility and melancholy, and a dramatic tenseness created, first, by the surprising and odd harshness of the *forte* woodwind chords at the beginning, and later sustained by the figure in the timpani based on the sinister interval of E flat–A natural.

The performance of this aria was one of great flexibility of rhythm and beauty of instrumental texture; it alternated between tension and superbly moving passages of *dolce* phrasing, between tenderness and excitement, elation and despair; it included a moving allargando to lead into the final Poco allegro section of the aria and an unauthorized *stringendo* to assist the building of Florestan's jubilant climax. This *stringendo* had a wonderfully dramatic effect, for all that it showed Toscanini to be capable of committing one of the very sins he most deplored in other conductors, who, he said, "always make a rallentando on a diminuendo and an accelerando on a crescendo". The dramatic purpose of this *stringendo* was obvious, however, immediately one heard the instrumental postlude to the aria. Florestan is meant to sink exhausted; exactly what had exhausted him and how much was something Toscanini made abundantly clear by the force of the climax and limpness of the postlude. It was a wonderful realization of the dramatic strength of Beethoven's music.

The dialogue in the *Melodram* that follows was included in Toscanini's recording, and at once the opera became even more alive than before, to make one regret more than ever that the entire dialogue could not have been dubbed in afterwards.

The duet between Leonore and Rocco was another of those familiar pieces of music which Toscanini presented to the listener as a brand-new experience apparently unrelated to any other music of the same name one might have heard before. In this case it was the revelation of the astonishing instrumental colour of the whole episode, the remarkable sound of the double-bassoon making its sinister effect against a background

of miraculously controlled dynamics in the rest of the orchestra
—a characteristic instance, particularly in the diminuendo to
ppp of the last three bars, of Toscanini's ability to make the
quietest *ppp* an audible, musical noise.

The trio for Leonore, Florestan and Rocco was another
example of Toscanini's preoccupation with the details that
affect orchestral colour, achieved this time by an insistence
that the string figures which run through the scene should
not be played with any less singing tone just because they were
figures and not "tunes". In consequence, a peculiarly warm
sound came from this accompaniment. There was also an
intriguing little "throw-away" *decrescendo* coda to remind one
that no fewer than eight of the sixteen numbers in *Fidelio* end
extremely quietly with what one might call under-the-breath
exit lines.

The quartet which follows the entrance of Pizarro included
one unforgettable moment that stood out amidst all the intense
dramatic force Toscanini injected into the scene: the phenomenal effect, as Leonore reveals her identity as Florestan's wife,
of the dynamic sequence of diminuendo from *ff* to *piano*, to *f*,
piano, and a diminuendo to *pp* of the reiterated figure for oboes
and bassoons:

Ex. 56

The suspense created by these five simple bars was one of the
most astonishing touches in the whole of Toscanini's astonishing
performance of *Fidelio*. By the way the opera was produced for
gramophone records we were unfortunately denied Jaquino's
dramatic spoken announcement of the Minister's arrival, so the
second (louder) trumpet call off-stage is followed at once by
the resumption of the quartet—but with such a preliminary
orchestral outburst that one is given a potent musical reminder
of the situation.

The last number before the change of scene for the Finale,
the duet for Leonore and Florestan, offered another display of
Toscanini's sense of instrumental balance, of the importance of

a singing tone for the simplest string figures, his exciting representation of the elation of the lovers by an inspiring, taut yet flexible rhythm and another wonderfully timed, charming coda.

Scene 2

The Finale started off with as tremendous a crescendo as Toscanini knew how to produce for the march, building up to its climax with a masterly vigorous demonstration of rhythm and the essential part played in it by precise note-values.

The preliminary huzzahs and "Heils" at an end, Toscanini next set about showing that solemn *maestoso* music is not necessarily dull music, by allowing the tempo to move easily and so leave time for moments of warm *dolce* playing; and inspiring an immaculate performance of the detail in the figures accompanying Rocco's dramatic narrative. The supreme moment came, however, at the sequence which begins when, against sustained *p dolce* chords for strings, Don Fernando decides that Leonore shall remove Florestan's chains, and which develops as a superb hushed ensemble accompanied by wind and pizzicato strings.

How Toscanini made this passage sound, how infinite he made the breadth of the long wind phrases, how musical and *cantabile* the strings' subordinate pizzicato, has been preserved in this recording of *Fidelio*; and it remains one of the great Toscanini mysteries—unanalysable and inimitable.

The beauty of this Sostenuto assai was something which, whenever I have heard Toscanini's performance of *Fidelio*, has seemed quite unnecessarily shattered by the resumption of the formal winding-up of the Finale. But once you have resigned yourself to the prospect of a typical trumpets-and-drums *strepitosissimo* Finale, Toscanini's recording still has rewarding incidents well worth detailed consideration—particularly, I would say, the wonderful luminosity of the orchestral texture in the sequence ("sempre più piano") for Florestan and the male chorus, when the scintillating triplet figure for first violins is punctuated by chords for clarinets, bassoons and horns and more of those typically "singing" pizzicatos from second violins and violas of which Toscanini alone seemed to know the secret.

This was, in its way, another of those astonishing revelations of "what is there" in a score one thought one knew pretty well until then. The final mark of Toscanini's genius, however, was to be found perhaps in his illumination of the least interesting pages of the score—namely, the repetitively conventional cadences of the concluding Presto molto. His sense of timing, here as in the last pages of the Finale of the Fifth Symphony, gave these bars a logic and inevitability which convinced the listener (who needed some conviction in the light of less fortunate experience) that not only was there not a single chord of C major too many, but that the last one to be played was the most important of all.

For a great many people *Fidelio* is an opera they hear more as a duty than a pleasure. They know it is a masterpiece, and having paid their respects to it they tend to pass on to other less demanding operas. And one cannot altogether blame them, for *Fidelio* is perhaps the most demanding opera ever written, with virtually no moments of relaxation in the music. The spoken dialogue certainly gives one a breather in the theatre, but it does not alter the fact that the music, with the possible exception of some of the playfulness in Marzelline's aria, is on a consistently lofty plane and, as there always is with such music, there is a constant danger of its becoming a crashing bore unless the performance matches the inspiration of the composer.

Toscanini, having had personal experience of the difficulties encountered in its enjoyment, may have felt passionately on the subject of political liberty; a great many of us do. But it was not this personal belief that made his performance of *Fidelio* so outstanding, as is sometimes implied; after all, he gave a remarkable performance of *Otello* without, so far as we know, having had to go through the personal experience of smothering his wife with a pillow to be able to do so. The greatness of Toscanini's *Fidelio* was the result of a phenomenal perception of the score and a faithful reproduction of what the composer intended. Whatever a composer's philosophy, whatever his political beliefs, it is only through music that he can express them, and the most worthy champion of human rights among conductors in the world is not going to make *Fidelio* intelligible to us unless he enables Beethoven's music to speak for itself.

Toscanini enabled Beethoven's music to speak more clearly, more eloquently, more forcefully than most of us can remember, and in doing so made us forget the shortcomings of *Fidelio* as an opera and realize in full the drama of music inspired by an indestructible ideal and expressed with all the fire and conviction of which Beethoven's genius was capable.

MISSA SOLEMNIS in D, Opus 123
[1818–1823]

Lois Marshall (soprano)
Nan Merriman (mezzo-soprano)
Eugene Conley (tenor)
Jerome Hines (bass)
Robert Shaw Chorale
NBC Symphony Orchestra

GREAT BRITAIN: HMV ALP 1182/3
RCA RB–16133/4
U.S.A.: Victor LM 6013
1953

1. Kyrie

When Toscanini first conducted Beethoven's Missa Solemnis in London, I was a little surprised that it was not regarded, as the English still regard the Verdi Requiem, as a little too dramatic for local taste. On reflection I realized that, of course, Beethoven is a classic in England (he was German, after all, and therefore beyond suspicion), whereas Verdi is still suspected of a slight lack of musical breeding being, when all is said and done, only an Italian. With the possible exception of Verdi's Requiem, however, Toscanini never conducted anything more dramatic in a concert hall than the Beethoven Mass. And it was precisely this understanding of the dramatic element in Beethoven's music that made his performance of the Missa Solemnis an uniquely exciting experience.

To describe the performance of a Mass as "exciting" may sound a little irreverent to those to whom religious music, in order to qualify for the Diploma of Sanctity, must be sombre, slow and—too often—soporific. But the Mass, while it is a solemn ritual, is not a dull one; it is a ritual which inspires meditation, awe, peace of mind and tremendous jubilation— all those elements most prominent in Beethoven's setting of the Mass, and incomparably expressed in Toscanini's performance of it.

Toscanini's perception of the drama of the Missa Solemnis was apparent when the performance was only two beats old— in the three arresting timpani notes which create in a most remarkable and unanalysable manner that atmosphere of awe and wonder one encounters in *The Magic Flute*. A moment later, however, in the rich, warmly phrased passage in which the strings play a prominent but not principal part, there was every indication that the dramatic element was not to be stressed at the expense of the lyrical.

But while previous experience of Toscanini's performance of Beethoven prepared one for this familiar conception of contrasting moods, it could not give one any indication of his conception of all the unique features of this Mass—namely, Beethoven's unparalleled use of dynamics, which play a prodigious part in this score and which one can imagine less honest conductors than Toscanini exploiting to achieve all kinds of fanciful "effects". Toscanini, we know, had no time for "effects" of any kind, but by his uncanny sense of contrast and balance, he made the dynamics of the Missa Solemnis a factor of superb eloquence. So remarkable, indeed, was Toscanini's instinctive feeling for this aspect of Beethoven's music that one rushed to one's score on hearing the chorus's opening "Kyrie" to find out what he had done that one had apparently never heard before. All he had done was to reproduce "what is there". Each time those first three tremendous cries of "Kyrie" occur the last syllable is sung *piano*. It always is, of course, but it never sounds quite so astonishing and arresting as it does here.

Toscanini adopted an easy-moving tempo for the Kyrie ($\textstyle\frac{1}{2}$ = ca. 56) that was always flexible enough to allow one to get the full value of such passing details as the short plaintive duologue between clarinet and bassoon as the chorus are concluding the first long choral passage before the soloists start their quartet of "Christe eleison". This whole movement displays a remarkable range of dynamic light and shade, of dramatic contrasts heightened by Toscanini's masterly grading of the rapid diminuendo from *ff* to *piano* in the space of a bar, by the electrifying hush of a *piano* immediately after a tremendous crescendo, by his control over choir and orchestra that always ensured that the music was clearly audible and not just hinted at, as, for instance, in the beautifully realized *pp–ppp* of the chorus's "Christe eleison" leading back to the reprise of the opening orchestral introduction and second singing of the "Kyrie eleison", and in the lovely sound of the final diminuendo from *f* to *pp* in the last four bars of the movement.

2. Gloria

It was not just that Toscanini had made the last bar of the Kyrie so quiet, but that the Gloria opened with a tremendous *ff* in its own right which made the contrast even more dazzling. The dramatic force and exhilaration of the opening passages (the proclamation of the words "Gloria in excelsis Deo") was immense, and not even the obvious damping down by engineers of the volume in the recording altogether disguises the intensity of the sound heard by those of us who enjoyed Toscanini's Missa Solemnis "live".

The lightning, dramatic changes of mood in the part which follows are largely achieved by the composer's equally startling changes of dynamics. But not of tempo or rhythm; and this was something Toscanini demonstrated again and again in this work of Beethoven's, though not in all the composer's symphonies. In the symphonies one often encountered the hinted-at breath-pause between a *ff* and a sudden *piano*. In the Mass, on the other hand, Toscanini kept the rhythm going strictly and in doing so increased the impact of, for example, the unexpected *piano* on the low choral bass notes of "et in terra pax . . ." and particularly, on the two occasions it occurs, of the hushed *pp* of "adoramus te" which follows, without a moment's break in the rhythm, a tremendous general *ff*.

These things, as I have suggested, are all plainly marked in

Beethoven's score; Toscanini let us hear that they were. What Toscanini may be said to have added to the score were such things as the composer could only hope for—such as the physical warmth of the *cantabile* accompaniment to the solo tenor's "gratias agimus tibi" (with the strings' pizzicato accompaniment as characteristically *cantabile* as ever), and the "extra something" held in reserve for what appears to be the only *fff* passage in the score, which occurs at the word "omnipotens". (In the recording this climax has obviously been "ironed out", and the *fff* is virtually no louder than the *ff* before it. The imaginative listener with a score can use the volume control at this point and by comparison at least give himself some idea of how much louder Toscanini made these bars than the engineers would have us believe.)

Toscanini's performance showed how rich this whole Gloria movement is in dramatic contrast; he brought great lyrical beauty to the peaceful Larghetto of "Qui tollis peccata", a moving pathos to the phrases to which the word "miserere" are set, tremendous excitement and vigour to the fugue, "in gloria Dei patris", and an unimaginable fervour with his almost ferocious rhythm in the final Amen and the chorus's excited "glorias" in the coda.

3. Credo

Those qualities found in the Gloria Toscanini found again in the Credo, another movement of varied emotional contrasts and powerfully dramatic music. The most immediately noticeable thing about his performance of the Credo was how unponderous were the rhythm and tempo he adopted. So often one has heard the opening phrase sound heavy and pedestrian, as though the mere presence of trombones in the orchestra became an intolerable millstone round the conductor's neck. As in the Gloria it was Toscanini's mastery of Beethoven's dynamics which coloured the drama of the Credo—the sudden *piano* of "et invisibilium", the mystery of the *pp* (following on the *ff*) at the words "ante omnia saecula", the gentle lyrical phrasing of the woodwind accompaniment to "Qui propter nos homines".

Some of the instrumental balance in this movement was quite

exquisite and showed how often we have been led by insensitive performance to regard Beethoven's orchestration as heavy-handed. In the whole "Et incarnatus est" sequence Toscanini inspired a delicacy of touch in the *pp* woodwind passages which suggested that Mendelssohn did not learn about the orchestra only from Mozart. This whole episode, marked *pp* in wind and string parts all through until the crescendo in the last bar, was a model of articulation and warm *cantando* phrasing. The bright D major cadence of the tenor's "Et homo factus est" was contrasted superbly with the whispered awe of the preceding passages and was no less impressive for the Andante being regarded by Toscanini as "con moto".

The harrowing realism of Beethoven's picture of the Cruci-fixion was heightened by the tremendous power of the orchestral hammer-blows which represent the nailing to the Cross. Toscanini's *f* and *sfp* were so intense that one went to the score to discover with surprise that Beethoven used no timpani to make his effect. Toscanini proved that he had no need to.

There was so much that Toscanini illumined in this score that it becomes increasingly difficult, as each movement proceeds, to discuss the details without having to give a note-by-note commentary—which, of course, is virtually what his performance of the Missa Solemnis warranted. In the end one can do little more than list the outstanding general features of a miraculous revelation of a miraculous score and hope that by doing so future generations will be stimulated to go and do likewise. After the Crucifixus, Toscanini successively brought an immense pathos to the passage beginning with "sub Pontio Pilato passus" and ending with a wonderful four bars of *p–dim.–pp–più dim.–ppp* at the final "et sepultus est", an outburst of characteristically vigorous rhythm with the change to Allegro molto for the rising excitement of "et ascendit in coelum", and a lovely clarity to the counterpoint of the long building up (without violins) of "et vitam venturi saeculi" and its subsequent climax.

In the bar immediately before the four soloists start their "Amen", Toscanini added a slight *allargando* to Beethoven's diminuendo indicated for chorus and orchestra—unauthorized, but again perfectly timed and somehow "in character".

The last sixteen bars or so of the Credo had a particular

enchantment in Toscanini's performance. He made music where others made only exercises of the hushed ascending scale passages for strings and woodwind. It was a superb example of his genius for creating an audible *pianissimo* in which every detail—especially in the rapid scales by strings in the final full-orchestra *pp*—was dazzlingly clear.

To these wonderful moments of Beethoven were added a couple of moments of Toscanini in the Credo. Purists may note, but I trust without regret, that according to what one hears in the recording, he doubled the bassoon parts with horns in the passage beginning "credo in spiritum sanctum", which includes a series of phrases for the bassoons such as:

Ex. 57

He also had the trumpets in the Allegro con moto "et vitam venturi saeculi, amen" double the whole of the violin phrase instead of only the first four notes shown in the score:

Ex. 58

These examples of instrumental deviation from the score are noted merely for the record. I do not recall having heard anybody make any comment on the matter one way or the other.

4. Sanctus

At a first hearing it seemed that Toscanini was curiously subdued in his performance of the thirty-four bars of the Adagio with which the Sanctus begins. One expected a greater intensity in the playing of one of Beethoven's most original passages of orchestration, even though he brought a wonderful sense of breadth and lovely singable phrases to it.

The purpose of this underplaying, however, was clear immediately he came to the sudden burst of sunlight which ushers

in "Pleni sunt coeli et terra gloria tua". The contrast was
electric. In the same way there was tremendous elation in the
rhythmic Presto of the "Osanna" to contrast with the solemn
Sostenuto of the Praeludium. This sequence, which accompanies the Elevation of the Host, was singularly beautiful in
Toscanini's performance.

The Benedictus ("Andante molto cantabile e non troppo
mosso") is a movement which I must confess I have always
found to be an over-sentimental conception. The solo violin—
dolce and *cantabile* though it may be—is something which in this
context strikes me as inappropriate and distracting. That is a
purely personal opinion and one which in its time has obstructed my objective view of Toscanini's performance of this
episode even when, as it was in London, the solo violin part
was well performed. In the recording the soloist took such a
romantic view of his part that it struck me as less suitable than
ever, and I wondered after hearing it whether, if the obbligato
had been played by all the first violins instead of by one,
Toscanini would have permitted any such interpretation.

The violin solo apart, however, I found much that was
lovely in the recorded performance—the broad, smoothly
flowing tempo, the masterly balance of the *pp* trombone and
trumpet passages, and the quite superb effect of the dramatic
diminuendo on the last word of the chorus's "in nomine
Domini" each time it occurs. This was Toscanini and the
dramatic, not the sentimental, Beethoven again.

5. Agnus Dei

What one can scarcely avoid thinking of as the Finale of
Beethoven's Mass was naturally the dramatic climax of
Toscanini's whole performance. The long Adagio which
begins this last movement was taken at a slow tempo (about
$\downarrow = 52$), and from the first plaintive phrase in the bassoon to
the final whispered supplication of the chorus's "miserere"
assumed a poignancy of quite remarkable intensity. Once
again it was almost entirely a matter of Toscanini's meticulous
observance of "what is there"—of dynamic variety, and particularly of a strict, unwavering rhythm which gave the music
something of the character of a slow march. Just as the drama

of the Adagio might appear to some to be contrary to their idea of "religious" music, so too, I think, might some of the lightness of Beethoven's orchestral touch in the Allegretto vivace of "Dona nobis pacem" which follows. It will be noticed that I refer to "Beethoven's orchestral touch" so that there should be no suggestion that Toscanini in any way introduced into the music anything not clearly shown in the score. After the elegiac colouring of the Adagio, Beethoven deliberately lightened his orchestral texture for the Allegretto, and Toscanini faithfully reproduced the change.

Drama is not long absent from this last movement, however, and we were back in remarkably unecclesiastic surroundings when Toscanini came to the excitement of the recitative and the distant trumpet calls. This whole Agnus Dei is filled with a variety of moods and contrasts, of course, which Toscanini was not slow to perceive. For all that the melodrama of the recitative is followed by a return to the placid Tempo I⁰ of "Dona nobis pacem", the mood of the music is one of rising excitement which Toscanini expressed with characteristic vigour, starting with the buoyant rhythm of the choral fugue and raising the music's blood-pressure still more with the rhythmic ferocity of the orchestra's Presto fugal sequence. It was this Presto which culminated in Toscanini's climax: the soprano's sustained cry of "Dona". The return once more of Tempo I⁰ relaxed the tension and the movement came to an end with a wonderful series of *p*, *sempre più p*, and *pp* passages. What may be considered the Coda of the Agnus Dei was, like the rest of the movement, rich in a masterly interpretation of Beethoven's dynamic markings, particularly of the sudden breath-taking *piano* and the arresting *sforzato* which emphasized the reiterated plea of "pacem".

But these were mere details of a performance which filled the listener most of all with a sense of having experienced a great drama, now finally resolved by the serenity of these last pages of the Agnus Dei.

BOITO
❧[1842–1918]❧

PROLOGUE: MEFISTOFELE
[1868]

Nicola Moscona (bass)
Columbus Boys' Choir
NBC Symphony Orchestra

GREAT BRITAIN: HMV ALP 1363
U.S.A.: Victor LM 1849
1954

My familiarity with the Prologue to *Mefistofele* is limited, like my familiarity with Verdi's *Te Deum* which is on the other side of this recording, to experience of Toscanini's performances of it. I do not know how other conductors perform it, so that my only possible standard is the one presented by Toscanini—which, on reflection, is not at all a bad standard to have.

Messrs Ricordi's full score of the Prologue is stamped with the words "Corrections of June 1955. The Prologue and Epilogue include modifications made by Maestro Toscanini". These modifications consist, in effect, of no more than titivations of Boito's orchestration—the piccolo added for brightness in the Scherzo movement, for instance, the doubling up of first with second violins from time to time, and so on.

But while these may be the modifications and corrections of June, 1955, they do not by any means always tally with Toscanini's recorded performance of March, 1954. The Ricordi score, for instance, shows Boito's orchestra to include a serpent and an ophicleide; but not even Toscanini's respect for a composer's wishes extended to the training of musicians to play obsolete instruments, so the common-or-garden tuba was used instead.

Comparison of the Ricordi "revised version" with Toscanini's recording shows a number of differences—differences which, if the non-professional reader will allow me, I will enumerate for the benefit of conductors who I hope will continue to perform Boito's individual and attractive music. Toscanini's modifications, as they are to be heard in the recording, all add to the general effectiveness of the score, and there is nothing to object to in the continuance of the timpani roll on page 3 (bars 2 to 4), page 7 (bars 1 and 2), and page 9 (bars 3 to 5). The string tremolo included as part of the *correzioni del giugno 1955* in bars 5 and 6 on page 4, and bars 5 and 6 on page 10, has been replaced in Toscanini's recording by a pizzicato passage which seems to double the ascending arpeggios of the two harps. There may well be other variations of the official score to be heard in the recording; the instances I have cited are those which were most readily apparent to me.

Toscanini's performance of the Prologue to *Mefistofele*, however, was not just a demonstration of the conductor's skill as an editor. There was characteristic vigour and clarity in the Scherzo passages (Toscanini adopted $\quad = 152$ as his basic tempo for this as against the prescribed 144), and a particularly charming realization of the *Scherzo vocale* for the chorus of cherubs. This was a most enchanting episode which vanished far too quickly, but not before one realized what an original dramatic conception it was. Toscanini never lost his unique gift of presenting a work so that its impact on the listener was as powerful and arresting as its impact must have been on its composer's contemporaries. Boito, we have tended to forget, was something of a revolutionary in the Italian opera house. Toscanini made sure we should never forget it again.

BRAHMS
❦[1833–1897]❧

SYMPHONY No 1 in C Minor, Opus 68
[1876]

GREAT BRITAIN: HMV ALP 1012
U.S.A.: Victor LM 1702
1951

SYMPHONY No 2 in D, Opus 73
[1877]

GREAT BRITAIN: HMV ALP 1013
U.S.A.: Victor LM 1731
1952

SYMPHONY No 3 in F, Opus 90
[1883]

GREAT BRITAIN: HMV ALP 1166
U.S.A.: Victor LM 1836
1952

SYMPHONY No 4 in E minor, Opus 98
[1885]

GREAT BRITAIN: HMV ALP 1029
U.S.A.: Victor LM 1713
1951

VARIATIONS ON A THEME BY HAYDN,
Opus 56a
[1873]

GREAT BRITAIN: HMV ALP 1204
U.S.A.: Victor LM 1725
1951

All the above were performed by the NBC Symphony Orchestra

IN music, as in food, it is not unusual to find things which disagree with one, or which one just simply doesn't like the taste of. As some people do not like oysters or garlic so I cannot get on with the orchestral music of Brahms. His songs and his violin concerto, yes; but his orchestral music is so nearly physically repugnant to me that it can be a painful experience.

Curiosity, my devotion to the Maestro, or its inclusion in a programme containing music by other composers often led to my listening to Brahms's orchestral music conducted by Toscanini, but it was not a pastime I willingly repeated. Indeed, it almost broke my heart that Toscanini should have made what was clearly going to be his last appearance in London in a couple of all-Brahms programmes in 1952. I did not go to either of the concerts, for not even Toscanini could cure me of my allergy.

Whatever one's feelings about Brahms's music, however, there is no doubt that Toscanini made it sound different—and for me, at any rate, very nearly tolerable. In spite of one or two amendments to the orchestration of the First Symphony Toscanini could not alter the purely physical character of Brahms's music, nor convince me that a composer who could think of sound in terms of a trio for such irreconcilable bedfellows as violin, horn and piano, was making any more pleasant noises by his constant use in his symphonies of oboe and horn playing a lyrical tune in octaves. The changes Toscanini made in the First Symphony were largely concerned with doubling some of the less effective woodwind parts by horns and adding a couple of bars for timpani in the last movement.

The familiar characteristics of Toscanini's orchestral performance were found in profusion in all his Brahms—the wonderfully matched dynamics, the effortless transitions from one tempo to another, the eloquent *cantabile* that effected even the strings' pizzicato and the lovely *sotto voce* playing that sounded as though the strings were muted. Apart from the instrumental changes he made Toscanini did not give a literal reading of the First or any of the other three symphonies; his performances abounded in spontaneous rallentandos, such as the slowing-up that leads to the Poco sostenuto of the Coda in the first movement which is not indicated in the score at all. But Toscanini did not dawdle either, and it was refreshing to hear him keep to the tempo and not slow up for the pompous hymn-like phrase which suddenly interrupts the Finale of the C minor Symphony.

Toscanini applied all his powerful, ferocious intensity to Brahms and almost persuaded one in the Allegro giocoso of the Fourth Symphony that Brahms was going to write us a scherzo. It was Brahms himself, however, who scotched that by introducing the triplet phrases which first occur at the eleventh bar and irrevocably slow up not the tempo, but the *thought* of the music. Compared with the recording I thought that Toscanini used to take this movement slightly faster in pre-war days; but even then it never became genuinely fast music as Beethoven, Mozart and Mendelssohn understood the term.

From a purely technical point of view Toscanini's performance of the four Brahms Symphonies was something I never heard surpassed and I cannot imagine—prejudice or no prejudice—that there is anything to be done to them that Toscanini did not do. It is possible that the out-and-out Brahms enthusiast may find them lacking in some special Brahmsian quality; but for myself, rightly or wrongly, if I *must* have Brahms then I prefer it the way Toscanini did it.

The Haydn Variations, by their very nature, particularly suited Toscanini and he found in the fifth variation—Vivace— some Brahms which at last he could regard as music genuinely fast enough in thought and tempo to be presented as a breathtaking experience.

The passage of the years changed one aspect of Toscanini's performance of these Variations and it was a change for the better. When I first heard him play the *grazioso* 6/8 variation (No VII) he used to "bounce" the rhythm in a disconcertingly un-*grazioso* way. In the recording he appears to have let it find its own natural lilt and the whole character of the music is improved as a result.

CHERUBINI
❧[1760–1842]❧

SYMPHONY in D
[1815]
NBC Symphony Orchestra

GREAT BRITAIN: HMV ALP 1106
U.S.A.: Victor LM 1745
1952

T HE author of the HMV sleeve notes to this recording
writes that Cherubini's symphony was first performed in
London "on May 1st of that year [1815], but not
again publicly in this country, it is believed, until 1952." Now
while all Toscanini's concerts in London inclined to be so
exclusive as to rate as private functions so far as the public
getting tickets for them was concerned, in fact he performed this
unusual symphony at Queen's Hall in May, 1937, and I
heard him do it. And in common with many others who heard
it, Cherubini's symphony left a strong and unexpected impression. I doubt quite frankly whether anybody but Toscanini
could have made quite the same impression with it; on the
other hand, it was not entirely a matter of the hypnotic power
of the Magic Baton. In the same programme there were
Tommasini's Variations on "The Carnival of Venice", of
which I recall nothing beyond the theme (which I already knew
anyway).

Toscanini made Cherubini's symphony memorable by his
unique gift for re-creating music in such a way that it sounded
brand new and unusual. At the time Toscanini played this
work of Cherubini's in London the composer was generally
accepted as an historical figure whom Beethoven, for some
reason, had greatly admired (as, it appeared, had many other
composers of note), but who otherwise did not rate more than

an academic mention in other people's life-stories. The last thing we thought of him was that he had any musical character or individuality of his own, that perhaps Beethoven had not been so mistaken in his regard for his contemporary.

Toscanini proved to us how wrong we were in our prejudice and demonstrated clearly how Cherubini had come to deserve the reputation he enjoyed during his lifetime. Here was no dull old stick, but a composer of considerable vigour and originality. There was an attractive spontaneity about the first movement and much lyrical warmth and charm in the Larghetto cantabile—in which Toscanini did not hesitate to stress the adjective. The Minuet was spirited and unusual, with witty Rossinian touches which completely disposed of the fashionable allegation that Cherubini was a solemn, austere composer. The movement revealed many ingenious touches of orchestration, particularly passages for woodwind which Toscanini played exquisitely and made to sound as light-fingered as if they had been written by Mendelssohn, who himself lived to be one of Cherubini's most devoted admirers and propagandists.

Toscanini's performance of the Finale was no less convincing than that of the other movements; he gave it a splendidly vigorous treatment, for it is a movement based on a strong and insistent rhythm which Toscanini's characteristic regard for the full value of dotted-note phrases made a most stimulating episode.

The performance of this symphony by Toscanini demonstrated conclusively that the neglect of Cherubini was not the fault of the composer, but of those conductors who, while accepting the composer's reputation as a man whose music was fit only for the library, had not bothered to go into the library to study the scores, or if they had, had not bothered to rid their minds of the traditional view of Cherubini as an outdated pedant whose place in history had been assured by the lucky chance of Beethoven having mentioned his name.

REQUIEM MASS in C minor
[1817]

Robert Shaw Chorale
NBC Symphony Orchestra

GREAT BRITAIN: HMV ALP 1412
U.S.A.: Victor LM 2000
1950

Toscanini's recording of this Requiem by Cherubini was my first experience of the work, so that almost instinctively I find myself wanting to discuss what was virtually New Music to me instead of studying Toscanini's performance of it. I can imagine nothing that would have delighted Toscanini more than to hear a listener admit that; nevertheless, his part in making this unfamiliar music come to life was so large that in the end the final experience must rank as a fifty-fifty contribution by composer and conductor.

Hearing Cherubini's Requiem for the first time I wondered whether what general critical opinion considers the composer's greatest failings were not, on the contrary, some of his most admirable virtues—particularly his alleged "austerity". The C minor Requiem, as Toscanini presented it, abounded in drama from start to finish, but a great deal of the power of that drama sprang from that very austerity which one finds in the liturgical form of the Requiem Mass—a lengthy business to listen to and exhausting to sing, but in its stark simplicity—in its "austerity", in fact—an intensely dramatic experience. As usual, the secret of Toscanini's performance was to be found largely in his meticulous observance of the composer's directions—in Cherubini's case, particularly of his original use of dynamic and orchestral contrasts, and in general of such comparative details as full note-values and accents.

Thus the work Toscanini presented proved to be one of considerable variety and invention. Amid all the stark drama there were moments of unexpected lyrical warmth and pathos, and at no time did the composer's contrapuntal ingenuities serve any solely academic purpose: they were always a means to a dramatic end, a vigorous, urgent factor in the creation of a dramatic and emotional intensity.

The balance and clarity of the instrumental texture was as remarkable a feature of Toscanini's performance as ever, with the long *sotto voce* "Pie Jesu" an astonishing tour de force in which the virtuosity of the execution characteristically never obscured the meaning of the music for a moment. Drama, lyricism, rhythmic vitality, orchestral and contrapuntal skill— Toscanini found all these elements in Cherubini's Requiem to appeal to him, and a comparatively unknown work, unspoilt for the listener by tradition, and still less by over-familiarity, at once became a refreshing and thoroughly stimulating experience which threw light on a new and intriguingly different corner of the musical world. It was an excursion which, made in Toscanini's company, was typically rewarding and illuminating.

DEBUSSY
❦[1862–1918]❧

LA MER
[1905]

I. *De l'aube à midi sur la mer*
II. *Jeux des vagues*
III. *Dialogue entre le vent et la mer*
NBC Symphony Orchestra

GREAT BRITAIN: HMV ALP 1070
U.S.A.: Victor LM 1833
1950

ALTHOUGH Debussy is known to have written quite a large part of this study of the sea and its moods while on a visit to romantic, sun-drenched Eastbourne in southern England, I have never been altogether convinced that The Sea in question was the English Channel. Nor, it was quite clear, was Toscanini either. For him the sun that rose on Debussy's sea blazed at noon from a Mediterranean sky, the winds that blew, the waves that played had the warmth of southern sunlight in them, and if there are some who believe that the dialogue of wind and water on a clear day in the Mediterranean has not the force and unnerving swell of the final movement, then let them take the day boat from Nice to Calvi in high summer. Indeed, by beginning in the later part of Debussy's first movement and continuing with the rest of the work, the listener will have as clear and vivid a picture of that crossing from France to Corsica as he could wish for. Luncheon is served at a time shortly before Debussy's first movement comes to an end. The rest of the piece will then be discovered to re-create by musical means almost any sensation or emotion the listener may feel about the sunlit six-hour crossing.

It must not be thought from my slight preoccupation with what I consider the true local colour of *La Mer* that I am anxious to interpret the work as a kind of musical travelogue. The general Mediterranean air of these three symphonic sketches is apparent to me, not thanks to any preconceived notion or even from a native prejudice in favour of the climate of southern Europe, but entirely to Toscanini's performance of the music.

The principal feature of *La Mer* is what is known, a little loosely but according to usage and the jargon of music criticism, as orchestral "colour". Toscanini presented that "colour" with such unmistakable Mediterranean clarity that there was never any question of the geographical inspiration of the work. Or, rather, of the apparent geographical inspiration. If by some remarkable chance Toscanini may have misunderstood Debussy's intentions then the fault was entirely the composer's for having in that case meant one thing and written another, for surely no music was ever more definitely Latin in its intensity and vividness and in the absence of half-tones.

Since Debussy is regarded as an impressionist in music it is perhaps natural to compare the effect of *La Mer* with that of the school of French painting of which it is the musical counterpart. I would go even further, indeed, and compare it to an individual aspect of that school—namely, the *pointillistes*. At any rate, close scrutiny of the picture presented by Toscanini's performance of the work revealed that the effect was achieved by the accumulation of innumerable minute details applied with immense care and precision.

This was particularly noticeable in the way in which, if one focused one's attention on instrumental passages in the score which performed no more useful function than that of contributing to the general "atmosphere" and colour-effects, these passages could be heard clearly to consist of strings divided into eleven distinct and different parts. So often with Debussy's scores one was tempted to dismiss such apparent extravagances with the rather patronizing thought that Oh, well, it was a nice idea and if it didn't really come off it didn't matter; it looked pretty on paper.

But with Toscanini if things *could* sound then they did, and there was rarely a time when, if one happened to be curious to know what the second clarinet was playing in an ensemble, one could not hear it. It was the early realization of this that caused me never to take a score to a Toscanini rehearsal after my first experience had demonstrated that it was entirely unnecessary. All that was in the score could be heard coming from the platform and in the case of *La Mer*, Toscanini reassured us that Debussy was no theoretician of the orchestra: he was a master-craftsman. Debussy's master-craftsmanship, however, did not mean that his scores were exempt from Toscanini's tampering and tinkering with the orchestration. More than once in *La Mer* there could be heard passages which Toscanini—it is said with the composer's knowledge and approval—reinforced by judicious doubling. There is one noticeable and extremely effective instance of this to be heard in the recording when the timpani continue to play the part heard in the fourth bar after Figure 8 in the score for another four bars, instead of observing the *tacet*, and so double the notes played by violoncellos and basses.

When one hears that Toscanini conducted *La Mer* more often than any other item in his repertoire except the Prelude to *Die Meistersinger*, it is perhaps not surprising, for it is a work which was perhaps the most ideally suited to his physical temperament, as it were. It gave him unparalleled opportunity to indulge in his delight in sheer beauty of sound and to express his prodigious sense of rhythm. There were few more lovely sounds to be heard in Toscanini's entire repertoire than that of the famous passage for divided violoncellos in the first movement, few phrases more gentle than the little trilling passage for violins in the "Jeux des vagues" (he spent ages grading the dynamics of these eight bars at his Queen's Hall rehearsal), nor more excitingly robust and stirring than the tremendous rhythmic drive of the last movement. His performance of *La Mer* was one of Toscanini's most remarkable and enlightening achievements.

IBÉRIA
[1909]

I. *Par les rues et par les chemins*
II. *Les parfums de la nuit*
III. *Le matin d'un jour de fête*
NBC Symphony Orchestra

GREAT BRITAIN: Not available at the
time of going to Press
U.S.A.: Victor LM 1833
1950

Whatever its merits as a composition, as an essay in orchestral writing *Ibéria* is even more remarkable than *La Mer*. The instrumental resources required by the later work are in fact larger than those demanded by the earlier, but in practice a great deal of Debussy's orchestral writing in *Ibéria* is infinitely more subtle, and depends for its effect on the most exquisite, almost chamber-musical touch.

There is perhaps nothing quite comparable in the three movements of *Ibéria* to the great inundation of sound that is encountered in the final movement of *La Mer*, but there is no lack of vigour in the music. Toscanini's tremendous rhythm added an unexpected excitement to *La Mer*; in *Ibéria* one expected it all along—and got it. He observed very faithfully the composer's metronome markings in the first and second movements ($\flat$ = 176 for "Par les rues et par les chemins" and $\flat$ = 92 for "Les parfums de la nuit") but adopted a tempo in the last movement sometimes nearer $\flat$ = 120 than Debussy's indicated 112. Whether Toscanini's tempi were "official" or not, in no case was there the slightest suggestion of the orchestral detail suffering from the vigour and general intensity of the performance.

Three words inevitably recur in any assessment of Toscanini's performance of *Ibéria*: rhythm, colour and detail, for these were the elements present from the first beat of the first bar of the work to the final *sec* and *fortissimo* chord in the last. As one discovered in *La Mer* those passages of instrumentation which

one considered the composer to have included rather optimistically, at last made their effect in full. The clarity of the
detail, in short, was miraculous, and the most incidental
features had a sparkle and brilliance without parallel in routine
performances of the work. The listener, and particularly the
student, who makes his first acquaintance with *Ibéria* through
Toscanini's recording is to be envied; he will never, until he
hears someone else conduct it, know how often the rest of us
have had paste instead of diamonds foisted on us when we have
heard others conduct Debussy's score, how long we had to wait
to hear the passages for six violins at Figure 32, the delicate
filigree of the *pp* woodwind at Figure 38, or the two violins with
their solo figuration at Figure 58.

Some have complained that the middle movement could
have sounded more luscious in Toscanini's performances. It
could only have done so, I believe, by demanding a richer tone
from the strings, which would have been at the expense of the
detail. As it was, there was no lack of warmth in this episode;
the southern night was as richly scented as could be imagined.
If it did not sound as luscious as, for instance, the orchestral
version of *La Soirée dans Grenade*, then it is because the composer
did not intend to orchestrate it that way. In fact, he never
orchestrated *La Soirée dans Grenade* at all. The orchestral
version is purely an arrangement made by Piero Coppola after
Debussy's death. As in *La Mer* it is the light that changes in
Ibéria; there are no half-tones, no mist; just a variation of the
intensity of light. Cézanne's demonstration that shadows are
composed of colours helps a great deal in understanding
Debussy's impressionism. The composer himself protested that
he was no impressionist. In his way, Debussy was perhaps the
most remarkable Impressionist of them all. Like some superhuman physics master he succeeded in making heat and light,
as well as sound, "visible" to the human ear.

It was never my intention in this study to reflect too much on
composers, their significance and place in history. On the
other hand, Toscanini had the unique effect of changing one's
whole view and assessment of a composer by a single performance of a single work. One came to expect it with his
interpretation of Beethoven, even of Wagner. But somehow,
because the composer had lived in our own time, one had not

expected it with Debussy; he was one of us, he was a "modern" and we knew all about him. That Toscanini could, as he did with his performances of *La Mer* and *Ibéria*, in fact throw as searching and brilliant a light on modern music as he did on the classics was perhaps one of the most astonishing facets of his art. One may regret that he did not record more of Debussy's music, that he did not conduct *Pelléas et Mélisande* after 1929, perhaps in particular that he never performed the companion pieces to *Ibéria*—*Gigues* and *Rondes de Printemps*. But these, in the end, are merely the regrets of the gluttonous. Toscanini, with *La Mer* and *Ibéria*, not only did Debussy proud: he did us proud too.

ELGAR
❧[1857–1934]❧

"ENIGMA" VARIATIONS, Opus 36
[1899]

NBC Symphony Orchestra

GREAT BRITAIN: HMV ALP 1204
U.S.A.: Victor LM 1725
1951

OWING to the geographical circumstances of my musical
education it was not until I returned to England in my
late 'teens that I first encountered a form of music
which its champions distinguished by the term "English
music". The national adjective, it seemed, explained everything; so that when I encountered a particularly ruminative,
motionless and nearly timeless piece of music, my indifference,
impatience and clearly expressed view that I could have passed
the time more entertainingly at the movies, were invariably
met by a little lecture on the quality of Englishness whose
importance, it was clear, had eluded me. Apparently, the
standards I applied to other music which bored me did not
apply to English music. If I was bored by English music it
was obvious that I did not understand it and was missing the
point.

It was inevitable, therefore, when Toscanini came to conduct
Elgar's Enigma Variations in London, that he should be
criticized for failing to capture the subtle, elusive quality of
Englishness in the music. My personal feeling of relief that
Toscanini did not try to capture anything of the sort was
equalled by the delight I experienced when the late Sir
Landon Ronald, the finest and most authoritative of all Elgar
conductors with the possible exception of the composer himself,
came to Toscanini's defence, replying to the critics that Elgar

did not write "English" music: he wrote great music, as Toscanini had clearly demonstrated in the finest performance of the Enigma Variations he had ever heard.

Toscanini's last performance of the Enigma was in 1952, his first in Turin in 1902; so that for half a century the conductor knew and obviously loved this music of Elgar's. While his performance may not have satisfied the Anglomaniacs when they heard it, it came as a revelation which demonstrated to the more sceptical among us that the music was really much better than one had thought hitherto.

Everything there was in Elgar's score in the way of "what is there" Toscanini saw with unrivalled clarity and precision. In the first statement of the theme the accompaniment for violas and violoncellos received special attention, as Mr Bernard Shore recalls in his *The Orchestra Speaks*, when Toscanini said to the lower strings: "It is only 'armony, yes, but it is lovely music and it must be alive. For me it is too dead." This remark might serve as a motto for his whole approach to this work, which in every respect received a virtuoso performance. The predominant element was that of striking contrasts; Toscanini established the character and mood of each of the fourteen variations with miraculous, instantaneous certainty, so that the very first bar of each variation created the atmosphere of what followed.

Thus one remembers the lovely clear texture of the first variation, the *staccatissimo* lightness and speed of the second; the great charm and warmth of No 3, and the tremendous vigour of No 4; the feathery touch of the woodwind interlude contrasting with the broad opening string phrases of the fifth variation; the lyrical gentleness of the sixth; the brilliance and irresistible exhilaration of the one-in-a-bar Presto of the seventh ("Troyte"); the grace and tenderness of the string passages and the ravishing *rit.* at the end of the eighth; the sonority and audibility of the *ppp* opening of "Nimrod" (No 9), the unforgettable climax that shook you out of your seat and the wonderfully graded diminuendo to the *pianissimo* of the next three, final bars; the enchanting phrasing of the accent in the little 4-note woodwind figure that made the "Dorabella" intermezzo so charming; the lightning speed and excitement of No 11; the pathos of the twelfth variation; the rich texture and warm lyrical beauty of the strings in the thirteenth; and the energy and exuberance of the Finale.

Toscanini, in short, presented in his inimitable way, every aspect of the Enigma Variations with such superb conviction, showing such genuine feeling for the lyrical passages and giving the fast, *scherzando* movements such a tremendous, irresistible rhythmic impetus, that one could not care less in the end whether the music sounded "English" or pedigree Eskimo. It was, as Landon Ronald had said, and as perhaps one was persuaded against one's better judgment, great music.

GLUCK
❦[1714–1787]❧

ORFEO ED EURIDICE – Act II
[1762]

Orpheus Nan Merriman
A Happy Shade Barbara Gibson
Robert Shaw Chorale
NBC Symphony Orchestra

GREAT BRITAIN: HMV ALP 1357
U.S.A.: Victor LM 1850
1953

I HAD often wondered why Toscanini, to fill up the odd side
of his 1929 recording of Mozart's Haffner Symphony, had
chosen the Dance of the Blessed Spirits from Gluck's
Orfeo. I presumed it was merely that he took great delight in
the purely sensuous quality of that particular piece of music;
I did not envisage his being interested in the rest of Gluck's
opera, somehow. Toscanini's performance of the second act of
Orfeo, however, showed that I could not have been more wrong
in my assumption. Not only did he put tremendous life into
music which can so often sound disconcertingly static (Gluck's
musical pulse, if not quite so like a slug's as Nietzsche said
Wagner's was, still did not beat in what is known as an "up-
tempo"), but by placing the Dance in its proper context
enhanced the effect of the solitary excerpt we had known all
these years.

The sense of context, indeed, was what impressed one above
all when it came to Toscanini's performance of this second act
—for what, after all, is context in opera in the end but contrast?
The second act of *Orfeo* is constructed of what, in the simplest
terms, are the contrasts of Good and Evil. Or Rest and Unrest.
Or Calm and Clamour. At any rate, of two complete opposites.

Toscanini brought a tremendous ferocity to the music of the first scene in Hades, and a sublime serenity and lyricism to the second part in the Elysian Fields.

Perhaps only those who have suffered the average German performance of "Orpheus und Eurydike" can really appreciate what Toscanini did for them by bringing all his clear-eyed Italian sense and sensibility to bear on a work which, with the best will in the world, seemed formerly to be a dead loss as anything more than a stage in the technical development of opera. He injected life into the four-square and unimaginative rhythms of the Furies' ballet music; his stepping up of the tempo to $\downarrow$ = 144 may have been academically incorrect, but it was artistically entirely justified by the drama and movement it gave the music. Moreover, instead of this scene sounding, as it usually does, rather pathetic in its naive attempts to depict the demonic terrors of Hades, the music was in some way renovated and restored to make the effect it must have made on its first audience; and the tolerant smile one wears while watching the antics of children vanished in the face of something which had ceased to be child's play and had become a dramatic reality.

It was dramatic reality, indeed, which Toscanini gave more than anything else to Gluck's score; the demons' music was as evocative of reality as the storm in the Pastoral Symphony and there was a bite and strength and an impellent rhythm in its performance which was—to me, at least—a revelation of what had so long sounded something more suited to study in the library than performance in the theatre.

The transition from Hades to the Elysian Fields was one of the master touches in Toscanini's performance, with a diminuendo from the music of the Furies so expertly and characteristically graded that one was inevitably reminded of the way he played the passing of the storms in *Rigoletto* and *Otello*, in the Pastoral Symphony and the *William Tell* overture.

The serenity and almost visible colour and light of the music in the Elysian Fields were quite incredible. The whole scene, with its charm and beautifully phrased lyrical passages, the wonderful clarity of the instrumental detail in the accompaniments to Orpheus' "Che puro ciel!" and to the supremely happy and contented Happy Shade, the "singing" of the strings' pizzicato and the indescribable atmosphere of contentment and innocence, combined to make this one of the loveliest of all Toscanini's achievements. And the rallentando on the last four chords of the Act, which Mr Alec Robertson described in *The Gramophone* as having "the effect of a grand classical gesture", was a stroke of genius.

HAYDN
⁅[1732–1809]⁆

FOR one who had so much admiration and affection for Haydn's music Toscanini was remarkably reticent about giving practical demonstration of his feelings in the matter. He appears to have performed only eight of Haydn's total output of 104 symphonies, and of those eight only three were played more than ten times each between the years 1926 and 1954.

According to published statistics, No 88 in G was performed twelve times, No 99 in E flat thirteen times, and the "Clock" Symphony twenty-seven times. Of those three most popular works No 88 was recorded in 1938 and has since disappeared from the catalogue, No 99 was never recorded at all,* while the "Clock" Symphony, first recorded in 1929, was replaced by a LP recording made in 1947 which, while it has been issued in the United States, is not available in Great Britain as I write, although it has been scheduled for release and allotted a catalogue number. A fourth Haydn work, the Symphony No 98 in B flat, which Toscanini played three times in all, was recorded in 1945 but withdrawn before it could reach England, and a fifth, the "Surprise" Symphony, which he played for the first time on June 20, 1943, and for the second and last time exactly ten years and four days later, was recorded in 1953 and has also yet to be issued in England.

It is not, to be frank, an altogether satisfactory state of affairs. Toscanini's Legacy should have been much richer in Haydn.

* See Supplement, pages 361–363.

SYMPHONY No 101 in D ("Clock")

[1794]

Philharmonic-Symphony Orchestra of New York

GREAT BRITAIN: HMV D 1668–71
U.S.A.: Victor M 57
1929

NBC Symphony Orchestra

GREAT BRITAIN: RCA RB–16138
U.S.A.: Victor LM 1038
1947

His performance of the "Clock" Symphony was all we knew of Toscanini and Haydn for many years and his early recording of it became a classic. Though nearly twenty years separated the two recorded performances listed above, they have the most important basic principles in common. In later years Toscanini inclined to take things faster, but whereas the metronome will show the Presto of the first movement to have been about ♩ = 144 in 1929 as against something like 152 in 1947, the slightly faster tempo in no way affected the astonishing clarity and buoyancy of Toscanini's performance. The little run-up by the first violins into the main tune of the Presto remained a masterly demonstration of Toscanini's unerring, instantaneous setting of a new tempo. The transition from the Adagio introduction to the Presto was always quite breathtaking.

Throughout this first movement Toscanini maintained an appreciably flexible tempo, and the flute player was always given time to breathe when he played his difficult little spotlit solo at bar 203, by the introduction of a comfortable, gentle *meno mosso*. (Toscanini made the repeat in this movement in his later recording, not in the first.)

The famous slow movement and its tick-tocking accompaniment proved paradoxically to be the most flexible movement of the four in the matter of tempo. Toscanini, the Human Metronome, varied his beat in this movement between 76 and 88, with 80 roughly the basic tempo of the earlier performance and 84–88 that of the later. In short, one could not set a metronome and just leave it in either case, for Toscanini strayed from the idea of a strict tempo with remarkable wilfulness. The joy of this movement, however, was never so much in Toscanini's easy, liberal interpretation of Haydn's Andante as in the effortless grace and *cantabile* phrasing of the melodic line, which made it one of the most memorable slow movements in his entire repertoire.

The Trio of the Minuet that follows provided another instance of Toscanini's consideration for the shape and comfort of a phrase. Even though in the later performance he took the movement as a whole a little faster than his original 1929 tempo of $\downarrow$ = 152, he allowed the flute player that necessary elbow-room in which to relish the melodic line of his part.

The Finale was another of those peculiarly enchanting Toscanini performances which left you breathless from sheer delight at the end of them. He expressed Haydn's sense of fun and his general high spirits in a way he only ever matched with his playing of Rossini's overtures. He made the effect of every one of the composer's points, understating them at times, but never throwing them away, and certainly never over-playing them. There is one intriguing difference to be noted between the 1929 and 1947 performances of this last movement. In the earlier recording Toscanini, when he came to the dramatic development section, stepped up his basic tempo of some 152 beats to create extra excitement. In the later version, having adopted a slightly faster tempo (about 160–168) at the outset, he had to broaden it when he came to this tense little contrapuntal interlude; to have continued at the particular Vivace he first thought of in this case would have obscured the polyphonic texture of the music. In both performances the double-fugue episode was a fascinating display of clarity and detail; in the earlier version it seemed to raise the blood-pressure of the music, in the later the sudden braking of the tempo introduced a wonderful note of tension.

Either way, the "Clock" Symphony was one of Toscanini's most entrancing and invigorating conceptions.

SYMPHONY No 94 in G ("Surprise")
[1791]

NBC Symphony Orchestra

GREAT BRITAIN: RCA RB–16138
U.S.A.: Victor LM 1789
1953

This is a work I had never heard Toscanini perform until I encountered this recording and I will admit that in view of what I had been told of Toscanini's "decline" as a conductor of the classics towards the end of his life I approached the record with considerable misgiving. My apprehension could not have been more misplaced. It proved to be one of his most entrancing Haydn performances.

On reflection, perhaps what went for one Haydn symphony conducted by Toscanini went for all of them. The principal Vivace assai of the first movement (the repeat, incidentally, was observed) was entirely enchanting; there was immense grace in the phrasing of the *dolce* passages, and an atmosphere of great charm which was not disturbed for a moment by what seemed at first to be a rather hectic tempo. The tempo was in practice never too fast to obscure the detail, and so long as the detail of a Haydn symphony was clear then the tempo was right. So far as Toscanini was concerned this was virtually a case of Q.E.D.

If there was one moment that stood out as more ravishing than another it was the *grazia* of the whole of the phrase which leads to the delightful cadence:

Ex. 59

Toscanini allowed this to play itself; he did not linger over it or exaggerate the charm of the falling seventh, and so sentimentalize it. It was a typical instance of that peculiar sense of timing possessed by Toscanini which instinctively made the composer's point in the only possible and logical way. It need hardly be added, I hope, that all these nuances and subtleties occurred within the framework of an exhilarating rhythm.

The slow movement offered two surprises: Haydn's familiar little joke and Toscanini's presentation of it. What was surprising about Toscanini's contribution was the realization that one had not, after all, come to know Toscanini as well as one thought, and that the way he performed Haydn's "surprise" should still have come as a surprise in itself. Toscanini made Haydn's joke doubly effective by taking such a literal view of it. Instead of doing what so many conductors do—that is, nudge us and tell us that this'll make us laugh—Toscanini gave the chord a maximum *ff* which was always music, never just a loud bang, and kept the tempo going so that there was no hint of a pause or hold-up of any kind. The continuity was unbroken and point added to the joke by the air of complete lack of concern. The theme continued as if nothing had happened, which, according to legend, was surely Haydn's point: that having woken his slumbering audience he denied all knowledge of having disturbed them in any way.*

The whole of this slow movement had a rare charm in Toscanini's performance, and from the point of sheer sound there was a quite remarkable balance and matching of tone between the two intruments in the duet for flute and oboe (bar 83 onwards). So often one has wondered, when the oboe has stood out like a sore thumb, why Haydn did not write the passage for two flutes instead; but with Toscanini it was a wonderfully blended passage played with the uncanny smoothness and tenderness that made the oboe-and-bassoon coda of the movement such a ravishing episode.

How fast Haydn's Allegro molto should be it is difficult to say. Toscanini took the so-called Menuetto at a speed which can only be described as something of a lick—♩. equalling roughly 116. Personally, since the movement so obviously anticipates the scherzo of Beethoven (the first four bars of the theme could be played as a not-very-distracting counter-

* Toscanini achieved the same effect in what may be called Rossini's "Surprise" overture—*L'Italiana in Algeri*—which, like Haydn's slow movement, continued on its quiet way after a loud and apparently irrelevant interruption. (See page 193.)

melody to the opening of the Scherzo of Beethoven's Fourth Symphony), I do not find this vigorous tempo at all disturbing. In a way this particular movement is symbolical of the social changes of the time. It may be called a minuet, for convention's sake, but husky Tyrolean peasants seem to have taken the place of courtiers in the dance. Whether Toscanini's interpretation of Allegro molto was over-generous or not, the tempo was invigorating and not too fast either for the orchestral detail or to deprive the rhythm of a thoroughly infectious lilt. The Trio was taken at the same speed, of course.

A Haydn Finale, one began to recognize after a while, was a typical Toscanini tour de force, and the last movement of the "Surprise" Symphony was no exception. He extracted all the fun and high spirits implicit in the music and played it with a vitality, brilliance and impeccable clarity of detail which made it a most unusually exhilarating experience.

SYMPHONY No 88 in G
[1786]

NBC Symphony Orchestra

GREAT BRITAIN: HMV DB 3515–7
U.S.A.: Victor M 445 and LCT 7
1938

Although this recording has disappeared from the catalogues of two hemispheres it is not too much to hope for that one day, even if only for documentary reasons, it may be reissued in the Complete Works of the Maestro. Whatever technical experts may think, it remains one of his most entrancing Haydn performances, and there were not so many Haydn recordings by Toscanini that we can go around gaily deleting them right and left from the lists just because the "fi" isn't "hi" enough.

From the point of view of performance this recording of No 88 provided an object lesson in the interpretation of a Haydn symphony. Toscanini, merely because he was concerned with a composer who was an eighteenth-century "classic", did not hesitate to apply his characteristic vigour to Haydn's Allegro in the first movement. Nor, because the rhythm and attack were robust and high-spirited, did this mean that the texture of the development section (Toscanini observed the repeat in this first movement as in that of the "Surprise" Symphony) was any less clearly defined. There was little Toscanini ever did that was more exquisitely conceived than the *pianissimo* passage for strings that begins this episode.

The slow movement was one long *cantabile* phrase played as *dolce* as Toscanini knew how. Above all, the easy-moving tempo and the refusal to ask for an exaggeratedly luscious string tone when the violins get the tune on the G string avoided all suggestion of sentimentalization and *Schmalz* with which so many conductors afflict this movement. Toscanini let it play itself—the way he would have sung it if he had been able to.

The Minuet—unequivocally Allegretto this time—was attacked with that robust disregard for what one might call traditional "eighteenth-centuryness" which was such a refreshing feature of Toscanini's performances of Haydn's symphonies. There was no lack of charm in this Minuet; it was just that it had immense virility as well. Toscanini's essentially masculine approach made a delightfully earthy and rather exotic affair of the Trio; he gave such unexpected emphasis to Haydn's wrong-footed *sf* accents that even when each section was played a second time (as the score demands) one was still caught out by them. Which was Haydn's intention all along, of course. The *da capo* repeat of the Minuet provided one inimitable touch: a momentary broadening of the tempo with an infinitesimal breath-pause on the up-beat that brings back the theme *ff* for the last time.

It was the Finale, however, which I will confess really made me include the Symphony No 88 in this study at all. The present inaccessibility to the public of Toscanini's recording is hardly a credit to the industry, but it will not deter me from continuing to discuss it. It was in every respect a superbly typical Toscanini performance of a Haydn finale. More than most, however, Toscanini's finale of No 88 was particularly enjoyable for its detail. The rhythmic vitality, the prodigious clarity of the instrumental texture, the sense of fun and general exuberance were all there. In addition there were one or two moments of rare and peculiar charm which cannot possibly be transcribed in the everyday notation of music. They concerned what can only be described as a kind of catching of the breath as the first two notes of the main tune returned to the Rondo. There was the smallest hint of a *tenuto* the first time, when the flute joined the bassoon with the tune—*dolce*—at the twenty-fourth bar, and a suspicion of it on similar occasions afterwards until, when the theme played by flute, violins and bassoon across two octaves came back at bar 158 (after the development) with such a ravishing catch in the breath that the notes almost warranted a full-blown "rit." over them. Perhaps these things could be metronomically explained and documented, but I rather think not. The secret of his sense of timing was something Toscanini took to the grave with him. Especially his timing of the Haydn finales.

MENDELSSOHN
❧[1809–1847]❧

I FIND it difficult to realize that, as I write, there is no recording available in England of Toscanini playing the Scherzo from Mendelssohn's *Midsummer Night's Dream* music. For many of us, the recording of the Scherzo on the eighth side of his performance of Haydn's "Clock" Symphony was one of our very earliest experiences of Toscanini altogether, and for those who did not hear his performance of it in London in 1930 the recording did much to convince them that an experience which had quickly become legendary was, after all, no fairy story.

How it has come about that for the first time for more than twenty-five years there should be no Toscanini Mendelssohn Scherzo I do not know, particularly as in 1947 he recorded the Overture, the Intermezzo, the Nocturne, the Wedding March and the Finale (as well as the Scherzo) in as near a "complete" selection of this lovely incidental music as he ever performed. But even that record—which never reached England—now seems to have been withdrawn and is no longer in the Victor catalogue. However, since it is surely not possible even for such a crazy mixed-up industry as the gramophone business to leave us without a *Midsummer Night's Dream* Scherzo for good and all, I make no excuse for referring to Toscanini's performance of a piece of music which was among his most exquisite conceptions.

The Mendelssohn of the Scherzos of the *Midsummer Night's Dream* music and the Octet, the Finale of the Violin Concerto, was the composer with whose death the true Scherzo, the ability to think in terms of genuinely fast music and to express that thought in clear orchestral language, disappeared from German music—apparently for good. For Toscanini I believe Mendelssohn was Mozart Without Tears; in a way that he was rarely able to relax with Mozart, Toscanini was able to enjoy all the

148

brilliance and vivacity, invention, tunefulness and quick-wittedness of Mendelssohn without ever—as he admitted happened with Mozart—feeling that he was missing the point of something below the surface. So it was no surprise to discover that one of the most thoroughly uninhibited and characteristically spontaneous of all Toscanini's performances was the one he always gave of the *Midsummer Night's Dream* Scherzo.

Here all Toscanini's magic was displayed—the perfect instrumental balance and "matching dynamics", the irresistible rhythm and lightness of touch, the translucent quality of the orchestral texture combined to produce what one can only describe as a magical realization of a magical score. It was a bewitching occasion equalled but never surpassed even by Toscanini himself.

SYMPHONY No 4 in A ("Italian"), Opus 90
[1833]

NBC Symphony Orchestra

GREAT BRITAIN: HMV ALP 1267
U.S.A.: Victor LM 1851
1954

This Symphony was something of a "natural" for Toscanini, of course, and its performance was full of characteristic touches and illumined detail, as well as of occasional departures from the letter, though not the spirit, of Mendelssohn's score. One of the first of these departures was to be noted as early as the sixth bar of the opening movement, when Toscanini took the throbbing wind-accompaniment down from Mendelssohn's indicated *forte* to a *piano* in order, one presumes, to have something to "crescendo from" eleven bars later. The quality and clarity of the instrumental colour of this first movement was a wonderful achievement; the tempo was a fast Allegro vivace somewhere in the neighbourhood of $\downarrow$. = 160, but it was a tempo which did not disfigure the detail of the superbly brilliant staccato playing, prevent Toscanini adopting a broader tempo when he felt it was called for (during the episode begun by the second subject, for instance), or detract from the quite entrancing effect of the little string phrase which begins at bar 103 with:

Ex. 60

I could not resist quoting that passage, for it was something I found myself playing again and again in the recording and wondering how it was that Toscanini, in looking to see "what is there", somehow saw so much more clearly than other conductors that what was there was what Mendelssohn had written there—neither more nor less.

As though impatient to get to the development section Toscanini did not make the repeat in the first movement. He went straight to the second-time-bar, an action which I must say did not outrage me as much as it seemed to outrage some of my contemporaries. It is true that by not making the repeat Toscanini deprived us of twenty-three bars by Mendelssohn which were never heard at all, together with the 186 we would have heard again if the exposition had been played *da capo*. But I must confess that I was so fascinated by the prospect of what was to come next, by the whole urgency of the performance, that I never found myself automatically rising to my indignant feet to lift the pick-up and put it back to the beginning again—although I admit I should have liked to have heard the passage again which I have quoted in Ex. 60.

For my taste, however, this was an ideal performance of Mendelssohn, with every detail crystal clear, especially in the dazzling treatment of the *fugato* episode of the development, and every one of the composer's typical counter-melodies being "sung" for all it was worth—not just because it was an ingenious passage of counterpoint but because it was, in fact, what I have said: a counter-*melody*.

The second movement, Andante con moto, moved easily at

about ♩ = 76, a tempo which some found a little on the fast side, but which for me rescued the music from the fate worse than death to which so many conductors so often condemn it —namely, the leaden, flat-footed funereal pace now fashionable for the Adagio of the Chorale of the Two Armed Men in *The Magic Flute*. At Toscanini's tempo this movement became unexpectedly intriguing, acquiring an air of conspiracy almost, which made one wonder how much Bizet knew of Mendelssohn's coda to this movement before he wrote the introduction to the smugglers' scene at the beginning of Act III of *Carmen*. Probably nothing at all, of course, but that does not make the association any less immediate or powerful. Toscanini's observance of Mendelssohn's markings, and the understated, inexorable *moto perpetuo* of the movement nevertheless created an absorbing air of drama about the whole thing ("moto", let it be said, does not necessarily mean fast). There was a logical and quite appreciable broadening of the tempo in the *legato* sections of the movement (violinists will recognize them: the flute plays Paganini's "La Chasse" in G), but for the most part it was the irresistible, cat-like tread of Toscanini's rhythm which was the most fascinating element of all. (According to my score Toscanini added a couple of trills to the B flats played by the first violins in bar 71. They were clearly needed on circumstantial evidence.)

The third movement was so charming, the playing of Mendelssohn's flowing phrases so smooth and soft-toned, that for a long time I was convinced the strings were muted during the first and last of the three sections in the recording. Closer listening showed that Toscanini had not been disputing the composer's instructions: the whole effect was characteristic of his remarkable ability to play music quietly without its ever deteriorating in tone. It was the volume, not the quality of the sound that was lower.

The Finale, taken at the handsome Presto of about ♩ = 184, was a ravishing experience, with composer and conductor at their respective bests. Toscanini's contribution was a masterly demonstration of his control of dynamics and instrumental balance, an inspired rhythm and a vitality which made this last movement an uniquely stimulating affair. Like the *Midsummer Night's Dream* Scherzo, Toscanini's performance of the Finale of the "Italian" Symphony was as near ideal as one could imagine, rich in unforgettable detail like, for instance, the perfectly balanced sound of the crescendo–diminuendo chords played by the wind on the figure of the Saltarello rhythm (at bars 156 and 160). Toscanini made one alteration to Mendelssohn's orchestration: he had the timpani follow the Saltarello rhythm of the violoncellos and basses instead of playing the straightforward roll written by the composer (bar 214 *et seq.*). It is certainly an improvement and helps to bring out the rhythm in a tutti which otherwise smothers the violoncellos and basses.

The general excitement and exhilaration of Toscanini's performance of this whole movement was so invigorating that the sad minor-key echo of the theme of the first movement of the symphony in the closing pages had an unusual poignancy. Toscanini found drama even in a Mendelssohn symphony.

SYMPHONY No 5 in D minor ("Reformation"), Opus 107
[1830]
NBC Symphony Orchestra

GREAT BRITAIN: HMV ALP 1267
U.S.A.: Victor LM 1851
1953

Toscanini's preference for this well-meaning work over Mendelssohn's "Scotch" Symphony is a puzzle that has never been solved. It is not by any means Mendelssohn at his best, so that one's interest in the recording is more or less limited to what Toscanini did with unsympathetic material. He gave an intense performance that was in every way typical of his greatness and in doing so succeeded in making this symphony a more attractive proposition than usual. There was a great tenderness in the little slow movement that prefaces the somewhat sanctimonious Finale, and he took the 3/4 pseudo-scherzo at a slower pace then one expected, and so introduced a curious atmosphere of gothic rusticity which suggested the dancing peasants of Dürer. It was suddenly Mendelssohn being very German. But where the composer offered a chance for Toscanini to extract charm from this particular music the conductor most certainly took it, and I found that my instinctive resistance to the nonconformist mood of the beginning of the movement had by the end been completely broken down by the grace of the later passages. So far as detail is concerned, the recording presents some wonderful instances in this movement of the peculiar "singing" pizzicato Toscanini always inspired in his string players; and there are some quite exquisite diminuendo passages which are model displays of his unique flair for the dynamic balance of music, so that every player makes a diminuendo of the same density and at precisely the same moment as everybody else. In the end I found this little mazurka-like episode was something I came back to very often —to the virtual exclusion, I will confess, of the other parts of a work which by and large does not entrance me. The most encouraging thing about it, on the whole, is that the Dresden Amen is played neither so often, nor for such long stretches, as it is in *Parsifal*. Unfortunately, however, the fact that a symphony is different in one detail from *Parsifal* does not automatically make that symphony unusually beguiling or very interesting. (In both contexts the "Dresden Amen" is surely a ridiculous anachronism. It was even less appropriate to *Parsifal* than to the Reformation, being the invention of a seventeenth-century German composer.)

All in all, though—in Toscanini's performance, at any rate— the second movement compensates for the stuffiness of the rest of Mendelssohn's "Reformation" Symphony. It is a gem in its own right.

MOZART

⊰[1756–1791]⊱

ONE of the most memorable musical experiences I have ever had was of a performance of Mozart by Toscanini; equally, one of the most dismal musical experiences I have ever had was of a performance of Mozart by Toscanini.

How can this be explained? What was it in Toscanini's musical make-up which could reveal, gloriously and unforgettably, as though for the first time, the unique, miraculous quality of *The Magic Flute*, but would lead him to regard *The Marriage of Figaro* as inferior to *The Barber of Seville*? It is obvious that Mozart was always something of a problem to Toscanini himself, and there is an interesting observation made by the conductor which supports this, in Adriano Lualdi's book, *L'arte di dirigere l'orchestra*, in which he is reported as saying to the author:

> "*The Marriage of Figaro* is beautiful; I heard a performance many years ago conducted by Richard Strauss and I was entranced. But I thought, and I confessed it to somebody who was with me: there is something about it which I cannot understand, which eludes me and which is lacking in me. *The Barber of Seville* is a magnificent opera, but there are some poor moments, unnecessary pages which aren't beautiful and need cutting; but compared with *Figaro*, how much sunlight, and variety and genuine gaiety there is in this music!"

Perhaps it was Mozart's peculiarly aristocratic quality which Toscanini could not understand, his—to an Italian—perplexing way of showing the shadows of human sadness cast by the sunlight of comedy. Just as there is no parallel to Mozart in the other spheres of music, so there is certainly none in the Italian opera house where opera is in the end basically either *seria* or *buffa*; it cannot combine the features of both. Unhappily, the Italians have never recognized that what to them are Mozart's greatest faults are in fact the virtues of genius, that the vast scope of the emotional canvas of *Don Giovanni*, for instance, is precisely what makes the work the stupendous and mercifully unclassifiable opera it is.

Toscanini, I think, always suffered from the impossibility of being able to pigeon-hole Mozart's music conveniently, and consequently he never truly recognized what Mozart intended. Certainly, there is no need to hold a Mozart score up to the light or turn it back to front; similarly, there is no guarantee if you follow Toscanini's maxim and "see what is there" in a score that you will necessarily understand it. It can, in fact, as Toscanini's own example proved, be a most unsatisfactory hit-or-miss process altogether, which can lead as easily to a superlative performance of the Jupiter Symphony as to an abysmally disappointing performance of the great G Minor (K. 550).

Nevertheless, while I always felt that in some way Toscanini was never quite old enough or experienced enough to understand Mozart fully—in the sense, that is, that Bruno Walter understands Mozart—I would be doing less than justice to Toscanini's genius if I did not try and recall something of his performance of *The Magic Flute* at Salzburg in 1937.

THE MAGIC FLUTE

Except that it would be difficult otherwise to explain how he came to perform his Rossini overtures so brilliantly, one might almost say that sophistication was the characteristic which Toscanini most notably lacked above all others. That, at least, is what his inability to understand *Figaro* suggests, although perhaps it would be fairer to say that while he acquired a certain sophistication over the years, a sophistication sufficient to make the most of Haydn and Rossini, Toscanini did not possess the natural inborn sophistication necessary to be a great conductor of Mozart. His lack of this particular instinctive sophistication explains Toscanini's temperamental indifference to *Figaro* and *Così fan tutte*, the two most sophisticated comedies in the entire history of opera; it also explains how he came to give an unforgettable performance of *The Magic Flute*, the one opera of Mozart's to which the sophisticated approach is not absolutely necessary. Indeed, *The Magic Flute* is a work which thrives on a naive, child-like treatment, and it was this which Toscanini brought to his conducting of it—a kind of wide-eyed innocence and extrovert enthusiasm which distinguished categorically between Good and Evil. There was none of the half-tones of *Figaro* to worry him. Monostatos was as black as he was painted and his music sounded like it.

The speed of Monostatos' eccentric little aria in Act II ("Alles fühlt der Liebe Freuden") was one of the high-spots that have stayed in my memory of Toscanini's Salzburg performance. It was a moment of quicksilver lightness which had the immediate effect of achieving what the composer intended —a musical scene which drew unerringly the malicious character of the little blackamoor and at the same time made him, by the very fussiness of the orchestral accompaniment, ridiculously pompous. Monostatos' musical prancing in that performance left no doubt that he wore button-boots which were too tight for him. He was, as Mozart meant him to be, a laughable, not a frightening figure.

Papageno's music Toscanini gave what I can only call an authentic peasant accent. It was a musical accent which seems to have been native to Toscanini, and which he immediately recognized and drew out of the music in which it occurred—in the scherzos of Beethoven, Haydn's rondos and the trios of his minuets, sometimes in Schubert.

The most surprising aspect of Toscanini's *Magic Flute*, however, was his perception of the peculiar serenity of Mozart's music. Earlier experience of Toscanini and the Blessed Spirits in Gluck's *Orpheus* * had taught one that the conductor whose reputation had been built largely on the prodigious dramatic power of his interpretations, could relax in a most convincing and lyrical way, but it had not prepared one for the tremendous breadth of his conception of the more solemn passages of *The Magic Flute*. In this way Sarastro's "O Isis und Osiris!" seemed to be sung and played in one long breath, so that it sounded, it has been said, "as if even the rests were filled in a miraculous way with unending music". A generation which is increasingly fed on the idea that Toscanini never did anything but "drive"

* Originally HMV D 1784 and Victor 7138 (both deleted). Now included in Act II of Gluck's opera on HMV ALP 1357 and Victor LM 1850 (1952).

music relentlessly cannot be reminded too often that his slow movements could be almost uncanny experiences of that "unending music" which he drew from *The Magic Flute*.

One other quality he emphasized in Mozart's score and that was what one might call the "primeval innocence" of the music for the Three Boys; but perhaps this was to be expected, for Toscanini's ability to give an orchestral texture an unparalleled clarity in performance was one of his most remarkable and, it seems, inimitable gifts. The contrast to this air of innocence provided by the angry outbursts of the Queen of the Night was understandably a "natural" to Toscanini, to whom the expression of drama in music was first nature and an instinct which coloured his whole musical outlook.

Only in one instance did Toscanini fail in *The Magic Flute*. On reflection it was a point at which one should have been prepared for failure, for its success normally involves a willingness to recognize Mozart as a forerunner of romanticism in music and to give it full rein: in other words, to understand those strange, bewildering undercurrents of Mozart's mind which Toscanini admitted were foreign to him. As befits a giant, Toscanini's failure in *The Magic Flute* was on a gigantic scale, for he failed at the most poignant moment in all Mozart—the instrumental postlude to Pamina's heart-rending aria "Ach, ich fühl's":

Ex. 61

There is nothing in those few bars to indicate that they are in any way "different" from anything else in the aria. There is no suggestion of a change of tempo, of any rubato or even of a sentimental *ritenuto*. This was one of the occasions when Toscanini should surely have held the score up to the light, and he would have seen clearly that Mozart was expressing something too deep for Pamina's words, giving voice to an emotion which certainly no well-behaved "classical" composer like Mozart should have known how to feel, let alone translate into music. Toscanini's resolute refusal to permit the slightest hint of romanticism in Mozart was a laudable one on the whole, and it was a rule which in general would seem to benefit Mozart rather than not. Unfortunately, of all composers Mozart is the one about whom no hard-and-fast rules can be made. Toscanini no doubt made his own hard-and-fast rules early in life and he let us—and Mozart—down when he failed to recognize the one moment in *The Magic Flute* when all such rules must be broken.

That it was a disappointing moment, this matter-of-fact, almost thrown-away curtain line to Pamina's moving scene, goes without saying; that it should, and could, have happened at all, however, was very typical, for it showed how obstinately and sometimes misguidedly Toscanini could stick to a principle.

Unless there exists somewhere an illegal but certainly fascinating recording made from the broadcasts of Toscanini's *Magic Flute* in 1937 posterity will have to make do with his performance of the Overture to the opera, made with the BBC Symphony Orchestra in 1938 (HMV DB 3350—Victor 49-0903). It is an admirable synthesis of all that was best in Toscanini's performance of the opera itself and shows how superbly he brought to life that side of the opera he understood.

SYMPHONY No 35 in D ("Haffner"), K. 385
[1782]
Philharmonic-Symphony Orchestra of New York

GREAT BRITAIN: HMV D 1782–84
U.S.A.: Victor M 65
1929

Just as all the generally accepted rules of musical behaviour have to be broken sooner or later to make the most of Mozart, so Toscanini in his performance of this extremely extrovert symphony disregarded many of his most treasured principles. The first to suffer was that proclaiming the Sacrosanctity of Tempo, though, it must be said, not until Toscanini had made

a vigorous statement of the first bars of the Allegro con spirito
of the first movement at about ♩ = 160:

Ex. 62

The bars immediately following these (in which the octaves in
bars 3 and 5 were unexpectedly short notes) were another
story, however. Mozart's habit of following a bold opening
with a gently contrasted second phrase (cf. the first subject
of the Jupiter) is admirably illustrated at the start of the
Haffner:

Ex. 63

Toscanini made no pretence of maintaining the rigid 160-
beats-a-minute of the first five bars when he came to this second
passage. If he did not play it "a piacere" he caressed it lovingly,
dawdling over the second and fourth bars of the phrase and
taking his time over getting back to the first tempo which
returns at the last note shown in Ex. 63. The unhurried return
to the basic tempo was even more marked when the whole
passage is repeated in its original key in the form of a pseudo-
recapitulation. Here Toscanini delayed things until the last
possible instant which produced a sudden last-moment
accelerando back to *a tempo*.

The first movement of the Haffner was altogether well suited
to Toscanini's temperament. It is a movement which, depending more on ingenious little twists and turns of a single theme
than on straightforward division into the familiar compart-
ments of sonata-form, demands that clarity of inner parts in
the orchestral texture which Toscanini seemed uniquely able
to procure from an orchestra. A glance at the score shows
that there is scarcely a bar in this first movement when some

instrument or other is not developing a variant or having contrapuntal fun with the opening theme (the subdued second part
of the phrase cited in Ex. 63 somehow gets lost altogether and is
only ever heard again on the occasion of the solitary repetition
I have mentioned).

Though Toscanini played one or two little tricks with the
tempo of this first movement they were tricks prompted by the
shape of the music itself. The slight slowing up in order to
enable the strings to "sing" the phrase

Ex. 64

brought a relaxed lyrical charm which was by no means out of
place in a movement so naturally full of contrasts. That
Toscanini should also find drama in the first movement of the
Haffner was not surprising; but it came easily, without forcing,
so that by playing "what is there" he heightened the rather
sinister effect of the development section which leads back to the
repetition of the first theme and begins with:

Ex. 65

The second movement, Andante, Toscanini also approached
in a relaxed manner, giving the tune grace and charm and
allowing it to "sing" at a comfortable ♪ = 80:

Ex. 66

It was in this movement, however, that he revealed what I
can only consider his inexperience of the composer, for he fell
into the trap which lures so many performers of Mozart to
disaster: the trap baited with "expression".

To the experienced Mozart conductor or instrumentalist there is little that needs "expressing" in the string passage:

Ex. 67

But Toscanini, like so many much less eminent than he, held the score up to the light and decided that what he read there should sound like this:

Ex. 68

"Leaning" on phrases like that, instead of letting them breathe themselves out, is a common habit among performers of Mozart, and I have never discovered how the practice originated. I can only suppose it was started by the romantics, who were always searching for sighs in music.

This movement is altogether an object lesson in what happens to Mozart if you ignore Toscanini's maxim about "the thing is to play *a tempo*"; the whole thing can degenerate into something perilously like an operatic *scena* before you're through and all kinds of "expression" creep in to distort the simple line of this cadence

Ex. 69

so that the final phrase is melodramatized—as Toscanini melodramatized it—into:

Ex. 70

As he made the first repeat in the slow movement of the
Haffner, and the passages I have mentioned have their formal
counterparts in the second part of the movement, Toscanini's
idiosyncrasies were heard several times and were clearly the
result of deliberate personal reflection on all aspects of the
question. But it was queer that a man who could blithely
countenance the near-romanticism of Ex. 70 should have been
so reluctant to put a little more into the instrumental postlude
to Pamina's "Ach, ich fühl's" quoted on page 157.

Toscanini's tempo for the Minuet of the Haffner always
came as a surprise: it was so unexpectedly slow. Accustomed
as one was to this particular Minuet being played sometimes
as fast as ♩ = 132, to hear Toscanini start it off at no more
than 112 seemed to presage a pedestrian performance. Toscanini's purpose, however, became clear at the fifth bar of the
tune. At his slower tempo, the phrase

Ex. 71   Menuetto

gave him what he was clearly looking for in this movement:
the charm of the Minuet. Indeed, the accent is on charm
throughout the entire movement and Toscanini did not hesitate to drop to a tempo of 100, or even less, for the Trio and its
warmly-scored graceful lines:

Ex. 72   Trio

It was an unconventional performance and the entirely unofficial *ritenuti* in the Trio did nothing to detract from the
effectiveness of Toscanini's conception of the movement. He
kept his accent on charm going to the end, and there were few
more enchanting moments than his final reiteration of the
bars in Ex. 71 with which the movement finished.

The Finale, Toscanini appeared to notice clearly, is marked
Presto, an Italian expression which he translated into terms of

♩ = 160—a tidy tempo which he maintained from the first statement of

Ex. 73

and maintained—particularly, it was noted—when he came to the second subject:

Ex. 74

This was always a moment which brought a gasp of astonishment from elderly English conductors whenever they heard it, for it had long been almost traditional at this point in the symphony to change gear down to something more dignified. It was nothing to do with the competence of British orchestras; the BBC Symphony Orchestra took it in its stride when Toscanini played the symphony at Queen's Hall in 1935, just as the same orchestra, in the long whispered string passage which leads to the third statement of the first subject, made one wish Toscanini could have been persuaded to conduct the Overture to *The Marriage of Figaro* (also in D major) more than a paltry couple of times in his career; there, at least, was an aspect of *Figaro* which could not have eluded him.

The whole of this Finale, indeed, has something of the irresistible effervescence of the *Figaro* overture, and Toscanini made each of its wittiest points—namely, the three different phrases which lead to the three reprises of the opening theme—with infallible skill and all his miraculous sense of timing.

I have discussed the old 1929 recording of the Haffner because that was more or less the performance I heard Toscanini give in the concert hall. Since then, however, there has been a new recording:

SYMPHONY No 35 in D ("Haffner"), K. 385
[1782]

NBC Symphony Orchestra

GREAT BRITAIN: RCA RB–16137
U.S.A.: Victor LM 1038
1946

This makes an interesting comparison with the earlier performance, revealing differences which are sometimes for the better and sometimes not. The differences are largely those of tempo. The later performance as a whole is slightly faster, and though the basic tempo of the first movement is roughly the same 160 as before, Toscanini did not seem to maintain it so strictly, so that one finds that some passages and phrases are faster towards the end than they were at their first statement at the beginning of the movement.

The Andante of the slow movement is now definitely Andante con moto, but I am sorry to say that instead, as one hoped, of this giving Toscanini less time in which to make his mistakes of style it did not eradicate them by any means. Perhaps the "leaning" I showed in Ex. 68 is not quite so marked, and the melodrama of Ex. 70 not quite so blatant, but it is still not Mozart as he should be played. It is odd that Toscanini, who was so admirably careful about not sentimentalizing Haydn in the slow movement of Symphony No 88 (see page 146), should have sentimentalized Mozart in the slow movement of the Haffner—especially since, in his later years, Toscanini was considered to have lost so much of his gentleness. His alleged ruthlessness and inelasticity would have done no harm here at all. As it is there is an exaggerated and out-of-place rallentando in the cadence at the end of both the first and second sections.

The Minuet and its Trio are both appreciably faster in this later recording, though it is the Trio which is now the more charming episode. Toscanini still made his final *ritenuto* at the end of the Minuet, but he never did it with quite the ravishing effect of the earlier performance.

The Finale, too, is faster than before, but there is still no lack of detail, the rhythm never degenerates into a gabble, and the second subject is still effectively played *a tempo*. It is not the ideal Toscanini Mozart, but it is certainly not so unsatisfactory as I had feared from hearsay of his latter-day activities.

SYMPHONY No 41 in C ("Jupiter"), K. 551
[1788]

I first heard Toscanini conduct the Jupiter in New York in 1933. It was the second of two items which comprised the first half of a concert in Carnegie Hall. The first item was the eight-year-old Mozart's earliest symphony, written in Ebury Street, London, in 1764, No 1 in E flat (K. 16), a work which it was clearly a sudden whim of the conductor's to contrast with the composer's last symphony, for he never played it again, either with or without the Jupiter for company.

Toscanini used a tiny orchestra for the early symphony—ten violins all told, as I remember—and he did not greatly add to the number of strings when he came to play the Jupiter immediately afterwards.

Five years later I heard Toscanini play the Jupiter again in London and it was a remarkable demonstration of that consistency which experience of his music-making showed to be one of his most astonishing characteristics. The London performance in 1938 differed in no apparent respect from the performance I had heard in New York in 1933; the two occasions combined to make a sufficiently deep impression that though it is now nearly twenty years since I heard Toscanini's Jupiter, all but the smallest details of his performance have remained in my memory.

As with his unrigid treatment of the second part of the opening passage of the Haffner (see Ex. 63), Toscanini allowed the contrasting section of the Jupiter first-subject to have its lyrical head and did not try to fit it into the tempo of the first couple of bars:

Ex. 75

But once that lyrical phrase took its place in the symphonic development (which is only fourteen bars or so later) the typically careful dotting of crotchets and quavers which was the foundation of Toscanini's unshakable rhythm permitted no further suggestions of rubato. Tenderness there most certainly was—particularly in the shaping of the line of the second subject,

Ex. 76

but there was no slackness, and the first movement, with its fascinating and ingenious development section, seemed to come to an end with the sort of electric crackle which may well explain how the symphony came by its nickname.

The slow movement of the Jupiter Symphony is marked "Andante cantabile", two expressions which Toscanini always took very literally. "Andante" meant "moving", and "cantabile" was just what it suggested. Unlike the slow movement of the Haffner, the score of this Andante is liberally decorated with expression marks—crescendo leading to *forte* followed by a sudden *piano* and the like—but Toscanini allowed none of this to interfere with the long smooth and continuous line of the music. Considering how disappointing his Mozart could be and how easily he made elementary mistakes of phrasing and exaggeration, the slow movement of the Jupiter was one of Toscanini's most noble achievements, seemingly unmarred by what—when we study his Haffner slow movement closely— can only be regarded as a perplexing inexperience of Mozart's style. It was wonderful music—Mozart played as Tauber sang him.

The Minuet bears the careful direction "Allegretto", perhaps as a hint that, whatever else it may be, it is not one of your slow and stately *tempo-di-minuetto* court dances this time. Toscanini brought a characteristic elegance of tempo and phrasing which gave the opening

Ex. 77

a curious shimmering quality.

In the Trio, Toscanini gave a hint of lingering a little on the opening phrase (and on each of the other seven occasions it occurred), so that it sounded rather like this:

Ex. 78

But this may have been the effect of a slightly slower tempo. There was, however, no hint of dawdling in any attempt by Toscanini to give the Trio a veneer of "charm". It is not that sort of Trio, and any attempt to do anything but let it gently take its course will only result in a saccharine coyness. This, at least, is a Mozartean pitfall Toscanini never fell into with the Jupiter.

The Finale of the Jupiter under Toscanini was one of those miracles of music-making about which there is virtually nothing to be said to those who never experienced it, and in trying to recreate something of the impression made by Toscanini's performances in 1933 and 1938 I fear I may be telling something of a fisherman's tale—almost, indeed, an immortal instance of the one that got away.

The considered opinions set down above, however, though

they relate in one case to an experience nearly twenty-five years old and which may not be held by those who know Toscanini's recording of the Jupiter made in 1946 and released in the United States by Victor as LM 1030,* will nevertheless, I believe, be endorsed by any who heard Toscanini play this symphony on one or other of the occasions I have mentioned.

Though Robert Charles Marsh in his *Toscanini and the Art of Orchestral Performance* dismissed the recording of the Jupiter with: "This is a set to forget", the performance is in fact not nearly so forbidding as one might fear from such a pontifical brush-off. On the contrary, this recording is, and will continue to be, remarkably helpful in reconstructing Toscanini's characteristic performance of this symphony.

The recording of the first movement displays all those elements to which I have already referred. (It also includes one to which I have not: a shocking change of intonation, dynamic and general quality in the 3-bar modulation that leads to the E flat of the development section. Was Toscanini really so fussy about tape-joins and the rest of the *chi-chi* as we were told? It is hard to believe it, for this was not a posthumous issue and so he must have approved it.) Unless one remembers Toscanini's tempo for this first movement from firsthand experience of his interpretation, the recorded performance may strike the listener as being too fast. That was exactly how it struck me when I heard this record for the first time. But as Denis Matthews has so rightly said: a Toscanini tempo might seem fast once, but very rarely a second time; and so it was with the opening Allegro vivace of the Jupiter. All the detail, particularly the contrapuntal detail of the development section, was wonderfully defined, and revealed fascinating, unexpected aspects of a score one thought one really knew by now.

The slow movement (taken at about ♪ = 96) proved to be a beautifully flexible performance, with Toscanini not hesitating to quicken the tempo as he went along, despite all his views on the Sanctity of Tempo, or to broaden it considerably with a good rallentando thrown in to lead to the recapitulation. There was also—by a conductor who was thought to be so unyielding in such things—a rallentando in the final seven notes

* Not available in Great Britain at the time of going to Press.

of the movement. It was a rallentando which Bruno Walter does not make and he is surely the most yielding of Mozart conductors. (Walter's *a tempo* is certainly the same speed as Toscanini's rallentando at this point. But Toscanini's relative slowing-up was noticeable and obviously justified by the *tenuto* written into the horn part at that juncture.) In spite of all one had been led to expect and fear from reading about this recording before hearing it, the slow movement proved to be a warm and extremely *dolce e cantabile* performance.

The Minuet (with ♩ = about 168) had great elegance and clarity. The Trio, in spite of what I suggested earlier, was taken at the same tempo and without any hint of the pause shown in Ex. 78. On reflection, of course, it would have been a little illogical and out-of-character if Toscanini *had* played the phrase with a *ritenuto* of any kind, just as it would have been if he had, in fact, taken the Trio at a slightly slower tempo than the Minuet, which is what I thought I remembered him doing. It seems, therefore, that the retard was purely an illusion which may have been caused by the change of tone-colour to a gentle *piano* for wind after the *forte* of trumpets and drums that preceded it.

The Finale in the recording I can well imagine coming as a shock to many people, for ♩ = 160 is indeed Allegro molto; but once again one becomes used to it on a second hearing. The main thing is that the wonderful counterpoint of this final fugal exercise is clear and eloquent, and there are even moments when Toscanini, to add emphasis, dropped to a slightly more deliberate tempo. He did this for a moment or two in what may be regarded as the development of the second subject. The performance of this Finale, as it comes out on the recording, is not without blemish, although much of the fault lies with the machine rather than with the man. The detail is all there, as it always was with Toscanini, but the recording somehow does not give it the chance on this occasion that it should, and one consequently finds oneself having to listen more closely than usual. Technically, the Jupiter was obviously not the product of a good session.

My main criticism is of what I consider the quite unjustifiable hurrying-up of the music towards the end of the movement and an accelerando in the Coda which, for the first time in my experience of Toscanini, made the final bars sound awkward and unsymmetrical so that the end did not come when one expected it.

None of this, however, entirely spoilt my enjoyment of this record, nor did it erase the memory of the "live" performances, and for that reason it seems to me that it will be of greater value to those of us who have had first-hand experience of Toscanini's Jupiter than to those who have not. The listener who is hearing Toscanini conduct the Jupiter for the first time through the medium of this recording will not be able to do what the rest of us can—namely, have our memory put the performance right where it goes wrong.

SYMPHONY No 40 in G minor, K. 550
[1788]

NBC Symphony Orchestra

GREAT BRITAIN: RCA RB–16137
U.S.A.: Victor LM 1789
1950

Whereas I found that my memory of Toscanini conducting the Jupiter produced a better performance than his recording of it, in the case of the G Minor exactly the opposite occurred. This late recording presents an incomparably better performance than I ever heard Toscanini give in person; his playing of it at Queen's Hall in 1937, for instance, was a very dismal experience indeed.

In this later performance Toscanini treated the main theme far less roughly than when I had heard it previously; he did not altogether lose his tendency to "lean" on Mozart's phrases, but it was only disconcertingly noticeable at moments during the dramatic development section of the movement (he also allowed the tempo to run away with him a bit during this sequence).

He cannot be absolved, however, from one or two instances of more serious misunderstanding of Mozart's style. The second subject was treated far too sentimentally; the tempo was slowed down for it and resumed only when the crescendo got under way nearly twenty bars later (this was a fault more noticeable at the second than at the first time of playing). And a few bars from the end there was a rather uncalled-for *stringendo*. But on the whole this proved a far more satisfactory and enjoyable affair than the memory of bitter experience had led one to expect, and throughout it there was a wonderful clarity of texture and polyphonic detail.

The slow movement was frankly disappointing. It was a hard, unsympathetic performance, even though there were un-authorized—and unnecessary—retards, diminuendos and increases of tempo. Compared with my last experience of this slow movement, played by the Vienna Philharmonic under Bruno Walter, I am afraid Toscanini never began to be in the same class. It was due to nothing more or less than Toscanini's complete lack of the right temperament. What Toscanini said about *Figaro*, he might well have said about this movement: "There is something about it which I cannot understand, which eludes me and is lacking in me." It was a sad reflection that both he and his listener could be so unmoved by one of the most lovely and moving of all slow movements.

The Minuet, on the other hand, demanded of Toscanini no more than that he should see "what is there", and it was a lovely performance with a strong, almost ferocious rhythm, all the clarity that Mozart's ingenious counterpoint demanded, and the Trio taken at the same tempo and given such a beautifully balanced instrumental texture that one could forgive Toscanini when he hurried for a couple of bars towards the end of it. This, in short, was the most satisfactory movement in the entire symphony.

The Finale might have equalled the Minuet in this had it not been for Toscanini's strange belief that the second subjects of the two fast movements in this symphony should be what I can only call "sloppy-ed up". When he reached the second subject of the Finale he dropped the tempo by something like twenty beats a minute which even at the vigorous—though highly variable—Allegro assai he adopted was still a noticeable gear-change. He never did it in the Haffner; why on earth did he think it was necessary in the G Minor?

Except for this completely false note the Finale was otherwise an exciting performance, with a development section played with rare vigour and clarity.

Though I believe I knew why Toscanini's Mozart could so often be disappointing, it does not ease the feeling of disappointment that he should have failed in his interpretation of the G Minor. This, one thought, was surely a "natural". It had drama, it had an original orchestral texture, it had depth of feeling and brilliance, and the fingerprints of genius on every note of it. It had everything, it seemed, that Toscanini looked for in music—except the power to touch his soul.

It is a sad thought.

SYMPHONY No 39 in E flat, K. 543
[1788]

NBC Symphony Orchestra

GREAT BRITAIN: HMV ALP 1492
U.S.A.: Victor LM 2001
1948

Toscanini is reported to have performed this symphony only once between the years 1925 and 1954, and this is the recording made of that solitary occasion—a broadcast in 1948. It would be easy to dismiss this performance with the observation that in that case Toscanini had obviously played it once too often— not only easy, but too damn true. All men of genius are expected to show human weaknesses like the rest of us. But I do not see why, like Toscanini, they should do so at the expense of Mozart. The Maestro's favourite epithet at his rehearsals was "Vergogna!"—"Shame!" It is an epithet which might well be shouted back by posterity to everybody concerned with the performance and publication of this recording—from Toscanini to those who considered for a moment that the world would be a better place for hearing the lovely, graceful minuet of this Symphony taken at a speed of $\downarrow$ = 192.

But in a way I suppose we should be grateful. It is the supreme demonstration by a master of How Not to Do It Yourself.

DIVERTIMENTO No 15 in B flat, K. 287
[1777]

NBC Symphony Orchestra

GREAT BRITAIN: HMV ALP 1492
U.S.A.: Victor LM 2001
1947

It is sadly ironic that the most nearly perfect of Toscanini's recorded performances of Mozart should have been of this comparatively unimportant Divertimento—a recording made, Toscanini confided to Howard Taubman, "for the benefit of his colleagues, the conductors, not particularly for the public. Fed up with the wrong tempi, he wanted to show what the right pacing should be." (In passing, I cannot imagine what kind of colleagues Toscanini had that they could possibly go wrong with the tempi in this work. Even he got them right. . . .)

Be all that as it may, however, the outcome of this magistral demonstration was an enchanting performance in which Toscanini avoided all those mistakes he persisted in making nearly every other time he played Mozart. It may be that the Divertimento is not so accident-prone, as it were, as the G minor Symphony, for instance; but even so Toscanini, had he put his mind to it, could still have found opportunity to indulge in his love of "leaning" on the notes in the slow movement. Apart from an occasional change of the bowing, an entirely enchanting rallentando at the end of the second movement (Toscanini omitted only No 5 of the six movements), and a strange moment of hurrying in the Finale, however, this was a performance founded on the solid basis of a literal observance of Mozart's expressed intentions. It was literal, that is, in all except the observance of Mozart's original conception of the first violin as a solo concertante instrument. The technical standard of modern orchestral string playing now makes it possible for the first violin part written for the one to be attempted by the many; but while one may feel ten times more anxious about the safety of ten daring young men on a flying trapeze than about the safety of one, the performance does not necessarily become ten times more attractive as a result.

I am not being a purist in this; it is just that the whole style of writing for the first violin calls for a solo performance, and while no doubt it was a source of great satisfaction to the old Maestro to know that he could call on a body of players of such unusual dexterity and general virtuosity, the musical gain to Mozart was nil. Besides, Toscanini was inconsistent in his practice: if the first violin part was not to be played by a soloist then why was the cadenza in the Adagio played by only one player? It should surely have been played by *tutti*.

The final effect, however, was one of great charm and brilliance, and it came as a great relief to be able to sit back and enjoy a performance which from the first moment was clearly going to provide no anxious moments for the listener. On the contrary, it provided one split-second moment that was quite ravishing: the phrasing of the two C's of the final bar of the "recitative" before the coda of the Finale gets under way. The dynamics and "breathing" of these two quavers was pure, inimitable, unmatchable Toscanini.

BASSOON CONCERTO in B flat, K. 191
[1774]

Leonard Sharrow (bassoon)
NBC Symphony Orchestra

GREAT BRITAIN: Not available at time of going to Press
U.S.A.: Victor LM 1030
1947

This performance was great fun, not least for the cadenza in the first movement being apparently based on the tune of "Ta-ra-ra-boom-de-ay!" Again this concerto showed that when the intellectual demands of Mozart's style were not beyond him Toscanini could give an enchanting account of his music. Neither the Bassoon Concerto nor the Divertimento, however, ever begins to compensate for the disappointment of Toscanini's failure to leave behind him an adequate recorded performance of the last three Mozart symphonies.

PUCCINI
≼[1858–1924]≽

LA BOHÈME
[1896]
(Property of G. Ricordi & Co)

Mimi	Licia Albanese
Rodolfo	Jan Peerce
Marcello	Francesco Valentino
Musetta	Ann McKnight
Colline	Nicola Moscona
Schaunard	George Cehanovsky
Bénoit *Alcindoro*	Salvatore Baccaloni

NBC Symphony Orchestra

GREAT BRITAIN: HMV ALP 1081/2
U.S.A.: Victor LM 6006
1946

Toscanini's association with Puccini was a long one; it began with the world première of *La Bohème* in 1896 and ended thirty years later with the posthumous performance of the incomplete *Turandot*. My own generation, however, has more or less grown up without experience of Toscanini's conducting of Puccini's operas. After he had left La Scala in 1929 there was no Salzburg Festival to give us unexpectedly a Toscanini *Turandot* or *Manon Lescaut*, as it gave us a Toscanini *Falstaff*, *Magic Flute* and *Fidelio*. Indeed, the nearest I myself ever got to hearing a "live" Toscanini performance of any Puccini music was the concert version of the Intermezzo and third act of *Manon Lescaut* given at the reopening of La Scala in 1946—a tantalizing experience, and frustrating, inasmuch as it indicated so clearly what one had missed by not hearing Toscanini conduct Puccini in his opera-house days.

The golden-jubilee recording of *La Bohème* made in 1946 was therefore a most welcome event, and if it did not altogether fill all the gaps in Toscanini's repertoire of operatic recordings, at least it gave us a powerful idea of his conception of Puccini's music and an authoritative interpretation of a masterpiece by the man who had launched it on its universally successful career half a century before. Just how authoritative this performance can be regarded we know from Puccini himself, for in spite of the repeated quarrels between composer and conductor, Puccini never doubted that Toscanini was the supreme interpreter of his music. He would not have entrusted *Turandot* to him if he had. And Toscanini for his part, though he had many reservations about Puccini's music, conducted *La Bohème* not only with all his characteristic fire and conviction, but also —and this was so important with this opera—with affection.

ACT I

Perhaps more than any opera except *Carmen*, the final dramatic effect of *La Bohème* depends on the atmosphere created in the first act. The ultimate sadness of the story is that of Dante's "time of happiness recalled in misery", the contrast of Mimi's death with the carefree gaiety and high spirits of the Bohemians in their normal surroundings.

Toscanini established the gaiety and high spirits from the very first bar with such vigour and rhythmic vitality that it came as a surprise to discover that his tempo was almost exactly the same as Puccini's prescribed metronome marking. As so often with Toscanini the speed was not excessive; the idea of his "driving" the music proved to be an illusion and, in fact, closer study of his performance, particularly of this first act, showed an abundance of beautifully timed, flexible *ritardandi* and the rest. Above all, the tempo was never too fast to blur the detail of this score.

As always, Toscanini drew something that one had never heard before out of even the most familiar score. What I heard for the first time in his *Bohème* was the full beauty of Puccini's very personal woodwind writing, which Toscanini's miraculous sense of instrumental balance and his meticulously careful grading of tone revealed in all its peculiar warmth and colour. (There is a wonderful example of this at the first mention of the Café Momus, when the woodwind play *pp* the tune which opens Act II.) The same characteristic preoccupation with the purely physical quality of the sound of Puccini's score pro-duced—again for the first time in my experience—a wonderful richness and crystal-clarity in the many passages for divided strings. Time and again in the recording of this performance the most intricate and—as one had hitherto imagined—most optimistically-scored figures for strings *divisi* "came off" in an unbelievable fashion.

Brilliance and general *brio* were perhaps the qualities most immediately apparent—and welcome—in Toscanini's per-formance of *La Bohème*. But they were not qualities exploited at the expense of the even more important elements of lyrical warmth and charm. In the recording Toscanini added his own quota of charm by frequently singing (with clear diction) at the top of his voice—usually at those moments when one most wants to join in oneself.

One of the most remarkable features not only of this, but of virtually all Toscanini's recorded operatic performances, was the excitement generated by the intensity of the music as a whole, regardless of the quality of the individual vocal per-formances. In other words, it was always the composer, not the singers, who made the greatest impact on the listener.

This was certainly the case in the last scene of this first act of *La Bohème*. From "Che gelida manina" until the fall of the curtain one was hardly aware of how good or bad the singers were. All one was conscious of was the gradual blossoming of the music, the growing warmth and eagerness of the two young lovers into whom Puccini breathed life. The whole of this scene had immense charm and conviction in Toscanini's per-formance; the *dolce* passages were exquisitely phrased and infectiously *cantabile*, the tempo was flexible with more than one unauthorized *ritenuto* making itself heard, and always that "singing" tone which affected even the pizzicato playing.

The last few bars of the act were notable—apart from the lovely sound of the orchestra—for allowing us to hear the part Puccini wrote for the tenor, and so sparing us that inevitable anxiety one feels, no matter who is singing, when the equally inevitable high C approaches. Puccini gave the soprano a high C; the tenor is intended to sing no higher than E. Toscanini insisted that Puccini's wishes should be respected.

ACT II

The vigorous tempo of the fanfare which raises the curtain on the Latin Quarter proved in Toscanini's performance to be the ♩ = 112 shown in the score. Just as he set the mood of the first act so exactly in the first bar of the score, so Toscanini immediately created the atmosphere of this act, an atmosphere greatly helped by the inclusion of boys' voices where Puccini demanded them. (This may not seem an unusual feature to those who live in the United States or Italy, but in England the use of boys' voices in the theatre is regarded almost as child labour and is so obstructed by rules, regulations and laws about bedtime for the young that it makes for a quieter life to use women's voices instead in this scene.)

The second act of *La Bohème* with Toscanini was largely remarkable for its display of purely technical mastery—of wonderful transitions from one tempo to another, of new and exciting revelations of Puccini's orchestration and the maintenance of a superb and irresistible rhythm from start to finish, which made the whole act into a kind of large-scale theatrical scherzo. Flexibility there most certainly was, when it was needed; Musetta's waltz song, for instance, had great charm and an easy grace about it.

Only one feature I found puzzling: Toscanini's complete disregard of the instructions "allargando e sostenendo" and "stentato" which occur in the score to bring the curtain down. I do not know what prompted this. All I know is that the steady *a tempo* makes the pay-off of the action a little dull. Either, I feel, there should be the *allargando e sostenendo* that Puccini marked, or one should go to the other extreme and treat the code to a brisk accelerando. At any rate, as Puccini obviously felt, the music needs something to make the point of its curtain line.

ACT III

Toscanini had the gift of bringing the whole smell and air and feel of the theatre to his studio and concert performances of opera in the most astonishing way, and there was little more vividly evocative in all his opera recordings than the orchestral introduction and background to the beginning of this scene.

It was not really Toscanini who created the atmosphere of the Barrière d'Enfer, but Puccini, of course, whose painting of the "audible scenery" on which the curtain rises is wonderfully sure and immediately effective. Toscanini's unique perception of "what is there", on the other hand, resulted in one of his most perfect physical realizations of a composer's intentions and illumined Puccini's score in a way which was unparalleled in my experience of this opera.

One of Toscanini's most effective touches in this scene, however, was not strictly a musical one. It was to do with the tone of voice used by the milk-sellers when they shout at the *douanier* to open the gates. Instead of the rather meaninglessly ejaculated "Hoppla! Hoppla!" one usually hears at this point, the women sounded extremely indignant at being kept waiting. Too often this, and the waggoners' shouts a few bars later, are regarded as vague expressions of "atmosphere" and local colour. Toscanini saw that they had definite dramatic meaning and ensured that we should know it.

The scene between Mimi and Marcello brings a new mood to the music, and Toscanini's expression of her unhappiness and despair was profoundly touching, not least for his own vocal underlining of Mimi's emotions.

At the end of the scene Toscanini made another personal contribution to the performance in the form of an alteration of the words. In place of Marcello's

> *Or rincasate, Mimì, per carità!*
> *Non fate scene qua!*

he substituted

> *Tornate a casa, ed io gli parlerò.*
> *Poi, tutto vi dirò.*

This was a reasonable modification, for it is not at all like
Marcello to speak to Mimi, whom he is trying to help, in such
rough terms as "Now go home, Mimi, for goodness's sake!
Don't make a scene here!" As Toscanini—or whoever altered
the lines for this performance—suggested, even if the rhyme in
the original Italian is not so strict, it is more in character for
Marcello to say: "Go back home and I will talk to him; later
I shall tell you everything."

As I cannot find this alteration in other recordings of the
opera I wonder whether it was an afterthought of Toscanini's
for the occasion, or whether he had always done it.

The entrance of Rodolfo brought an intenseness to the music
for the first time, which Toscanini sustained with his characteristically powerful grip on the rhythm, so that the syncopated figures in the inner parts of the accompaniment to
Rodolfo's fiercely ironic outburst at Mimi's behaviour had a
particular urgency. This ferocity (there is no better word for it)
contrasted wonderfully with the melting tenderness of Mimi's
Farewell.

Twice in the course of this scene there occurs a passage
which Toscanini accorded special treatment. The phrase
(which is repeated seven bars later) is accompanied by clarinet,
violins and violas and consists of

Ex. 79

In the string parts, which I have shown above, Toscanini
permitted himself a quite extraordinary embellishment in the
form of a clearly audible *portamento* between the second and
third beats of the first full bar. At least, so it sounds to me in the
recording; and since it apparently happens both times the
phrase occurs I am loth to regard it as an aural illusion caused
by the climax of the crescendo coinciding with the change

from, say, the first to the third position by the players. It is an odd sound, and I must confess that if it was intended I am not greatly enamoured of it. It is a bit of *Schmalz* which was disturbingly out of character for everybody concerned.

The Quartet which ends the act redeemed the sentimentality of the intentional or illusory *portamento* in no uncertain manner. Toscanini polished the details of this exquisite sequence of Puccini's orchestration to shine like diamonds, with every nuance of dynamics and rubato and instrumental invention making its telling effect. There was great lyrical warmth and tenderness in the Mimi–Rodolfo sequences, sparkle and ironic humour in the cantankerous exchanges between Musetta and Marcello. And, as usual, there was at least one moment in Toscanini's performance which was a revelation of something one had never noticed before. In this case it was the clarity of the ascending scale of harmonics in thirds played by the harp during the final receding, off-stage unison of Mimi and Rodolfo. It was a typical display of "what is there".

ACT IV

Toscanini's unique perception of Puccini's sense of the theatre made him instinctively pitch the note of Bohemian gaiety unusually high in the first half of this act. The *brio* was just that extra bit *brioso*, the bright busy-ness of the little theme associated with Rodolfo's and Marcello's work just that more than usually bright and busy, so that when the time came the contrast between the high spirits of the early stages of the action and the tragic reality of Mimi's last few moments was unbearably poignant and dramatic.

La Bohème seems to have been a work to which Toscanini was always adding contributions of his own. In this last act the mock-fandango ends a little unconventionally with Schaunard (or somebody) crying "Olé!" It is one of those things which I am sure Puccini would have wished he'd thought of. It does no structural harm to the music, and is entirely in character. The vigour and brilliance of the hammer-and-tongs "duel" that follows led me to look at Puccini's instructions: "Allegro spigliato $\downarrow$ = 132". Toscanini decided that the second half of the instruction was the clue to the music.

"Spigliare" means to expedite or dispatch, a term which Toscanini understood to imply a crotchet somewhere in the region of 152 instead of Puccini's hoped-for 132. The faster tempo proved, as it so often did, that what could sound ragged under other conductors could be amazingly clear and exciting under Toscanini. As I have said, the effect of this intensified gaiety was to heighten the impact of the serious action which follows, an impact I do not recall ever having experienced quite so forcefully in the theatre as in this studio recording by Toscanini.

From the moment of Musetta's entrance, with her despairing announcement that Mimi is ill, the whole mood changed so vividly in Toscanini's performance that the smile one might have had on one's face, listening to the antics of the Bohemians, was removed with a slap in the face like a hammer-blow.

The last forty pages of the full score of La Bohème, to anyone who has once succumbed to the spell of this opera are pages, like Hamlet's Niobe, "all tears". Toscanini, typically, drew tears in the least expected places—or rather, in places where it was not necessarily the singer who moved the listener, although perhaps that is what one should have expected. It was Toscanini, however, not Licia Albanese, who in the end brought an unanalysable pathos to Mimi's "Buon giorno, Marcello,—Schaunard, Colline, buon giorno . . .". A look at the score explains nothing—sustained notes for flute and piccolo, divided muted strings, four chords on the harp. One can only put it down to something like the equivalent among conductors of a great actor's gesture or spontaneous facial expression.

The last episodes of La Bohème with Toscanini were filled with details of this kind, some more easily analysable than others. Colline's farewell to his coat, for instance, sounded faster than usual (in fact, it was as near as makes no difference to Puccini's prescribed $\flat = 63$), but it would inevitably have dragged if the tempo had been allowed to spread itself as it is usually allowed to do.

The purist, on the whole, had a pretty thin time with Toscanini in this opera, for to off-set any complaints that he took things too fast, Toscanini could introduce an entirely unauthorized but completely justified rallentando, like the one in the orchestral phrase leading immediately to Mimi's "Sono andati?". Not only did Toscanini take liberties with the tempo, but in this same scene he made a very noticeable alteration in the orchestral accompaniment, which was not so much a matter of re-scoring as of re-writing the trumpet parts. After Mimi's quotation of "Che gelida manina" it will be remembered that she breaks out coughing and the orchestra plays (with the trumpets as indicated)—

Ex. 80

Toscanini altered the trumpet part to sound, from what I can make out from the recording, something more like

Ex. 81

What prompted Toscanini's unpredictable revision of something which, in my experience of the original, has generally made its effect, I cannot imagine. As usual, there is no harm done. I only wonder why he picked on that particular bar in the score to change Puccini's orchestration. It is a puzzling incident altogether.

Whatever its reason, however, this tampering with the trumpets in no way disturbed the effect of Puccini's drama. The whole of this last scene, from the point where Mimi and Rodolfo are left together, was almost unbearably moving in its sadness, with little details that tore at the heartstrings such as the emotional intensity of the string-tone accompanying Mimi's echoing of "Mi chiamano Mimi", and the wonderful audibility of the *pppp* passages as Mimi is discovered by Schaunard to be dead.*

The final couple of pages of *La Bohème*, harrowing enough at any time, were wonderfully moving, the more so perhaps because of the conductor's own touchingly pathetic vocal contributions to the general sadness of the situation.

I have always loved *La Bohème*, but never so much as I love it now that I have heard Toscanini's performance of it. This was surely the way Puccini heard it when he wrote it.

* To refer to the "audibility" of a *pppp* may seem paradoxical, but it is a remarkable fact that few conductors can control dynamics so that however quiet the music may be the audience can still hear it. Furtwängler was the arch-druid of the cult of the inaudible *pianissimo*.

RAVEL
⊰[1875–1937]⊱

DAPHNIS AND CHLOË – Second Series
[1912]

NBC Symphony Orchestra

GREAT BRITAIN: HMV ALP 1070
U.S.A.: Victor LVT 1025
1949

TOSCANINI's performance of these Symphonic Fragments was in the nature of a virtuoso display of his delight in the purely sensuous appeal of music—a display of such stupendous virtuosity, indeed, that one finds oneself further away than ever from discovering the secret of his genius. It is not enough to say that he saw "what is there" in the score. The question to which there seems to be no answer is: how did he manage to make the things he saw sound as he made them sound?

Experience of *Daphnis and Chloë* before I heard Toscanini conduct it did little to convince me that a great deal of what Ravel wrote in his score had not been done more for the look of the music than the sound of it, and that the composer had really been a trifle over-optimistic if he had expected half of what he put down on paper to be audible.

When Toscanini came to play it, however, this music changed much of its character; where there had been merely a vague "wash" of colour before there was now a texture made up of a mass of discernible, sparkling detail which combined, like the dabs of colour of the *pointillistes*, to create a complete picture. Not only did details like Ravel's bird-imitations stand out at last, and various hitherto inaudible harmonics, but the division and sub-division of the strings into fourteen parts or so made aural sense for the first time. Once one could *hear* that the violins were *divisi* into four, the violas into two parts and so on, there was some reason for having all those small black notes sprawling all over the page after all.

The balance and clarity of the instrumental texture in Toscanini's performance was something that defies description as it defies all attempts to explain how it was done. The familiar "matching dynamics" were in frequent evidence, of course, and particularly in the first pages of "Daybreak", when the flute figures are echoed at exactly the same dynamic level by the clarinets.

Even after considerable previous experience of Toscanini the sheer volume and force of the climaxes in *Daphnis and Chloë* still came as a surprise, just as one was astonished to notice—as though for the first time—the purpose and effectiveness of so many of Ravel's dynamic markings, especially his subtle use of crescendos and diminuendos which had formerly seemed to have no particular artistic importance.

While Ravel was careful to give metronome markings for most of the tempi in this Suite, he neglected to provide any for the Animé which heads the final Danse Générale. Toscanini regarded this as being worth roughly $\quarternote = 176$, an exhilarating tempo clearly inspired by the words (referring to the action of the ballet) found in the score: "Joyeux tumulte". The last movement of this score in Toscanini's performance was precisely that. The vitality and the excitement stimulated by Toscanini in this Finale was something that had to be heard to be believed. It was a tremendous, exhausting experience, and yet never for a moment did this overwhelming inundation of rhythm and brilliant orchestral sound degenerate into mere din. The *batterie* crashed and banged, the brass bellowed and brayed with a vigour that left the listener limp, but never for a single beat was the music in Ravel's score obscured. The only details which were obscured in any way (the two-octave *glissandi* for strings, for instance) were obscured by the sheer physical impossibility of making them audible. It was the composer's, not the conductor's fault that some of the things written in the Danse Générale should have remained merely the paper transactions of music.

For the rest, for sheer exuberance and beauty of sound, a *Daphnis and Chloë* like Toscanini's is not likely to prove an everyday experience again in a hurry.

ROSSINI
❧[1792–1868]❧

As far as I know, Toscanini only ever conducted two Rossini operas in his life. One was a comedy, *The Barber of Seville*; the other was a "grand opéra", *William Tell*. And yet, in the concert hall, one of the things one always most looked forward to, because they all had such an air of authority and authenticity about them, was Toscanini's performances of overtures to Rossini operas which—one was rather surprised to discover—he had never conducted at all. One was surprised because many of the operas were, and still are, in the general Italian repertory and it seemed a little strange that in all his huge operatic experience Toscanini should never have devoted time or attention to such enchanting works as *La Cenerentola* or *L'Italiana in Algeri*.

If he neglected the operas, Toscanini at least recorded eight of their overtures (omitting, for some reason, *Tancredi* and *The Siege of Corinth*). Some of these recordings are available in one country, some in another; some have been deleted from the catalogues, some have not yet made their appearance in them. The complete list, however, is as follows:

LA SCALA DI SETA * [1812]

SEMIRAMIDE * [1823]

LA CENERENTOLA * [1817. Overture composed 1816]

LA GAZZA LADRA * [1817]

L'ITALIANA IN ALGERI * [1813]

* Consult the Table of Original and Current Record Numbers, pp. 388–389, for the breakdown of Toscanini recordings of Rossini issued in the United States and Great Britain.

THE BARBER OF SEVILLE * [1816. Overture composed 1813]

IL SIGNOR BRUSCHINO * [1813]

WILLIAM TELL * [1829]

Average experience of Toscanini's methods and outlook enabled most people to know what to expect when they came to his performances of the Rossini overtures. That they were invariably given more than they expected, however, goes without saying, of course; for over and above what one came to regard as the everyday features of Toscanini's, but unfortunately of nobody else's, performances there were those inimitable touches of genius which made his interpretations so unpredictable and intensely personal. Rossini's music provided Toscanini with unparalleled opportunity for the demonstration of his immense rhythmic vitality and his uncanny sense of instrumental clarity and dynamic balance, to display his ability to bring charm, brilliance and an air of incomparable spontaneity and effervescence to overtures which are too often merely an exhibition of din without precision.

Toscanini's regard for precision was, in fact, one of the factors which as much as any other made his Rossini outstanding. The famous "Rossini crescendo" occurs in each of the overtures listed above, and in most performances they are allowed to degenerate into an occasion for general rowdiness. Toscanini, as in all such matters, never lost sight of the music, and he made the effect of these crescendos something very far out of the ordinary by establishing with great precision the detail of the orchestral figure on which each crescendo is built.

I referred in the chapter on Beethoven's Seventh Symphony (page 75) to Toscanini's peculiar achievement of a diminuendo which sounded as though a *forte* chord had been slowly faded down to *pp* by a master hand at some control knob, so that it was only the volume that was "graded down", never the tone or expression.

The same thing applied in reverse to these Rossini crescendos. It was as though the quiet, exquisitely phrased initial figure

---

* Consult the Table of Original and Current Record Numbers, pp. 388–389, for the breakdown of Toscanini recordings of Rossini issued in the United States and Great Britain.

was slowly "faded up" to its maximum volume without loss of precision or coarsening of the tone in any way. (This gift of making music sound louder without making it so loud that you couldn't hear it was rarely better demonstrated by Toscanini than in the storm of the *William Tell* overture.)

Toscanini's performances of Rossini's overtures were not only invariably an exhilarating experience, but in many cases were to be regarded as interesting instances of Toscanini in the role of editor. He did not do much in the way of retouching Rossini's scoring; at least I do not regard as "retouching" his retention of the traditional pizzicato accompaniment during the long 5-bar solo in octaves for clarinets in the Maestoso introduction to the overture to *La Cenerentola*—even though the score most recently published (in 1952) bears the words "Edited from the autograph MS and Foreword by Renzo Bossi" and suggests that the relevant string passage from bar 16 onwards should be played *arco*.

For the most part Toscanini's editing was a matter of meticulous regard for the individual player's comfort. Whenever he was to conduct the overture to *La scala di seta*, for instance, he sent the first oboe player of the orchestra a manuscript version of his part in advance—a copy, that is, of Toscanini's careful modifications of Rossini's original part for the instrument. The extent—and effectiveness—of these modifications, the subtlety of Toscanini's revision, are something everybody who intends to conduct this overture should study. It is an easy enough curriculum to follow, for it is no more than a matter of comparing the recording with the score and noting where and how often Toscanini introduced the use of *legato* in the oboe's solo passages in place of Rossini's obviously optimistic (and, in practice, monotonous) use of *staccato*.*

Comparison between recording and score is something recommended for any study of these Rossini recordings made by Toscanini. Much of his intriguing deviation from the letter of

---

* Comparative study will prove easier, I fear, for the English student than for the American. The overture to *La scala di seta* was recorded by the BBC Symphony Orchestra and is therefore, for contractual reasons, still current in Great Britain. What Mr Terence MacDonough is heard to play on HMV DB 3541 is the oboe part as revised and approved by Toscanini. Also, as this was recorded at 78 rpm, study is facilitated in these days by being able to play it at 33⅓ or even slower, and so note the phrasing more closely.

Rossini's scores, however, was the result of that characteristic-ally spontaneous perception not only of "what is there" but also of what it would do no harm to have there instead. The score of *La scala di seta* is almost forbiddingly devoid of helpful hints for conductors. Toscanini's performance of the overture was one of endless enchanting nuances—the sudden un-expected accent in the unison violin passage leading to the over-ture's second theme (which Toscanini took *meno mosso*, although there is no hint of a slower tempo in the score), the exquisite lightness of the chattering passages for the two oboes in thirds, the surprising, but dramatically and stylistically correct, intro-duction of the occasional crescendo and rallentando which was instinctive.

Toscanini's performance of the overture to *Semiramide* drew attention to what might be called "editorial details" which were more apparent in performance than on paper. The most immediately intriguing touch, apart from the wonderfully timed moments of *ritenuto* in the pizzicato accompaniment during the slow introductory section, affected the strings' first theme of the Allegro:

Ex. 82

The final D of the phrase was played by the violins as a harmonic on the D string—a clear-as-a-bell note, without vibrato, reached with the tiniest suspicion of a *glissando* from the A preceding it. It was a breath-taking moment that passed almost before one was conscious of it at all. More remarkable than this first little gesture was Toscanini's matching of it a few bars later, when the same theme was repeated an octave higher. The charming effect of the harmonic D in the first phrase was reproduced in the second by Toscanini's unique sense, not of "matching dynamics" in this case, but of matching tone.

In the second case, however, the final D was not a genuine har-monic; by having the violins use a "white" tone, the famous vibratoless *ton blanc* of Ysaÿe, Toscanini created the illusion of a harmonic and so matched the sound of the first phrase. (There was some ravishing woodwind colour in the thrown-about arpeggios of the accompaniment in the last recapitulation of this.)

From his performance of the *Semiramide* overture there is much for the student to learn about when Toscanini did and did not use the cymbals. Even when, as in *William Tell*, it includes "gran cassa e piatti", the score gives no specific indication of when the bass drum is meant to play alone and when it is joined by cymbals. Convention suggests that the two instruments should play together, the single note in the part they share in the score being intended to serve for both of them. To avoid the almost incessant din that would be caused by following this convention, Toscanini rationed the cymbal clashes and limited them to points in the music where they gave the greatest emphasis. In the case of *Semiramide* no *piatti* are called for at all, but Toscanini included them nevertheless on the ground, one supposes, that the nature of the music needed them, while it did not need them in *La Cenerentola*, for instance, where similarly only the *gran cassa* is indicated.

Apart from Toscanini's preference for the pizzicato I have already mentioned, his editing of the *Cenerentola* overture consisted largely of his introduction from time to time of retards which sounded so logical and natural that one was surprised to learn they were not in the score.

Toscanini's divergence from the score of the overture to *La gazza ladra* began in the very first bar. The three famous side-drum rolls, both on this and the second occasion on which they occur, are written to be played respectively *piano*, *piano* and *piano–crescendo–forte*. Toscanini observed the composer's markings of the second two rolls, but played the first one unmistakably *forte*, giving the second the effect of an answer in the distance. (He repeated this procedure when the passage was heard again at bar 51.)

This overture of Rossini's was one of Toscanini's most effective conceptions, for he gave the *marziale* introduction immense elegance and charm and the main Allegro a very characteristic *brio* and clarity, while his two crescendo episodes were a masterly and exciting demonstration of the building-up process I have already mentioned.

The late Constant Lambert's immortal view that the opening
of the overture to *L'Italiana in Algeri* depicted a drunken hus-
band creeping upstairs late at night, knocking over the grand-
father clock and continuing on his way as though nothing had
happened, was always superbly illustrated by Toscanini's
performance of the opening phrase. This was a perfect example
of his feeling for the right tempo and above all for the importance of unwaveringly adhering to it. The crashing *f*
unison C did not impede the progress of the stealthy pizzicato
for one moment longer than it took to play in strict tempo;
there was not the slightest hint of a pause, and the pizzicato
went on its way as though nothing had happened.

Two instances of Toscanini's editing were noticeable in this
overture. The first resulted in this phrase for strings:

Ex. 83

In the orchestral score the group of four semi-quavers is written
as all in one bow. Toscanini added the accent shown above
and played the notes staccato.

The other noticeable departure from the orchestral score,
which was really noticeable enough to qualify as an addition
to it, was the heavy, effective accent imposed where I have
shown it in this phrase for unaccompanied violoncellos and
double basses:

Ex. 84

In Rossini's original there was nothing of the kind to be seen;
it seems to have been entirely Toscanini's idea, and without it
the passage would certainly strike one as a little dull and uninteresting. Toscanini's treatment of this overture was altogether on the liberal side. He obtained a remarkable cut-
diamond brilliance and precision in the *forte* chords which

punctuate the statement of the main Allegro theme and its recapitulation without for a moment allowing these chords to degenerate into mere loud interjections; they always retained their music quality. But he encouraged something bordering— for him—on rubato in some of the rapid little phrases for the solo flute (once again he considered the player's comfort), and was not above allowing a suggestion of *stringendo* in moments of excitement before returning to the basic vigorous tempo.

The overture to *The Barber of Seville* was the first recording of Rossini conducted by Toscanini, in 1929, that we ever heard, and for that reason his performance of it was always something of a classic. Listening to the latest recording it is still an ex-hilarating experience, with all the typical sparkle of the orchestration, the exuberance of the rhythm and the dynamics and inimitable Rossini *brio* as clearly defined and enthusiastic-ally presented as ever it was.

Whatever he felt about the operas that followed them, Toscanini's performances of Rossini's overtures were a labour of great love, and if he did not reveal any unexpected emo-tional depths or hitherto unsuspected beauty it was because they were not to be found in the music anyway. What Tos-canini did, as nobody else did, was bring his own peculiar, irrepressible vigour to bear on the music of a composer who possessed this quality in a greater degree than any other who ever lived. The famous "Rossini crescendo", it seemed, might almost have been invented for Toscanini.

Of the other two Rossini overtures Toscanini recorded, the comparatively unfamiliar jeu d'esprit which is the prelude to the very gay little comic opera, *Il Signor Bruschino*, was an enchanting product of Toscanini's inimitable sense of timing.

The remaining overture, *William Tell*, was perhaps the most remarkable performance of all. It seemed impossible that this glorious old war-horse of a work could be so filled with life that it sounded as fresh and spontaneous as though one were hearing it for the first time. But that was what happened. Toscanini's presentation of the four so-familiar, "corny", so-easily-parodied episodes of this overture, demonstrated with tremendous con-viction the effect Rossini must have had on his contemporaries. In its way, indeed, the *William Tell* overture offered a remark-ably concentrated synthesis of Toscanini's outstanding qualities.

The opening Andante section, with the five solo violoncellos, enabled him to indulge in his love of the sheer physical beauty of sound; the Storm showed how infallibly he could draw music from the most shattering *fortissimo*; the pastoral epilogue revealed all his lyrical gentleness, his gift for making music so warmly *cantabile* that even a pizzicato accompaniment "sang"; and the final Allegro vivace was everything one had learned to expect—a wonderful display of tremendous vigour and rhythm, clear-cut detail and cumulative, infectious excitement.

Hearing the overture to *William Tell* played as Toscanini played it, one at last understood why Rossini's contemporaries respected him as they did. In its way this was one of the most remarkable of all Toscanini's achievements. Perhaps his demonstration of Rossini's true calibre as a composer—and one can have few doubts about it after hearing this performance—will encourage more people to look at the score of the rest of *William Tell* again. They may not see "what is there" quite so clearly as Toscanini; but they would have to be stone blind not to see more than they do at present.

SCHUBERT

❧[1797–1828]❧

SYMPHONY No 8 in B minor
("Unfinished")
[1822]

NBC Symphony Orchestra

GREAT BRITAIN: HMV BLP 1038
U.S.A.: Victor LM 9022
1950

1. Allegro Moderato

SINCE Toscanini apparently did not conduct the work at all between December, 1930, and October, 1939 (or if he did, then he certainly did not do so in my hearing) this recording has had to provide me with my only experience of Toscanini's performance of the work. And I must admit my first hearing of it was something of an ear-opener: a familiar, hackneyed work that every conductor for years had been messing about with in a desperate attempt to give life, some new "angle", to music which had become limp with maltreatment and lack of care and attention, was suddenly revealed in all its original power and glory.

Toscanini's direct and dramatic approach to this symphony was quite startling in its difference from accepted traditions or habits, so startling, indeed, that it successfully obliterated all memory of other performances, so that one can no longer think of it in terms of "whereas other conductors do so-and-so, Toscanini did such-and-such". One glance at Schubert's score and one can now imagine no other way that this symphony should be played. Toscanini, as nobody else in my experience, most faithfully revealed it for what it is: one of the most original and personal works in the whole history of music.

Dramatic tension and a warm, infectious lyricism dominated

Toscanini's performance—and not inappropriately, for these were the elements that dominated all Schubert's music; he would scarcely have become the greatest of all song-writers if they had not. Schubert's unequalled genius as a song-writer is something which is sometimes forgotten when his instrumental music is under consideration. The absence of the human voice to perform it did not in any way change the composer's fundamental conception of music as something essentially *cantabile*, whether it sang in the tones of drama or of a gentle lyricism. The composer who thought of music like that could not have wished for a more loyal champion than Toscanini. There is drama in the very first note of this symphony and it continues, in varying degree of intensity, throughout the two movements.

The listener unacquainted with Toscanini's ways may fear that he is going to hear an exaggerated over-dramatization of Schubert's score. Let him rest assured that he will hear nothing of the sort: he will hear what Schubert wrote, and having heard it, will ask himself what possible way there is of playing the restless little semi-quaver figure for violins accompanied by the pizzicato of the rest of the strings, which follows the grave opening bars of the movement, but with the so clearly audible but still mysterious *pp* Toscanini saw Schubert had indicated.

Toscanini adopted a tempo of about ♩ = 120 for the first movement of the Unfinished, and he kept to it virtually throughout, with one unexpected and highly effective *ritenuto* at bar 251 which leads into the return of the lovely second subject. He allowed no slowing-up for the second subject itself; it was the instrumental colour, the whole atmosphere and gentle character of the melody that made the contrast with the drama of the first part of the movement. "Cantabile" this section most certainly was, and there is little I remember so ravishing as the phrasing and tonal quality of the strings on the two occasions they came to the passage: *

Ex. 85

* This, of course, is heard in B major the second time.

The performance was rich in superbly pointed details like this—in the sudden significance of an apparently unimportant *sfz*, in the restful contrast with what has gone before which is made each time by the simple 3-bar modulation that introduces the second subject, in Toscanini's characteristic insistence on exact note-values which was the basis of his prodigiously strong rhythm, in the familiar "singing" quality of the pizzicato and the uncanny "matching dynamics" which were such a remarkable feature of Toscanini's performances of Beethoven.

Like other great Toscanini performances this was not lacking in its particular breath-taking moment. For me this came at the end of the powerfully dramatic conception of the Coda: in the quality of the diminuendo made by the orchestra on the final chord. This had all the intensity and melancholy, expressed by the same miraculously balanced and synchronized dynamics, of the diminuendo of the final chord of the slow movement of Beethoven's Seventh Symphony as Toscanini played it (see page 75). All the score indicates is three bars of *ff* with a diminuendo sign in the fourth bar. To what degree of "unfortissimo" that bar is to diminish the composer does not say; but what Toscanini thought Schubert meant he judged to perfection.

2. *Andante con moto*

This movement, which Toscanini took at some ♪ = 92, consists of the same principal elements as the first; there is a drama and there is Schubert's unmatched lyricism—both aspects of music which were Toscanini "naturals". It is the lyrical element, of course, which predominates in this slow movement, played by Toscanini with a great tenderness and all his incomparable feeling for beauty of line created by his insistence that the tunes should be *dolce* and *cantabile* within the framework of an easy but steady *con moto* tempo. The recording of this second movement of the Unfinished, indeed, is a wonderful display of Toscanini's ability to say all that the composer asks should be said without "hamming" or wanting to burst the confines of a 3/8 bar.

Toscanini's recording of this slow movement is something I have come back to frequently, for its performance, like that of the first movement, is unusually full of touches which become more obvious and intriguing with each hearing. Among these I count the quite unbelievably clear *ppp* of the syncopated string accompaniment to the second subject; it is so quiet that one thinks at first that the strings must surely be muted, until a crescendo leads to an unmistakable natural tone and we realize that it has all been a matter once again of Toscanini's unique control of dynamics.

Toscanini naturally made the most of the dramatic aspects of what I always think of as "the loud bits" of this movement (the four episodes are clearly visible at regular intervals on the surface of the record), but his most memorable dramatic touch was to be found in the final dying-away pages of the movement. The dimenuendo echoes in the coda of the little cadence

Ex. 86

assumed a strange pathos which gave the last moments a peculiar melancholy, like the slow fall of the curtain at the end of some drama that has not been a stark tragedy, but wistfully sad. I found myself listening to this slow movement of Toscanini's many more times than I had anticipated.

SYMPHONY No 9 in C
[1828]

NBC Symphony Orchestra

GREAT BRITAIN: HMV ALP 1120
U.S.A.: Victor LM 1040 (withdrawn)
1947

A critical study of Toscanini's performance of this symphony is complicated a little by this 1947 recording, the only version available in England, having been replaced in the United States

by the later one made in 1953 (LM 1835) to which the English
have not yet had access. I can only hope that the final version
comes closer to my personal experience of Toscanini's playing
of the work in London in 1938 than the 1947 recording, which
serves both as a positive and a negative aide-mémoire by
reproducing some of the best features of what I heard in 1938
together with some new and less admirable features, which
serve as stern reminders of How Not to Do It.

In analysing the 1947 recording I shall inevitably have to
point out certain things which Toscanini did *not* do in 1938,
and by not doing them so achieved an altogether finer and more
worthy reading of the symphony than he has bequeathed us—
so far as we in England are concerned, at least. If, as I hope,
the 1953 performance proves to have eliminated what are not
altogether trivial shortcomings then posterity will have an
inspiring model to emulate. If not, then all I can hope is that
this analysis will enable the student, by inference and comparison, to piece together, from what I have to say and from
what is good in the 1947 recording, some sort of composite
sound-picture of Schubert's Ninth Symphony as Toscanini
made it sound.

1. *Andante – Allegro ma non troppo*

The basic tempo of the opening Andante in the recording was
somewhere in the region of ♩ = 96, but this was far from being
a metronome-bound performance in any of the four movements.
Sometimes Toscanini's deviations from a strict tempo were
justified, at others they were not. As a general rule, they were
justified when the tempo dropped below the speed first adopted
and unjustified when it exceeded it.

On the whole, however, the recorded performance of the
first movement reproduces fairly faithfully the more memorable
elements of Toscanini's 1938 reading of the music: there is a
great spaciousness and smoothness of motion in the Introduction, a superbly conceived transition to the Allegro which
puts into practice Schumann's description: "The transition
from the Introduction to the Allegro is something quite new.
There appears to be no change of tempo; we find ourselves
transported—we know not how." Schumann's words referred

to this Schubert symphony; they could have applied equally to
every change of tempo Toscanini ever made.

What was not good in the recording was Toscanini's tendency
to quicken the tempo in the course of building to a climax. It
did not sound right and it came as no surprise, in consequence,
to discover on reference that there was no *stringendo* in Schubert's score to run concurrently, as it were, with the big
crescendo to the climax of the exposition. In his "live" performance of this movement Toscanini's refusal to let the
tempo run away with him increased the intensity of this
building-up of the climax in a way that was never equalled in
the recording. (In the concert hall the *fff* attained in the
exposition was overwhelming, of course; in the recording the
engineers have obviously kept it to themselves. It is no louder
than the *ff* nine bars earlier.) As Toscanini retorted when he
was shown not to have observed the metronomically precise
tempo, "Man is not a machine." But the variation, or, rather,
instability of tempo which characterized this recorded performance, demonstrated that the otherwise laudable determination of man not to be a machine could sometimes
strike at the very root of rhythm. Rhythmically Toscanini's
1947 recording was most uncharacteristically lacking in precision. The first movement displayed precision of phrasing,
of dynamic balance, of all the detail one came to expect from
a Toscanini performance; but it lacked the rhythmic precision
which had been such an invigorating feature of the work as
Toscanini had played it in 1938. Then there had been about it
that unique air of inevitability, of logical development as
irresistible and impressive as the flow of a great river to the sea.
It was these qualities which were missing from the 1947
recording, and not even the broadening of the tempo in the
last pages of the Coda was altogether able to compensate for
their absence.

2. *Andante con moto*

The first point of difference between the 1947 recording and
the 1938 performance of this movement was in the seven introductory bars for strings with which it begins. The engineers,
or Toscanini, or both combined, have placed on record as

nearly inaudible a *piano* as I have ever heard from Toscanini. As recorded, indeed, one has to have the volume control up so high at the beginning of this movement that otherwise the initial *piano* is so weak that it cannot look Schubert's genuine *pp* in the face seventeen bars later. This is neither characteristic nor particularly artistic, and is altogether a disconcerting feature of the recording.

My memory of this movement, as I heard Toscanini play it at Queen's Hall, is again of the wonderfully inevitable unfolding of the composer's ideas which one encountered in all Toscanini's Beethoven performances. Having decided on how much *moto* his Andante was to have, Toscanini kept to it, but never so strictly that he could not stretch it a little when the music demanded room to breathe. The deviation, in effect, was always in the direction of expansion, never contraction. In his 1947 recording, on the other hand, it seemed that whenever Toscanini was confronted with a dotted note sequence, he could not resist hurrying. It happened in the first movement, it happened in this movement; it happened again in the last—which quite coincidentally meant that all the development sections of this symphony were subjected to an unnatural stimulation which deprived them of most of their effectiveness.

In the recording of the slow movement, however, the essential *cantabile* nature of the music was by no means altogether lost, though sometimes, in order to emphasize it, Toscanini had to slow things down more than might have been necessary if he had not hurried other things up so much meanwhile. As performed in this recording it must be admitted that it is not a model of metronomically strict tempo. The basic ♪ varies between 132 and 144 (with occasional instances of less than the first as well as of more than the second), and in consequence the rhythm never really settles down to that sense of ease and effortlessness which made most of Toscanini's slow movements such a rewarding experience. By the end of the movement, indeed, one was conscious of an unnaturally high quota of *allargando* and *meno mosso*, introduced to reinforce a lyrical line which had suffered one or two shocks to its structure in the course of the performance.

In isolated detail and beauty of phrasing, in such moments as the famous and mysterious diminuendo passage for horns and strings which leads to the first recapitulation of the principal subject (at bar 160), and the wonderfully articulated figure that then appears in the accompaniment for the first time, the recording reproduced many of the essential features of Toscanini's London performance. What it did not do was to leave one with that feeling of contentment, of music being played with such spontaneity one felt it was being improvised before one's ears, which was how this lovely movement could sound and, I know from first-hand experience, had sounded, under Toscanini.

3. Scherzo: Allegro vivace

This movement was always a very vigorous affair with Toscanini, but never so vigorous that, as the recording shows, the basic $\downarrow. = 96$ could not fluctuate quite appreciably in either direction when necessary. If the Scherzo lacked one special quality in Toscanini's performance it was that of the peculiar mellowness and charm and unmistakable Vienneseness found in Schubert's music. It was a quality which eluded Toscanini as Mozart's greatness eluded him, because it is not something written in the score; it was something clearly quite foreign to his whole nature, and one has only to remember his grotesque performance of "The Blue Danube" to realize *how* foreign.

Toscanini's 1938 performance certainly had more charm than that in the recording, but I believe that was largely because the BBC Symphony Orchestra provided him with better woodwind playing than we hear from the NBC Orchestra in the later version. The American oboists, for instance, cannot compare with those in the English orchestra; instead of singing like birds, they twitter.

This lack of tonal charm is particularly unfortunate in the Trio, which Toscanini took more broadly on purpose, so that Schubert's natural graciousness could have room to stretch its wings; but even rather harsh instrumental treatment did not altogether obscure the fundamental *dolce* of the conductor's conception. The *cantabile* passages for strings, wherever they occurred in the movement, were naturally played for all they were worth, but on the whole the brilliance and vigour of this Scherzo were more suited to Beethoven than to Schubert.

(For the purist: Toscanini observed the first repeat in the Scherzo, ignored the second and omitted both repeats in the Trio.)

4. Allegro vivace

The really outstanding difference between the 1947 performance and the one given in London in 1938, I believe, was to be found in the performance of the Finale. Once again the later version lacked the rhythmic stability and precision of the older one; the fast tempo was constantly running away with Toscanini, and where he formerly created excitement and developed the emotional intensity of the music by the maintenance of a firm compelling rhythm, he now tried (or hoped), and failed, to do the same thing by the different and mistaken method of speeding up. The music lost its natural impulse, and Schubert's exuberance, which had carried things along before, was no longer allowed to speak for itself.

This did not happen all through the 1947 Finale, but it did occur often enough to make one apprehensive of the next occasion, and certainly it served to remind one of the steadiness and greater effect of the Queen's Hall performance. It was the dotted-note passages which led to trouble, as they had done in the first and second movements, especially when they were being played by strings alone.

Although the opening stages of the Finale in the recording were played with a virile and infectious rhythm by Toscanini, it was not until he reached the second subject proper that I felt I was almost hearing the 1938 performance again. I have naturally no recollection of the metronome speed on that occasion, but when I heard the theme again in the recording at approximately ♩ = 116 it sounded as I remembered Toscanini saying at rehearsal it should sound—"like a tune you whistle in the street walking home at night":

Ex. 87

I was pleased to hear again, too, his characteristic diminuendo each time in the last four signing-off bars of this thirty-two-bar theme. Schubert hinted at no such diminuendo in his score, but I doubt if he would have objected to Toscanini's introduction of it. It was one of those typical and very welcome luxuries that Toscanini used to throw in for good measure.

The resumption of what I consider the True Tempo of the second subject in the recording had a beneficial effect on the general rhythm of this last movement, so that when the theme occurred in the development section in conjunction with the dotted-note figure it was the tune which kept the rhythm steady. It was only when an obvious climax was building, or when it was heard on its own, that the dotted-note sequences got out of hand and upset what should have been the even tenor of the music.

I do not for a moment wish to suggest that the 1947 recording of the Finale should be dismissed as of no consequence whatever. Like any Toscanini performance it was rich in typically ravishing detail: * but it was not the entirely satisfying, perfectly timed and exhilarating experience the 1938 performance had been.

If the 1953 recording has eliminated the faults and blemishes I have inevitably had to criticize in the 1947 performance, then nothing could be better. If it has not, then I fear we are left with no evidence of what was in my lifetime one of Toscanini's most stimulating and enlightening performances. All I can hope is that by my comparisons between what I heard in 1938 and what I hear in the 1947 recording the reader may end up with some idea of how this C major symphony sounded under Toscanini. In spite of the absence of *viennoiserie*, it was as near an ideal conception of the music as one could imagine.

---

* I would draw the student's attention particularly to the wonderful diminuendo that starts at bar 146 and occurs again at bar 734 and to the addition of a *sforzato* in the tremolo passage for violins in bars 434 and 442 (echoed in each case, by the violas two bars later) with which Toscanini anticipated Schubert's own markings as they appear a few bars later on in the episode. It was a logical piece of interference entirely justified by the whole scheme and mood of the music.

RICHARD STRAUSS
❧[1864–1949]❧

ONE of the principal differences between the Italians and the Germans is that whereas the Italians enjoy vulgar music and whistle it, the Germans admire it—and write a book about it. Which is why all the vulgar tunes ever written by Verdi can never detract from his position in music, while those written by Richard Strauss have time and again succeeded in disfiguring what might otherwise have been masterpieces. Though one hesitates, in view of the public knuckle-rapping once suffered by Dr Vaughan Williams, to use such a term as "beer-garden music", it is clear—now that Strauss's lifework can be viewed as a whole—that it was precisely the composer's genius for melodic anticlimax, his lack of what one can only call musical breeding that was at the root of all Strauss's magnificent failures. From *Don Juan* and *Tod und Verklärung* to the *Alpine Symphony*, from *Salome* and *Elektra* to *Die Liebe der Danae*, there was always that streak of inescapable beer-garden vulgarity and bathos, that lapse of melodic, harmonic and orchestral taste at the critical moment into depths Lehár, Oscar Straus and Kalman would have despised, and that element of the commonplace which Constant Lambert described as providing "a subtle but all-pervading aroma" in Strauss's music.

Toscanini, I fear, did little to disperse this all-pervading aroma; indeed, by that very attention to detail which added so much to the music of Beethoven or Verdi, he succeeded in showing how much of Strauss's orchestral writing is best left to the general mush and haze of the routine performance of his music. Done Toscanini's way, a great deal of remarkably trite detail in the form of chromatic runs, which are better seen on paper than heard in practice, came to the fore; equally a great deal of equally trite detail not even Toscanini could make audible and so happily reassured many sceptics that—as they had always suspected—what Strauss had written was in many cases visual not aural decoration.

The music of Richard Strauss occupying the somewhat lowly position in my affections that it does, so far from being made to sound more attractive by Toscanini's performances, in fact sounded less impressive than ever. On the whole, that is; most of Strauss's music contains at least a moment or two of fascinating invention, and Toscanini naturally made them sound better than I had ever heard them sound before; but in the end I was not convinced that I was being given more to get my teeth into than a gorgeous exhibition of exciting orchestral noise. It was not Toscanini's fault that the music was not better; he did his best.

DON JUAN, Opus 20
[1889]

NBC Symphony Orchestra

GREAT BRITAIN: HMV ALP 1173
U.S.A.: Victor LM 1157
1951

With this, as with the other three symphonic poems by Strauss he recorded, Toscanini did all that the composer asked of him and, in the matter of rhythmic vigour and orchestral brilliance, undoubtedly quite a lot more than the composer could reasonably have hoped for. This *Don Juan* was a characteristic virtuoso performance in which the spirit of the initial Allegro molto con brio was sustained throughout; even the slower lyrical passages seemed to glow with the same urgency and intensity.

The fire and lyrical warmth of the performance, indeed, were its dominant characteristics, with Toscanini apparently adding his own little touch to the love scene. The last note in the second of the phrases played by the solo violin at this point in the recording has acquired a grace note which seems to me to be Toscanini's personal contribution, for it is not in my score, nor do I recollect ever having heard it before. Such was Toscanini's way, on the other hand, that it may well have been there all along and that, as so often happened, one did not notice it until he came to conduct the work. In the matter of orchestral detail Toscanini's whole performance of *Don Juan* was like that, of course.

TOD UND VERKLÄRUNG, Opus 24
[1890]
NBC Symphony Orchestra

GREAT BRITAIN: HMV ALP 1404
U.S.A.: Victor LM 1891
1952

When Toscanini came to London with the New York Philharmonic-Symphony Orchestra on his tour of Europe in 1930, Ernest Hall, first trumpet of the BBC Symphony Orchestra, deputized for a member of Toscanini's orchestra who was ill, and played in the programme which included Strauss's *Tod und Verklärung*. Mr. Hall was full of admiration for his American colleagues and in the course of relating his experience in the Strauss work remarked that "with Toscanini you're not blowing into the mouthpiece—you're biting it!"

Toscanini's *fff* climax of *Tod und Verklärung* was certainly one of the grandest moments of sheer orchestral din ever created; it did not raise the musical value of Strauss's work to any extent, for by the very clarity of the texture we were ironically more than ever aware of the trite tonic-and-dominant beergarden Strauss, but as a purely physical experience of instrumental volume it was unforgettable.

The whole of Toscanini's *Tod und Verklärung*, indeed, was a physical rather than an emotional or spiritual revelation; for the first time in one's experience one was able to hear the detail of the opening Largo and appreciate every nuance of the sentimental passages for solo violin, and to hear clearly the musical-box, harp-and-woodwind noises which Strauss made whenever he wanted to write that "beautiful" music which obsessed him throughout his career.

Every performance of Toscanini's was an experience and his *Tod und Verklärung* was no exception. But it was the conductor that was the fascination, not the composer.

TILL EULENSPIEGEL, Opus 28
[1895]

NBC Symphony Orchestra

GREAT BRITAIN: HMV ALP 1404
U.S.A.: Victor LM 1891
1952

This was, to me, the most satisfying of all Toscanini's performances of Strauss, for the simple and very good reason that it has always struck me as being the best piece of music its composer ever wrote. *Till Eulenspiegel* is Strauss at his natural level; it does not set out to be "beautiful" or Philosophically Significant. It does not contain a single moment of the cheap and nauseating sentimentality which reduces to the level of the lowest common denominator such superficially different scores as *Elektra, Der Rosenkavalier* and *Ariadne auf Naxos*. It cannot be cut, nor is there a single orchestral part in it that needs rescoring on the ground of inaudibility or ineffectualness. It is, in fact, within the limits of Strauss's talent, a perfect work —vigorous, spontaneous, unself-conscious, inventive and thoroughly likeable. Its composer may have written longer, more profitable and high-sounding music in his time; he never wrote anything more immediately appealing and certainly nothing more honest and personal.

Toscanini perceived with characteristic insight all the best and most peculiar qualities of *Till Eulenspiegel*, and though some of the details of his performance may sometimes come as a surprise there is not one of them which is not justifiable and—in the end—an improvement on the routine interpretation to which we have had to become accustomed. Like so many of Toscanini's performances, though, it was one which one accepted wholeheartedly only at a second hearing. Thus I was uneasy about the quickening of the tempo in the episode of Till's address to the university professors, but not once I had heard the delicious way Toscanini played the skittish snook-cocking polka-like music to which Till makes his rapid and characteristic exit. These dozen-odd bars, which I had heard played in so many different ways in my time by so many different conductors (and by few of them in such a way that one altogether disagreed with what they did), suddenly sounded right, logical and "in character" at the speed Toscanini played them. Perhaps Till Eulenspiegel became less Teutonic and consequently more quick-wittedly Latin in his get-away from an awkward situation, but if so it did not do anything but good in the process.

Till Eulenspiegel, the more one thinks of it, was a work with which Toscanini could hardly go wrong. It is the only one of Strauss's symphonic poems which is based on a rhythm and tempo which are more or less constant (it is a Rondo, after all), and it is full of a simple, unsentimental charm which Toscanini could always point with such effortless grace without ever disturbing the vigorous fundamental sweep of the music.

No Toscanini performance of even the most familiar music was ever without that peculiar surprise which sent one to the score, only to discover that what one had just heard was something that had been in cheap miniature-score reprints for a generation and more. My own personal ear-opener was in the last few bars of the Trial Scene, when Toscanini introduced what seemed an entirely unauthorized *allargando* to the final death-sentence pronouncements of the Judges. As so often, it proved that one did not know a familiar score as well as one kidded oneself. Why, of all the conductors I have ever heard conduct *Till Eulenspiegel* it should have been an Italian who first made me take note of the composer's words "etwas breiter" at that point, I cannot imagine. But that was one's experience with Toscanini time and again. He saw what was there, no matter what language it was written in.

Toscanini's view of the Epilogue was a little perplexing; it was so slow. But just as his tempi could seem fast on a first hearing but right on a second, so his slow tempi could also sound right on re-consideration. Because one was used to a more offhand interpretation of the Epilogue at a tempo to match—as the composer indicated—that of the first five bars of the work, it was a shock to find that Toscanini should disregard Strauss's instructions to the extent of playing the Epilogue as slowly as he did. But after the tremendous exhilaration and unaccustomed brilliance of what had gone before, this contrast had an unexpectedly dramatic and melancholy effect—the second time one heard it.

In terms of the metronome, Toscanini's tempo for the Epilogue was not in fact so much slower than that of the opening of the work, which it was supposed to match; it was the context that made it seem so, and in the context I think it was most certainly right.

DON QUIXOTE, Opus 35
[1898]

Frank Miller (violoncello)
Carlton Cooley (viola)
NBC Symphony Orchestra

GREAT BRITAIN: HMV ALP 1493
U.S.A.: Victor LM 2026
1953

All that applied to Toscanini's performance of the other Strauss works applied to his performance of *Don Quixote*. This recording proves an admirable reminder of the *Don Quixote* we heard Toscanini give at Queen's Hall in 1938, which was a splendid example of his genius for presenting a panoramic view of a work composed of a thousand minutely-drawn details. It was all there—the all-embracing breadth of the conception, the powerful rhythm, the brilliance and clarity of the smallest, most insignificant little orchestral figure, the wonderfully balanced richness of sound and precise dynamic grading.

One particular feature of Toscanini's performance was that of giving warmth and charm to those passages of Strauss's music which so often sound arch and coy—a characteristic caused largely by Toscanini's exact observance of the composer's markings and the complete avoidance of any exaggeration. Or almost complete. In the very last phrase played by the solo violoncello in the final bars of this recording of the work, Toscanini introduced a very marked downward *glissando* to the instrument's bottom D from the D an octave above. There is no suggestion of this to be seen in the score, for the only markings there are *dim.* and *pp.* It is a convention, however, which has the sanction of the composer, for in Strauss's own recording of the work that *glissando* can be heard. The only difference between Toscanini's version and this precedent is that Toscanini's *glissando* is more marked than Strauss's, which, while clearly noticeable, is more the result of a graceful change of position by the player than the unmistakable slide we can hear in this recording. It seems that Toscanini's Don Quixote sighed more deeply as he died than the composer's.

GIUSEPPE VERDI
⌇[1813–1901]⌇

IN the final estimate of Toscanini it may be found that
perhaps it was his Verdi which was the greatest revelation
of all. The immense power of his Beethoven was something not easily forgotten, but it must be admitted that we had
at least caught glimpses of those titanic peaks before, if through
a comparatively misty atmosphere. Weingartner and Bruno
Walter had opened our eyes to them even if, in the end, they
did not illuminate them with quite the same dazzling light
which Toscanini brought to bear on them. The mountain
range of Beethoven's symphonies did not lack grandeur, beauty
or strength as Weingartner or Walter showed them to us, but
Toscanini succeeded in blowing away patches of mist which
obscured some of the detail. With him it was always a clear
day with visibility almost unlimited.

Verdi, on the other hand, was something we were glimps-
ing almost for the first time. Though it was the last thing the
composer ever intended, a Verdi opera has become primarily a
"singers' opera". When it is treated to top-class singing the
vocal performance tends to upset the dramatic balance of the
work as a whole, while when it is treated to bottom-class
singing the same thing happens, of course. In neither case are
we getting the full, genuine flavour of Verdi's music; familiarity
with the composer has bred an astonishing contempt for his
instructions and intentions, and while critics and laymen are
mostly agreed on his greatness, it is an agreement they have
reached more by instinct than thanks to any help from the
majority of the conductors who accompany a Verdi opera.
And "accompanying" a Verdi opera, whether the vocal performance is good, bad or indifferent, is exactly the job to which
the conductor has been relegated in far too many modern opera
houses.

In the circumstances, then, it is hardly surprising that a

Verdi opera conducted by Toscanini should have proved such an overwhelming experience, for though his antagonism to singers as a race was not quite so violent as it was always made out to be, there was never any question that he regarded the composer's intentions as of paramount importance.

The sad aspect of it all is that Toscanini should have recorded so few of Verdi's operas, and not one of those was recorded until nearly twenty years after he had ceased to conduct anything but "festival" performances in a theatre.

The Verdi opera recordings which have come down to us, however, must be regarded as unique, inasmuch as there is not one of them on which Toscanini's performance does not throw a new and exciting light, not merely on isolated moments and hitherto unrevealed details, but on the character of each opera as a whole. Sometimes Toscanini's approach to the work may come as something of a shock to the listener, when he finds that the music isn't being played in the manner to which he has been accustomed. This, however, does not in any way necessarily mean that Toscanini's way was either the wrong one or even unduly eccentric. Most of the things done by the conductor, which some may consider to be little less than sacrilege, more usually prove to be the result—unpleasant and upsetting at first—of shifting the emphasis in opera from the singers on to the composer, an action which is not, in my opinion, altogether to be deprecated.

Toscanini was always a composer's conductor by nature and he proclaimed his intentions in this direction often and forcefully; it was a prejudice which it was nowhere more welcome to encounter than in his performance of the music of Verdi.

RIGOLETTO – Act IV
[1851]

Rigoletto   Leonard Warren
Gilda   Zinka Milanov
Duke   Jan Peerce
Sparafucile   Nicola Moscona
Maddalena   Nan Merriman
NBC Chorus and Symphony Orchestra

GREAT BRITAIN: HMV ALP 1453
U.S.A.: Victor LM 6041
1944

This, for me, was perhaps the most tantalizing recording Toscanini ever made. As tantalizing, I imagine, as his recording of the last scene of *Götterdämmerung* must have been to the Wagner enthusiast. One can only imagine how the earlier acts in the opera would have sounded.

And yet, after hearing Toscanini's performance of this last act of *Rigoletto*, when I read through the full score of the first three acts to myself again I found that my whole conception of Verdi's music had changed. My experience of Toscanini's performance of Act IV enabled me to hear in my mind's ear things in the earlier part of the opera which I had never heard before, and to discover dramatic excitement in passages which numberless routine performances had rendered ineffective.

Now while this ability to imagine, up to a point, how Toscanini would have conducted the first three acts of *Rigoletto* is some personal consolation to me (and I believe to most people, for I cannot see how Toscanini's revelation of Act IV can fail to influence one's view of the rest of the opera), it is hardly a solid enough factual foundation on which to base a study of his interpretation of the complete work. All we can do is be grateful that his Legacy included any of *Rigoletto* at all and to make the most of it.

As with all Toscanini's performances it was the sum of the parts which made up the whole, and the tremendous drama of this last act of *Rigoletto* was built on the perfection of numberless details which contributed, among other things, to the creation of a remarkably theatrical atmosphere. From the first note of the brief string phrase which raises the curtain of this act Toscanini was conducting nowhere in the world but in an opera house. Once created, this atmosphere of the theatre was sustained throughout the recording, and to me it was so strong that I could almost hear the audience of an Italian gallery joining in the tune of the introduction to "La donna è mobile".

To show that he did not hold with purism for purism's sake, Toscanini ignored the *pp* marking of the first "chuck-chuck" bar of the introduction to the Duke's aria. He played it with a *ff* to match the *brio* of the tune, and in doing so added a great air of excitement and expectancy to the introduction.

The aria itself Toscanini regarded with benevolent indulgence. He permitted no dawdling, but allowed all the natural *espansioni* to make their effect. There was no high B for the tenor to end on, but he was not discouraged from hitting one in the course of the cadenza in the penultimate bar—a cadenza which closely resembled the brief flourish with which Caruso ended the aria.

Though for most people the Celebrated Quartet from *Rigoletto* does not begin until the tenor's "Bella figlia dell' amore", Verdi's score is, in fact, headed "No 12. Quartetto" several pages earlier than that, and it is the bustle and excitement of the Allegro episode leading immediately to it that adds to the dramatic effect of the Quartet proper. Toscanini made this introduction to the Quartet a characteristically thrilling affair, in which the reiterated trills in the orchestra had a peculiarly exhilarating quality.

The singing of the Quartet itself in the recording was nothing out of the ordinary, but with Toscanini's guidance the performance was as irresistible as any I ever heard—the sort of performance one quite unwittingly joins in oneself because its whole air of *cantabilità* is so infectious. As one would expect, Toscanini permitted no loitering among the singers' favourite notes, but it was nonetheless an unusually flexible performance, with several instances of the spontaneous *stringendo* and *ritenuto* and, of course, with the natural (but still not officially indicated) *espansione* leading to the climax of the scene, which is perhaps the most infectiously *cantabile* moment in the whole Quartet.

Toscanini's concessions to traditional practice in this number did not, however, run to the cadence on which it ends. Here he forbade the soprano's familiar top A flat followed by her D flat *in alt*. She sang what Verdi wrote, and so, for the first time in one's life, enabled one to hear the Quartet end on the *ppp* (or thereabouts) that the composer intended. If ever one was grateful for Toscanini's literal observance of a composer's wishes it was then. It was an entirely different sound from what one was accustomed (in the name of "singers' operas") to hear.

The next episode ("No 13. Scena, Terzetto e Tempesta") was fired by Toscanini with a dramatic intensity which was almost indescribable. Following the uncanny suspense of the first passages, for sheer excitement it is difficult to think of anything more compelling than the ferocious vigour of Toscanini's rhythm and tempo of the sequence which begins:

Ex. 88

Toscanini's basic tempo for this was in the region of $\downarrow$ = 104 —fast, but dead right in that it did not force the pace in any way. The drama and the music could both stand this unusual intensity—at least, in Toscanini's hands. His sense of timing and his prodigious reserve of strength ensured that when the storm finally broke it was a *tempesta* of quite shattering violence and conviction, dying away with some characteristic revelations of orchestral detail in those last bars when the humming of the off-stage chorus is heard again.

For the remainder of the act, described so laconically in the score as "No 14. Scena e Duetto finale", one detail after another emerged from Toscanini's performance to discover new dramatic significance in familiar music. Again, many of these touches were Toscanini's own invention. Although Verdi marked it *piano* the 3/8 bar which precedes the Duke's reprise in the background of "La donna è mobile" was played *forte*, reverting to *piano* when the Duke starts singing. The effect of

Toscanini's unorthodox action was uncannily dramatic, pulling the listener up with a sudden violent jerk which was quite unnerving. Incidentally, the singer studying the part of Rigoletto can note from this recording how Toscanini revised the baritone's startled "No, no! . . . no! . . ." sung while the Duke is singing. By spacing the three words through five instead of four bars, the first "No" coinciding with the second syllable of the Duke's "mobil", the second and third "No's" with his "vento" and "-cento" respectively (which is how they occur in the score), Toscanini added an extra urgency to Rigoletto's growing incredulity.

The purist, indeed, will have an unhappy time altogether with Toscanini's recording of this last scene; he will encounter a broadening of the tempo where none is indicated, a disregard of an accelerando which is. But in the place of strict observance of the letter of the score he will hear an inspired interpretation of its spirit. He will hear, too, a characteristic demonstration of Toscanini's sense of rhythm in the tense syncopation of the accompaniment to Rigoletto's first words to Gilda; a wonderfully clear realization of the orchestration, showing the origin of what Verdi called his "vaporous" orchestration in the last scene of *Aida*, that accompanies Gilda's dying "Lassù in cielo"; and a moving—and infectious—*cantabile* from the orchestra in the four bars of Rigoletto's pathetic plea to Gilda not to die, "Non morir mio tesoro . . .".

These are the things to be noted among "what is there" in the score. It was Toscanini's genius that removed the film of over-familiarity obscuring the original picture and, by his unique gift for the musical counterpart of picture-restoring, revealed Verdi's score in all the glory of its original colouring and design.

This recording of the last act of *Rigoletto* may be tantalizing and even frustrating in its way. But there is no doubt to my mind that to hear it and study it throws light not only on the first three acts of the opera, but virtually on all the Verdi that Toscanini did not have time or opportunity to record as a part of his Legacy.

LA TRAVIATA
[1853]

Violetta Licia Albanese
Alfredo Jan Peerce
Germont Robert Merrill
NBC Symphony Orchestra and Chorus

GREAT BRITAIN: HMV ALP 1072/3
U.S.A.: Victor LM 6003
1946

Dog, if not according to the canons of music criticism at least according to those of respectable journalism, does not eat dog. Nevertheless, since in law a dog is allowed one bite I shall claim this legal indulgence in reporting that it was my disagreement with the reception by some of my younger colleagues of Toscanini's *Traviata* recording which was among the first things that prompted me to write this book.

To be honest, it was a disagreement which arose only on reconsideration of their opinion. To begin with I found myself in reluctant and extremely depressed accord with their views. In course of time, however, obstinately and sceptically I began to play this recording of La *Traviata* again and found that I was coming to learn more and more about Verdi's score from the experience—a score I considered I already knew well enough, for in my student days in Berlin it had been one of the three obligatory "set books" for a would-be conductor. The others were *Carmen* and *Figaro*.

Gradually, I began to see what had happened. My colleagues had approached the whole matter from an angle that was strange to me. Many of these fellow-critics are inclined, in their commendable devotion to the propagation of *bel canto*, to rate the reverence of the memory of a long-dead singer whose voice we no longer hear above the rights and merits of a long-dead composer whose music we do. In short, they were unhappy because Toscanini's *Traviata* was not a "singers' opera" (an art-form Verdi did not recognize), and they did not find in the performance things which it would not normally occur to me to look for; indeed, I began to wonder whether we had all even learnt the opera from the same scores. How else, I asked, could they abuse Toscanini's performance so roundly and yet not remark that probably for the first time in many decades they had heard things *put back* into *La Traviata* which Verdi had originally written, but which a lazy, slip-shod singer-dominated tradition had removed or altered beyond recognition? Needless to say, the things which Toscanini put back have been clearly visible in the score all along. It was not that Toscanini was suddenly able to lay a privileged hand on a newly discovered or revised autograph of Verdi's opera; it was just that he refused to acknowledge the validity of bad habits and ignore what the composer intended. He saw, in fact, "what is there".

These are all features of Toscanini's interpretation of Verdi which I hope to demonstrate in this chapter; and in the case of *La Traviata* in particular, rightly or wrongly, I refuse to accept or dismiss it, in the way it has been dismissed, as an insensitive performance deserving such epithets as "unyielding", "inflexible", "overdriven" and "unfeeling".

Sometimes I think I know what they mean by it, but I think they are making a grave mistake in most instances—mainly in criticizing Toscanini before they have studied Verdi's score carefully enough to see what is in it that made Toscanini do what he did, for it is only the composer who can prove Toscanini wrong. At other times, I think they are being deluded, as audiences were often deluded by Toscanini, into thinking that the music was being played faster than in fact it was. This was always a perplexing aspect of Toscanini's performances and was largely due, I believe, to the strength of his rhythm and the clear-cut lines of the orchestral sound, which somehow combined to give the impression of unusual speed. Certainly in the case of *La Traviata* there are several quite remarkable instances of Toscanini's tempi being *slower* than those indicated by the metronome markings in the score. Indeed, if some of the metronome speeds shown in Ricordi's orchestral score published in 1914 were followed literally, then we might well complain with some justification of the music being "overdriven" and the rest.

Toscanini's modifications of the metronome markings, however, are something I will point out when we come to them. These markings do not occur regularly throughout the score, and there are whole sequences devoid of any metronomics of

any kind. I suggest that at these points the student should make
a note of Toscanini's tempi and add them to his score. He will
be surprised how often Toscanini made them slower than the
average conductor or coach does.

ACT I

The Prelude to Act I of *La Traviata* was for many of us our
first introduction to Toscanini as a conductor of Verdi and the
famous recording he made of it in 1929 (with its companion,
the Prelude to Act III) was for a whole generation a constant
reminder that we had been born too late to hear Toscanini as
an opera conductor. Later experience in the 1930's of *Falstaff*
at Salzburg did not entirely compensate for being denied a
legendary *Traviata* at La Scala in 1922.

Today, in its 1946 version, the Prelude to Act I of this opera
is still a superb synthesis of Toscanini's approach to Verdi.
There is drama in it, tenderness and that unique ability to
make mere instruments "sing"; and it shows a characteristic
understanding of Verdi's highly personal orchestration. No
performance of this particular Prelude which I have heard has
ever combined the warmth and clarity of Verdi's score so
successfully and convincingly as this.

For the young conductor there is one exemplary passage,
illustrating Hans von Bülow's maxim: "Diminuendo means
forte; crescendo means *piano*". In other words, as Felix von
Weingartner explains in his reference to this apparent paradox
in his treatise on conducting, you must have something to
diminuendo and crescendo *from*. Toscanini underlines the
importance of this in the last three bars of the Prelude when,
although the first violin part is still marked to be played at
the same *pp* as when it began its staccato countermelody to the
violoncellos' tune eighteen bars earlier, he makes them play
louder at the beginning of the *allargando* in order to make the
point, first, of the diminuendo, and then the final *morendo*:

Ex. *89*

(As a matter of simple metronomics it is interesting to note that where it is suggested in the score that the whole Prelude should be performed at $\downarrow$ = 66, Toscanini always took the first part as slowly as 52 or 54, and only adopted the official 66 when the big E major "con espressione" tune began. For all Toscanini's proclaimed insistence on tempo, this Prelude was a model of how rubato could be used.)

Verdi's *Traviata* is an opera which, like *Carmen* and *La Bohème*, depends on the creation of an atmosphere of musical cheerfulness to point the final dramatic impact of its tragedy. The sadness of the Prelude to Act I, however, has no counterpart in the noisy introduction to *Carmen* or the high spirits of the few bars which raise the curtain of *La Bohème*. But the curtain of the first act of *La Traviata* rises on as brilliant and cheerful a sequence of music as one could wish for. Toscanini follows the Prelude with a busy festive tempo ($\downarrow$ = 168) for the indicated "Allegro brillante e molto vivace", creating instantly an atmosphere of carefree social activity which permeates the entire first act. And it is not, let it be pointed out, an atmosphere created by the use of fast tempi. In fact, where the score indicated the Brindisi as $\downarrow$. = 69, Toscanini starts off the instrumental introduction at a slower speed, somewhere near 66 reaching 69 as the drinking song gets under way, exceeding it when the chorus comes in, and returning to a steady but by no means inflexible 69 beats to the minute when the two soloists, Violetta and Alfredo, share the "middle" section of the tune, which starts

Ex. 90

It is surprising, indeed, in view of what we have been warned to expect, how relaxed this whole number sounds, a quality which is not lost when the conductor quickens the tempo towards the end as the famous staccato passage for the chorus gradually builds up into its wonderfully effective crescendo.

From time to time during this recording, as in *La Bohème*, the sound of Toscanini humming and singing is an audible accompaniment to the performance. This out-of-tune, rather plain-tive sound was a feature of many Toscanini occasions, fairly audible to those sitting close to the platform in the concert hall, and quite clearly so to any radio audience; and it is interesting to note exactly which passages he chose to fortify with a personal note or two. Some of the tunes you would have most expected him to sing he passes by in silence, while others—often obscure and unexpected snatches of them—he suddenly sings at the top of his voice. He helps the beginning of the Brindisi along in this way, for instance.

Some people have shown disapproval of this and consider Toscanini's habit disturbing. To those of us brought up to hear opera from the gallery in Italy, on the other hand, there is no distraction at all. In any Italian opera house the Brindisi in *La Traviata* is inevitably sung by *all* the occupants of the *loggione*; it is only in the smarter parts of the house that the singers on the stage can be heard in comparative silence. A conductor's occasional overheard joining-in on a gramophone record is nothing to disturb any experienced opera-goer, and with Toscanini I find it occurs usually at those points when one most wants to join in oneself anyway.

On the whole, so far as this first act goes, I think it would be fair to say that while Toscanini's tempi take a bit of getting used to at times, they sound right in the end. The tempo of the waltz sequence, for instance, is a shade faster (84) than the metronome marking of 80, but one extra step every fifteen seconds is not going to turn a dance into a shambles, nor does it obscure the detail of the back-stage band playing for dancing. Too often the "banda" is allowed more or less to fend for itself; Toscanini took as much trouble over it as over the main orchestra.

The duet, "Un dì felice", began by Alfredo,

Ex. 91

is taken a shade faster than indicated (100 instead of 96) but does not, I consider, suffer in the process. So far from sounding "overdriven" or "inflexible", it is treated with a generous amount of *rubato*, as anybody will learn who tries to match a metronome strictly to it; and where the tempo is strictly applied, as in Violetta's coloratura decoration to the number, it gives the tense brilliance which the music implies.

The final departure of the guests which follows this scene is one of Toscanini's most effective moments, and he gives a special point to one half of Hans von Bülow's maxim about diminuendos and crescendos by observing the clear indication in the score made by Verdi (who also knew a thing or two about conducting): "*pp* and staccato, beginning *ppp* to make a crescendo".

This is a tremendous sequence, reaching a *ff* climax in the characteristically rhythmic and powerfully sure syncopation in violins and woodwind which follows the chorus a quaver's length behind:

Ex. 92

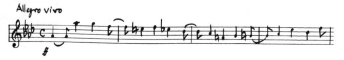

There now follows Violetta's solo scene, beginning with "Ah fors'è lui". This, the metronomic marking suggests, should be taken at ♪ = 96. Toscanini not only takes it virtually at 92, but allows plenty of time for the singer to make her *tenuto* when such phrases occur as

Ex. 93

The tempo of the next section, "A quell' amor", has been known to horrify some of my colleagues, for they are accustomed to hear prima-donnas dawdle lovingly and sometimes too long over the passage:

Ex. 94

It is marked, it will be noticed, to be sung "con espansione". Once again Toscanini will be found to be beating a tempo slower than the officially recommended ♪ = 96. The main difference between Toscanini and other conductors is that he does not consider the tune will stand as much "espansione" as they do, and I, for one, find little to object to in this moderation. (Toscanini makes the usual cut in this sequence, omitting the second verse, as it were.)

There is no metronome indication for the final pages of the scene. Toscanini interprets the "allegro brillante" as roughly ♩. = 96, and the result is appropriately *allegro* and *brillante*, with an added *allegria* supplied by the aged Maestro himself, who repeatedly sings the opening phrase of "Sempre libera . . ." ahead of his own beat. Mme Albanese takes this unconventional competition in her stride and the act ends with all concerned entirely and gaily in character.

ACT II

Scene 1

Toscanini takes more notice of the words "Allegro vivace" than of the metronomic injunction ♩ = 132, which in all conscience is a dragging tempo at which to raise the curtain or expect the strings to play:

Ex. 95

Toscanini tends to set a fast tempo throughout this first scene of the second act and in general the music is improved by it. Certainly there is nothing "overdriven" or suggestive of hyper-tension in the easy Andante (a term Toscanini always understood to mean "going", not "slow") at which he takes Alfredo's "De' miei bollenti spiriti" and we find at least a couple of occasions during the aria when a metronome set at a basic ♩ = 80 wanders way ahead of the conductor's flexible

rhythm and willingness to spread himself in such phrases as
the soaring:

Ex. 96

Toscanini's insistence that one should "see what is there" in a
score is fortunately forgotten after Alfredo's aria. The *cabaletta*
to "De' miei bollenti spiriti" is cut, as it nearly always is—on
the grounds, one presumes, that it is a very dull piece of music
—and a brilliant bridge passage for unison strings, which does
not appear in any of my scores but may well have been written
by Verdi himself (or by Toscanini, for that matter—it is a link
a student could do quite competently), leads to the entrance of
Violetta, followed, after a moment or two, by Alfredo's father,
Giorgio Germont.

The dramatic scene in recitative between Violetta and Germont is given one quite unusually effective touch by Toscanini.
It occurs as Germont reads the documents Violetta shows him
as proof that she is keeping his son, not his son keeping her.
On paper perhaps it is a ludicrously unimportant passage; in
Toscanini's performance it becomes the understated and
wonderfully effective moment that Verdi must have intended:

Ex. 97

Moderato

It is a moment of drama which is memorable in this performance for its restraint, its almost literal observance of the
injunction "moderato". There is little in the way of expression
marks to help a conductor; the diminuendo sign is purely
spontaneous and leads from an unspecified dynamic (the last
dynamic marking of any kind in the score is a long way back—
in the *cabaletta* that has been cut). Toscanini makes these four
bars as dramatically eloquent as almost anything in the entire

work: by noticing that because the composer did not make a conventionally *agitato* diminished-seventh comment on the situation, it did not mean that Verdi was making no comment at all.

It is not long after this that Germont embarks on the first of his addresses—"Pura siccome un angelo"—which Toscanini wisely takes at about ♩ = 96. To insist too strongly on the "moderato" of the Allegro moderato indicated in the score (and with ♩ equalling 84, at that) is to drag out music which can come perilously near to being monotonous at the best of times. By keeping the tempo moving Toscanini holds the listener's interest, and he adopts the same tempo for Germont's later passage—"Un dì quando le veneri". At Violetta's moving "Così alla misera",

Ex. 98

the music expands perceptibly and the development of the scene into a duet (with "Dite alla giovine" taken at ♪ = 104, an easy and convincing tempo) proceeds in a relaxed and moving manner. It is a sequence full of tenderness and with a powerful emotional high-spot reached as Toscanini has the orchestra underline Verdi's poignant phrase on the two occasions on which it occurs towards the end of the duet—

Ex. 99

The whole of this Violetta–Germont scene is filled with little touches which become apparent only on hearing the performance again and again—details, for instance, like the leaden pizzicato of the strings in the sostenuto passage of musical dialogue following immediately on the cadenza for the two voices which ends the "Dite alla giovine" duet; and the restoration of the string chords to those parts of the bars in

which Verdi originally intended them to be played. In the
final bars immediately preceding Germont's exit into the
garden it has long been a convention to play the chord
accompanying Violetta as she tearfully repeats "conosca il
sacrifizio" not on the first beats of the bar (as they are written
in the score), but for some reason three beats later, a habit
which is not only puzzling but disturbs the whole pattern of
Verdi's carefully and dramatically accompanied quotation.

The story of Toscanini's *Traviata* is one in which the restoration of Verdi's original thoughts plays a great part, and I was
very surprised that so little notice was taken of what struck me
as an epoch-making act of restoration by Toscanini—epoch-
making because for the first time for a generation or more a
bad habit had been ruthlessly eliminated.

In the original score Violetta's great passionate outcry as she
tears herself away from Alfredo is written

Ex. 100

In ninety-nine out of a hundred performances of *La Traviata*
in bars 11 to 14 of the phrase the value of the notes is altered so
that what one hears is roughly

Ex. 101

How or why this habit started I do not know, unless some
bright person decided that since that was the way the passage
was played in the Prelude to Act I, Verdi must have made a
mistake in not marking it to be played that way in the first
scene of Act II. Posterity, in short, took it on itself and without
authority to create a tradition; certainly it was not a practice
ever countenanced by Verdi: many years after he had com-

posed *La Traviata* he wrote the phrase in an autograph album
precisely as it appears in the score and in Ex. 100.

By restoring it to its first form Toscanini gives the whole
passage that heart-breaking dignity which is so characteristic
of Violetta in this whole scene. The half-time-value version is
a hysterical snivel compared with the unbearable desperation
of the long and moving phrase with which Verdi intended
Violetta to say her final and tragic farewell. The only sign of an
uncontrolled emotional upset, the suggestion of Violetta break-
ing into tears—out of our sight and Alfredo's—is made by the
few bars of agitated epilogue supplied by the strings as Violetta
rushes from the scene, a passage Toscanini impregnates with
such tremendous dramatic power that it seems as if the whole
orchestra were playing.

Toscanini, it is true, suggests a *stringendo* in the last bars of
Violetta's "Amami, Alfredo!", but at no time does it lapse into
the traditional half-value version. The conductor's preparation
for the whole phrase is incidentally one of the most dramatic
sequences in his whole performance of *La Traviata* and is a
superb example of Toscanini's characteristic genius for building
up a crescendo of overwhelming force and excitement. It is a
crescendo dependent on pure dynamics; that is, there are more
instruments playing at the beginning of the *pp* trills,

 Ex. 102

than there are in the final moments of the crescendo leading to
the passage in Ex. 100. The crescendo, in fact, is not assisted
by the addition of mechanical devices; sheer weight of instrumental numbers is not what counts, but the intensity with
which the emotional contents of the music can be expressed.

Toscanini, we begin to discover in this *Traviata*, was an enemy
of tradition when it was bad and its champion when it was
good. Thus he refused to accept the familiar way of mutilating
"Amami, Alfredo!"; similarly, he agreed with the traditional
cuts made at the end of Scene I of Act II. After taking "Di
provenza il mar, il suol . . ." at an oddly conventional ♩ = 60

as recommended in the score, he agreed with the general view that with that aria Germont had said enough for the time being and proceeded to make the traditional cut which prevents Alfredo's father embarking on a couple of verses of another number altogether, which several generations of audiences have decided they can be spared without harm.

Scene 2

As with the opening of Act I the atmosphere of carefree social activity is created from the first moment of this scene. "Allegro brillante" is taken at its full face value by Toscanini (and at $\textstyle\downarrow = 168$, like the opening of the first act) and remains the basic motive power of all the wonderfully effective ensembles and chorus numbers which pass the time of day until Violetta's entrance at the beginning of the gaming scene.

The card scene in Toscanini's hands has a tremendous tension and urgency. Indeed, the keynote of the whole of this second scene of Act II is an emotional tension which is barely relaxed in the music at all; the feverish nervousness of the situation is captured superbly by taking at a tempo of $\downarrow$. equalling between 96 and 100 the restless figure which forms the background to the musical dialogue:

Ex. 103

Toscanini does not let this tempo drop, not even for Violetta's despairing cry:

Ex. 104

It has long been a convention to expand this phrase each time it occurs in this scene, slowing down the tempo considerably in order to allow Violetta to make her pathetic point more markedly. There is no authority for this in the score whatever. It is just another bad habit, but in this instance I believe I know its origin. It springs from bright people again, but this time from bright people knowing Verdi in general better than *La Traviata* in particular.

In *Il Trovatore*, written a year before *La Traviata*, there is a passage (in Leonora's "Tacea la notte") which is almost identical with this one of Violetta's. The key, the 6/8 time, the tempo are the same; and even the orchestration is very little different:

Ex. 105

The only vital difference between the two passages is that in *Trovatore* there appears above the tune the significant words "con espansione". It is obviously the precedent thought to have been created in the earlier opera which has led to the unauthorized application of "con espansione" to the similar passage in the later *Traviata*. It seems to me to be going a little further than even Toscanini feared, when you hold up the score of one opera to the light and see the expression marks which concern another opera altogether.

Since this treatment of Violetta's "Ah perchè venni, incauta!" has become almost musical protocol, it is small wonder that there are some who consider this card scene of Toscanini's unnecessarily rigid and inflexible.

The tenseness and edginess of the social atmosphere increases as the music to this scene proceeds, an effect Toscanini achieves largely by making the most of directions like "Allegro agitato assai vivo" to build up Alfredo's bad temper into a white-hot fury. At Alfredo's public denunciation of Violetta with the phrase,

Ex. 106

Toscanini suddenly and dramatically holds the tempo back. The word "sostenuto" in the instruction "Allegro sostenuto" has its effect; the unexpected slowness of the tempo ($\downarrow$ = 96) gives Alfredo's outburst a tight-lipped, vindictive and almost vicious fury which I have never experienced before. The tense, throbbing quavers in the strings, which introduce and accompany Alfredo's first words, assume a menacing quality by their very reticence and sulky understatement. (The listener who is not bothered by such things will probably be delighted and intrigued by Toscanini's very audible singing as Alfredo's first phrase reaches its cadence. The sudden doubling of the vocal line over two octaves for a couple of bars has a magnetic effect on the old *violoncellista*, who joins in loudly as the violoncellos have their first—and last—properly *cantabile* tune for some time.)

Anybody who tries to match a metronome strictly to Toscanini's performance of the final ensemble of this act (beginning with Germont's "Dov'è mio figlio?") will find it an unrewarding task. The basic $\downarrow$ equals about 52, and the notorious old martinet of unbendingly inflexible singer-driving tempi has a high old time with it and, in fact, conducts the whole scene exactly as he feels, indulging in *espansioni* and generally exploiting a most unorthodox *rubato* to allow this moving and lovely ensemble to "sing" and blossom as lyrically as it should. Toscanini sings with it all, of course, but it is unlikely that you will hear his voice above your own as you listen. The whole performance is far too infectious.

ACT III

The statistician will note that when Toscanini recorded the Prelude to Act III of *La Traviata* in 1929 he took three minutes forty-five seconds over it, whereas the same music in this complete recording made of the opera in 1946 took three minutes thirty-three seconds. The impartial listener will observe that in neither case did Toscanini begin to approach the speed of $\downarrow$ = 66 the score suggests, and that it was only a slight dawdling over the last couple of bars of the Prelude in the earlier performance which made any difference in the timing. In both cases, however, the student would do well to learn from the conductor's superb control of the last trill of all and his translation of the baldly written

Ex. 107

into the lingering and affecting

Ex. 108

Once more Toscanini makes the atmosphere Verdi creates at the rise of the curtain (the orchestral introduction to Act III, of course, is meant to be played with the curtain up) hang about the action in a remarkable way, and it is by the incredible sense of dramatic apprehension and understatement he engenders that we become increasingly convinced we are listening to an unique performance of Verdi's music, conceived in Toscanini's mind as a *theatrical* occasion (I do not doubt for a moment that Toscanini, who was quite ludicrously short-sighted, found himself in this recording giving cues to singers on a stage which while it did not exist in reality, was a very real object in Toscanini's mind).

The conductor's sureness of touch is wonderfully evident in the way he disregards the officially prescribed metronome speeds in this last scene. Indeed, listening to Toscanini's gentle approach to it with ♪ = 69 one wonders who ever considered playing the delicate chamber-music accompaniment to Violetta's reading of Alfredo's letter at anything like the score's recommended ♪ = 88:

Ex. 109

A moment later there is the same instinctive feeling for the natural pulse of the music. Toscanini takes "Addio del passato"

at a basic, flexible $\downarrow$. = 44, and the singer can enjoy all Verdi's invitations to be "dolente", and so on, in a comfort which would be impossible if the conductor literally observed $\downarrow$. as 50. This whole aria (the customary cut of the second verse is made) is one of the most moving scenes in the whole performance. It has a desolate sadness.

The contrast made by the Bacchanale a moment later is almost shocking in its violence, and it is characteristic of Toscanini's whole conception of *La Traviata* that this little incident, taken at a breakneck Allegro vivacissimo, should "register" so strongly. So often it is almost thrown away.

Toscanini now creates a mood of tremendous excitement with another masterly crescendo as Alfredo approaches and sustains a suitably breathless tempo for the reunion of the lovers.

The scene which follows—the duet "Parigi, o cara"—came in for a lot of criticism in this particular recorded version, largely on the grounds that once more Toscanini was setting too rigid and unsympathetic a tempo. Closer study, however, shows that this is largely an illusion again. Whether or not it is the fault of the mechanics of recording that neither singer is heard using the *mezza voce* the score demands I do not know, but the tempo is considerably slower than the official $\downarrow$ = 112, being somewhere near 100, with reasonable allowance made for *tenuto* phrases in the voice parts. If this allowance is not considered generous enough, then I plead to being more easily satisfied than some, since I am quite happy with the result on this occasion.

The closing pages of *La Traviata* are made in every way as dramatically convincing as one would expect from a conductor like Toscanini. Again the tempi are nearly all slower than the metronome markings in the score, particularly the *pp* funeral-march thumping of the full orchestra in the ominous figure which seems to have strayed into *La Traviata* from the Miserere in *Il Trovatore*, and in the short final quintet it leads to.

Strangely, unlike many other moments in his performance of the opera, there is little in the last scene of Toscanini's *Traviata* that can be, or indeed needs to be specifically analysed. The cut made by omitting the reprise of the tune of "Gran Dio, morir sì giovine" is one normally made in performance, and he restores the exclamations of grief uttered by the company at the fall of the curtain after Violetta's death. But otherwise it is simply a case of playing "what is there" and giving a characteristic intensity to the final *ppp* echo of the tune in Ex. 109 and the short crescendo leading from it to Violetta's triumphant cry of "Oh gioia!"

At the end, as with nearly all Toscanini's performances, whether of symphonies or of operas, one has that remarkable feeling of having heard a work whose logical conclusion has been foreseen from the very first note, and to which the whole performance has been inevitably and inexorably building up.

Almost more than to any of the other Verdi operas recorded by Toscanini I find myself returning to his performance of *La Traviata*. Whether it is because of the purely personal affection I have always had for this particular opera, or whether I unconsciously went to the defence of something so many other people regarded as a goose in order to prove it was a swan, it is certain that constant re-hearing and study of Toscanini's performance has revealed new aspects of Verdi's opera each time, until this recording, with its brilliance and vitality, its dramatic intensity and unexpected and highly effective moments of understatement, convinces me that this is the way I want to hear *La Traviata*, and the way it should be directed.

UN BALLO IN MASCHERA
[1859]

Amelia	Herva Nelli
Riccardo	Jan Peerce
Oscar	Virginia Haskins
Ulrica	Claramae Turner
Renato	Robert Merrill
Samuele	Nicola Moscona
Tommaso	Norman Scott

NBC Symphony Orchestra and Robert Shaw Chorale

GREAT BRITAIN: HMV ALP 1252/3/4
U.S.A.: Victor LM 6112
1954

The last music Toscanini lived to conduct included passages incorporated in this recording of *Un ballo in maschera*. He was then over eighty-seven years of age, a fact scarcely worth mentioning were it not that this opera of Verdi's, belonging to the end of the composer's second period, which had begun with the immortal trio of *Rigoletto*, *Il Trovatore* and *La Traviata*, is one which demands unusually vigorous treatment. And yet that an old man should have been able to give Verdi's opera all it demanded in the way of physical effort alone was something one somehow took for granted with Toscanini. He had never shown any signs of age (although he suffered from arthritis for a while when he was in his sixties), and it did not occur to us that it was at all unusual for a man of seventy-seven to embark on what was virtually a new stage of his career when he recorded the first of his seven complete operas in 1944. One's reaction was largely one of relief that he had made the decision —or at worst, that it was about time too.

The physical vigour entailed in the performance of *Un ballo in maschera*, however, is nothing to compare with the astonishing intellectual vigour which characterizes every bar of Toscanini's conducting of it. It is an opera of vivid contrasts, of dazzling light and sinister shade, of romantic conventions and unexpected touches of comedy, of long moving lyrical passages and tense, stirring dramatic climaxes. Toscanini did not ignore a single one of these aspects of the work and, as with his performance of *La Traviata*, it is an experience which not only highlights the obvious high-spots, as it were, but makes musically interesting all the "ifs" and "ands" and "buts" of Verdi's musical language.

It was in his performances of Verdi, indeed, that we were most clearly aware of Toscanini's assessment of the details of the score. In a Beethoven symphony there are few passages of prose, and no sequences of music introduced for the purely mechanical, but nevertheless essential, purpose of getting on with the plot. The problem of getting on with the plot is one perennially facing the composer of opera who—presumably— chooses the medium in the first place because his natural inclination and preference is for writing lyrical and dramatic music. Action and librettist, however, frequently present him with situations and words of a most unprepossessing and musically uninspiring nature, which only the fundamental technique of the composer, with his inspiration ticking over (not going all out because he is not going anywhere in particular at that moment), can cope with. A composer like Verdi, with the librettos he was given, was presented with more than his fair share of this particular problem. As a superbly competent technician with an understanding of the theatre surpassed only by Mozart, Verdi "ticked over" confidently and reassuringly; the plot—where necessary—thickened and progressed to the accompaniment of quasi-recitative punctuations by the orchestra. But because these competently constructed passages have virtually no interest for the singers their significance in the scheme of things—as viewed by the conductor hired merely to "accompany"—has dwindled to almost nothing.

Toscanini, defiantly regarding Verdi's operas as "composer's operas", has restored what can only be called the self-respect of these conventionally unglamorous operatic sequences. I have indicated how Toscanini took Verdi's side in *La Traviata*; he was no less the composer's champion in *Un ballo in maschera*, where he again made *musical* sense of the conversational and action music linking the lyrical and dramatic scenes in such a way that at last we are able to hear them, not as the unavoidable and often dull trappings of operatic convention which, like the poor, are always with us, but as strong and vital links in the chain of the dramatic and musical evolution of the whole opera.

Toscanini's ability to "see" a Beethoven symphony, not as a suite of movements, but as an integrated, indivisible artistic conception, was matched by his unique sense of what one can only call the "smell" of a Verdi opera. Most Verdi operas have a distinctive atmosphere of their own, an atmosphere immediately discernible from the very first bars of the work. It is an atmosphere which penetrates the auditorium at most Verdi performances, however carelessly prepared; the full recognition of the potential strength of this atmosphere by a conductor like Toscanini can provide an overwhelming experience. The absolute certainty with which Toscanini was able to transmit this atmosphere was a peculiar facet of his genius and something which he retained from his earliest experiences until the end of his life. When Toscanini stood in front of his orchestra for the last time, it was to perform a Verdi opera. Nearly sixty years earlier he had made his first professional appearance in front of an orchestra—to perform a Verdi opera. The inbred sense of the theatre, of all that Italian opera means, was as gloriously unmistakable in the *vecchione* of eighty-seven conducting *Un ballo in maschera* as it had been in the *bambino* of nineteen conducting *Aida*.

The lyric theatre was in Toscanini's blood and it stayed there, its intensity increasing with more than half a century of experience, until his dying day. Whatever signs of senility he may otherwise have shown in the last years of his life, his performance of *Un ballo in maschera* demonstrates with supreme forcefulness that Toscanini was not only unalterably Italian, but that though he was more than 3000 miles away from the nearest Italian opera house, and seventeen years removed from his last experience of public operatic performance at all, he had lost none of his gift of being able to re-create the whole atmosphere of Verdi's lyric drama within the course of a couple of bars performed in a New York concert hall with a predominantly un-Italian cast of singers. It is for such things, surely, that one is finally grateful for the invention of the gramophone.

ACT I

Scene 1

It seems that by the time Toscanini's recording of this opera was issued in England—1955—the country and its critics had grown accustomed to what had been considered the conductor's lamentable maltreatment of Verdi. At least, with *Un ballo in maschera* we heard remarkably little about the singers being "driven" and the whole thing being played too fast. It was remarkable because where in *La Traviata*, as we have seen, Toscanini very often adopted tempi below the suggested metronome markings, in *Un ballo in maschera* he takes the music almost without exception quite enormously much faster than the metronome speeds shown in the score. The quiet reception of the later performance may be due to several things, of course: firstly, *La Traviata* was the first Verdi recording by Toscanini we had heard, and the experience, as I have suggested, was somewhat unnerving for many listeners; secondly, *La Traviata*, because it is immensely popular and has suffered over the years from being regarded as a "singers' opera", is a work which has not only had reprehensible traditions and habits foisted upon it, but about which listeners—and particularly critics—have very definite preconceived notions which they are unwilling to be talked out of.

Un ballo in maschera, on the other hand, suffers from none of these handicaps (in the context there is no other word) and in England at least it is an opera unhallowed by any "traditions", either good or bad, and in consequence might be regarded as an "open" subject free for all and unhampered by any particular sentimental associations.

As a matter of purely academic interest the student who cares to try out the official metronome times marked in the score will discover, I think, that they are almost eccentrically slow. He will also learn, however, that—as so often—it is the spirit not the letter of a Toscanini tempo which matters, that the presence of the word "vivissimo" in the instruction *Allegro vivissimo* will immediately invalidate the metronomic idea of 153 beats to the minute, because to Toscanini "vivissimo" takes the whole matter into the realm of something nearer 176 or even 184.

Indeed, there is one almost infallible rule in which the would-be conductor of Verdi should follow Toscanini and that is in the observance of what are the subordinate clauses of Verdi's musical instructions—the extra adjective or adverb like "brillante" or "vivissimo", "assai" or "sostenuto", "agitatissimo" or "quasi"—particularly "quasi", for this is the clue to the understanding of many Verdi subtleties and hints.

One thing emerges in the course of the Prelude which is directly relevant to the question of tempo: that Toscanini's faster-than-advertised tempi as a general rule result in a heightening of dramatic tension rather than in the lowering of it. The sinister "darkness" of the fugal theme associated with the conspirators in *Un ballo in maschera*

Ex. 110

is one of the most immediately striking moments of this performance and typical of what I have called the "smell" of this particular score. From the purely technical standpoint the first scene of Toscanini's performance is a fascinating example of his conducting, particularly of the tremendous strength and precision of his orchestral punctuation of Verdi's "conversation" music, the familiar exhilaration of the "bite" with which he always endowed the detail of the rhythm:

Ex. 111

and the superbly controlled, instantaneous changes of tempo which he always achieved so effortlessly and naturally.

Just as he made his changes of tempo so easily so, in *Un ballo in maschera*, Toscanini made his changes of mood and character. Early on in this opening scene we first hear music characteristic of that enthralling and remarkable creation, Oscar the page.

There could be no greater contrast with the dark conspirators'
music than the light and gaiety of Oscar's musical personality,
and it is a contrast pointed by Toscanini with a brilliance and
lightness of touch which are one of the most ravishing features
of the whole recording. The hand which made such magic of
Mendelssohn's *Midsummer Night's Dream* scherzo brought a
peculiar sparkle to the skittishness of the violin figure which
accompanies Oscar's first appearance:

Ex. 112

Renato's aria, "Alla vita che t'arride", which follows
shortly afterwards, is taken at a tempo which stresses the
implication of movement in the word "Andante". It is a tempo
which, frankly, is quite slow enough for any baritone aria dating
from this stage of Verdi's career and Toscanini, agreeing with
us, shortened the final cadenza into the bargain—not by much,
but enough to remind us that Verdi's musical footsteps were by
now headed in another direction and that a long cadenza was a
stylistic anachronism.

Renato's scene is followed by an admirable show of Toscanini's ability to make Verdi's getting-on-with-the-plot sound
musically interesting, and it was something achieved, I believe,
by the simple process of taking an interest in the music itself.
Until Toscanini, it seemed, nobody ever thought the Judge's
little scene and its accompaniment worth bothering about—a
few figures for strings here and there, but nothing you could
really call much of a tune. Toscanini, on the other hand,
clearly took as much trouble over these few moments of the
Judge's account of Ulrica's sentence of banishment as with
Oscar's brilliant aria which succeeds it that, as with so many
other things in music, what one formerly considered dull and
uninteresting was perhaps so only because the composer did
not always write completely foolproof music. The Judge's little
scene accordingly comes out as far more intriguing than one
remembers it from other conductors' offhand treatment of it.

The light-hearted brilliance and infectious gaiety which Toscanini drew from Oscar's solo after the Judge's scene was uniquely astonishing. The bare facts and figures of the metronomics are irrelevant, for the whole tempo and the atmosphere it created could not be more in keeping with the action and the characters, nor more exciting for the listener to experience. It is a superb curtain to a first scene which has been rich in musical variety.

Scene 2

One could ask for no more clearly defined change of musical scene than the bars which introduce us to Ulrica's cavern. Toscanini's tremendous dramatic sense made every possible point in the instrumental introduction, but without exaggerating either dynamics or expression marks. He let Verdi speak for himself. The purist will nevertheless note that Toscanini helped the composer out at one point. When Ulrica comes to the place in her scene where she relates that the supernatural voice spoke to her three times ("tre volte a me parlò"), flute and oboe in octaves twice play the sinister phrase heard in the introduction:

Ex. 113

On the first occasion in Ulrica's invocation the phrase is played by the second violins as well. In the score, when—a bar later—flute and oboe repeat the phrase the violins are for some reason not included. Either Verdi forgot to add the violins the second time, or the engraver of my orchestral score forgot to; in either case the relevant bar is left empty in the violin part. Toscanini, however, put this right and had the phrase played as Verdi must surely have intended it to sound.

The amount of detail which Toscanini brought to the ear in the whole of this Invocation was quite extraordinary, the result of his peculiar genius for creating clarity of instrumental texture in which he was never rivalled—whether it was in the meticulous

staccato of the rapid violoncello figures, or in the ability to make
the loudest tutti or the quietest brass *pp* always a *musical* sound.

This whole scene in Ulrica's cavern, indeed, was a model of
the interpretation of Verdi's dynamics by Toscanini, of the
care with which it appeared the most unsignificant unison
forte for strings had been approached and rehearsed, while the
climax of the Amelia–Riccardo scene was superbly timed with
Toscanini's unique ability to find—in terms of sheer volume
and excitement—plenty more where that came from.

Riccardo's *scena e canzone*—"Di' tu se fedele il flutto
m'aspetta''—was treated in an unusually flexible manner.
The "con brio" was emphasized, and there was a perceptible
(and exciting) quickening of the tempo when the famous
staccato passages occur at the end of the strophes:

Ex. 114

But plenty of time was allowed for the pauses and even a dis-
pensation from singing, as originally written, the phrase,

Ex. 115

Instead, the tenor was allowed to sing the last three notes of
the phrase an octave higher.

Not long after this *scena e canzone* Toscanini made further—and
most successful—modifications in Verdi's score, namely, in the
phrasing of the wonderfully effective passage for woodwind which
accompanies Ulrica's reluctant telling of Riccardo's fortune.
In the score the passage appears with the following phrasing:

Ex. 116

Toscanini re-phrased the sequence to be played in one breath:

Ex. 117

This process at once makes musical sense, for it gives the passage continuity of performance and matches the revision Toscanini made a few bars earlier of the phrase which is printed in the score as:

Ex. 118

but which was obviously—as one knows immediately one hears it played that way—meant to sound:

Ex. 119

Again, it is difficult to decide who is to blame: the composer, the engraver, the editor or a negligent copyist who couldn't be bothered to extend his phrase-marks to embrace more than a couple of notes at a time. There is no doubt, however, that Toscanini's phrasing is the obvious and right one.

Riccardo's famous "È scherzo od è follia . . ." was taken considerably faster than one usually hears it. But after the three flippant, shoulder-shrugging introductory woodwind bars which lead up to Riccardo's first phrase and are so delightfully perky and correctly unexpected after the astonished, almost speechless expression of horror by the rest of the company immediately before them, it is impossible to imagine any other tempo being appropriate. The tempo is almost certainly faster

than tenors unguided by Toscanini have ever sung it in their
lives, but the result is most satisfactory: it cuts down the time
available to the singer to dawdle on the traditional laughs at
the line "ma co- (ho-ho-) me fa (ha-ha-) dari- (hi-hi-) de-re . . ."
and it is absolutely right and comfortable for the general
ensemble which is developed almost immediately Riccardo has
had his first say. Taken at the slower, more conventional
tempo this quintet-cum-chorus sounds unnaturally heavy-
footed. Toscanini's tempo particularly suits the long soaring
phrases Verdi gives to Oscar to share with the orchestra:

Ex. 120

For the rest, the march-like final section of the scene was
introduced by Toscanini (seeing "what is there"?) with an
allargando in the fanfaresque couple of bars leading into the
Allegro assai sostenuto made very much earlier than Verdi
indicates, and the curtain is brought down to a glorious and
exciting din which closer examination of the score shows to
have been suggested by the phrase "tutta forza". At the point
where this phrase occurs it seems from the sound of it that
Verdi's instruction is being implicitly obeyed. That the final
pages are even louder, however, is yet one more instance of
Toscanini's ability to pull out one more stop than anybody
ever thought existed. In this case it was the one just called
"fortissimo".

ACT II

The "Preludio, Scena ed Aria" for Amelia, with which this
act begins, and the love-scene between Amelia and Riccardo
which follows, form what is perhaps the most remarkable
sequence of this whole recording. The effect of the long
orchestral introduction (which although it is labelled "Preludio" is intended to be played with the curtain raised) is that
of a synthesis of nearly all that Toscanini stood for in the
theatre—not quite all, for while this movement has tremendous
vitality and dramatic impetus and a ravishing passage of lovely

cantabile playing, the gaiety which the composer brought to moments of *Un ballo in maschera* in the person of the page Oscar, is, of course, absent. But if ever the accusation needs refuting that Toscanini habitually sacrificed the lyrical to appease the insatiable demands of strict, rigid and relentless tempo, this third side of his recording is all that is needed to throw the whole case out of court. Here there is such a wealth of detail, of beautiful sensitive phrasing, of exquisite dynamic shading, that in despair one falls back on recommending that the listener should merely do what Toscanini did: take the score and "see what is there". How else can one explain that all the conductor did when he encountered two bassoons, three trombones, one tuba, timpani and bass drum all playing

Ex. 121

was to have them play *pianissimo*, as Verdi said?

Nothing, on the other hand, will ever explain how Toscanini managed to make *music* heard in that phrase, and not a growl or rumble. However, my intention in this study has been all along not to "explain" how Toscanini did anything, but to draw attention to what he did and why, and it is in the smallest details of his performances that the most fascinating aspects of his genius are to be found. (Toscanini's treatment of the brass throughout this score was exemplary, for Verdi reverts unmistakably at times to the noisy habits of his earlier operas when three trombones and tuba threatened structural damage to any theatre that ever performed *Nabucco* or *I Lombardi*. Toscanini, while restraining none of their dramatic power, guided the loudest *ff* into the disciplined channel of music, not noise.)

One of the many lyrical passages in this scene provides a curious instance, audible in the recording, of the unorthodox approach sometimes made by Toscanini to instructions found in the score. In the course of the sequence which may be said to begin the duet proper with Riccardo's gentle 6/8 "Non sai tu

che se l'anima mia", a phrase is reached which is marked to be
sung "con entusiasmo":

Ex. 122

Instead, as one might surely expect, of the pace quickening to
keep up with Riccardo's *entusiasmo*, it in fact slows down for this
phrase and the tempo of the passage which follows gradually
broadens towards the Più lento of Amelia's lovely confession
of love for Riccardo. The result of this slower tempo is to
heighten the emotional effect of the music, and add intensity to
the great warmth of Riccardo's outpourings underlined not
long before by the two tremendous crescendo–diminuendo
passages for the strings in the singer's phrase which begins:

Ex. 123

Riccardo's next important passage—"Oh qual soave brivido"
—is marked to be sung "a mezza voce dolcissimo" and accompanied by three wind instruments marked *pp* and a harp and
strings marked *ppp*. Toscanini insisted on *everybody* observing
these instructions (including Riccardo) and the experience is
quite startling. Not only does it prevent the duet which
develops from degenerating into what has been described in
other performances as a "bawling match", but it enables one
for the first time to enjoy—among other things—the full effect
of the remarkable figure for strings which is a feature of the
passage:

Ex. 124

All in all this third side of Toscanini's recording is a superb and exciting revelation of Verdi's scoring and nowhere, I think, more than in the astonishing *cantabile* prevailing in the lyrical passages. Lyrical passages in Verdi, it should be remembered, are usually meant to be shared by both singers and orchestra, and it is the emphasis laid on this fact by Toscanini that makes this whole scene so memorable. Everybody sings.

There is tremendous excitement to be enjoyed in the final moments of *entusiasmo* which bring the duet to an end; but when you change from Side 3 to Side 4 of this set it is the long warm phrases like Riccardo's "Non sai tu che l'anima mia" and Amelia's "Ma tu, nobile, me difendi dal mio cor" which remain in the memory.

The scene which follows with the appearance of Renato is remarkable, at the end of Amelia's first lengthy solo phrase,

Ex. 125

for the addition by Toscanini of a woodwind accompaniment in unison with the soprano, which does not occur in the full score. It sounds, from what I can hear on the recording, like piccolo, flute, oboe and clarinet in octaves (the wind instruments which have been supporting Amelia's vocal line for the two previous bars). Why it would have been added I cannot imagine; it serves virtually no useful purpose and, in fact, is scarcely audible but for a rare lack of co-ordination between singer and instruments at this very point. Unlike Toscanini's addition to the score shown in Ex. 113 this can scarcely be considered an improvement. It is a quaint illogical little touch altogether.

The trio between Amelia, Riccardo and Renato almost immediately following is taken at a tremendous speed (and why not, since it is marked "Presto assai"?), so that what can usually be an exciting experience becomes quite breathtakingly so in its scherzo-like deftness of touch and the astonishing clarity of the instrumental detail in the accompaniment to this remarkable near-patter-song.

Lightness of touch is the outstanding feature of the music from this point to the end of the act, which is dominated by the delicious passages for the conspirators. Toscanini made the most of Verdi's indication that Samuel should be accompanied by violins playing "con eleganza", and there can be few occasions when this whole scene has so effectively given the impression of suppressed cynical laugher—from the moment Samuel first recovers from his initial astonishment at the spectacle of Renato having (apparently) kept a rendezvous with his own wife, to the relish with which the final unaccompanied reflections are made by the conspirators off stage to make this superbly effective "curtain".

If Side 3 of this *Ballo in maschera* left an impression of warmth and supremely *cantabile* lyricism, this side reflects the sense of fun as well as the *eleganza*, unfortunately rare in other composers, which Toscanini always found in Verdi. These two sides, at any rate, show conclusively that *Un ballo in maschera* is an opera of far greater musical and dramatic variety than its generally-accepted reputation as an uneven work of art might suggest, and its revelation is typical of Toscanini's performances of Verdi.

ACT III

Scene 1

The early stages of this scene in the recording are noteworthy for a strange lapse in Toscanini's direction of the ensemble when —for a couple of bars only—the orchestra lags behind Amelia. It is a reassuring reminder that Toscanini was occasionally subject to human failings and is to be treasured for just that reason.

The erstwhile *violoncellista* comes out in Amelia's great "Morrò, ma prima in grazia", when Toscanini lets the solo violoncello have his head with his obbligato, though not to the extent of allowing him to dawdle. Amelia may be asked by the composer to sing "con dolore" but Toscanini allows no suggestion (which the metronome markings of $\downarrow = 48$ would imply) that we are having a pre-view of Amelia's funeral cortège; instead, it moves —Andante—easily and flexibly at a thoroughly natural speed.

Flexibility, indeed, is a forceful characteristic, not only of the rhythm, but of the whole spirit underlying the tempo of Renato's "Eri tu", which follows shortly after Amelia's exit.

In this aria, with its alternation of tension and relaxation of tension, Toscanini varied the tempo considerably, and frequently, from the Andante sostenuto which starts the short and incisive instrumental introduction. In these first five bars (one of them a silent bar) the tempo is appreciably faster than when the voice begins. Similarly, the long-phrased "middle" —when the accompaniment features mainly flutes and harp— is taken at yet another and slower tempo. The difference between the instrumental introduction to "Eri tu" and Renato's last *a tempo* bars represents the difference roughly between 66 and 54 beats to the minute respectively—not much on paper, but nevertheless perceptible, and indeed fairly obvious, in practice. Nobody can complain that "Eri tu" is "driven" anyway, even though it never drops as low as the score's ♩ = 52.

The arrival of Samuel and Tom brings back the famous conspirators' *fugato*—a wonderfully sinister conception of Toscanini's —and before long we are in the midst, first, of the martial exaltation of the three men as they take their oath; then in the uncannily contrived tension of the music which accompanies the placing of the names in the urn—an admirable sequence of orchestral writing for the *ppp* thumps of bassoons, trombones and tuba (see Ex. 121), and little chromatic runs for strings, punctuating the fateful-sounding *legato* of the trumpet solo:

Ex. 126

The climax of this sequence, the *fortissimo* as Amelia approaches the urn to pick out the ballot paper, is a terrifying moment from which Toscanini drew that little bit extra in the way of dynamic force beyond the power of other conductors.

The remainder of the scene is worth remarking for the easy, unhurried precision of the syncopated passages shared by Amelia and some of the orchestra (a peculiar Toscanini achievement which never ceases to astonish—and depress—by its apparent inimitability), and for the return of all the fabulous sparkle and *leggerezza* that goes with Oscar's music in this performance.

Scene 2

Toscanini, who was intent on giving us not only every note that Verdi put in the score of *Un ballo in maschera* but, as we have seen, also one or two that he didn't, was naturally not in any mood to cut the *Romanza* sung by Riccardo at the beginning of this scene. (Personally, I never imagined that he would; but it seems, according to the writer of the notes that go with the records, that this *Romanza* is sometimes omitted. I must admit its omission is something I have not experienced in any performances of the opera I have ever heard.) On results the tenor appears happily at home with Toscanini's Andante in this lyrical episode to make the contrast with what follows even more startling. As in *La Traviata* Toscanini takes a particular interest in the off-stage dance band; he starts off the "Festa da ballo" at a tremendous speed (roughly 176–184 beats a minute) and permits no suggestion of the *banda* being anything but in a purely literal, physical sense "off-stage". Its manners, habits and general way of life are otherwise fully integrated in the score as a whole and it is expected to play a *musical* part in what's going on.

Oscar's last show-piece, "Saper vorreste", is something one finds oneself looking forward to, and, hearing again all the *eleganza* with which Toscanini endowed it, one is sorry when it is all over and that there should be no more like it to come. Toscanini's presentation of Oscar was one of the really great features of this whole performance. The role is a piece of musical characterization which Verdi made far from foolproof; it is only too easily made ridiculous by over-playing, by an excess of coyness, or exaggeration of the delicate accompaniments from a genuine vivacity into an intolerable skittishness. Toscanini avoided all these possible pitfalls; he struck a miraculous balance and in consequence Oscar remains in the memory as an outstanding musical creation.

As the *Festa da ballo* proceeds the second back-stage orchestra of strings is heard to be given the same attention by Toscanini as the earlier *banda*; it plays its mazurka with great charm, an imperturbable charm indeed which once more heightens the impact of Verdi's dramatic strokes. This imperturbability may

in fact be a little illusory, inasmuch as I will not swear that
when the pit-orchestra violins begin their reiterated

Ex. 127

there is not a hint of a *sforzando*, or at least of an accent, on the
third note of the phrase each time. But, as I say, this may all
be an illusion; Toscanini brought the pit-orchestra violins into
a sudden perspective and that, combined with the typical
unemotional working to rule of the stage band behind them,
may account for the impression I get. Certainly I have heard
few more dramatic moments in opera than the calm, casual,
disinterested musical reappearance of the string band on the
stage after Riccardo has been stabbed. There was surely never
a band which had more obviously been playing all the time
than this one. Once more there is no suspicion of a "join"
between the assembled company's furious Prestissimo and the
return to the "I° tempo" of the string band.

There remains Riccardo's death scene, an episode of phrases
liberally marked with "dolcissimo", "dolcissimo con espansione" and "cantabile", and leading to the climax of the whole
work—the final ensemble passage which Toscanini leads from
a hushed *pp* to a tremendous, thrilling *ff* climax and back to
nothing in the course of four bars to Riccardo's dying "Addio
per sempre, miei figli . . .".

If ever one needed proof of Toscanini's gifts as a "composer's
conductor" it is surely to be found in this one short episode of
Un ballo in maschera. There have been half a dozen thrilling
moments in what has gone before; there have been climaxes of
tremendous brilliance and dramatic power. But as Verdi
intended, it is this last climax which is meant to top them all.
Toscanini, who understood Verdi as I believe no other conductor has ever understood him, brought all the power he ever
commanded to bear on this climax and make it everything the
composer ever dreamed of. It is a stupendous moment.

There are so many things to be said about Toscanini's performance of *Un ballo in maschera*, so many things to be remem-

bered, admired, and cherished that a neat summing-up is virtually impossible. It is in numberless ways an unique and stimulating experience. And yet, though I reflect on the elements which contribute to this experience—Toscanini's sense of lyricism, of drama, of gaiety, and (above all) of timing—the recording of this particular opera has had one curious effect on me which I have not experienced with the others. For some reason when I had finished listening to the records it was not long scenes that kept running through my head afterwards, but tiny snatches of phrases—the group of three decorated notes of the conspirators' laughter, the sound of the final reprise of the mazurka, the sinister *pp* brass figures, the details of the accompaniment to Oscar's two arias. I attribute no great importance to this, except that the more I reflect on Toscanini's treatment of *Un ballo in maschera* the more fascinating do I find the details that made up the whole remarkable experience.

AIDA
[1872]

Aida	Herva Nelli
Amneris	Eva Gustavson
Radames	Richard Tucker
Amonasro	Giuseppe Valdengo
Ramfis	Norman Scott
The King of Egypt	Dennis Harbour
A messenger	Virginio Assandri
A priestess	Teresa Stich-Randall

Robert Shaw Chorale
NBC Symphony Orchestra

GREAT BRITAIN: RCA RB–16021/2/3
U.S.A.: Victor LM 6132
Recorded in 1949 with additions made in 1954

Apart from anything else, the release at long last of this recording of *Aida* (which many in England had long resigned themselves to believing was no more than a myth) filled a great sentimental gap in Toscanini's legacy of performances of the music of Verdi. We had had a recording of *Un ballo in maschera*, the first Verdi opera Toscanini had ever heard; we had had a recording of *La Traviata*, whose two preludes had been the first experience of Toscanini conducting Verdi for so many of us; we had had a recording of *Otello*, at the first performance of which Toscanini had played the violoncello; we had had *Falstaff*, which Toscanini had first conducted in Genoa at a time when he could appeal successfully to the composer to decide a dispute over a detail of tempo; and we had had the Requiem, which Toscanini had conducted at La Scala when Verdi died.

But we had not had a recording of *Aida* to complete Toscanini's performance of the great triptych of Verdi's maturity—*Aida*, *Otello* and *Falstaff*—or remind us that it had been *Aida* that Toscanini had conducted as a nineteen-year-old boy at Rio de Janeiro, when he made his spectacular and legendary start to his spectacular and legendary career.

Toscanini's recording of *Aida* seems to me, however, to have a further significance beyond the obvious and sentimental association with Toscanini's debut: when Toscanini first conducted it *Aida* was Verdi's latest and, in all likelihood, last opera. It was also the opera which had shown the greatest advancement and development of the composer's style and so came as the greatest shock to his contemporaries. We who today are able to look back on Verdi's development as a whole and can see how that development was to lead inevitably (as it seems to us who are so wise after the event) to *Otello* and *Falstaff*, cannot really imagine how *Aida* must have sounded to contemporary audiences. It was experience of Toscanini's miraculous re-creation of the contemporary impact of Beethoven's symphonies which made me, at any rate, so desperately anxious that Toscanini should bequeath us a performance of *Aida*. He alone, I knew, was capable of presenting Verdi's opera with the impact it had had in Verdi's lifetime. That this lifetime had also overlapped into Toscanini's was an added stroke of luck, and in a purely chronological sense gave Toscanini's performance an extra authenticity, a special "link" which nature and coincidence denied to other conductors. But, as we have seen in the case of Toscanini and Beethoven's symphonies, contemporaneity was not everything; identification with the composer's aims and objects was what mattered, and it was this that in the end was most important in Toscanini's performance of *Aida*.

ACT I

Scene *1*

If there is one feature of the Prelude to the first act that is more immediately noticeable than another in this recording it is that very flexibility which Toscanini was considered to have suppressed so ruthlessly. The warmth and subtlety of the phrasing of the whole movement has that exquisite translucence which we first heard when Toscanini played us the two *Traviata* Preludes; each bar of it is superbly *cantabile*, and so far from being mercilessly subjected to a rigid tempo, the great *ff* tutti climax of the orchestral introduction, which Toscanini has made one realize is not the mere curtain-raising formality other conductors would have us believe, is taken at a considerably stepped-up tempo. This climax, of course, is the moment of conflict between the gentle and pathetic theme associated with Aida, and the stern, march-like tune which accompanies the Priests throughout the opera. The quickening of the tempo at this point is characteristic of Toscanini's method of creating dramatic excitement whenever such moments occur in *Aida*.

Studio performance or not, Toscanini created a thorough, superbly theatrical atmosphere in this *Aida*; he made no concessions to any non-theatrical convention, and in doing so brought to a mere gramophone record more of the true colour and smell of an opera house than any other recording of this work I have ever heard. Recalling more than half a century later his famous debut with *Aida* in Rio de Janeiro, Toscanini said that he could still summon up "even the smell of the theatre that evening". This recording proves that this was no mere sentimental reminiscing of an old man, for it smells not only of the Theatro Lyrico on June 25, 1886, but virtually of every performance Toscanini must have given of *Aida* in a theatre afterwards.

The moment the curtain rose (one can describe it no other way) Toscanini immediately communicated that peculiar knack which Verdi shared with Shakespeare of presenting two characters in the middle of a fascinating conversation, whose first words are of such import and significance that one wonders what they had been talking about up to the moment we first hear them.

This opening conversation in *Aida* is only thirty-two bars long. Toscanini made them understandably memorable, for the only orchestral accompaniment comes from the violoncellos divided into three parts. The former *violoncellista*, who had learned his *Aida* in the orchestra pit of a touring company, took great care over this sequence. So many conductors regard it as a rather eccentrically scored recitative; Toscanini recognized it as a lovely, musically-interesting sound.

The apprehension with which those who are convinced that Toscanini was a Human Metronome are sure to approach the Romanza called "Celeste Aida" is likely to be fearsome; they will discover it to be entirely unjustified. Apart from adopting a tempo slower than the officially prescribed ♪ = 116 (Toscanini took it at about 100), within the framework of that tempo the aria was allowed to sing itself with remarkable freedom of rubato and phrasing. The orchestral texture was made to sound entirely ravishing, with every note of one of Verdi's most original passages of orchestration receiving individual attention. It was an accompaniment, yes; but an accompaniment written by a genius of the orchestra whose simplest pizzicato "chuck-chucks" Toscanini always made sound different from any other composer's.

The student who, like myself, may have been puzzled for many years by an oddly contradictory instruction in Verdi's score of this aria, may be interested to know how Toscanini dealt with it. In the bar immediately preceding Radames' last singing of the words "del mio pensiero tu sei regina . . .", the clarinet, bassoon, first violin and violoncello parts are indicated to be played "dim.", but under the notes of each instrument there appears the familiar "hairpin" sign for a crescendo. Toscanini decided the composer's instructions cancelled themselves out, played the whole passage *piano* and threw in a little *ritenuto* for good measure.

The purist, or for that matter the ordinary opera-goer, will probably be struck (if he is not horrified) by a spectacular departure from the text at the end of "Celeste Aida" in Toscanini's recording. Richard Tucker, as Radames, is heard to repeat his closing words—"vicino al sol"—on a middle B flat, in the bar in which most tenors are still usually struggling with the high B flat which customarily ends the aria.

Again, this was a characteristic Toscanini solution of a problem. As Verdi wrote them the dynamic sequence of the last five bars of the tenor part is: *pppp—ppp dim.*—leading (a little oddly, after the *dim.*) to *pp morendo*, which is an increase in volume. Disregarding the rather eccentric introduction of a diminuendo between the *ppp* and the final *pp*, it will be observed that the passage is in fact a gradual crescendo from the first to the final mention of the words "vicino al sol". The final *pp*, however, carries the qualifying instruction "morendo", though whether this means that the volume is greater or less than at the *pppp* start of the phrase, it is difficult to decide. Verdi's experience of the conductors and orchestras of his time led him to exaggerate his dynamic markings when he wanted his music to be played really quietly. In order to get a genuine *pianissimo* he had to underline his request by marking the effect *pppp*, and the score of *Aida* abounds in such heartfelt pleas for quiet playing.

The confusion in "Celeste Aida" is that if we accept *pppp* as equalling the *pp* Verdi wanted, *ppp* must equal *p* and the final *pp morendo* equal *mf*. Toscanini, however, recalled that Verdi himself obviously realized in the end that it would be something of a miracle if ever a tenor was found who could do anything but bawl out his top B flat, for when the composer was asked by the tenor Ernesto Nicolini to transpose the whole aria down a semitone to A and so make a final *pianissimo* top note easier, he refused, but suggested the compromise adopted by Toscanini. It seems to me to settle the whole question admirably, though I would like very much to know how often Toscanini resorted to this variant and when he first did so, for none of his biographers has mentioned it so far as I know.

At risk of appearing wise after the event, I was not surprised to learn that Toscanini spent a great deal of time in rehearsing

the orchestra in the scene which follows with the theme
associated with Amneris's jealousy:

Ex. 128

He is reported to have told his violins: "Don't play the ordinary
staccato you learned at school", and one can hear the result,
for in spite of the *pp* there is nothing delicate or graceful about
the first five notes. They were given a quite remarkable
quality of dramatic tension, with the bows gripping the strings
and giving the phrase a peculiar "bite" which was particularly
characteristic of the *agitato* music throughout Toscanini's
performance of *Aida*. Toscanini's creation of tension was not
so much a matter of instrumental tone as of the tremendous
rhythmic precision which is found, for instance, in this whole
scene between Amneris, Radames and Aida, where the few
short passages of syncopation are particularly notable for the
driving rhythm which made this typical Verdi device so
wonderfully effective in Toscanini's performance.

The big fanfare which follows the Trio and introduces the
King in this recording may surprise some of the critics, for
Toscanini unexpectedly observed a familiar theatrical tradition at this point and brought the sequence to a close with an
emphatic *allargando* which is not indicated in the score. Toscanini, one finds, observed quite a few of the traditions common
to this opera, nearly all of them concerned with the spontaneous
quickening or broadening of tempo not shown in the score.
One tradition he did not observe, however, was that which so
often regards the Messenger as nothing more than a necessary
evil and a character of no musical value. Toscanini, instead of
looking on these twenty-three bars as no more than a matter-
of-fact announcement, gave the little scene a sense of the
tremendous urgency and fierce excitement which, after all, one
might expect on first hearing of the invasion of one's country.
The tension this created gave extra significance to the choral
outbursts of "Guerra! guerra!" by the Egyptians, and served
also to explain the elation of the March which ends the episode.

This March, which is introduced by the first of several of the Maestro's own vocal contributions to this recording, may sound a little fast on a first hearing; in fact, Toscanini took it scarcely a beat faster than the official 88 recommended by the composer as the right metronome marking for the Allegro maestoso. Toscanini regarded it as Allegro, but did not detract from the Maestoso element. It was both a virile and a noble conception.

There is one interesting point to be noted during this and the other processional moments in *Aida*, and that is how the cymbals are not immediately damped after each crash of a crotchet on the first and third beats of each bar. Toscanini allowed them to ring between each stroke, cutting them short only when the rest of the orchestra ended a phrase on a short note. By allowing the cymbals to "sing" Toscanini created the intriguing illusion that even the unmelodic percussion instrument was making *music*, not merely a din. He also introduced the cymbals, off and on, when they are not shown in the score.

As the March ends, and the procession leaves the stage, Toscanini introduced a conventional note, which I was surprised to find him doing, in making the traditional accelerando in the final couple of bars. It surprised me (I will not go so far as to say it disturbed me) because I have never understood the purpose of this sudden, last-minute quickening of the tempo and I was hoping that Toscanini might agree with me—and with the composer who suggests no such nuance in his score. It is a harmless convention in all conscience, but nonetheless a puzzling one.

Toscanini's handling of "Ritorna vincitor!" was another of those miraculous revelations of great music which we had hitherto considered we knew all about. This time it was not just the lyrical beauty and the wonderfully delicate orchestral texture which was so astonishing—one expected that, anyway—but the mood of horror and despair created in the earlier part of the scene, as Aida realizes for the first time the full significance of what she has said in praying that Radames may return victorious. Here Toscanini found drama indeed as Verdi must have conceived it, and offered the experience of an aspect of *Aida* which I, at least, had never before encountered in performance.

The shimmering translucence of the string parts in this aria, the shading of the dynamics ranging from *ppp* to *ff* with a wealth of *cresc.–dim.* passages, the easy flowing tempo, the rhythmic tautness of the syncopated figures, were features of Toscanini's performance that gave it a peculiar atmosphere of its own. There was fierceness, but there was incomparable gentleness (including a couple of spontaneous instances of *tenuto* which will surprise the listener brought up to believe Toscanini was heartless and unyielding) which was one of Toscanini's noblest musical emotions and one which a generalizing posterity is reluctant to give him credit for or to recognize when it encounters it.

Scene 2

The sound Toscanini created at the beginning of this scene in the Temple of Vulcan was most theatrically evocative and gave the music a wonderful air of mystery and sacred ceremony, largely, I believe, by differences in tempo which contrasted the rather brisk, businesslike four-in-a-bar invocation of the Priestess with the free and much slower tempo adopted for the chorus of Priests in the distance.

Toscanini, indeed, made remarkably free with breath-pauses, unexpected *tenuto*, *ritenuto* and *allargando* phrases when he came to the Dance of the Priestesses—little touches which were matchless examples of his immaculate sense of timing. Two technical points to be noted, one of them a departure from the composer's written note, occur in this Dance. The first concerns the detail of the trills in the three flute parts in the phrase:

Ex. 129

Too often these trills are made to sound casual, and given the status of little more than a couple of rapidly executed grace notes and left at that. Toscanini extracted full value from the trills and made them sound as though the players had had all the time in the world to play them. The second point to be

heard is in the four bars immediately following the one illustrated above, and on another couple of similar occasions in the
course of the Dance. In each case the oboe is shown in the
score to sustain a high B flat—*pp* the first couple of times and
ppp the last time. Toscanini introduced a long crescendo to the
phrase whenever it was heard—quite without authority, so far as
I know, but with great effect. It is a crescendo that affects only
the oboe, for the rest of the orchestra continues on its way, with
the flutes observing the composer's instruction to play *dolcissimo*.

If critics were as honest as they would have us believe they
are knowledgeable, there ought to be as much comment on the
occasions when Toscanini took music *slower* than composers
indicate, as on the occasions when he was alleged to have taken
it so much faster. Time and again in his performances of Verdi
one found him adopting a slower-than-usual tempo. Just such
an instance cropped up in this scene of *Aida*. The *grave* of
Ramfis' invocation to the gods, with its throbbing accompaniment of trombones, which Verdi asks to be played at $\texttt{J} = 66$,
Toscanini took appreciably slower.

This final sequence, which brings the first act to an end, is
rich in fascinating and spontaneous detail, as, for instance,
Toscanini's addition of *sfz* to the *ff* timpani part from time to
time, his reinforcement of Radames' part in the ensemble by
the voices of the Priestesses, and his systematic slowing up of the
tempo for each phrase sung by the Priests in answer to the off-
stage chorus of Priestesses. None of these things is an "effect",
except in the sense that the result of what one hears is "effective"
and a credit to the music.

ACT II

Scene 1

Toscanini took the opening passages of this scene at an admirably brisk and unsentimental pace (Verdi prescribed his Allegro
giusto as $\texttt{J} = 108$ while Toscanini interpreted it at about one
notch higher on the metronome—about 112), and in doing so
avoided making it the dragging, ponderous sequence less confident conductors so often make it. Brisk and unsentimental the
tempo most certainly was, but it was not inflexible; there was a
perceptible hint of broadening whenever the word *dolcissimo*

occurs in the score and a definite *ritenuto* on each occurrence of the phrase which leads into the smooth singable tune which is marked *dolcissimo*, namely the little woodwind "sign-off"—

Ex. 130

The peculiar charm which Toscanini always seemed uniquely able to bring out of Verdi's music makes an enchanting appearance at the end of this sequence—a slight lingering over the last phrase (marked "grazioso") sung by the women's chorus before the repetition of Amneris' pathetic aside which leads into the ballet music for the Little Moorish Slaves. It is clear from the recording what kind of Amneris Toscanini imagined, for the class of the character's *music*, as distinct from the pretty unimpressive performance of it by Miss Gustavson, is unmistakable; all the warmth, jealous ferocity, pathos and anger which the singer did not seem able to impart by her singing, are unmistakably expressed in Toscanini's tempi, his affectionate caressing of the melodic line associated with all Amneris' music, in every gentle nuance and dramatic emphasis in the score whenever the character appears.

The remarkably undistinguished performance of Amneris in this recording will clearly depress those who regard *Aida* as another "singers' opera". I doubt if it depressed Toscanini very much. As far as he was concerned, Verdi had been served as faithfully as he himself knew how, and that is what has made this recording such a supremely valuable item in Toscanini's Legacy. Singers, after all, can change from one performance to another; Verdi's music, on the other hand, goes on for ever, his intentions and achievement eternally to be seen in the pages of the score—by those who have eyes to see "what is there". So it seems to me that while the recorded performance of *Aida* is vocally a little unexciting, its over-all presentation of Verdi's case, as it were, is tremendous. The conductor who can make the orchestral detail as plain as Toscanini did, who can create the warmth and dramatic fire, reproduce the fascinating nuances of this recording will have a blue-print of *Aida* into which any averagely competent company of singers can be "slotted in" without for a moment depriving the *composer* of his rights. A cast with Destinn, Caruso and whom-have-you can obviously illuminate a performance of *Aida* in an unforgettable manner and, with an uninspired conductor, might even contribute more to the understanding of Verdi than a cast of lesser talents in the same circumstances. The great conductor, however, will in the end inevitably "re-create" Verdi's score with greater conviction and fidelity, because it is the conductor who is entrusted by the composer with ultimate authority. Singers are never more than the servants of the composer; nor is the conductor ever more than a servant. But in operatic, as in other households, there is—or should be—a strict order of precedence and importance among the servants. And it has never struck me, any more than it can ever have struck Toscanini, that there was any question who should be the senior servant in an opera house.

The natural setting of *Aida* being an opera house, Toscanini, as I have suggested, allowed no hint of any other atmosphere to influence his conception of the music. The whole performance smelt of the theatre, and nowhere more than in the admirable sequence of ballet music which serves for the Dance of Little Moorish Slaves while Amneris is being dressed for dinner in this first scene. The sparkle and excitement Toscanini brought to this short interlude was superbly evocative, even in its recorded form. He did not consider it as a musical episode which permitted elderly gentlemen in the audience to relax, and therefore to permit an elderly conductor to relax, too, when he came to it. The *Danza di piccoli schiavi mori* was an occasion for a quite exquisite realization of Verdi's score, of attention to detail and dynamic balance and an effective stepping-up of the tempo for the "trio" which constitutes the middle section; and, of course, since this is dance music, a characteristic display of an appropriately irresistible rhythm.

It is the examination of the unexpected details of Toscanini's performances of Verdi which is so often so rewarding. Ballet music is ballet music no matter who conducts it in Grand Opera —as a rule—and one tends not to give it a second thought. Toscanini gave it far more than a second thought and let us hear it as a supremely effective additional splash of colour in Verdi's most ambitiously colourful score.

When the women's voices return after the dance music, Toscanini joined them with characteristic fervour clearly audible in the recording, and enthusiastically joined in again at moments during the great duet between Aida and Amneris.

The over-all effect of this duet (as distinct from the purely vocal performance in the recording which does not rise to great heights at any time) is a wonderful indication of the extent of Toscanini's perception of the dramatic characterization of Verdi's score. It was a perception which never failed to grasp that it was the sum of the parts that made the whole; with the result that numberless details of the scene which usually go for nothing assumed the importance the composer had intended.

Toscanini saw that the opening sequence for strings and timpani, for instance, which accompanies Amneris' hypocritical concern for Aida's happiness, was as subtly characterized as the same kind of sequence it so clearly anticipated—namely, the accompaniment to Iago's "Era la notte" in *Otello*. Toscanini's portrayal of Amneris as a human being transcended all the shortcomings of the artist who sang in this recording, and one may experience a superbly dramatic unfolding of the Princess's character, from the insincerity of her comforting friendliness towards Aida to the passionate sincerity of her anger as she traps her into admitting that Radames is her lover. Aida herself stands out as all that Verdi made her: one of his most pathetic and noble heroines.

There is a certain amount of pathos and nobility in the purely vocal and histrionic sense in Herva Nelli's performance; the pathos and nobility of the character as a complete musical conception, however, was provided by Toscanini and his realization of Verdi's score—particularly in the sequence where Aida, having checked herself as she was about to reveal her own royal identity, falls on her knees to ask Amneris' mercy and forgiveness and confesses that she loves Radames and lives only for that love:

Ex. 131

In the recorded performance the poignancy of this little passage came less from the voice than from the remarkably plaintive orchestral accompaniment—a small handful of wind instruments, with a melancholy arpeggio figure for the solo bassoon. Toscanini could influence singers up to a point; instrumentalists he could usually succeed in getting to play as near as humanly possible to what he knew the composer wanted. How successfully he could make an orchestra speak on Verdi's behalf, and so present the composer's case convincingly and eloquently, was shown again and again in such details as the accompaniment of this particular passage in *Aida* and in the texture of the strings which accompany Aida's despairing "pietà" which ends the scene.

Scene 2

The first sixty-two pages of the orchestral score of this scene are devoted to marches and dances which Toscanini made remarkably stirring and enjoyable with an immense show of rhythmic vitality, excitement and precise interpretation of note-values by no means lacking in those exquisitely timed little moments of rubato and *dolcezza* which he always uniquely found time for.

There was one of these warm and unexpectedly lyrical touches at the beginning (*cantabile*, of course) of the passage for women's voices which leads to the solemn gait of the Priests' theme-song. The "Grand March" itself, played by "Egyptian" trumpets, Toscanini made as refreshingly jubilant and thrilling as one has ever heard it—and it is, basically, a thoroughly thrilling tune, although it has become a hackneyed one.

The ballet music, as I have suggested already, was something Toscanini made stand out as *music*, not merely as an exotic interlude, and his performance of this *ballabile* was an intensely invigorating experience. His tempo was slightly above Verdi's indicated Più mosso $\downarrow$ = 144, but the result is so exhilarating, so full of theatrical atmosphere that one would have little patience with any corps de ballet who, in an opera house, complained that Toscanini's tempo was too fast. One would send for another, more lively corps de ballet.

The ballet music in this scene includes one quite delightful, unauthorized touch, a gesture from a former violoncellist to his colleagues, which occurs each time at the passage:

Ex. 132

Toscanini decorated the little group of four notes on the second beat in the violoncello part with a *sforzato* accent and a quick diminuendo. Again, it is not one of those aspects of Toscanini's genius one would ever ask any young conductor to emulate. It is an example not to be followed, but to be enjoyed for its own sake as a manifestation of Toscanini's having been born with certain instincts which less fortunate mortals will never acquire in a lifetime.

There remains one thing to be said about the return of the choral hymn of praise and rejoicing, and that is that Toscanini succeeded in making it sound even louder, build to an even greater climax, than the first time it was heard.

For the student-conductor there are two details to note in the scene which follows: the first fanfare by the stage band to punctuate the King's proclamation sounds to me to have been re-scored by Toscanini, the trumpets' E in the chord of C major being doubled by trombones, while a wonderfully effective unison crescendo in the trombone parts is made in the third bar of

Ex. 133

instead of in the bar afterwards, which is where Verdi indicated it to begin. (The bar-earlier crescendo is made again when the choral phrase is repeated immediately after.)

The pomp and circumstance at an end, Toscanini returned to the drama with tremendous intensity at Aida's recognition of her father, Amonasro, and his account of how he had fought and lost. Then, in a moment, there was a heart-breaking

tenderness and warmth in the strings' playing of the music as
Amonasro turns to plead with the King for the lives of his
fellow-captives:

Ex. 134

The great ensemble which builds up from this point showed
the so-called "inflexible" Toscanini not only observing every
single nuance of tempo shown in the score but inventing
several of his own—among them a considerable *ritenuto* to
return to *a tempo* after the *stringendo a poco a poco* which occurs
when Ramfis and his bloodthirsty brethren are demanding
death and damnation for all in answer to Amonasro's plea for
clemency; a generous *allargando* in the bars immediately before
Aida's unaccompanied cadence leads back to a reprise of
Amonasro's tune shown in Ex. 134; the introduction of a
markedly slower tempo in the middle of an Allegro, when the
voice of the Egyptian populace is heard pleading for mercy for
the unhappy prisoners (they take Radames' side against the
Priests, who do not appear to be very popular with the crowd
in this story); and an occasional stepping up of the tempo as the
music grows in dramatic intensity, together with a traditional
accelerando as the tune of the Grand March brings the act to
an end.

So much for "inflexibility". But if Toscanini did not dawdle
quite so much over this final ensemble as some would have
wished him to, there is none who can deny that the whole
movement from Amonasro's "Ma tu re" to the fall of the curtain has, even in a gramophone recording, a unique quality of
"theatre" and tremendous excitement. Which is, after all,
rather what one imagines Verdi had in mind.

ACT III

Toscanini is reported to have told his orchestra during
rehearsal of the beginning of this scene: "The stars are shining.
How shall I explain this? It is not water, not fire, not stars, but

poetry." Compared with his abruptly musical explanation of the opening of the Eroica * this was a somewhat confusing and over-colourful way of describing Verdi's Andante mosso, and I must confess that if I had been a member of his orchestra I would have found it difficult to find fire, water, stars or even poetry in what I had to play as a first violinist (repeated G's across three octaves, starting on the open G string and coming back to it four times a bar), a second violinist (*tremolando* on D–G in the third position on the A string), a violist (pizzicato G across two octaves), or any of the violoncellists (who play nothing but a sustained harmonic G in one octave or another for thirty-two bars).

The orchestra's bowing, intonation, volume, tone and solo flautist, however, in the end added up to what Toscanini sought and the result is a magically poetic and evocative sound in which every exquisite detail is audible.

Toscanini's tempi in the opening stages of the Nile Scene were generally below the metronome markings of the score—69 against 76, 50–52 against 60, 80 against 92. The unexpected rallentando and *allargando* appeared from time to time, too, a particularly noticeable slowing-up occurring in the two *morendo* bars immediately before Aida's voice is heard for the first time. These departures from the strict letter of the score are of no great importance, but they serve to show once again how often so much of Toscanini's "inflexibility" was purely imaginary.

The slow tempo adopted for Aida's "O patria mia" (80 against Verdi's 92) did not drag the aria for a moment. Instead, it gave the music room to breathe more freely than I had ever heard it before. To begin with the little oboe phrase which forms the instrumental introduction to the aria proper assumed a quite ravishing *cantabile* quality and there seemed—as there had seemed in the case of the flutes I have mentioned on page 260—to have been all the time in the world for the oboe to give full value to the trills without any hint of over-emphasis, even though in the second part of this oboe solo (just before the change of time to 6/8) Toscanini permitted a perceptible rallentando at the end of the phrase. This, so far from violating the Spirit of Verdi by being unauthorized by the

* See page 39.

composer, added an extra shade of pathos to a scene which is already intensely pathetic. It was, in fact, a sudden, magnificently typical touch as characteristic and stimulating as the inflexion of a great actor's voice in a classic Shakespeare speech we have all known backwards since our school days.

Toscanini's performance of "O patria mia", as it has come down to us in the recording, is an endless source of astonishment. Dramatically, the pathos of the whole conception is wonderfully moving; musically, it is à revelation of Verdi's quite revolutionary orchestral colouring and the masterly effectiveness of such details as, for instance, the plaintive little figure played by violins and violas in unison during the second of Aida's strophes.

The duet between Aida and Amonasro was a superbly faithful reflection of Verdi's rapid changes of mood from the *agitato* and *appassionato* to the *dolcissimo* and *cantabile*. Again it was a performance full of surprising and breath-taking details, the result of Toscanini's split-second timing of the unexpected pause and the barely perceptible *ritenuto*. One of the most lovely of these moments was the faintest hint of a breath-pause between the crescendo and the sudden *ppp* of the phrase which begins:

Ex. 135

Toscanini's genius for showing us things in a score that one had never seen before was particularly apparent in this whole scene between father and daughter. Amonasro's angry outbursts have the incisive ferocity of Iago's music; Toscanini evoked tremendous drama from the passage in which Aida is disowned by her father. The rhythm of this 6/8 Allegro episode was superbly controlled, and by its very strictness and intensity heightened wonderfully the pathos of the passage which follows as Aida lies at her father's feet, and declares that she will be worthy of her country.

This was another characteristic revelation of something which, so far as my own experience of the opera was concerned,

I had never hitherto encountered. Toscanini made the passage quite uncannily moving, and by doing no more than observing "what is there". There was no secret attached to it; the process was simplicity itself. All Toscanini did was to respect the accents and pay full attention to the dynamic balance and note values in the string figure which runs through the whole movement:

Ex. 136

To declare that "all" he did was to observe the letter of the score is, of course, one of the least satisfactory ways of describing the way Toscanini ever performed anything. He would tell you himself that "all" he did was remain faithful to what was written in the score; but he knew as well as the rest of us that that was only half the truth. The other half was unanalysable, the result of some uniquely privileged insight into the composer's mind which could evoke from the violins' repeated figure a sound of almost unbearable sadness and despair.

The beginning of the duet between Aida and Radames Toscanini took at a tempo slightly above par—108 to Verdi's 100—and in doing so increased the feeling of excitement as Radames (*con trasporto*) embraces Aida again; this same excitement underlies the long sequence in which the trumpets play their series of martial figures, *leggerissimo e staccato*, like some distant call to action to inspire Radames' unwittingly tactless promise that when he has defeated her countrymen he will claim Aida as his royal reward for his prowess. Radames' enthusiastic reflections in the course of this were liberally decorated by Toscanini with moments of *tenuto* and elasticity that tradition, if not the score, permits.

When the tempo changes to "più animato" and Amneris' jealousy theme returns at Aida's mention of the Princess's possible vengeance, Toscanini adopted Verdi's officially prescribed metronome marking of 144 and for the rest of the duet for the most part accepted the composer's recommendations. Certainly no single detail was neglected; the *pp* figure repeated for ten bars or so in the strings, when Aida first puts forward her plan that her lover should desert Egypt and escape with her to Ethiopia, suddenly acquired a dramatic significance far beyond anything one had ever associated with it before. Instead of being, as it had always sounded previously, merely an instrumental accompaniment, it became a sinister and ominous comment on the vocal line.

That part of the duet which begins with Aida's *dolcissimo* account of the new country she and her lover are to fly to—"Là . . . tra foreste vergini"—was made unusually moving by Toscanini's restraint and understatement. The three flutes and their wonderfully seductive accompaniment gave to what is virtually a pipedream of Aida's a remarkable quality of remoteness and other-worldliness. The gentleness and beauty of the phrasing of this episode, with its admirably judged moments of rubato, both authorized and spontaneous, combined to create a deliberately lyrical atmosphere which, by contrast, made Aida's sudden accusation that Radames does not love her more than usually dramatic and unexpected.

Toscanini brought a remarkable intensity to these fifteen-odd bars of dialogue between tenor and soprano, especially in the tremolo string crescendo leading to Aida's final "Well then, let the axe fall on my head and on my father's." Having raised the temperature of the music in this way, Radames' exultant decision (made "con appassionata risoluzione") that he and Aida should flee into the desert was launched by Toscanini on the wave of a thoroughly exhilarating tempo, faster (though not much faster) than Verdi's Vivo assai of $\downarrow = 92$ and in the circumstances the only possible speed at which the music would any longer be effective. To have taken it slower would have killed the drama stone dead and allowed the excitement, so carefully built up to a high pitch, to sag and end in anticlimax instead of continuing with ever-increasing force and impetus.

This instinctive concern of Toscanini's for the intensity of the drama of Verdi's operas may have resulted in tempi which did not always agree with the metronome, or with traditional standards of behaviour in "singers' operas"; to me, however, they were in nearly every case justified by the drama of the situation which, as Toscanini presented it, was automatically

more potent and on a higher plane than one experienced elsewhere. In consequence, it seemed to me that, in the case of this
scene in *Aida* for instance, if the great feeling of release from the
tension of the previous passage was to affect not only Radames,
but the audience as well, then it could only be achieved at a
tempo appropriate to the degree of tension that had been
created up to this point.

Except that it seems to need saying so often in order to
convince the sceptic, it is almost unnecessary to report that in
the course of this last stage of the scene between Radames and
Aida, Toscanini naturally observed all the pauses, instructions
to play "col canto" and "molto rit." indicated by the composer
without, in so doing, depriving the music of any of its natural
exuberance.

From now until the end of the act Toscanini increased the
excitement and drama steadily, with inevitably one or two
moments of quite startling originality and illumination—
notably in the clarity of the *pp* string phrase which follows
Radames' astonished "Tu!" when he learns Amonasro's
identity, and the white heat of the next phrase which follows
ff on his incredulous "Amonasro!"

Every Toscanini performance abounded in moments such as
these; *Aida*—perhaps because one imagines one knew it so well
—seems in this recording to have been unusually rich in them;
this third act particularly so.

ACT IV

Scene 1

The first delight in Toscanini's performance of this scene was
the purely physical one to be derived from the exquisite balance
of the rippling figures for two flutes which accompany the
repetition of Amneris' jealousy theme. Again this was something one was apparently hearing for the first time—not
instead of, or more than, but *as well as* the agitated string theme;
just as a little later, after a tender and thoroughly flexible
treatment of Amneris' reflective and sentimental soliloquy, the
entrance of Radames, accompanied by six remarkably tense
bars in which Verdi produced an orchestral sound entirely

new for him, sounded as surprising as it must have sounded to the composer's contemporaries.

Tension was naturally the element that dominated Toscanini's performance of the scene between Amneris and Radames, and he created it by his characteristic control over the rhythm; but it was a grip that was never too tight that it did not relax to allow the lyrical element in the music to breathe freely and warmly whenever the drama demanded it. So it was that Amneris' big *cantabile* sequence, in which she offers to give up her crown for Radames' sake, emphasized by its exquisite phrasing and instrumental detail the quite remarkable excitement and tension of the passages which followed: the Princess's announcement that Aida is still alive and her passionate determination to be revenged.

There are few instances in Verdi's operas of sustained excitement and dramatic tension comparable with the development of Amneris' love-turning-to-hate scene and Radames' refusal to be affected by it. It is a scene whose over-all effectiveness is due to the composer's unusual concentration on detail, his concern with sudden accents and dynamic contrasts in the orchestra, with abrupt and exciting changes of mood and tempo—in short, with all those dramatic touches in a dramatic score which Toscanini instinctively picked out and highlighted with rare and dazzling conviction.

As Toscanini's recorded performance of *Aida* progresses it becomes increasingly difficult to quote from it; every other bar demonstrated—— To be honest, every other bar demonstrated nothing—except that Toscanini saw "what is there"; but so faithfully and clearly that all one can do is refer the reader, the listener, the student and critic to the orchestral score of *Aida* and the Toscanini recording and leave them all together.

The Judgment Scene which follows the departure of Radames and his guards starts with numerous repetitions in the major of the solemn tune associated with the Priests. Toscanini obtained a wonderful singing tone from the lower strings in this, first from the double basses in their long solo passage, and then from the violas and violoncellos in unison, to contrast superbly with the *tutta forza* of the climax of the theme in the minor as the Priests invoke the spirit of the gods to descend on them—a climax which Toscanini made quite frightening in its intensity.

The trial of Radames, it will be remembered, is in three parts, each consisting of Ramfis' allegations, Radames' silent refusal to defend himself and the Priests' unanimous verdict of "Traitor!" After each of these verdicts Amneris sings the same pathetic phrase in which she beseeches the gods for pity. Tradition has usually permitted the singer to linger over the plaintive tearful cries of "Numi, pietà", so that one was a little taken aback on a first hearing to discover that Toscanini took the phrases faster than one was accustomed to. Reference to the score, however, showed that if Toscanini was not giving the passage its characteristic pathos at the traditional tempo he was doing so at the official one. His ♩ = 120 was what Verdi asked for.

Toscanini's performance of the remainder of this scene showed how remarkably dramatic and moving it can be and so rarely is. There was tremendous drama in the pronouncement of the death sentence, the Priests' repeated cries of "He is a traitor", the shattering distortion by the orchestra of their theme as they emerge from the subterranean chamber where the trial takes place, and in their final echoing "Traditor!" when they have left the scene. There was a desperate pathos in all Amneris' vain entreaties to the Priests to spare Radames' life, and a superb orchestral sound, treated with great breadth and with an unsolicited *tenuto* thrown in (indicated in the example below), to accompany the last plea made by Amneris in which she is not interrupted by the Priests—namely, the passage which begins:

Ex. 137

And there was drama again in Amneris' final invocation of the curses and vengeance of heaven on the Priests, and in the wonderfully theatrical atmosphere of the relentless and ferocious music which brings down the curtain.

Scene 2

Toscanini's performance of this last scene was something of such incredible tenderness and beauty that it is virtually unanalysable. His tempi were almost invariably slower than Verdi's metronome markings—52 against 60, 72 against 80, 52–60 against 63—and the orchestral texture was of a prodigious translucence. The famous passage of what Verdi called his "vaporous" orchestration, which accompanies Aida's first signs of delirium, sounded as crystal-clear in its detail as a piece of chamber music.

And above all Toscanini brought out the tragic tenderness of the music, allowing the melodic line to "sing itself" and again making the occasional unsolicited but logical *tenuto*, especially in the lovers' last farewell to earth—"O terra, addio". From the purely sensuous point of view Toscanini made of this scene something one had never experienced before; his phenomenal sense of dynamic balance and instrumental colour revealed more clearly than ever that *Aida* was Verdi's most original and ambitious essay in orchestration. The sheer sound Toscanini drew from the score was entirely ravishing and supported two of my favourite theories: that the orchestra is always more eloquent when it whispers than when it bellows, and that over the years more has been contributed to the art of orchestration by music heard in the opera house than in the concert hall.

As I come to the end of each hearing of Toscanini's *Aida* recording I find that, paradoxically, what runs through my head after the experience is not the memory of instrumental details so much as of passages in the vocal line. It is paradoxical because this particular *Aida* was not blessed by very distinguished singing, except from Richard Tucker, and the vocal parts were not therefore memorable in the sense one usually understands the term. In some curious way, however, Toscinini, for all his ruthless rejection of bad traditions and refusal to permit such a thing as "a singers' opera", always succeeded in focusing one's attention on the singers' music—in other words, on the human characters created by the composer; so much so that it was almost as though the less outstanding the singers the nearer we came to the true Verdi. This was not altogether literally the case, of course, but it is significant I think that the least vocally remarkable performance of a Verdi opera recorded by Toscanini should have been the one in which, to me, the *characters*, as distinct from the artists who portrayed them, stood out most clearly.

This *Aida* was chronologically the last of the Toscanini performances of Verdi that I heard. As I said earlier, its release filled a sentimental gap; but most of all, like Toscanini's recordings of *Otello* and *Falstaff*, it showed the true stature of Verdi. And that, in the end, was perhaps Toscanini's most dedicated aim in life. The issue of the recording of *Aida* in the United States was originally planned to celebrate Toscanini's ninetieth birthday; it came instead as the first of his posthumous gifts to posterity. And it was an imperishable one.

OTELLO
[1887]
(Property of G. Ricordi and Co.)

Desdemona	Herva Nelli
Otello	Ramon Vinay
Iago	Giuseppe Valdengo
Cassio	Virginio Assandri
Emilia	Nan Merriman

NBC Symphony Orchestra and Chorus

GREAT BRITAIN: HMV ALP 1090/1/2
U.S.A.: Victor LM 6107
1947

To me Toscanini's recording of *Otello* was his supreme achievement, not least because it was something one had never dared hope to live to hear. With the exception of his *Traviata*, *Ballo in maschera* and *Aida*, most of the more important items in Toscanini's great legacy of records consisted of music I had heard him play in person—Beethoven's nine symphonies, *Fidelio* and the Mass in D, the Verdi Requiem and *Falstaff*. In addition I had heard performances of *The Magic Flute* and *Die Meistersinger* at Salzburg. His recording of *Otello*, on the other hand, was something entirely out of the blue. Like *La Traviata*, *Un ballo in maschera* and *Aida* it was an opera he had not conducted since his last season at La Scala in 1929 and the news that he had performed it in a couple of broadcasts in New York during 1947 added to the feeling of frustration among those of us in Europe who had been denied the Maestro's activities for so long.

There was still worse to be suffered when a friend of mine brought back from America what can only be described as a bootleg recording of a couple of passages from Toscanini's *Otello* performance—or, more accurately, of passages from an orchestral rehearsal of the performance which had been secretly recorded. It is a fascinating episode of eavesdropping which was most kindly, though doubtless illegally, duplicated for me thanks to that marvel of modern science known as "dubbing". This is understandably among my most treasured possessions and I would not mention it if it had not so vividly reminded me of the enthralling experience of a Toscanini rehearsal, and particularly of the perseverence and concentration he lavished on what might seem almost frivolous detail. The sequence of the rehearsal recorded was from the first act, beginning at the "Fuoco di gioia" chorus and ending after a couple of refrains or so of Iago's Brindisi. In the course of the first half of the passage there occurred the phrase, played by the oboe in unison with the clarinet and flute and an octave below the piccolo:

Ex. 138

Toscanini made the oboist play his phrase nearly a dozen times until it matched the phrasing of the other instruments. After this typical instance of the fantastic acuteness of Toscanini's ear the rehearsal continued with a great deal of singing, shouting and pleading from the conductor. The direct consequences of that rehearsal are to be heard in this recording of *Otello*, for what I did not realize at the time I listened to that bootleg excerpt was that the eventual broadcast performance was recorded on transmission.

Even so, the *Otello* records took six years to reach us in England and it looked during most of that time as though my eavesdropping souvenir was to remain my only, tantalizing glimpse of what Toscanini's *Otello* might have been.

In a way, the fierce attack of this rehearsal excerpt gave quite a formidable indication of Toscanini's approach to Verdi's greatest opera, and it was clear from the orchestral passages alone, which was all—apart from the conductor's excruciating out-of-tune la-la-ing—one could hear of the Brindisi, that the character of Iago was going to be presented to American radio audiences in a light which few of us can have imagined existed before. And, indeed, so it proved to have been when, at last, the recording of *Otello* was issued in this country.

The predominant characteristic of Toscanini's whole conception of *Otello* is the evil he distills from the musical character of Iago, a quality so strongly accentuated that it is not just the musical line or mood which is affected, but the very sound of the instruments themselves undergoes a change, so that the strings, for instance, wheedling and insinuating one moment are suddenly shown to bare their teeth viciously and menacingly the next.

This great shifting of the opera's musico-dramatic centre of gravity towards Iago is something I have not encountered in performances of *Otello* before, and its effect is tremendous. It is also dead right, for not only was it the character of Iago that first attracted Verdi to the idea of Shakespeare's tragedy as a subject for an opera, but *Iago* was the original title by which composer and librettist referred to the project for a great part of the time they were working on it together.

It is Toscanini's instinctive perception of the dramatic power and importance of every detail in the score of *Otello* (including insistence on the use of horns in D and A *basso* where they are demanded in Verdi's score, instead of having everything played indiscriminately by horns in F, which is the common practice), that makes this recorded performance such an overwhelming experience. We need not marvel at the vitality of a man of eighty conducting a performance such as this; he was still seven years younger than when he came to conduct *Un ballo in maschera*. It remains a uniquely stupendous item in the whole unique and stupendous legacy of Toscanini's work, because while it is impossible for anyone to say for certain that the conductor did this or did that, because he was privileged to have played in the orchestra at the first performance of *Otello* in 1887, there is nevertheless about the whole performance an air of indefinable authenticity and authority. In the end, however, I believe it will be found that this quality has far less to do with the personal association of composer and conductor sixty years before the recording was made, than with Toscanini's preoccupied reflection ever since then on the letter and spirit of Verdi's music. In other words, if Toscanini had been born too late to play at the first desk of violoncellos at La Scala on February 5, 1887, it is highly likely that he would have approached the task of conducting *Otello* in the same way.

It was a work supremely well suited to his temperament, as every bar of this recording testifies. But above all it was a score to which, more than any other—and perhaps in the end because he *did* have such privileged access to Verdi as a young man—he brought a special sense of intense personal dedication, and in which he saw far more clearly than anybody else the ultimate truth and significance of "what is there".

ACT I

If ever an opera gave an immediate indication of its dramatic calibre in its first couple of bars it is Verdi's *Otello*. No less certainly does the performance of the same bars reveal the calibre of the conductor who is to take charge of it all. Toscanini gave the whole of this opening sequence of stormy terror and excitement a dramatic impetus of quite fantastic intensity and vigour. This was the seemingly inimitable Toscanini who could raise the roof with the greatest of man-made dins and yet never for a moment suggest that the sound was anything but entirely musical It was a supreme example of his powerful control of the dynamics of the music, his effortless building of climaxes for which he was always able to call on a reserve of energy from himself and the musicians under him, so that a Toscanini *ff* was somehow always just that much louder, more thrilling—and more musical—than other people's.

The sound and fury of this storm scene, unleashed at a basic $\text{♩} = 80$, was not so overwhelming that Toscanini hadn't time to notice a moment of thumbnail musical characterization by Verdi in the midst of it all. Iago's first line in the opera is a general factual observation that the mainmast of Otello's ship has split. His second, addressed in confidence to Roderigo a couple of bars later, is a prayer that the sea will prove Otello's grave, and it is accompanied by fiercely accentuated inter-jections by bassoons, violoncellos and double basses in octaves:

Ex. 139

(L'al-vo fre - ne - ti - co del mar sia la sua tom-ba!)

Amidst all the turmoil of the crowd, the sudden evil quality of those bars was brought out in high relief by Toscanini with arrestingly dramatic effect as a malevolent aside audible above the sound of the storm—a perfect instance of seeing "what is there", for it is as clearly marked by the composer as it is habitually ignored by the majority of the conductors of this score.

The detail in this first long sequence of Act I was repeatedly and astonishingly brought out by Toscanini, but typically never at the expense or misrepresentation of the over-all dramatic picture. There was no searching for subtleties where none exists—that was never Toscanini's custom; but, above all, the flow of the music was maintained in such a way that in spite of changes of time and tempo the whole scene had an almost symphonic continuity, a rhythmic inevitability which took in its stride the sudden nobility of Otello's entrance, the scherzo-like *pp* Allegro vivace ($\text{♩.} = 120$) of the chorus's 6/8 "Vittoria! Sterminio!", and the wonderful dying-away of the storm and the popular excitement which leads, after a restful couple of bars from the chorus, to the first extended passage of conversation between Iago and Roderigo.

The scene which follows, the chorus of "Fuoco di gioia", was a sparkling, fiery affair which on first consideration seemed a little fast at $\text{♩} = 126$ or so, but which proved, like so many of Toscanini's fast-sounding tempi, to be absolutely right, relaxed, and comfortable for all concerned. This whole sequence was a peculiar miracle of detailed phrasing and orchestral clarity, the instrumental texture owing nothing whatever to tricked-out "hi fi" or anything like it—as I know from the dubbing of a dubbing of a dubbing of whatever was the original, basic, illicit, under-the-seat, low-infidelity source of the recording of the orchestral rehearsal in my possession to which I have already referred.

Toscanini's approach to the next scene, the Brindisi, was almost ferocious in its attack. This was "Allegro con brio" indeed, and noticeable for a perceptible flexibility of tempo which varied between one "verse" and "chorus" and another, and for a refreshingly literal respect for the absence of any suggestion by the composer that there should be a pause between the 4/4 orchestral introduction and the four 6/8 "vamp-till-ready" bars before Iago's entry. The tradition prevalent in the modern opera house of making a pause between the two sections seems to be based on the entirely irrelevant precedent of the empty bar between the orchestral introduction and the "vamp" in the Brindisi in *La Traviata*. With the Brindisi in *Otello* it was a case not so much of Toscanini putting something back into the score, as of suggesting why he, at any rate, could never have taken it out. To have made the unauthorized pause in those bars would have upset the conductor's whole conception of the scene which follows, by interrupting its rhythmic continuity. The Brindisi in *Otello* is not just a drinking song; it is part of the plot, and Toscanini concentrated on letting the music tell its story, with the result that we do not need to *see* Cassio staggering about to know he is drunk. All his lurching and befuddledness is illustrated by the orchestra's incisive cross-rhythms and the open fourths and fifths accompanying his sozzled attempt to remember the tune of the first part of the Brindisi. Toscanini made this a magnificently exciting scene which grew irresistibly towards its inevitable brawling climax and Otello's intervention in the Cassio–Montano quarrel.

Toscanini gave this entrance of Otello's an unchallengeable authority, and a simple matter like the chord of G major which emphasizes Otello's command had a sudden arresting effect one never anticipated. More remarkable still, however, was

the force and stern ferocity of the little 6-note motif for the
strings which punctuates Otello's questions and reproaches:

Ex. 140

Too often that figure is regarded merely as a handy conjunction in a passage of dramatic quasi-recitative. Toscanini
gave it the status of an expression of Otello's musical character,
and it immediately assumed a dramatic purpose. Because of
the tension and force Toscanini infused into this little scene it
contrasted just that much more effectively with the lyrical
warmth and beauty of the Love Duet which follows to end the
Act. On the Duet Toscanini brought to bear all his belief that
singing is the basis of all music, and he created an unforgettably
rich experience by literal observance of the composer's directions and with virtually no deviation from the metronome
markings in the score.

So closely, indeed, did he adhere to these markings that
when we arrive at the great and moving passage towards the
end—

Ex. 141

many have been shocked by what they consider to be Toscanini's "insensitive" treatment of the tune.

It can, certainly, come as something of a shock on a first
hearing, for one has grown accustomed over the years to conductors spreading themselves at this point and expanding the
tune with an almost Wagnerian generosity. Verdi, however,
clearly intended no such thing, and Toscanini respected that
intention. He observed the metronome marking and slowed
the tempo where the composer writes "poco più lento", and
the result was moving, without for an instant allowing sentiment to degenerate into sentimentality. The greatness of this

Love Duet lies in the unique nobility of its conception, in the expression of a passionate love rising above mere sensuality. Toscanini's *poco più lento* and the crescendo to the *forte* and its diminuendo was never for a moment exaggerated; Verdi's instructions are simple, Toscanini obeyed them, and once again it was as though a new score had been born.

ACT II

As though he were anxious to get on with the performance after the interval Toscanini returned to the score of *Otello* with an extremely brisk interpretation of the Allegro assai moderato of the short instrumental prelude to this Act. Instead of the indicated ♩. = 72 for this opening, Toscanini took it somewhere in the region of 84 or more; but so far from causing any structural damage to the music the faster tempo gave it an added urgency and emphasized Iago's apparently incessant plotting and planning in his pursuit of vengeance. The articulation of the instruments concerned in this introduction was so clean, however, that there was no feeling of the tempo being rushed, and indeed the graceful line of the almost eighteenth-century smoothness of the string writing acquired an added elegance.

No sooner has Cassio left Iago alone on the stage, however, than we realize the purpose of Toscanini's first tempo when the quiet opening phrase of the introduction was translated into the angry

Ex. 142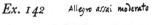

Played at the more usual tempo these triplets sound sadly tame and un-menacing; Toscanini's way with them brought us with unexpected suddenness to the terrific unison tutti which prefaces Iago's "Credo". All the evil in Iago's musical character that Toscanini had been slowly fomenting comes to the boil with this scene. It was a deliberately rough portrait of "honest Iago" soliloquizing honestly, without having to hide his true feelings behind a mask of honeyed tones and hypocrisy. So it was that we found a full measure of roughness in the phrases which Verdi marked to be played "aspramente",

Ex. 143

and in the piercing oboe trills which reinforce them.

Throughout the "Credo" Toscanini combined in a masterly fashion a feeling of almost pathological tension with un-expectedly relaxed moments of *cantilena*, among them one bar well worth listening for when Iago was encouraged to make use of rubato when he sings:

Ex. 144

The gentle, leisurely phrasing of this passage was superbly typical of Toscanini's faculty for translating a passage into terms of the human voice and allowing the human process of natural breathing to determine the whole shape of the tune. Like the astonishing, held-back notes of the Haydn finale (see page 147) the exact technical process of this moment in the "Credo" is unanalysable. It is something which just happened and it has fortunately been recorded for us to hear it.

The last phase of Iago's soliloquy—beginning at the *poco più lento* shortly after letter G in the vocal score—was remarkable not so much for the lovely playing of this remarkable under-stated variant of the original unison "Credo" theme, as for the long pauses Toscanini made between Iago's reflections on death and what happens after it, and the dark *pp* interjections of the orchestra. This was an unforgettable piece of instinctive "theatre" on the part of a man who never gave a "concert performance" of an opera in his life. This "Credo", if nothing else, proves that.

Iago's great scene had now firmly established his musical

character, and it dominated the opera from this point on with ever-increasing intensity. One of the immediate consequences of this was the conspiratorial string accompaniment to Iago's one-sided conversation with Cassio, which Toscanini treated with an almost Mendelssohnian lightness and staccato touch.

The scene after this, between Iago and Otello, was a masterly sequence of understatement which the conductor kept flowing so that there was no jerkiness in what can too often be merely a string of instrumental interjections. The reticence of this and the observance of "Assai moderato" made Otello's outburst just that much more telling when it came. Toscanini's gradation of the emotional tones of this whole scene was quite uncanny as each bar reveals with increasing irresistible force the slow and inexorable process of Iago's undermining of Otello's faith and love. There was something quite terrifyingly sinister and evil in the insidious pp of the full orchestra in the crescendo–diminuendo chromatic phrase in which Iago tells Otello to beware of jealousy, and in the whispered menacing passage which accompanies his reference to the "green ey'd monster which doth mock the meat it feeds on" and is heard again so effectively in the instrumental introduction to Act III:

Ex. 145

There were few moments in all the music I heard Toscanini conduct more immediately astonishing and enchanting than his sudden transition from the grim uneasiness of the scene between Iago and Otello to the sweet and gentle E major of the off-stage chorus serenading Desdemona with its flowers, bag-pipes, mandolines and guitars. It was a magical moment and typical of his unparalleled gift of being apparently able to create an atmosphere a split second earlier than even the composer can have hoped to make his effect.

This whole scene had an intoxicating charm (not the least of it contributed by Toscanini's careful observance of Verdi's request that the strings play "con eleganza") which had the effect of an almost physical change of air, and ended with an object lesson in how the long sustained passage for the first violins at the end of the scene should be phrased so that it does not sound like something that has strayed from Kreutzer's Studies.

The atmosphere of charm created in this whole little interlude is firmly established and maintained by Desdemona to contrast with Otello's angry outburst a few moments later, which once and for all destroys the calm of their marriage. The ensemble which begins as Emilia picks up Desdemona's handkerchief,

Ex. 146

was a movement Toscanini took very much nearer ♩. = 60 than the 50 marked in the score. The result of this I found was to make the original marking sound drably ponderous and to deprive the scene of much of the effectiveness of the *pp* orchestral tutti and the lyrical beauty of the whole conception. The "singing" quality of this quartet movement was remarkable, but kept superbly under control—largely, I think, by Toscanini's quickening of the "official" tempo which prevented the instruction "Largo" being over-generously interpreted and broadening too much, and so running the risk of sentimentalizing what is a restrained, and deliberately not-too-highly-coloured, lyrical sequence.

In the final scene of the Act—the duet between Iago and Otello—Toscanini built up the tension and sheer ferocity of much of the music to a stupendous and awful climax. Once more the final effect was achieved by Toscanini's concern for what may be called the contributory factors which help to develop the drama and its music, and by the fullest exploitation of the carefully designed light and shade of contrast in Verdi's music.

The final curtain of this Act in Toscanini's performance would have lacked a great deal of its power if the conductor had not previously emphasized in his own unique way the whole subtle charm and hypocrisy of Iago's whispered passage, "Era la notte".

Charm was not a quality Toscanini was generally credited

with bringing to, or drawing out of music. The popular idea
was that he "drove" music to the exclusion of all else. Drama,
rhythm—these were the predominant features of his art. In
fact his ability to bring charm to music was very highly
developed; but perhaps because it was never used at the wrong
time, but always perfectly, if unostentatiously, suited to its
context, it was not an aspect of Toscanini's musical personality
that was obvious. But charm was something which Toscanini
could find in abundance in music—when it was necessary. It
was necessary in Iago's wheedling "Era la notte", and Toscanini gave this scene an irresistibly seductive quality. The very
sound of the orchestra, the hushed *ppp* of three flutes and an
oboe, convinced not only Otello, but the audience as well of
Iago's evil sincerity and authority—which is a much rarer
achievement than is generally realized. Otello *has* to be convinced; the words he has to sing tell him so. But they do not
necessarily always tell the audience.

Once again, with this remarkable episode Toscanini saw
"what was there" in the score and there was surely never music
which was in consequence more repulsively, convincingly
serpentine in its insinuation. The outstanding feature of this
performance was the utter lack of over-emphasis of any kind.
You listen to the music; you look at the score; there is nothing
remarkable or "subtle" about the performance, nothing in one
that is not in the other. Its simplicity is almost frustratingly
unanalysable—and indescribable.

I remember a performance of *Otello* by the Scala company at
Covent Garden in 1950 conducted by Victor De Sabata in
which an extremely effective touch was added to "Era la
notte". In the bars immediately following Iago's last quotation from Cassio's alleged dream—"Il rio destino impreco che
al Moro ti donò" ("Cursed fate, that gave thee to the Moor"),
Verdi wrote this for the strings:

Ex. 147

The Scala conductor, with considerable but unauthorized imagination, had his strings play the passage with a pronounced slithering, reptilian *glissando* at each rising interval:

Ex. 148

I will admit that this orchestral "gimmick" made quite an impression on me. I even thought that perhaps Verdi might have approved if he had heard it.

It was not until I heard Toscanini's recording that I realized how completely unsubtle, exaggerated and altogether wrong this would-be subtle, understated and "clever" interpretation of Verdi's score proved to be. The comparison, indeed, was laughable. What did Toscanini do that De Sabata didn't? He played it exactly as Verdi wrote it, placing the accents where they are marked in Ex. 147, observing the simple instructions "dolcissimo" and "ben legato", and not imagining some between-the-lines hinting at a subtlety not clearly indicated in the black and white of the score.

In one respect, which is purely personal, I find Toscanini's treatment of "Era la notte" a little disturbing in this recording. I keep going back to it and playing it again—a process which does not improve the condition of the record and which interrupts the dramatic continuity of this tremendous finale.

The last bars of all—the astonishing *pesante* sequence of major chords (consecutive fifths and all) which brings down the curtain—Toscanini took a little faster than one is used to. There is no metronome marking for reference at this point; the only reference for the tempo of the whole passage, indeed, is the dramatic context of what has gone before. Toscanini's tempo had the urgency and excitement of the context.

ACT III

Toscanini continued his development of Iago's musical character with a briskly incisive, sinister performance of the short orchestral introduction to the Act; but it is less to this, than to the short scene which opens the action that I would draw particularly the student's attention.

This is a scene of straightforward "conversation music" between Iago and Otello, played by strings only in a quasi-recitative manner, punctuating the dialogue with occasional *legato* phrases and off-beat chords—fifteen bars of actual accompaniment in all. With his passionate regard for the importance of detail in all music but particularly in opera, Toscanini once more made otherwise insignificant phrases sound *musically* important. He ended with a characteristic stroke by somehow maintaining a natural unbroken rhythm, so that there was no hint even of a change of bow between the *fff* and *p* of the phrase:

Ex. *149*

Within a moment, as Desdemona enters, those same fierce strings were exuding that lyrical warmth and charm which Toscanini invoked so expressively and there was a moment of expert phrasing at the end of the little movement in E major which was ravishing. There was little in the whole performance of *Otello* more poignantly enchanting than the way Toscanini played:

Ex. *150*

How he succeeded in doing what he did with that one bar and a bit, I have no idea—but like his opening of Beethoven's Fifth Symphony it is there in perpetuity (one trusts) as an example of phrasing for all who may ever want to earn their living as conductors, and for the armchair musicians who would have us believe that all Toscanini could do was "drive" music.

At this stage of Toscanini's performance of *Otello* detailed comment becomes difficult. All the charm and drama—the entrancing *grazioso* lyricism of Desdemona, and the mounting agitated, hysterical suspicion of Otello—had been so carefully emphasized and developed by Toscanini earlier in this performance that everything one heard at this point of the story was virtually an instance of "the same, only more so . . .".

The charm which coloured Desdemona's entrance recurred
with particular grace—and a typical Toscanini view of what
Verdi meant by "con eleganza" as unanalysable as the
cadence of Ex. 150—when Desdemona suddenly brings back
an air of sanity with her disarming:

Ex. 151

The ferocity and violence of what follows was doubly underlined by the quality of innocence which Toscanini extracted
from Desdemona's music in this scene, not only in the little
movement cited above, but also—and particularly—in the
heart-breaking despair and sincerity of her pleading in the long
warm tune which begins:

Ex. 152

This, and the few bars just before it where there is another
sequence of typical Verdi "thumping" of *ppp* brass in his best
"Miserere" manner, were two wonderful examples of the sheer
beauty of sound which Toscanini was uniquely able to persuade from an orchestra. In the first passage there was that
astonishing articulation which we noted before (in *La Traviata*),
and in the second an inimitable breadth and warmth to a tune
which—in Toscanini's case—was almost superfluously marked
"cantabile". He could never have done it any other way. There
was also, incidentally, an intriguing little extra added by Toscanini to the instructions in the score at Desdemona's cadence:

Ex. 153

Behind Desdemona's last G, Toscanini added a crescendo to the
orchestra's *ff* semibreve. This may have been purely accidental,

due perhaps to the players suddenly giving more to their notes than they thought they were capable of; but whatever the reason it was an unexpected and exciting effect. (There was a similar unauthorized crescendo a little later—two bars after letter P in the score—made this time either in accordance with Bülow's principle of "having something to diminuendo from", for it leads to a *ppp*, or because the rest of the strings are influenced by the only crescendo marked at this point, which is to be found in the violoncello part. I mention these two divergencies from Verdi's score not merely to show that Toscanini could ignore the letter of a score, but to show that when he did do so it was with immediately noticeable dramatic effect.)

Otello's short solo scene after Desdemona's exit provided another experience of Toscanini's uncanny insight into the music of Verdi's masterpiece. He induced a *ppp* unison from the strings in their recurring downward chromatic passage which was so quiet that it sounded as though it was being played muted, and yet there was never for a moment any suggestion of the theatrical exaggeration which, for instance, made the notorious Furtwängler *pianissimo* so laughable at times— not so much because it was often musically indefensible, but because it was often musically inaudible, and therefore served no immediately apparent purpose. Indeed, reflecting on Toscanini in general and on his performances of opera in particular, it is remarkable how there is never any suggestion of exaggeration of a composer's intentions. He never "hammed"; and that was one of the great differences between him and nearly all other conductors. The effect of Toscanini's *ppp* in the orchestra behind Otello's monotone was not to cause one to cry "How astonishing!", but "How right!"

At the end of the scene, in the last eight bars before Cassio enters and the fourth side of the record ends, one may well remark "How astonishing!" as well as "How right!" on encountering another break with a careless tradition. Toscanini made *no* conventional and unauthorized *allargando* when he reached the fierce repeated G flats of the phrase which begins:

Ex. 154

Toscanini kept strictly to the tempo and it had the impact of a series of tremendous hammer blows. Once more, on hearing the authorized version, as it were, one wonders how or why on earth a meaningless convention came into being in the first place.

After the noble and sustained passage for strings which accompanies Iago's meeting with Cassio and Otello's over-hearing of it, the music becomes a kind of protracted scherzo, ranging from the delicate charm and lightness of the sequences between Iago and Cassio, the gloomy frustrated comments from Otello, to the warm lyrical outbursts of Cassio, which Otello is intended to misunderstand.

This whole scene, including the fast 6/8 passage for Iago which can so often sound like a Gilbert-and-Sullivan patter song, was as light-fingered and quicksilver in its texture as one can believe Verdi ever hoped it to sound.

From the end of this scene which is interrupted by the off-stage fanfares, to the end of the Act the music moved inexorably along its inevitable dramatic path conducted—in the sense of being guided—by Toscanini to its unparalleled climax. There was little—or rather, there was too much—to be singled out for isolated analysis. The strength of the whole sprang from the strength of the smallest details—from the ability to extract musical interest from figures and phrases serving merely as accompaniment, and similarly to ensure that dramatic stresses and accents, such as loud tutti chords off the beat, remain always a purely musical sound, and not a loud bang. Above all, Toscanini's rhythmic strength, combined with his uncanny control over the dynamics of the music, was what made this whole scene and its climax such a tremendous experience.

From the purely technical point of view of Toscanini's command of dynamics, I would refer to the remarkable sound of the phrase which is played when Desdemona is thrown to the ground by Otello,

Ex. 155

and the incredibly delicate staccato of the woodwind when
Desdemona begins the tune which starts off the great final
ensemble:

Ex. 156

ACT IV

Toscanini had moulded the whole dramatic shape of the
first three acts of *Otello* with such power and certainty that
even a listener ignorant of the entire nature of Verdi's opera
might reasonably have expected—particularly after the climax
of Act III—something disastrous to happen in the last act.

The atmosphere of the instrumental introduction, Toscanini's presentation of the tension and whole colouring of the
Willow Song, and the sinister, chilling effect of the moment
when Desdemona mistakes the sound of the wind for someone
knocking at the door were terrifying in their anticipation of
tragedy; while Desdemona's despairing cry of farewell to
Emilia became just that little more moving by being accompanied for a moment by what sounds like the familiar voice of
the Maestro himself.

Unexpected little touches there certainly were, particularly in
the wonderfully moving "Ave Maria" where Toscanini somehow managed to make the strings' phrases stretch to infinity.
One of those touches was the barely perceptible *ritenuto* which
occurred in the string passage leading up to Desdemona's "per
noi, per noi tu prega" and the return to Tempo I°:

Ex. 157

This was another of those breath-taking moments which had
to be heard to be believed and which were so characteristic of

Toscanini's genius for what can only be described as "timing", as the term is understood in tennis or boxing or golf.

The famous passage for double basses, which accompanies Otello's stealthy entrance and approach to Desdemona's bedside, was so menacing and sinister that one can only imagine what the effect of Toscanini's performance of it in the opera house can have been like.   Again nothing was exaggerated or "hammed"; the music was allowed to play itself and the suddenness and force of the two great tutti chords which occur as Otello steps back from the bed made an unnerving moment.

The second of the three occasions when the "love theme" from the Duet at the end of Act I is heard in the opera, follows now as Otello kisses the sleeping Desdemona. As before, Toscanini disappointed the more sentimental traditionalists by not dawdling over it, observing strictly Verdi's instruction of "più animato" and ♩ = 88. The time for the full poignancy of the phrase was not yet; there was a great deal of melodrama to go, and the excitement of the music from this point until Desdemona's dying words was a further object lesson by Toscanini in the art of not losing sight of the fact that Verdi, however *ff* the chords and ferocious the syncopated figures, was always creating *music*. His dramatic emphasis and plea for "tutta forza" was never allowed to degenerate into mere clatter. It is not just a louder bang that was heard as Desdemona is suffocated: it was probably the loudest chord of the diminished seventh ever created by man.

There were two other notable instances of the essentially musical importance to Toscanini of Verdi's melodramatic touches. One occurred as Desdemona speaks the first of her dying words—"ingiustamente . . . uccisa ingiustamente . . ."—and Toscanini, instead of allowing the phrase for violins, flutes and piccolo to be swamped by the *ff* of the rest of the orchestra, brought it out clearly over the general din, so that

Ex. 158

was not just an instrumental flourish, but had the bloodcurdling horror of a piercing scream.

The other detail was in the four bars immediately before Otello's "Niun mi tema . . ."—the descending chromatic passage for violins and the nerve-racking effect of Toscanini's wonderfully observed "diminuendo sempre" of these bars.

In the final moments of the opera the "love theme" is heard for the third and last time; perhaps this time, too, Toscanini may have sounded too matter-of-fact for those who are accustomed to a more *schmalzig* treatment of the phrase. But what *is* the way to play this theme? It occurs only three times; it is scored differently each time; its context is different each time and the composer's indications of tempo are different on each occasion. In practice, Toscanini took it in Act I slightly slower than the ♩ = 88 and observed the subsequent "poco più lento" in its last bars; the first time it occurs in Act IV (at a tempo marked "più animato") it was almost exactly the ♩ = 88 that is marked. Now, in its final form, where the word "cantabile" appears over the violin part instead of the "dolce" of the second time, Toscanini took it slower than in either of the two earlier cases and slowed up perceptibly at the final bar of the phrase proper (see Ex. 141).

Perhaps I am easily moved, but I confess that as the curtain falls on this recorded performance of *Otello* I feel the emotional effect of what I have heard in the last couple of pages of the full score is enough to last me for some time.

I wrote the phrase "as the curtain falls" quite automatically. This whole chapter, after all, has been concerned only with discussion of a studio performance of an opera, but the predominating atmosphere of the records made of that performance has been theatrical. To Toscanini, myopic to the point of fantasy, I do not doubt that this studio performance of *Otello* was as theatrically real as any production he ever conducted in an opera house. Perhaps the lighting immediately in front of him may have appeared different, and perhaps people didn't seem to be moving about as much as usual. But there is no doubt that the music he was conducting was being performed nowhere but in a theatre.

Knowing how Toscanini approached every type of music with a determination to perform it better than he had ever performed it before, perhaps it was inconsistent of me to suggest that this *Otello* was his greatest achievement. Nevertheless, it is my own feeling that *Otello* was in the end his greatest, worthiest monument. We can hope one day to hear comparable performances of Beethoven's Ninth Symphony or *Fidelio* by other conductors—if not in this generation, then perhaps in the next. But with *Otello* there is no doubt, I think, that there can never be another performance quite so authentic, so completely personal and thoroughbred in its expression of Verdi's intentions, for the same set of circumstances can never arise again.

The mantle of Verdi, the composer, has not so far been inherited by anyone; the mantle of Verdi, the man, the musician and his artistic integrity there is little doubt fell once and for all on the shoulders of the young violoncellist from Parma he first leaned over the Scala orchestra rail and spoke to at a rehearsal of *Otello*—Arturo Toscanini.

FALSTAFF
[1893]
(Property of G. Ricordi and Co.)

Falstaff	Giuseppe Valdengo
Fenton	Antonio Madasi
Ford	Frank Guarrera
Dr Caius	Gabor Carelli
Bardolph	John Carmen Rossi
Pistol	Norman Scott
Mistress Alice Ford	Herva Nelli
Nannetta	Teresa Stich-Randall
Mistress Meg Page	Nan Merriman
Mistress Quickly	Cloe Elmo

The Robert Shaw Chorale and NBC Symphony Orchestra

GREAT BRITAIN: HMV ALP 1229/30/31
U.S.A.: Victor LM 6111
1950

Falstaff, I believe, was the work above all others that Toscanini most loved and most enjoyed conducting, for Verdi's last opera had its particular place in his affections and, indeed, in his professional life also. Toscanini's first association with the opera dated from one of his early seasons at the Carlo Felice, when, in 1894, he had to appeal to Verdi, who always wintered in Genoa, to be proved right by the composer on a matter of some disagreement with the Carlo Felice cast over tempo or nuance in the opera.*

From those early days onwards Toscanini regarded *Falstaff* with a special kind of reverence. He included it in his first season at La Scala in 1898 and again in his first season at the Metropolitan ten years later; he chose it for the centenary celebrations of Verdi's birth at Busseto in 1913; he reopened La Scala with it after the First German War, when he became conductor, administrator and virtually stage-director of the entire concern in 1921; he conducted it at Busseto again in 1926, on the twenty-fifth anniversary of Verdi's death; he took the opera in the repertoire of the Scala company in 1929 when they went on tour to Vienna and Berlin; he conducted it in his first season of operas at the Salzburg Festival of 1935; he planned to conduct it again in 1951 at Busseto to commemorate the fiftieth anniversary of Verdi's death, and the idea of a Toscanini *Falstaff* was one of the great publicity angles to draw attention to the inauguration of La Piccola Scala in 1955. That Toscanini did not, in fact, take part in either of the two last-mentioned enterprises is neither here nor there: for sixty years he always thought of *Falstaff* as a work for a joyful occasion, and it was probably only his respect for the German temperament that prevented his opening the Bayreuth Festival with it.

Toscanini's famous principle of "seeing what is there" was never better proclaimed than by his performance of *Falstaff*. To say that he saw the work as a gigantic scherzo is to oversimplify things, though the predominant mood is one of astonishing vitality and gaiety; but whereas these qualities are readily apparent from the most casual look at what is there in the score, Toscanini somehow saw things in those pages which only his eyes could discern. It was as though Verdi spoke to him in a language which he and Toscanini alone could understand, for there is something uniquely authentic and peculiarly

* See the author's *Great Opera Houses*, p. 270.

toscaninianesco about a superbly exhilarating experience. Above all, of course, the whole performance makes the music sound so brand new that one feels, as a French critic said of the 1935 Salzburg performance which I heard, as though one were hearing the work for the first time "dans son texte original".

My memory of that performance, the only one I ever heard of a Verdi opera conducted by Toscanini in a theatre, has not so much been obliterated by the later recording as confirmed by it. Details which I remembered vividly from twenty years ago are there to be noticed as wonderfully executed and conceived as before—only more so. Because of the opportunity to compare the two experiences—or rather, to compare the memory of one with the reality of the other, I find more convincing than ever Toscanini's confession: "It has never seemed possible to me that I could have understood ten or twenty years ago something I understand today. . . ."

This ability to discover a new aspect of a familiar piece of music was one of Toscanini's unique gifts and there is today—as I remember there was in 1935—an almost unbelievable spontaneity and enthusiasm in the music which can have been equalled for sheer unexpectedness only by the experience of the première of the opera itself in 1893. Indeed, one does not know in the end what to marvel at more—the composition of the opera by a man in his eightieth year, or its performance by a conductor in his eighty-fourth. Perhaps it was appropriate that Toscanini should have provided a parallel to something of what Boito called Verdi's "Olympian old age" (a phrase which I am sorry to see the author of the analytical notes to this *Falstaff* recording has translated as "olympic old age", which is not quite what Boito intended). Verdi and Toscanini were both natives of the province of Parma; they spoke the same dialect; their temperament and vitality, their strength of character and unshakable artistic intransigence were qualities they had in common and typical of the contradictory nature of the *parmigiani*—so intensely and aggressively Italian in their nationalism one moment, and so sensitively conscious and parochially proud of the debt they owe to the rule and patronage of Marie Louise the next.

When Toscanini died, a fellow citizen wrote how the conductor had been all his life a typical "figlio del loggione"—a son of that famous gallery of the Teatro Regio of his native city which is unequalled in Italy for the fury of its criticism and the warmth of its affections. It was from the *loggione*, the writer said, that Toscanini inherited all his *furie* and *carezze* and I think that nowhere are these two characteristic qualities more apparent, more intensely developed than in his conducting of *Falstaff*. From the fierce fury and brilliance of the first chord of the opera to the warm caress of the midsummer magic of the music in Windsor Forest, this was a glowing, incomparable achievement.

ACT I

Scene 1

If ever one were to be asked by somebody who had heard neither what kind of opera *Falstaff* was and what manner of conductor Toscanini was, the answer is surely in the first note of the first bar of this recording. For if ever anything loudly and immediately proclaimed its whole purpose and intention and made the listener sit up and take notice, it is the sound of this opening chord of C major. It is played *fortissimo* and *allegro vivace* as the score indicates and for all such expression marks are worth in Toscanini's view of music.

Falstaff has been described as a great scherzo; it was not until I heard Toscanini conduct it that I realized it is something of a concerto for the piccolo as well. The conductor's unique concern for instrumental detail emphasized Verdi's quite astonishing exploitation of all the instrument's possibilities in all its moods—perky, lyrical, loud, soft, and pensive and subdued. High-fidelity takes no credit for this so far as the recording of *Falstaff* is concerned, for it is not due to any electronic ingenuity; it would have been audible in an acoustic recording, since it is the result of Toscanini's instinctive attitude to "what is there". The role played by the piccolo is such a revelation in this performance, indeed, that I was not surprised to find that there seem to be only about forty-one bars all told (and all but seven of those in the last scene of the opera) when the piccolo player puts aside the instrument to "double" third flute.

In the first few pages of the score of this recording we have a clear indication of what we are to expect. There is sparkle and dazzling brilliance, but there is an immense grace; there is a wonderful rhythmic vitality, but there are tenderness and a great elasticity; there is an infallible, if sometimes unexpected, choice of tempo, but there is an equally infallible sense of when a spontaneous (i.e. not indicated) *ritenuto* is not only permissible, but entirely stylistically and unanswerably right.

Quite early in the opening scene Toscanini makes what—according to the score—is an unauthorized *ritenuto* at Dr Caius' indignant:

Ex. 159

This is a nuance which may be justified as giving emphasis to Caius' words: "I shall force you to answer me!", and, a little later when the same kind of passage crops up again, to Caius' indignant complaint that when he had been made drunk by Falstaff's two ruffians, Bardolph and Pistol, his pockets had been rifled. It is not a *ritenuto* I remember having encountered in other performances of *Falstaff*, but heard in Toscanini's performance it fits in so naturally that one feels it was always meant to be there.

The next thing that made me sit up was not an unconventional treatment of a passage like the Dr Caius *ritenuto*, but the completely literal observation of what Verdi wrote in the score: the figure with which the trombones punctuate Dr Caius' oath that next time he gets drunk in a tavern it will be among honest people:

Ex. 160

Usually that phrase, and its counterpart two bars later, is played so explosively that the effect is deafening. Toscanini characteristically put music back into it once more by playing it *forte* instead of *fortissimo* and insisting on the clear articulation of the notes as the composer indicated.

Where the first bar of the opera in Toscanini's performance gives an immediate indication of how one aspect of Verdi's score is going to sound, there now follows an equally immediate indication of how another aspect is going to sound: we hear Toscanini's way with one of the numberless tunes which give *Falstaff* its uniquely generous quota of lyrical charm. The warmth and *grazia* Toscanini brings to the little tune of Falstaff's appreciation of the luminous properties of Bardolph's nose,

Ex. 161

was typical of the conductor's obsession with the need for instruments to "sing" with such infectious conviction that I find one invariably joins in oneself. It is Toscanini's full expression of the emotions of the music, the fierce contrasts he creates without hesitation from one moment to another which make this such a fascinating revelation of Verdi's score, so that one is consistently surprised by the unexpectedness, following the gentle lyrical atmosphere of the passage just quoted, of such things as the violent orchestral comment on the penniless Falstaff's defiant shout to the innkeeper for another bottle of sack.

It is the lightning changes of thought, the quick-wittedness of the music of *Falstaff*, in itself so hard to analyse, which makes this performance, of all the Toscanini performances of Verdi we know, so difficult to annotate. No mood is ever sustained for very long; even a "number" like Falstaff's discourse on Honour which ends this first scene, constantly changes from one mood to another so that the opera resembles a kind of musical mosaic which it is the conductor's job to put together in such a way that nothing is missing from the over-all picture. Toscanini's remarkable gift of maintaining the continuity of music makes this process of putting-together a fascinating experience for the listener. One may *see* the joins between the pieces in the score, where they are shown by time and tempo indications; but one never *hears* a join in this performance, and that is one of its characteristic joys. As an example of

Toscanini's unequalled ability to establish a new tempo instantaneously and surely, there are few better than the little *fugato* marked *Allegro presto* when Falstaff sends the page off with the two letters in the passage immediately preceding the Honour sequence. This was a superbly conceived demonstration of the meaning of the word "leggero" and the clarity of Verdi's part-writing.

Scene 2

The curtain rises on this scene, if you remember, with a sparkling passage for woodwind and horns which begins:

Ex. 162

It is pardonable to suggest that there can be a little confusion about the tempo this should be played at; the printed orchestral score marks ♩. = 108, while Verdi's autograph very clearly indicates 126. I have no theory to offer of why this disparity should exist, although it seems that Verdi may have had second thoughts on the passage altogether when the manuscript shows the last two notes in Ex. 162 with a slur over them and the printed score shows them detached, as they appear above.

Toscanini, ignoring the *texte original* and the revised version so far as the question of tempo is concerned, starts off with a dazzling ♩. = 138, which settles the matter of the right speed once and for all, but doesn't let us hear the effect of Verdi's original idea of a slur over the last two notes of the tune I have quoted.

I find Toscanini's acceptance of the printed score in this second matter the more puzzling because he was known to have gone back to the original manuscript again and again— and in the process, as we know, to have discovered between the pages of the score Verdi's moving little personal *envoi* to his opera in the form of a paraphrase of the passage in the libretto: "Va, va, vecchio John . . .".

What was it that decided Toscanini against accepting

Verdi's original phrasing of those two notes? Or didn't he notice the difference? It is impossible that this legendary myope, peering at the music with his nose pressed against the page of the score, can have overlooked the slur in the manuscript, for his perception of what was written was as acute as his hearing of what was played. It remains an intriguing and now, alas, insoluble mystery.

The short orchestral introduction in the recording is once more an indication of the nature of what is to come. Its *scherzando* gaiety and sparkle are mirrored by the Merry Wives throughout the action which succeeds it, and Toscanini's faster-than-official tempo is justified by the convincing quality of the laughter which follows Alice's reading of Falstaff's letter. Too often the indicated "Allegro più presto" at this point is lifeless and the laughter a little hollow and forced—largely because the basic tempo has so far been too slow for the Allegro to have anything to be "più presto" than, as it were. But lifelessness is the last thing encountered in this *Falstaff*, and in the bar immediately after the four women's laughter their indignant cries of "Monster!" are punctuated with an almost alarming ferocity by the brass. (As in his performance of *Otello* the orchestral punctuation by Toscanini of the dialogue sequences in *Falstaff* had immense clarity and thoroughly musical significance.)

Unexpectedly fast the general tempo may seem to be, but there is no doubt that again and again it proves to be right because it is relaxed and corresponds to the natural pulse of the whole performance. Only a relaxed performance by singers and orchestra could ever give the charm and clarity Toscanini brings to the famous nonet of the four women and the five men (who sing their 2/2 against the women's 6/8); this complicated little polyphonic, polyrhythmic passage is remarkable for its quite astonishing lucidness.

Those who may expect the worst from Toscanini—those, that is, who have been brought up in the past decade to regard him as the incorrigible slave-driver, who stands over the immortal lyrical moments of music cracking a relentless whip in the cause of "tempo"—can prepare themselves at this stage of *Falstaff* for one of the most moving, gentle performances of moving, gentle lyricism in all their born days.

Again the scene between Nannetta and Fenton is one which, on first hearing, gives the impression of being taken too fast; in fact it is played below the metronome's specified ♩ = 126. The clear orchestral texture, the urgency and warmth of the dramatic situation so wonderfully translated into music, give an illusion of speed which in reality is not there. Every tiny suggestion of *dolce* or *dolcissimo* marked in the score is made the most of, and a scene which, when it begins, one is almost inclined to regard as likely to be cold and casual, develops into something to bring tears to the eyes.

In this performance of Toscanini's I found myself more than ever grateful for Verdi's inspired reprise of the boy-and-girl duet after its interruption by the three older women, for if ever one felt there was something one wanted to hear again, it is this.

The reprise, like the unexpectedly restrained tempo of the first part of the duet, has its particular and unanticipatable surprise in Toscanini's irresistible slowing-up towards the end of the duet, in the passage beginning with:

Ex. 163

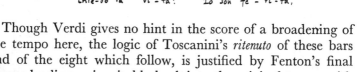

Though Verdi gives no hint in the score of a broadening of the tempo here, the logic of Toscanini's *ritenuto* of these bars and of the eight which follow, is justified by Fenton's final phrase leading so inevitably back into the original tempo with the thrown-away:

Ex. 164

Again it is a case of having to have something to perform faster than; hence Toscanini's affecting and effective *ritenuto* of the preceding bars.

For the rest, from this point on, the scene is largely a recapitulation of a great deal that has gone before, with the cross-rhythm nonetheless clear and intelligible for being scored more fully the second time.

The Coda to the whole scene is a paraphrase of the 6/8 passage which began it (Ex. 162). Toscanini takes this—now marked simply "vivace"—at such a speed that one bursts out laughing at the sheer audacity and high spirits of the whole idea. There is no metronome marking for this passage in the score, but it is logical to presume, as most conductors do, that it should be roughly the same tempo as at the start of the scene. Toscanini ignores this possibility and instead of reverting to his earlier ♩. = 138 settles for a brilliant rip-roaring 168 or thereabouts. It is the most exhilarating and unexpected moment in the entire performance, which bristles with exhilarating and unexpected moments. The only trouble is that one can no longer imagine it ever being performed in any other way. But that is one of the dangers of the whole business of the Toscanini Legacy.

ACT II

Scene 1

Having ended Act I at an extremely unconventional tempo, Toscanini began the recording of Act II with almost academic propriety at more or less the officially indicated metronome marking of ♩. = 80. He underlines the "vivace" quality of the Allegro vivace direction, not by speed this time, but by an exquisite lightness in the orchestral playing where every expression mark is given meticulous attention.

After such a scintillating beginning the music accompanying the arrival of Mistress Quickly and her exaggerated obeisances sounds quite remarkably slow. And so, in fact, it is. Toscanini interprets "assai moderato" as about ♩ = 60 instead of the recommended 80 of the score. The effect of this is intriguing and, I imagine, only possible if you have an artist like Cloe Elmo there to sing Mistress Quickly; instead of sounding, as it might so easily do, intolerably drawn out, it has a quite remarkably humorous quality, a mock-solemnity which is entirely in keeping with the composer's musical characterization. But, as I say, I think it needs a singer who can sustain the comedy convincingly if the idea is to come off. (Unfortunately,

I cannot remember any details of this scene in Toscanini's Salzburg performance of 1935, so I cannot say that it was necessarily one of his invariable habits to adopt this slow tempo. I can only presume that whatever he did on that occasion sounded right, and it is only now, after hearing a great many more non-Toscanini *Falstaffs* since that date than I had heard before, that it suddenly pulls me up with a jerk.)

The reader who, not having heard this recording of *Falstaff*, may fear that Toscanini's slow tempo deprives the performance of wit and humour may rest assured that nothing less likely can be imagined. The delicious touches to be found in the detail of this performance are endless and enchanting, as for instance the echo of the famous phrase "dalle due alle tre" by the violins and its re-echoing by the violoncellos two octaves lower:

Ex. 165

It is unfortunately hopelessly impossible to quote a fraction of what deserves quoting of this performance, for it abounds in intriguing little musical gestures and asides like this; but it is typical of the sort of things Toscanini did which were peculiar and, it seems, inimitable.

Lightness of musical touch is the prevailing characteristic of the scenes between Falstaff and Ford (it would be a dreary performance if it were not, in all conscience), with a specially noteworthy veneer of charm added to Ford's narration (in his guise of "Signor Fontana") of his hopeless passion for a certain Alice Ford:

Ex. 166

Charm, on the other hand, is understandably not one of the elements one expects to encounter in Ford's monologue. This

is made to sound quite exceptionally fierce and is characterized
by an orchestral attack—especially in the unison string passages
between Ford's short catalogue of the things he would sooner
trust than his wife—which crackles and spits in a way which I
remember impressed me so much in the Salzburg performance.

The ferocity of this scene establishes a powerful mood which
provides a superb contrast with the little sequence which
follows on Falstaff's return to the scene dressed up to the nines
for his visit to Mistress Ford.

The violins play

Ex. 167

a theme of delightful optimism and elegance which Toscanini
made unforgettable at Salzburg, and which he repeats in this
performance by the same device—that of adding a hint of a
glissando and a harmonic so that the third bar sounds:

Ex. 168

This was one of the immortal Toscanini touches which made
his *Falstaff* a unique experience.

Scene 2

The short instrumental introduction to this scene is indeed
ppp and *leggerissimo* and as evocative of mischievous feminine
conspiracy as one could imagine. Toscanini's tempo for ♩ is
nearer 152 than the 132 in the score, but although the score is
headed "Allegro brillante" in practice the effect is oddly
moderato. Once more it is a characteristically deceptive tempo,
in this case sounding not faster than it is in fact, but because of
the secretive nature of the music rather slower than one would
expect.

The elegance and delicate *scherzando* mood of this opening
recurs repeatedly throughout the rest of the scene (with

Mistress Quickly's fruity account of her meeting with Falstaff providing a richly comic interruption at the same solemn tempo of the previous scene), and Toscanini gives it a finely cut chamber-music quality to add extra point and a suggestion of ill-suppressed excitement to the little sequence for strings which accompanies the laying out of the "props" for the humiliation of Falstaff—the screen, chairs, laundry basket and so on.

These pages in the score, and particularly the enchanting quartet which is started off by Alice—

Ex. 169

are among the most ravishing moments in the whole recording. So far. There are more to come. In fact, more come almost immediately on Falstaff's entrance, when Alice's music is made to sound so seductive that one is on the point of wondering whether the joke hasn't gone too far.

There is also just a hint of an underlying sadness in Giuseppe Valdengo's singing of "Quand'ero paggio". His interpretation of Falstaff is generally and not unreasonably regarded as lacking in maturity; but in this particular little scene Toscanini suggests a regret in Falstaff's recollection of his youth, by taking the passage quite appreciably slower than one would expect—or indeed, than one usually hears. Instead of the score's $\bignote = 112$, Toscanini lets it make its point at an easy tempo of something like 100. It is an interesting touch and oddly wistful.

The return of Mistress Quickly, with her warning that Mistress Page wants to talk urgently to Alice Ford, introduces the semi-quaver figure ("Allegro agitato, pianissimo e molto staccato") which is the basis of the *moto perpetuo* on which the Finale slowly builds from this point onwards.

Toscanini's sense of tempo-continuity was never more clearly demonstrated than in this Finale. Metronome markings do not count; it is the pulse of the music which is irresistible and abolishes any suspicion of "joins" between one tempo or mood

and another. So it is that, as Verdi indicated with his instruction "Lo stesso movimento", the short duet for Nannetta and
Fenton hiding behind the screen, fits in with the over-all tempo
and excitement as though it were an ingeniously super-imposed
passage of counterpoint in a complicated polyphonic movement. This little intermezzo, incidentally, accompanied
largely by woodwind and horns, introduces a lovely sound
from the orchestra—again that crystal-clear chamber-music
quality which Toscanini inspired in the playing of this
miraculous score.

    There is one notable detail, another of those details which
Toscanini makes theatrically so effective that they get a laugh
all to themselves; it occurs in the mercurial passage of the
woodwind as Nannetta and Fenton are heard kissing behind
the screen:

Ex. 170

  (This is a wonderful perception of "what is there"—a
purely theatrical moment of wit making more impact in a
broadcasting studio performance by Toscanini than in a
hundred performances in the theatre by other conductors.)

    The Finale resumes with the great ensemble of the angrily
apprehensive men and the highly amused women, a movement
making its effect by being taken at a superbly strict tempo to
heighten the tension before the anti-climax of the discovery of
Nannetta and Fenton behind the screen, instead of the expected
Falstaff and Alice.

    The *moto perpetuo* takes over again, an astonishing example
of Toscanini's ability to polish an already brilliant score to the
point of dazzling and delighting the listener by the integration
of meticulously observed detail into an uniquely effective
whole.

    This Finale alone—particularly with its endless instances of
the conductor's power to maintain continuity of rhythm and
tempo so that not a moment of musical thought, or the quality
of the musical sound is interrupted by the sudden contrasts of

ff and *pp* in the accompaniment—is worthy of a lifetime of study by any student of conducting.

ACT III

Scene 1

"I do not know who taught it to me, but I repeat again and again this true saying: 'In a *pianissimo* every player should play so that he can no longer hear his own instrument; in a *fortissimo*, every player should play so that he can hear his own instrument above everything.' "

Perhaps in this maxim of Toscanini's we have at last a faint clue to one of his peculiar secrets: his prodigious control over the dynamics in music. The student conductor, at any rate, might bear it in mind and see what happens, though I fear he is not likely to achieve quite the effect that Toscanini, practising what he preached, achieved with the staggering crescendo to the tutti *ff sempre staccato* of the orchestral introduction to this first scene in Act III, based on the *moto perpetuo* of the previous scene. This is a magnificent din growing from the quiet rumbling of the double basses (starting *molto staccato e ppp* or merely *pp* according to whether you read the words above or below their stave in the orchestral score) to the ear-splitting repeated semi-quavers of the climax.

The anger and indignation of Falstaff, as he sits outside the inn after his ducking in the Thames, is wonderfully expressed in Verdi's music, and Toscanini brings all the necessary darkness to the general "black" mood by careful observation of the dynamics in such phrases as the gloomy:

Ex. 171

Toscanini's same sensibility to dynamics naturally colours the famous trill in the orchestra as Falstaff feels the wine warming his veins. This is always, in almost anybody's performance, a characteristically effective bit of Verdi's orchestral virtuosity;

as Toscanini plays it, it has the superbly dramatic effect of underlining Falstaff's angry irritation at the re-appearance of Mistress Quickly to such an extent that we in the audience find ourselves wholly on his side.

The brilliance of the climax of the crescendo trill makes Mistress Quickly's anti-climatic "Reverenza" superbly comic; and unexpected as well, of course, as infuriating. What man, least of all one like Falstaff, having recovered something of his equanimity after his adventures, wants to be interrupted in the middle of a highly salubrious draught of wine by a woman with some damn-fool message concerning another woman who has already landed him in enough trouble?

But precisely because Toscanini stresses Falstaff's irritation the scene which follows is remarkably convincing and persuasive. The success of Mistress Quickly's wheedling is immediate—as, indeed, it can hardly fail to be when we hear the ethereal sound Toscanini draws out of the three trumpets and one trombone at the phrase:

Ex. 172

The irritation and disgruntledness depart with Falstaff's exit into the interior of the inn with Mistress Quickly. From now on until the end of this scene, Toscanini's *Falstaff*—he would have hated to have heard it described like that—is a sensuous experience of quite astonishing richness and loveliness.

The whole performance has an air of *sotto voce* fun and elegance ("con eleganza" is the first expression to catch the eye in the orchestral score when Alice has finished relaying to the rest of the conspirators, the instruction Quickly is giving Falstaff about the midnight rendezvous at Herne's Oak) and ends with a coda of overwhelmingly magical charm. How it is done I have not the faintest idea. There are no tricks; there is no tempo that one can say is "better" than another; there are no unexpected dynamics; there is nothing Toscanini does which is not transparently just "what is there". It is a magical experience—the supreme performance of one of the supremely beautiful passages in all opera.

Scene 2

The closing moments of the preceding scene prepare us for the enchantment of the one that follows in a way which must be without parallel.

"Think for a moment," Toscanini once said, "how many musical devices—beautiful ones, certainly—Wagner needs to describe the night of Nuremberg. And look how Verdi does the same thing *with three notes*. . . ."

Which exactly the three notes were that Toscanini was referring to, I am not certain. They could be the B, A and G sharp of the phrase which is repeated in the strings at the end of Scene 1:

Ex. 173

or the three notes on the natural A flat *basso* horn heard in the distance as the curtain rises on Windsor Great Park in Scene 2:

Ex. 174

Either way, there is little doubt what Toscanini means; the one scene ends and the next begins with the most richly evocative midsummer-night music and it is music which in this performance has an exceptional warmth and charm. The *dolcissimo* echo by the woodwind of the Nannetta–Fenton theme (see page 304) after the first horn call, for instance— always a golden moment in the score—is burnished still more by the sort of unpredictable, unauthorized, irresistibly melting rubato which Toscanini alone seemed to know how to per- form, so that it sounded like a catch in the breath that was gone almost before you realized it had happened.

These first two phrases—the off-stage horn and the 2-bar echo of the young lovers' music—are quite unanalysably full of "atmosphere". Or so they seem to be until, with Toscanini's performance to help you, you go to the score and look for "what is there". It is as simple and inexplicable as that.

The atmosphere of this last scene, so firmly established in the first note of the orchestral introduction, is overwhelming in Toscanini's performance; and it is not merely the memory of a Salzburg production of a couple of decades ago that makes it so. It is as strongly and physically real and alive in the comparative daguerrotype of an LP recording, as it was to those of us who heard Toscanini conduct the opera in 1935.

In practice, the last scene of this recording is virtually impossible to annotate in any detail. From the first three or four bars Toscanini establishes almost what one might call a proprietary right to the music which it is useless to dispute.

Details there certainly are which emerge from the performance as it proceeds, but one fears they are less examples from which would-be conductors can learn, than by which they may be generally (and perhaps wisely) discouraged from any intention of pursuing their careers. In spite of the slender clue provided by Toscanini's maxim quoted on page 310, what can anybody really learn of his secret of the gradation of the dynamics of the passages based on the string phrase which accompanies Falstaff's entrance?

Ex. 175   Andante sostenuto

This motif ranges, from bar to bar, between *fff* and *ppp* in varying intensities of string volume—sometimes with first and second violins and violas in unison, sometimes with first violins alone, sometimes with the entire string orchestra sharing it in unison across two octaves. This much any fool can learn from the score, anyway; what I fear he cannot learn is how Toscanini succeeded in making the *ppp* a quieter form of the *fff*, avoiding inaudibility in one, coarseness in the other, and allowing music to be absent from neither.

A moment later we are back in the gossamer world that might almost be defined as "the *Falstaff* staccato" when Alice arrives on the scene and Falstaff proclaims his love for her.

Here again there is that wonderful lightness of touch and literal observation of such little Verdi instructions as "ppp ma sensibile".

Toscanini's unique sense of orchestral colour reaches what must be its supreme manifestation, however, in the nocturne enchantment of Nannetta's fairy song. Here the sheer sound is so exquisitely evocative that if one did not know that Verdi intended this music to take us into a world of midsummer play-acting, it might almost appear out of character. Which, strictly speaking, it always was, of course: the company are only *pretending* to be fairies, they aren't real ones. On the other hand, they are real to Falstaff; and also, one suggests, to Verdi and Toscanini. But it is always something of a paradox that a composer who spent his life writing flesh-and-blood-and-thunder music to express the flesh-and-blood-and-thunder emotions of love, hatred and violent death, should have ended his operatic career with a movement of magical fairy-tale make-believe.

The midsummer night's dream is shattered violently as the music starts on what is virtually the finale of the opera: the 6/8 introduction to the "pizzica" chorus. Toscanini's tempo at this point is notable as being the basic tempo of the whole of the rest of the scene; in spite of various little interludes of a different tempo, sooner or later we are always returning to what is the natural pulse of the music. In Boat Race parlance it is a high rate of striking—about 138 to the minute—but the sheer mathematics of the matter do not affect the final superb effectiveness of this whole performance.

Never for a moment, however, does Toscanini allow the music to become the slave of a rigid tempo; there are still moments of elasticity, of the little unexpected and breathtaking *ritenuto*. And particularly moments of that lyrical warmth and charm which distinguishes the entire score and Toscanini's performance of it. There is little in the entire opera more disarming than Falstaff's effusive recognition of Ford, nor more *graziosa* than the minuet-like music which accompanies the marriage of the two veiled and masked couples:

Ex. 176   Allegretto

In the finale of the Finale, the Coda to this gigantic genial hundred-minute scherzo—in other words, the fugue that brings down the curtain of *Falstaff*—the natural pulse of Toscanini's performance is sensed again. The indicated "Allegro brioso" is taken by the conductor in the spirit in which it is given by the composer: one can imagine nothing more literally *allegro* nor more joyously *brioso* than the crystal-clear polyphony and excitement of the performance of this superbly apt end to Verdi's opera. Here we see the joint creators of this musical mosaic—Verdi as designer, and Toscanini as practising craftsman-mosaicist—putting the final touches to the masterpiece which is Verdi's *Falstaff*.

This performance, perhaps like no other in the history of the work, is indeed "Verdi's *Falstaff*". And that, I am sure, is what Toscanini himself hoped he had achieved in these records. But it is difficult not to describe it as "Toscanini's *Falstaff*" too; in his inimitable revelation of the score what is the purest first-water Verdi is automatically the purest first-water Toscanini.

As the applause dies away at the end of the last record one is left with mixed feelings: a feeling of sadness, at the end of this great gaiety, that we shall never hear the like of Toscanini again, but also, more optimistically, that Verdi's *Falstaff* was surely predestined for this performance by Toscanini, as the supreme example of his ability to see "what is there".

MESSA DA REQUIEM
[1874]

Herva Nelli (soprano)
Fedora Barbieri (mezzo-soprano)
Giuseppe di Stefano (tenor)
Cesare Siepi (bass)
Robert Shaw Chorale
NBC Symphony Orchestra

GREAT BRITAIN: HMV ALP 1380/1
RCA RB–16131/2
U.S.A.: Victor LM 6018
1951

No 1. Requiem

Just as the first chord of *Falstaff* conducted by Toscanini indicated at once what class and manner of performance to expect, so the opening bars of his Verdi Requiem always suggested that we were in for a mercifully unsentimental view of a work which, for all its dramatic power and spirit, suffers more than its fair share of sentimentalization in performance. I was thinking in this connection particularly of a performance of the Requiem under Victor De Sabata during the Scala company's visit to England in 1950, when the opening page of the score was played so quietly as to make musical nonsense; at least, I do not see what musical sense there was to be found in such near-inaudibility that one had to *watch* the music being played instead of hearing it. But, as we have seen in the case of "Era la notte" in *Otello* (p. 288) Maestro De Sabata is given— though by no means alone in this world—to moments of exaggeration.

Paradoxically, where in nearly every other case Toscanini so noticeably put things back into Verdi's scores which an unjustifiable tradition had taken out, with the Requiem it was the things which were *not* there for the casual student to see in the score that made Toscanini's performance a unique experience. Certainly there were numerous instances of his inspired observance of literal instructions so often ignored by others;

but equally there were many inspired moments of interpretation of the *spirit* of Verdi's music which led one to wonder why nobody had ever thought of things that way before.

In this very first section of Toscanini's recording (apart from being able to hear what Verdi wrote as the curtain rises, so to speak) there are moments of remarkable literal fulfilment of the composer's hopes and intentions—hopes and intentions fulfilled by Toscanini's uncanny and inimitable control over orchestral dynamics and his conception of the whole line of the music.

As a model of these two phenomenal qualities there is little to compare with Toscanini's phrasing and unexaggerated treatment of the accents in the string passage accompanying the four sopranos' "dona dona eis, Domine:" and of the sudden *ppp* which follows it:

Ex. 177

Toscanini's remarkable gift of introducing the sudden *ppp* after a crescendo is something which, to me, remains un-analysable even after intensive study of the performances considered in this volume. Other conductors achieve something which they may consider approximates such a thing, but on inspection it is found that it is an effect obtained only by inter-rupting the rhythm of the whole, or by the introduction of a false note of theatricalism; one can almost see them suddenly crouching down on the rostrum to ensure that the orchestra—and audience—do not miss the great dramatic point.

Almost immediately after Toscanini has demonstrated the art of the post-crescendo *ppp*, we encounter in this recording the first of the conductor's—— I was going to say the first of his "departures" from the score. In fact he is not going away from what the composer wrote, so much as getting extremely close to it. When he consulted Verdi about a rallentando which seemed to him implicit in the composer's *Te Deum* but which was not indicated in the score, Toscanini was told that any true musician would know a rallentando was admissable at that point; Verdi had not marked it in the score because he knew that if he had done so the unmusical would instinctively and inevitably have exaggerated it out of all proportion.

Toscanini's whole reading of the Requiem was justified by Verdi's assurance to him regarding the *Te Deum*: the true musician will know instinctively what is needed. And this, I think, is borne out by the unqualified stylistic effectiveness of everything Toscanini did in this work.

The first entry of the tenor soloist, who begins the Kyrie, is made with the superbly arresting phrase:

Ex. 178

In the fourth bar Toscanini introduced a *tenuto* on the F sharp and allowed the singer to end the phrase in a comfortable, but not too much *ad lib*, tempo. His authority is not shown in words in the score. It is shown in the music, for it will be seen that the gentle pulsating rhythm of the strings is followed by a sustained chord in the second half of the fourth bar, suggesting that the rhythm may be interrupted at this point. This same rhythmic pattern in the accompaniment and the solo part is repeated by both composer and conductor in the imitation of the tenor's phrase by, first, the bass and then by the soprano. It is an illuminating instance of Toscanini's instinctive perception of how far—and no further—a tempo can be made flexible and still sound "right". This first movement included one other notable moment coloured by the unexpected introduction of an *espansione* of the otherwise smoothly flowing basic tempo. It occurs nineteen bars from the end when the four solo singers enter, after the hushed and dramatic "eleison" for women's voices echoed by the men's voices, with the phrase:

Ex. 179

The effect of Toscanini's *espansione* in this one bar, followed by a resumption of the tempo, is to give added point to the composer's return to the A major which is the prevailing tonality of the movement. It is also a moment which by its very breadth and warmth emphasizes the serenity which dominates the mood of this first number in the Requiem.

No 2. Dies Irae

If by some awful mischance everything of Toscanini's recording of Verdi's Requiem had perished except the Dies Irae, I feel we would still have been left with enough circumstantial evidence to be able to convince posterity that Toscanini's performance of the whole work was something without parallel. For just as the composer provides us with a synthesis of the complete Mass in the immense variety of mood and sentiment of this movement, so Toscanini revealed every aspect of the drama and lyrical richness of the work in his performance of this tremendous Sequence—and for once the adjective "tremendous" may be used literally as the noun "Sequence" is used in its liturgical sense.

For those of us who remember Toscanini's performances of the Requiem in London in 1938, the Dies Irae has perhaps an added, visual association, for it was in this movement that we saw as well as heard what may well have been the Biggest Bass Drum in the World. It was a monster instrument about six feet in diameter with, as far as one could see, only one side to it—in other words, it was like a huge tambourine but without the rattling bits of brass stuck in the frame. It had apparently been specially constructed for a performance of Verdi's Requiem at the Royal College of Music under Sir Charles Villiers Stanford and was brought out again on its first public appearance for many years for Toscanini's concerts. It made an imposing sound.

The question of the bass drum in the Dies Irae is not just a bit of *chi-chi*. Verdi made a particular point in the score of describing exactly how he wanted the instrument to be played. When it is first heard he indicated that "the cords should be very taut so that these off-beats sound short and very loud", while in the *ppp* punctuation of the bass soloist's "Mors stupebit", which follows the general hubbub of the Tuba mirum, the player is instructed to loosen the cords ("allentate le corde") and so produce a dull thud of tone.

All this and a great deal more was realized in this recorded performance, which opens in a stupendous fashion with a representation of Verdi's picture of Divine Wrath that is quite terrifying in its intensity. This was the Toscanini of the storms of the Pastoral Symphony, the *William Tell* Overture and the opening of *Otello* all rolled into one; and as in those classic performances the orchestral detail was of an unbelievable and supremely musical clarity, giving a crispness to such things as the fierce chords of G minor with which the movement starts, the trills of the horns and trumpets, the runs and arpeggios of woodwind and strings. Toscanini's preoccupation with detail made an unusually effective and sinister thing of the *pp* (but clearly audible) off-beats for flutes, piccolo, oboe and horns in the hushed passage "quantus tremor est futurus" leading to the Tuba mirum:

Ex. 180

This whole passage was so dramatically exciting that one was surprised on reflection to discover that Toscanini made neither a crescendo nor an accelerando, but in fact, as the score demands, adhered to a strict tempo, a steady *pp* ending with the prescribed two bars of *ppp*.

Toscanini's ability to create a more glorious and over-whelming musical din than any other conductor is hinted at in the recording of the slow-building fanfare which begins the Tuba mirum section; but it is no more than hinted at. To have heard this passage in the flesh is a privilege which those of us who experienced it may pardonably be permitted to boast about; not all the high-fidelity in the world, I fear, will ever succeed in re-creating the thrill of the original.

One thing, however, the recording succeeds in doing is to preserve for posterity the stirring sound of Toscanini's voice urging the players on as he drives towards the climax of the *crescendo e sempre animando* brass passages. As the full brass choir opens up at the bars marked "tutta forza" Toscanini can be heard, not singing this time, but shouting either "Più forte!" or echoing Verdi's words in the score, "Tutta forza!" It is difficult to distinguish the words, but the voice, like the result, is unmistakable. It is a touching moment.

With the temporary subsidence of the tumult of the Tuba mirum a note of dramatic tension and understatement is introduced with the bass's "Mors stupebit", a tension which Toscanini heightened by raising the tempo from the indicated ♩ = 72 to something like 80. Once again, although the dynamic accent in this little interlude is for the most part on *ppp*, there is no suggestion of exaggeration; the music is always plainly audible.

Except for a quickly dying reprise of the main theme of the Dies Irae, the dominant mood for the next few minutes of this movement is one of poignancy, a mood Toscanini sustained by allowing the music to "sing" without frills or tricks. He permitted himself an unexpected rallentando on the triplet of the first bar the last time the mezzo-soprano sings the phrase,

Ex. 181

but for the rest he made the music speak for itself by scrupulous observance of Verdi's instructions. In consequence there is something touchingly pathetic about the sound of the bassoon figure which is heard at the beginning of the mezzo-soprano's solo on Side 2 ("Quid sum miser tunc dicturus") and in the violoncellos' diminuendo chromatic run at the end of it, after the words "sit securus?"

As a model of phrasing and the interpretation of Verdi's markings, there is little I can think of to compare with the effect of Toscanini's literal way with the bar for violins, played an octave higher than the flutes and clarinets, as the soloists have their unison phrase to the word "secundus":

Ex. 182

It is a model because the dividing line between what is permissible (and moving) and what is not (and sentimental) is so
dangerously narrow. Toscanini's performance of the Requiem,
as I have already suggested, was full of such instances of
exceptionally unexceptionable and inspired divergences which
in their way may well prove to offer dangerous precedents to
conductors who do not possess Toscanini's sense of restraint and
timing.

   "Timing", indeed, was perhaps the rarest of all Toscanini's gifts and the least easily analysed. It was his sense of
timing, for instance, which permitted him to introduce a
stringendo towards the end of the first sequence of "Rex
tremendae majestatis", and to return so easily, without any
sense of interruption or heavy going, to "Lo stesso tempo"
which introduces the duet for mezzo-soprano and soprano,
"Recordare Jesu pie". Apart from the relaxed and telling
phrasing of the reiterated figure for violoncellos in this
duet, the episode is remarkable for the exemplary timing
of the pauses Verdi marks in the voice-parts at such
phrases as:

Ex. 183

Toscanini, knowing instinctively when to continue after a
pause like that, made the pause itself a magical moment of
music suspended in mid-air.

   The tenor's solo which followed is far more carefully anno-
tated by the composer than one would imagine from the way it
is generally performed. Consequently Toscanini approached
the *scena* (it is difficult to regard "Ingemisco" as anything less)
paying careful attention to Verdi's requests that the music
should be sung "dolce", "dolce con calma", and "dolcissimo",
and presenting us with a movement of immense *grazia*, filled
with lyrical warmth and entirely devoid of any suggestion of
sentimentality.

   In the bass solo immediately following on the tenor's *scena*,
we are accustomed to hearing a moving phrase to the words

"Oro supplex et acclinis" accompanied by the orchestra in this manner:

Ex. 184   Andante

The accents shown above are not what Verdi wrote, but they are what we usually hear. Toscanini, on the other hand, played the phrase as it appears in the score, namely:

Ex. 185   Andante

and at once it is infinitely more effective and so unquestionably right. It was the question once more of "what is there", as it was in the case of the literal acceptance of the accents marked in "Era la notte" (p. 288).

The rest of the movement was remarkable for several characteristic Toscanini touches—the easy-flowing tempo of the "Lacrymosa" which was taken only a fraction faster than the indicated ♩ = 60 (about 63) and which in its avoidance of heavy lugubriousness lost none of the pathos of Verdi's music; the typically telling *ppp* after the climax of the soprano's broken cries of "lacrymosa", accompanied by the wonderfully characteristic weeping figure marked "come un lamento" which Verdi used all his life to express tears; and the effective slowing up of the last three bars of all to allow the full flavour of the rich *pp* chords of the full orchestra to be enjoyed and also, one suspects, to give the effect of a "slow curtain" to bring this first act of a tremendous musical drama to a close.

No 3. Offertorio

The first refreshing difference between his and other performances was in the tempo at which Toscanini interpreted Andante mosso. He took it briskly and at once the pulse of the music was healthy and normal. It was a tempo sounding so unmistakably right that it was only curiosity, not incredulity, which led me to compare it with the metronome and to learn that against the score's 𝅘𝅥𝅭 = 66 Toscanini played it in fact only at 69, though sometimes expanding it to a tempo appreciably below the official 66.

Because of the intensely *cantabile* nature of the tunes in the first section of this movement, there is what seems a universal tendency to take it too slowly. In Toscanini's hands the music took on a new life, and he was not above throwing in an *animando* for good measure in the long crescendo to the climax of the solo quartet.

Fortunately audible in the recording is some hint of the lovely instrumental sound Toscanini always drew from the accompaniment to the first statement of the tenor's "Hostias" theme. The tremolando strings and the gradation of tone from *ppp* to *pp* and back again provide an exquisite instance of Toscanini's unique ability to make the pure sound of any orchestra he ever conducted unlike that of any other, or, indeed, of the same orchestra under any other conductor. (For the benefit of those who would have posterity regard Toscanini as the Great Slave Driver and Singers' Galley Master of music it may be pointed out that he took the Adagio 𝅘𝅥 = 66 of the "Hostias" at 54, which is very much slower than one usually hears it.)

There is what I imagine amounts to a proof-correction detail to be noticed in the course of this section. The tenor's first phrase ends:

Ex. 186

and is matched symmetrically at the end of the bass's solo in F a few bars later. The tenor's repetition of his C major phrase ends with the words "de morte transire ad vitam", the last word of which is later echoed in the minor by the soprano. In the orchestral score published by Ricordi in 1913, however, the soprano part appears thus:

Ex. 187

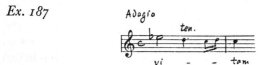

Toscanini, with precedent and formal logic behind him, regarded the expression "ten." in that passage as an engraver's error for the "tr." which appears in every other instance. He also permitted a suggestion of "ten." as well in performance, but that, after all, was a naturally polite gesture to allow a lady time to enjoy the trill the engraver would have denied her.

No 4. Sanctus

The Sanctus is the first, and indeed only, exclusively choral number in Verdi's Requiem; it is also the first movement of an entirely polyphonic character, for we are confronted not only with a first and second choir but with a double fugue as well, apart from a great deal of rewarding contrapuntal activity in the orchestra.

Toscanini's approach to the Sanctus was above all a powerfully rhythmic one, characterized by his unswerving insistence on giving the notes and accents their full literal value. As a result, a great deal of commonly thrown-away material in the brass writing was clearly audible, and there was a sparkle to the *leggero* passages for the strings when the "Pleni sunt cœli et terra" got under way which had the arresting, electric quality of the strings in the "Fuoco di gioia" sequence in the first act of *Otello* (p. 280).

To discomfit the purists the Sanctus ended with an apparently unauthorized and distinctly lengthy *ritenuto* in the final bars sung by the chorus:

Ex. *188*

Once more it was a departure from the letter of Verdi's score which added unmistakably to its spirit. What else *could* one do there, anyway?

No 5. Agnus Dei

This, I must confess, has always seemed to me the least satisfactory movement in the Requiem, largely because it introduces a rather austere, gothic note into something which has so far been so mercifully and opulently Latin in its conception. Even in Toscanini's performance I found myself wearying a little of the repetition of the theme and the deliberate aridity of the counterpoint, the orchestration and the harmony, and in consequence I have always inclined in this movement to listen primarily to what Toscanini was up to instead of to the composer—a state of affairs which was normally unthinkable, except where composers of very minor distinction were involved.

As a purely sensuous experience, on the other hand, Toscanini's Agnus Dei had something to offer the listener, and in this recording a great deal of the physical attraction of the orchestral sound has been recaptured, particularly in the tonal quality of the violins in their few *pp* bars of counter-melody in octaves when the chorus echoes the two soloists' "dona eis requiem sempiternam". And there is much to marvel at in the rich beauty of the final chord of the movement which Toscanini played throughout at almost exactly the indicated metronome marking of ♩ = 84.

No. 6. Lux aeterna

Toscanini's unique control over the performance of instrumental detail, and his ability to conjure up sounds and dynamic subtleties which we did not imagine we would ever hear, were matched to a certain extent by his ability to control and colour the human voice—a musical instrument of far less malleable material than any found in the orchestra. This second gift is apparent in the recording of this movement where there is to be heard unaccompanied singing by the mezzo-soprano, tenor and bass which is not marred by the disconcerting element so often encountered in this particular movement and caused by the determination of the individual singers to preserve their independence at any cost, so long as it is at the cost of a properly blended and balanced vocal trio.

Somehow, Toscanini succeeded in keeping his trio of soloists aware of the need for a sense of vocal proportion, and for once in a way one is not alarmed by the prospect of the second unaccompanied sequence when one hears the first.

The orchestral texture of the accompaniment of this section

was unusually delicate (including the *pp* but nonetheless ominous contributions from the trombones from time to time), and there were several passages of staccato figures and runs in the woodwind which Toscanini presented with a gossamer touch worthy of the last scene of *Falstaff*. The accompaniment throughout the whole movement is a masterpiece of imaginative orchestration; unfortunately it always seemed to take Toscanini to show us how superbly well those details did come off which one feared, from comparing the score with other people's performances, seemed unlikely ever to make their effect at all. It was not, we are now happily reassured, ever Verdi's fault that we did not see "what is there". Toscanini not only took care of the unobvious things in the score; he also ensured that we noticed the obvious things, by pointing such careful directions as the "dolcissimo con calma senza affrettare" Verdi expects in the performance of the final passage for flute and clarinet which brings the movement to an end.

No. 7 *Libera me*

With this great finale drama returns once more to the musical action of the Requiem. I make no apology for thinking of this Verdi Mass in operatic terms—"finale", "drama", "action", are words one uses instinctively in connection with it. Certainly there was never any doubt about Toscanini's belief in the dramatic significance of this last movement. The score is barely a few bars old before we hear the chorus repeating the soprano soloist's opening words in an unaccompanied whispered echo of the off-stage murmurings of the monks in the *Trovatore* "Miserere". A few bars later, as the soprano concludes her next solo phrase ("Dum veneris judicare sæculum per ignem"), there is a 5-bar phrase for the four bassoons on their own which Toscanini succeeded in making superbly sinister, instead of faintly comic as it can so often be. Indeed, the dramatic character of the Requiem, an aspect of the work which never ceases to astonish and disquiet the English, was never more clearly or convincingly revealed than in Toscanini's un-unashamedly operatic treatment of this final movement. "Unashamedly" is not the right word, of course; it would be only if there were any alternative way of approaching this finale. As it is, there is none. How else can one interpret the lyrical and dramatic intensity of the soprano's first long solo, except in terms of *Aida*? Or the Dies Irae (which returns with shattering effect in this movement) except, as we have seen, as a companion piece to the picture of the storm in *Otello*? Verdi's whole conception is operatic from start to finish, not least in his exploitation of the medium to present two points of view simultaneously, when the chorus continues to mutter its cries of "Dies irae" while the soprano repeats her "Dum veneris. . .".

It is significant, I feel, that the two most famous versions of the Requiem Mass should have been written by the two greatest of all opera composers: Mozart and Verdi. But then perhaps the words of the Requiem provide almost as fine and inspiring a libretto as you could wish to find anywhere.

The dramatic spirit of Verdi's music was something Toscanini absorbed so intensely that one is not surprised to find him acting as the composer's agent in an instance where he felt that perhaps Verdi had nodded for a moment. I do not know what authority Toscanini had for adding something to the score which was not originally there, but in this instance he added a bass drum roll (or, alternatively, introduced a bass drum roll a bar earlier than it is shown in the score) behind the word "quando" in the soprano's 8-bar phrase, which follows the unaccompanied repetition of "Requiem aeternam" and leads directly into the fugue of the "Libera me". The only accompaniment in the score is the fierce tremolo of strings which, in his recorded performance, Toscanini reinforced as I have described with a roll on the bass drum:

Ex. 189

Whether this bass drum roll is authorized by being shown in some score I have not seen, or whether Toscanini thought it all up on his own, there is not the slightest doubt that it sounds authentic enough by being superbly suited to its whole context.

Few things give greater pleasure to those of us who heard Toscanini during his lifetime than to encounter again and again examples of his remarkable consistency over the years. The most striking details I remember of his 1938 Requiem were not only the tremendously incisive rhythm of this final fugue, but his unique "timing" of the unindicated rallentando, the *ritenuto* or the *meno mosso* he contributed with such infallible justification and taste in the course of something of which the predominant impression was one of a strict, relentless and unwavering tempo.

All these touches have been repeated and preserved in the recording Toscanini made many years after I first heard him conduct the work—together, one must point out, with a touch which is not a repetition of anything I ever heard before, but which is now preserved nevertheless: a ragged moment of orchestral ensemble as the full orchestra gets going after its punctuations of the fugue subject. The brass runs away from Toscanini's beat, but it is a scarcely perceptible lapse and no more important than a champion steeplechaser's momentary hesitation at the last fence in a race he has well in hand.

For the benefit of the student who may wish to learn something of the art of rubato, or at least of flexibility within the framework of a seemingly rigid tempo, as practised by Toscanini, I would quote the rallentando Toscanini introduced into the third and fourth bars of this phrase which leads to the *stretto* of the fugue,

Ex. 190

and the *meno mosso* at the point where violas and bassoon are first heard presenting the instrumental version of the soprano soloist's extended "Libera me":

Ex. 191

Toscanini, in the recording, may be heard to pick up the tempo again almost immediately and build up to the superbly vigorous rhythm of the climax which was one of the unforgettable moments of his earlier performances: the fiercely incisive, accented *tutta forza* by orchestra and chorus of

Ex. *192*

a rhythm relaxed for the merest suggestion of a rallentando as the soprano comes down from the mountain of her high C to the broad plain of the unmatched drama of Verdi's whispered coda.

Once again, as one comes to the end of the recording of Toscanini's performance of Verdi's Requiem, one is conscious of having been through not only a great spiritual and emotional experience, but of having heard in all the glory of its original colouring music to match Michelangelo's Last Judgment. The clarity of the detail in this performance was fantastic, but never once did it distract one's attention from the grandeur of the whole conception nor disturb the inexorable development and progress of the music. It was, in short, a performance which showed Toscanini at his greatest.

Whether it has been wise to draw attention to Toscanini's "unofficial" interpretations of some aspects of the score I now begin to doubt. When and how to do what Toscanini did which is not marked in Verdi's score, it is impossible to say, for the success of all these gestures depended entirely on his inimitable gift of timing. My only hope is that these peculiarities will not be held up as models to imitate, but as further clues to the secret of his greatness. As for conductors, whether established or still students, one can do little more than beg them to note how Toscanini approached those instructions and indications which *are* written in the score and so come a little nearer to what Toscanini would certainly not have recognized, but which we, who have inherited this recorded performance of the Requiem, can see to be as near-ideal a performance as we are ever likely to hear again.

TE DEUM
[1898]

Robert Shaw Chorale
NBC Symphony Orchestra

GREAT BRITAIN: HMV ALP 1363
U.S.A.: Victor LM 1849
1954

This is one work by Verdi which I have never heard conducted by anybody but Toscanini, and about which, since I had never seen the score, I had no preconceived notions when I first heard him perform it in London in 1938. No study of Toscanini's performance, therefore, can be in any way comparative; Verdi's *Te Deum* has always been for me a work unaffected by good or bad traditions and free of all association with other conductors' methods.

It is virtually the only work discussed in this book about which I cannot at some point say that where most conductors do such-and-such Toscanini always did so-and-so. And thanks to the recording that has come down to us I am also mercifully absolved from having to listen to other conductors when I next want to hear this remarkable and movingly dramatic fruit of Verdi's old age. Now that I have seen the score and noted how clearly Toscanini has perceived "what is there" (as well as a lot more besides), I am content to consider this recording as the finest performance of the *Te Deum* I am likely to hear in my lifetime.

Of all Verdi's works the *Te Deum* was the one with which Toscanini was perhaps most closely associated as a conductor, for shortly after its first performance in Paris during Holy Week, 1898, he conducted the first Italian performance in Turin. It was also a work which contributed one of those typical incidents and anecdotes which go to make up the Toscanini Saga.

Howard Taubman tells the story in his *Toscanini*:

"In preparing Verdi's *Pezzi sacri* for chorus for their first performance in Italy, Toscanini was disturbed by a passage in the *Te Deum*. He felt that the music here required a ritard,

but there was no such indication in the score. He decided
to go to Genoa to consult Verdi . . . The composer . . . in-
vited his young visitor to sit down at the piano . . . When he
[Toscanini] came to the troublesome passage he gave it the
ritard that it seemed to him it must have.

"When he was finished, Verdi patted him on the back and
said: 'Bravo!'

" 'Then the ritard here,' Toscanini pointed to the place,
'did not offend you?'

" 'No.' Verdi smiled. 'It is what I want.'

" 'But you did not indicate a ritard.'

" 'I was afraid to,' the composer said. 'If I had written it
down, it would be played too slowly. A true musician would
sense that there should be a ritardando.' "

Inevitably, remembering this anecdote, one naturally listens
attentively to the recording, score in hand, in order to discover
exactly where Toscanini made the famous ritardando. I would
warn the reader, however, that this is a singularly unsatisfactory pastime. There are no fewer than five places in the
score where Toscanini made what may be regarded as an unindicated ritardando, together with a *meno mosso* which could
just qualify as a lengthy ritardando, and one spontaneous
accelerando which is neither here nor there.

More to be emulated, on the other hand, than the luxury of an
unidentifiable ritardando authorized by the composer, is Toscanini's wonderful revelation of the drama of this *Te Deum*. As with
the Requiem, Verdi the operatic leopard did not, and indeed
could not, change his spots merely because he entered a church
and decided to set sacred Latin instead of secular Italian words
to music. Like Beethoven in his Missa Solemnis, his religious
music was profoundly dramatic and he expressed his intensely
personal faith in the idiom that came most naturally to him.

It is not surprising, therefore, that the score of this *Te Deum*
should abound in those indications so familiar to us from Verdi's
operas—*dolce, dolcissimo, cantabile, con espressione*—in phrases
to be sung "as in the distance" and "sombrely, without
accents". It is supremely dramatic music and the fact that it
is a song of religious exultation and thanksgiving, instead of an
episode in some romantic tragedy, does not for one moment

mean that we smell incense instead of grease-paint or that the transept takes the place of orchestra pit and footlights. Nearly everything that Toscanini found in Verdi's operas he found in this *Te Deum*: moments of great lyrical tenderness, of tremendous excitement, powerful drama and uncanny tension, and, in the cadence (to be sung "sempre dolciss.") of "Sancta confitetur Ecclesia", even something of the grace and charm typical of *Falstaff*. The only element lacking was that of Verdi's peculiar brilliance and sparkle which cropped up so unexpectedly in both serious and unserious dramatic situations in his operas. But perhaps that was to be expected.

For the rest, there was little in all Toscanini's repertoire that provided a more illuminating experience than this otherwise unfamiliar *Te Deum*, or more satisfactorily epitomized all—or nearly all—that Verdi meant to him.

Francis Toye wrote of Verdi's *Pezzi sacri* that "as an epilogue, so to say, to the work of a lifetime the *Pezzi sacri* are worthy of the composer of *Otello*, *Falstaff* and the Requiem Mass". That is how Toscanini made the *Te Deum* sound. He could not have done more.

MISCELLANEOUS

*Nabucco—Chorus: "Va pensiero, sull' ali dorate"
*I Lombardi—Trio: "Qui posa il fianco" (Vivian della Chiesa, Nicola Moscona, Jan Peerce)
*I Vespri siciliani—Overture
*La forza del destino—Overture
*Luisa Miller—Overture
*Luisa Miller—Aria: "Quando le sere al placido" (Jan Peerce)
†*Otello*—Ballet Music (Act 3)
†*Inno delle nazioni*—Cantata (Jan Peerce)

NBC Symphony Orchestra

GREAT BRITAIN: *HMV ALP 1452
†HMV ALP 1453
U.S.A.: Victor LM 6041

These items from the collection known as "Verdi and Toscanini" may be considered as musical *canapés* prepared by the chef as samples of his *grande cuisine*. Like Toscanini's performance of the last act of *Rigoletto* they provide a tantalizing and frustrating experience; there is not one overture or number from any of the operas represented that does not leave one wishing one could have heard Toscanini conduct the rest of the work. Only the ballet music from *Otello* and the extremely occasional *Inno delle nazioni* leave one at all contented: the *Otello* excerpt because Toscanini recorded the rest of the opera, and the Cantata because there was no more of it to record, anyway.

The *Otello* ballet music has, in fact, been a source of considerable personal tantalization and frustration in its time. During the Second German War the BBC broadcast a programme sent on disc from the United States—one of those friendly international exchanges of culture and entertainment which the War gave us as a consolation for the boredom, terror and general discomfort we suffered. I introduced the broadcast with a fifteen-minute talk about Toscanini which I gave from a studio deep underground in Broadcasting House (my script bore the Censor's rubber stamps—"Passed for Policy"—"Passed for Security"). The music in the programme consisted of two items which neither I nor, I imagine, anybody else in the British Isles had ever heard conducted by Toscanini: the ballet music from *Otello* and the *Inno delle nazioni*.

The impact of the ballet music was perhaps just more powerful than it is in this recording: it was my first experience of Toscanini conducting music from Verdi's greatest opera. Then, as in this recording, he showed the *ballabile* to be a brilliant and exciting essay in near-exotic orchestration through which the thoroughly Italian musical voice of Verdi can be heard with the utmost clarity.

The Hymn of the Nations, written for the International Exhibition in London in 1862, has its peculiar place in musical history. Not only may Toscanini's wartime performance (recorded here) well have been the first—and last—performance of the Cantata since its composer took a reluctant call at its première in May 1862, but this recording of it offers posterity what I believe to be the only extant recorded example of Toscanini, the composer-arranger. Among the music he put on paper that has not been recorded, one must include the notoriously inept sequence he is said to have contributed to the posthumous completion of Puccini's *Turandot*. The gramophone record has immortalized, in this *Inno delle nazioni*, the Maestro's appendix to Verdi's ingenious treatment of the French, Italian and English national hymns with which the Cantata concluded: the spectacularly banal *Internationale* and *Star Spangled Banner*.

Nevertheless, as with Beethoven's Battle Symphony, there are moments in Verdi's *Hymn of the Nations* which Toscanini showed left no doubt about its composer's identity or of his ability to write exciting music under the least prepossessing professional conditions.

The remaining items in this collection of Verdi *canapés* were performed with all the fire and flexibility, lyrical fervour and dramatic intensity one came to expect from experience of Toscanini's conducting of Verdi. In every case—particularly in the earlier Verdi—he seemed to reproduce in a miraculous way the startling vigour and novelty of the music as it must have struck the composer's contemporaries when they first heard it.

The extent and inspiration of Toscanini's spontaneous contributions to these pieces, the masterly timing of rubato and unauthorized touches (such as the unindicated crescendo from the *ff* to the sudden *pp* at letter "N" in the overture to *La forza del destino*) are details which may well prove unwise examples for the student conductor to follow. So much of this sort of thing with Toscanini depended on his instinctive good taste and sense of style. But the spirit of dedication and integrity which was behind it is there as an inspiration for endless generations of conductors—if only they will recognize it.

Since the example and character of Verdi was in the end the most important single influence in Toscanini's life it is perhaps only right that this chapter should end with a reference to the chorus of the Jews from *Nabucco*—"Va pensiero, sull' ali dorate". Toscanini conducted this great and moving chorus at Verdi's funeral in Milan in 1901. This same piece of music was sung at Toscanini's own funeral in Milan in February 1957.

They could have played nothing else.

WAGNER
⟨[1813–1883]⟩

FOR my generation Toscanini's conducting of Wagner
meant a memorable performance of *Die Meistersinger* at
Salzburg in 1936 and such items as he might include in
his concert programmes—items in some cases very "adapted"
indeed.

Our immediate successors and posterity in general will be
even less favoured. They will have to be content with records of
the concert-hall items and little else. There were no Toscanini
performances of a Wagner opera after 1936, still less any complete recording of one, and while his performance of Brünnhilde's last scene in *Götterdämmerung* may be regarded as better
than nothing, even this was something of an arrangement, inasmuch as he began it with an orchestral passage which Brünnhilde should sing through but didn't, and then skipped about
eight pages to reach the place where she should and did.*

Perhaps Brünnhilde's Immolation Scene, which lasts almost
as long as the last act of *Rigoletto*, should not by rights be
regarded as a "snippet", but by Wagnerian standards it is
scarcely more than a *bonne-bouche*. In consequence Toscanini's
legacy of Wagner recordings includes nothing comparable to
his comprehensive repertoire of Beethoven and Verdi. Those
of us who happened to hear his 1936 *Meistersinger*, however,
will recognize that the few recordings he did leave are remarkably characteristic of his performance of this composer's music.

In spite of his professed devotion to Wagner we know that in
the end Toscanini derived greater genuine pleasure from the
music of Verdi; at least, that is what I infer from the words I
have quoted on page 312. Whatever distinctions Toscanini
may have made in his mind between two composers of such
irreconcilable views, there seems to have been little doubt that

---

* Victor LVT 1004 (1941) with Helen Traubel. Not available in Great Britain
at time of going to Press.

where the orchestral texture of Wagner's scores was concerned, the nearer the lucid, *cantabile* and generally pleasanter and more Italianate sound of Verdi's orchestra he could get, the better.

One of the immediate outcomes of this attitude to Wagner was that one heard *Die Meistersinger*, for instance, played with a brilliance and speed (not so much of tempo as of spirit) that one had never heard before and certainly never heard again.

The unique instrumental colour Toscanini discovered in Wagner's scores inevitably prompted second thoughts about the composer's music, and if not even Toscanini could convince one that *Parsifal* was anything but a slightly slow-moving piece, the sheer sound and delicate orchestral texture of his performances of the Prelude and Good Friday Music * presented a new aspect of Wagner altogether. If it did nothing else, it demonstrated more forcibly than ever that Wagner, in common with his colleagues down the ages, was always more eloquent as a Master of the Orchestra when he was whispering than when he was shouting his head off.

An inspiring rhythm was not one of Wagner's strong points and it said volumes for Toscanini's genius that he brought a sense of movement to some extremely pedestrian stretches of music. Toscanini, at least, created an illusion of activity in his familiar *Götterdämmerung* arrangement—Dawn and Siegfried's Rhine Journey †—without making it sound too hard work.

The force of Toscanini's climaxes made his Wagner in a purely physical sense a more exciting experience than one was accustomed to; the memory of the impact of such moments as the climax of Siegfried's Funeral Music and of the Prelude to *Tristan* is at least stirred, if not fully revived, by the recordings of these two items.‡ In each case it seemed impossible that more sound could be extracted from an orchestra and, as one learned early in one's experience of Toscanini's control and balance of dynamics, there was never a moment when that tremendous din ceased to be music. This was particularly true of the *Tristan* Prelude; not only did the intensity of the tone seem inexhaustible, but the climax was reached without any suggestion of

* Great Britain: HMV BLP 1033; RCA RB–16135; U.S.A.: Victor LM 6020 (1949).
† Great Britain: HMV ALP 1173; RCA RB–16135; U.S.A.: Victor LM 6020 (1949).
‡ Great Britain: RCA RB–16135; U.S.A.: Victor LM 6020 (1952).

driving during the gradual process of building up to the final
ff. The music just got naturally, spontaneously louder and more
exciting until the climax was as paroxysmal as its composer can
ever have hoped for.

The orchestral detail audible in all this was quite phenomenal, as it was in the Prelude to Act I of *Die Meistersinger*,*
where Wagner's famous contrapuntal juggling of all his themes
at once had the translucence of a Mozart string quartet.

My experience of Wagner conducted by Toscanini in the
theatre was, as I say, limited to the Salzburg *Meistersinger*.
But just as Wagner in his overtures and preludes was all for
giving the listener a synthesis of the tunes he was going to hear
for the following three or four hours, so Toscanini's performance of the first act Prelude provided one with a résumé of his
conception of the complete opera. His performance of the
Prelude, which has come down to us in his 1951 recording,
was rich in details for the musician to study and enjoy. The
basic tempo was ♩ = 112. Wagner, for some reason, did not
recognize the existence of the metronome and marked the
Prelude to be played "Sehr mässig bewegt"—or Molto moderato
—one of the least inspiring and helpful instructions any conductor can surely be faced with. Toscanini, however, accepted
Die Meistersinger as a reasonably cheerful opera and accordingly
attacked it as such from the very first moment.

And "attacked" is the right word, I think. The briskness
and merciful lack of moderation in Toscanini's idea of the *Sehr
mässig bewegt* of the Prelude was characteristic of his entire
conception of the opera. His tempi were flexible, and he had no
less hesitation, when he reached the first quiet moment in the
Prelude (at Bar 27), in slackening the tempo, than he had in
quickening it when he considered the general sense of the music
demanded it—whatever the composer may have indicated.
In short, everything that Toscanini did in the Prelude he did in
the opera: he brought lyrical warmth, rhythmic vitality, dignity
without pomposity and a superb brilliance of detail to a score
which so many can kill stone dead with the first beat of the
first bar. Toscanini kept the opera alive, and the time passed
quickly for the listener.

The Prelude to Act III of *Die Meistersinger* completed Tos-

* Great Britain: RCA RB–16136; U.S.A.: Victor LM 6020 (1946).

canini's synthesis of the opera in the concert hall, and, as the recording suggests,* it was a performance of such tremendous sadness and mellowness, revealing once again that astonishing clarity of texture which one had never considered possible with Wagner, that one almost forgave Toscanini the corny village-organist "concert" ending.

Toscanini's preoccupation with instrumental colour was naturally particularly apparent in the balance and tonal quality of the Prelude to Act I of *Lohengrin* † which was inseparable from its pendant, the Prelude to Act III ‡ in Toscanini's concert programmes. From the purely technical point of view Toscanini made of the first act Prelude a remarkable experience of sound and, as so often with familiar and hackneyed items, gave one a vivid idea of how Wagner's music must have sounded to its first audiences. The Prelude to Act III was a virtuoso display of vigour and general *brio* which never transformed the music itself into anything but the commonplace conception it is. Sousa would have thrown a trombone tune like that out of the window.

Finally, there was what to me was the most rewarding of all Toscanini's performances of Wagner in the concert hall: the *Siegfried Idyll*.§ Toscanini performed Wagner's one immediately endearing work with great tenderness and affection, and came nearer than anybody else to making the final cadence seem a reasonable length once the music settles down on the endless E which dominates the orchestra for all but eight of the last fifty-five ever-retarding bars. Tolerance of this last sequence depends entirely on the listener's personal belief that what Wagner has to say is worth saying, not once, but six or seven times. Toscanini almost convinced one that Wagner's famous last words, if not actually terse, were not quite so diffuse as usual.

Toscanini's genius lay in his being able to do this, not only in the coda of the *Siegfried Idyll*, but in the theatre with an

* Great Britain: HMV DB 21564; RCA RB–16136; U.S.A.: Victor LM 6020 (1951).

† Great Britain: HMV DB 21574; RCA RB–16136; U.S.A.: Victor LM 6020 (1951).

‡ Great Britain: RCA RB–16136; U.S.A.: Victor LM 6020 (1951).

§ Great Britain: HMV DB 6668–9; RCA RB–16136; U.S.A.: Victor LM 6020 (1952); LVT 1004 (1946).

outsize assignment like *Die Meistersinger* which, in the process of being polished up, acquired something not so far removed from a Latin wit in place of the slow-moving teutonic humours of Wagner.

Perhaps Toscanini's Wagner was considered "too Italian"; I do not know. But if it was, I would not rate that as anything but an advantage to all concerned.

SUPPLEMENT

BEETHOVEN
✢ [1771–1827] ✣

SYMPHONY No 3 in E flat, Opus 55 ("Eroica")
[1804]

NBC Symphony Orchestra

Victor
RCA-Italiana } LM 2387

1953

This recording of a broadcast in December 1953 took an oddly long time to reach us considering how frequently one read ten years ago that this was the set of all sets to wait for if only somebody would issue it. When I eventually heard it, through the courtesy of my friend Commander Keith Hardwick of the Royal Navy (whose two great interests in life—the wines of Bordeaux and the records of Toscanini—he shares generously with his friends), it was before this present supplement to *The Toscanini Legacy* had been considered. I listened to it, therefore, if not uncritically, at least in an unprofessional frame of mind which spared me making any conscious comparison with the 1949 recording.

Today, when it comes to writing about the 1953 version, I find that critical comparison is of little importance. The differences in detail may be great or trivial. Certainly, both performances are different from the first Eroica I heard at Carnegie Hall in 1933; but the two recordings and the three live performances I heard Toscanini give of this symphony all had one thing in common: they were supremely characteristic of Toscanini's uniquely dramatic view of Beethoven in general and of this symphony in particular. Above all, they were consistent in their intention, and it is this which makes the differences in detail largely irrelevant; a fraction of a second *più mosso* than the basic tempo here, the unmeasurable breath pause or *tenuto* there—these were in the end no more than reassuring signs that the performance as well as the creation of music is a human experience, not a mechanical exercise.

There is, however, one very noticeable difference in detail between the two recordings. It occurs in the last movement during the first

343

variation for violins and violoncellos, where according to my score
(the small Wiener Philharmonischer Verlag edition 1923) we have:

Ex. 193

Weingartner, in his classic study *On the Performance of Beethoven's
Symphonies*, (Dover Reprint, 1969) comments: "Some editions place
the pause over the E flat instead of over the D; this is wrong". This
means that my little score is wrong, which doesn't surprise me.

In a most uncharacteristic spirit of compromise Toscanini pauses
on both the E flat and the D in his 1949 recording, thus playing the
bar half-right and half-wrong. In his 1953 performance, however,
he plays it strictly according to Weingartner and pauses only on the
D. This is obviously the logical way of doing it, for by pausing on the
D the return to *a tempo* coincides with the resumption of the theme
in the second violins.

Although I have lived with memories and records of Toscanini's
interpretation of the Eroica for well over thirty years now, it is only
quite recently that I realized how, in one very important instance,
he broke sharply with tradition. This was in the slow movement
which begins

Ex. 194

Weingartner wrote: "Bülow has already pointed out that the
three first C's in the basses are introduced by grace-notes, and that
these, in contrast to the later, written-out demi-semiquavers [thirty-
second notes], must not be played as

Ex. 195

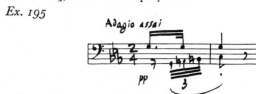

but that the G marks the first point of the bar which, however, is followed by the other notes in such quick succession that they form only one rhythmic value. The same holds good, of course, for the similar passage [in bars 105–6]. It is striking, however, that here the notes preceding the third C have a different notation from those in [the passage shown in Ex. 194], whereas in all other points the similarity is complete. I do not know of any reason for this, but of course the will of the master must be obeyed".

Toscanini, ignoring the printed notes, obeyed the master's will perhaps more faithfully than Bülow and Weingartner and knowing absolutely no reason for playing the grace-notes as they are shown in Ex. 194, habitually played them as it was said they must not be played, as in Ex. 195.

Toscanini's view seems to have been that since Beethoven couldn't make up his mind, he would do it for him. The result was not only symmetrical but, with its suggestion of the funeral drum, dramatically much more effective than the way Weingartner did it. I did not notice that Toscanini differed so completely from Weingartner in all this because Toscanini's approach always seemed the only possible way of doing it. His interpretation of the grace-notes was not peculiar to him; it was also followed by Pierre Monteux among others.

On one important matter concerning the Eroica, however, Weingartner and Toscanini agreed: that in spite of the assertion of an American critic (see page 46) that "everyone else slows down for it", the Trio of the Scherzo should, as Weingartner put it in his book, "be fresh and energetic without any change of tempo".

SYMPHONY No 7 in A, Opus 92
[1812]

New York Philharmonic Symphony Orchestra

GREAT BRITAIN: CDN 1028
HMV DB 2986/90

U.S.A.: Victor LCT 1013, CAL 352
1936

The first appearance of this recording as an LP in England five or six years ago on the bargain Camden label was a most welcome event because it brought back into circulation what is without question an immortal performance. My own original 78's had long been worn to shreds, for this was one of the classic Toscanini recordings of a work I had first heard him perform in the course of his 1933 Beethoven cycle at Carnegie Hall, and which he later played in two of his four festival seasons with the BBC Symphony Orchestra in London.

What I did not realise when the LP was released was that it was not exactly the same as the original 78 rpm issue. According to Mr B. H. Haggin, in his *Conversations with Toscanini*, it contains a different "take" of the *poco sostenuto* introduction to the first movement which is slightly faster than the one on the original release. The substitution was made in 1942, when the master of side one began to wear out, and is almost identical in tempo with the same sequence in the 1951 recording. I have to take Mr Haggin's word for it that the 1942 substitution is in fact faster than in the earlier pressings, for I no longer have my old 78's to compare it with. I must confess that I do not remember noticing that the original version was slower; however, Toscanini himself preferred his slightly faster introduction and was pleased to have the opportunity to use it.

A more striking difference between the 1936 and 1951 performances is to be heard in the slow movement. Both versions start out with an Allegretto of about ♩ = 72–76; but in the 1936 recording Toscanini keeps this as the basic tempo of the whole movement, allowing only the smallest deviations and moments of rubato. When he comes to the A major middle section in the 1951 performance, he races away *molto appassionato* and whips up the tempo with a vigorous *stringendo*. The speeding-up of this section results in a difference of no less than 14 seconds in the time taken to perform the sequence most affected—the 48 bars from the start of the A major section at bar 102 to bar 150, when the recapitulation begins. This is one occasion on which the stop-watch only confirms what is as plain as a pikestaff to the ear.

In discussing Toscanini's rehearsal of the Allegretto in the earlier part of this book (see page 74), I wrote that he "took longer over perfecting the opening and closing chords of this movement than over any detail I ever heard him concentrate on at rehearsal", and that he described the sound he wanted as "like a mirror".

If Toscanini achieved the effect he wanted it was more in spite of, than because of, his uncharacteristic use of a non-musical image. Since I wrote the passage on page 74, I have discovered that not only was Toscanini's "mirror" simile uncharacteristic, it wasn't even original. He got the idea from Weingartner's book on the Beethoven symphonies:

> My first music-master, Dr Wilhelm Mayer of Graz, found a beautiful, poetic comparison for this movement. The first A minor chord is, according to him, a look into a magic mirror. At first nothing can be seen; then forms appear, approach us and look at us with eyes which have seen another world, then pass on and disappear again—and only the dark surface of the mirror (the last A minor chord) remains. Poetic interpretations of pieces of music, which in general I am not disposed to favour, are absolutely individual and cannot be forced upon anyone. But it is often of value to learn what impressions are produced by great music on men endowed with imagination, and for this reason I have repeated what my teacher told me of his.

It is an interesting source for Toscanini to have consulted or rather, an odd thing for him to have extracted from it what he did. But it was exceptional. In all other respects Toscanini's performances of the Beethoven symphonies show that he had consulted Weingartner's book very thoroughly on all the instrumental aspects of the music, including the re-voicing, re-phrasing and at times rewriting of many of the wind passages in the Ninth Symphony, but he had not consulted Weingartner on interpretation. Weingartner himself was generally following many of Wagner's recommendations. Mirror similes or not, as far as the Seventh Symphony was concerned, this 1936 recording remains a unique reminder of Toscanini at his greatest as a conductor of Beethoven.

CONCERTO No 4 in G for Piano, Opus 58
[1805–6]

Rudolf Serkin

NBC Symphony Orchestra

GREAT BRITAIN: RCA RB–6628

U.S.A.: Victor LM 2797

1944

Like several of the posthumously released records discussed in this part of the book, this broadcast performance of Beethoven's Fourth

Piano Concerto was my first experience of the work conducted by Toscanini. It was not, however, my first experience of Toscanini conducting a solo concerto. The 1933 Beethoven cycle in New York included the Emperor Concerto played by Horowitz and the Triple Concerto played by Carreras, Piastro and Wallenstein. That same season Heifetz played the Brahms Concerto in D with Toscanini conducting.

Before I had actually heard this record of the Fourth Piano Concerto one of our local critics wrote that it provided "a unique opportunity to hear Toscanini in a Beethoven work for which I would have expected little sympathy from him". I was a little perplexed to read this, for apart from its having been the one Beethoven piano concerto he performed more often than the others, it seemed to me to be full of precisely those qualities which would appeal most to Toscanini—colour, good humour, rhythmic vigour, drama, lyrical episodes of great warmth and a work of tremendous vitality. And so it most certainly proved in practice.

The first playing of any Toscanini record of a work one knows, but has not heard him perform, has always had its own peculiar excitement—the unforgettable, eagerly awaited moment when one hears the first notes of the performance. This moment is delayed in the record of the Beethoven Fourth Piano Concerto because it is the solo instrument, not the orchestra, that has the first word. When, after five bars, the strings answer the piano it is a ravishing entrance which has all the magic one has come to expect of those famous first notes I referred to.

Taken as a whole the performance of the Concerto is the result of an unusually sympathetic musical partnership; the solo instrument is not accompanied by the orchestra, but complemented by it, and in the tuttis we have Toscanini's characteristic presentation of Beethoven that we know so well from the symphonies, rich in the perception of "what is there" and intensely, unmistakably individual.

The orchestral contribution itself is a fascinating demonstration of Toscanini's concern for detail. In the first movement (where the orchestral statement of the first subject is quite astonishingly ragged for five or six bars) we hear the familiar singing pizzicato tone, the fierce three-part chords in the violins which, however loud they may be played, are always music and never noise, the typical *cantabile* warmth of the strings in the second subject (bar 119)—a four-bar phrase heard alone for an exquisite fleeting moment before it is overlaid with variations by the soloist. There is great beauty too in the long hushed string passage from which the coda builds to its last few signing-off bars of *ff*.

Beethoven's astonishing slow movement is perhaps the high spot of the Serkin-Toscanini performance of the Concerto. The dialogue between the strings, with their grim, repeated unison phrases, and the piano with its inexpressibly sad replies is almost operatic in its eloquence and dramatic intensity. Once again it is something achieved by Toscanini's insistence on seeing "what is there"; when he sees the *p dim.* marked in the sequence that begins at bar 38, the effect is breathtakingly unexpected and we are faced once more with the fact that seeing "what is there" was only the half of it; it still does not explain why the wonderful *ppp* coda has never sounded quite so magical before.

The Rondo finale, marked Vivace, is pure joy—the first whispered, crystal-clear staccato statement of the theme, the sparkle and wit of the echoes and imitations in the piano-and-orchestra dialogue, the exquisite matching dynamics of woodwind and pizzicato strings, the ravishing *dolce* passages in the violas and violoncellos, the infectious, almost Rossinian exuberance and charm of the whole piece. These are only a few of the miraculous details which add up to one of the most exhilarating Beethoven performances Toscanini ever recorded, and which cannot be spoiled even by the electronic blemish of an unfortunate pitch wobble on the sustained A in bars 312–313. It is a recording I have returned to again and again as a stimulating demonstration of how the orchestra should sound in a Beethoven piano concerto.

BERLIOZ
⚔ [1803–1869] ⚔

ROMEO AND JULIET, Opus 17
(Dramatic Symphony)

Gladys Swarthout (mezzo-soprano)

John Garris (tenor)

Nicola Moscona (bass)

NBC Symphony Orchestra

U.S.A.: Victor LM 7034

1947

Of all the recordings released after Toscanini's death, this performance of Berlioz's astonishing work is undoubtedly the most important and exhilarating. Apart from anything else it is a sharp reminder, to those who saw in the Toscanini centenary commemorations no more than a perfunctory public genuflection to an historical monument, that over the years Toscanini lost none of his power to shock and startle the listener with a brand new and incomparable musical experience. From the first electrifying statement of the opening fugato theme by the violas, this performance is a dazzling revelation of one of the most original pieces of music ever written.

PART I

Introduction: Tumult and Strife—Intervention of the Prince. Prologue—Strophes—Scherzetto

Toscanini's unique understanding of Berlioz's peculiar idiom is immediately apparent in the brilliance and ferocity of attack in the violas' playing of the first bars of the Introduction. Berlioz's use of the violas in this score is highly individual; he exploited not only their warm, lyrical and melancholy quality, but also discovered in them dramatic characteristics not normally associated with the instrument. Toscanini brought all this out in his performance with the same instinctive sureness of touch that made the attention he paid to the piccolo in *Falstaff* such a joy. The bite and diamond-hard intensity of the opening phrase of the violas in *Romeo and Juliet* is one of the most arresting sounds Toscanini ever produced from an orchestra.

The vigour and brilliance of the first pages is followed by a really masterly interpretation of one of the most difficult passages in all orchestral music—the long instrumental recitative for unison brass which represents the Prince's intervention in the "turmoil and strife" of the Montagues and Capulets. It is difficult because it must be impressive without being pompous, authoritative without being dull, firm without being rigid. The effect of Berlioz's original conception —which is no less original for being an obvious development of Beethoven's idea of the instrumental recitative in the last movement of the Ninth Symphony—is increased in Toscanini's performance by the uncannily eloquent, *cantabile* character of the brass phrasing of a long, testing and mercilessly exposed passage.

The dramatic emptying of the scene which succeeds the recitative is a wonderfully imaginative stroke by Berlioz, and perfectly timed by Toscanini who never forgets for a moment of the hour and a half performance that the composer called his work a dramatic symphony.

The opening passages of the Prologue that follows are distinguished by some skilful unaccompanied choral singing in some of the most execrable French ever put on record, and punctuated by a chord of D minor for brass and timpani—one of those typical "hairpin" dynamics from *p* to *sf* and down to *pp*—which Toscanini controlled with such precision that it sounded as though he were turning the knob of a volume control.

The performance abounds in the most exquisite and fascinating details, among which I would count the eleven bars of the *Andante con moto e appassionato assai* which forms the choral and in-strumental coda to the section called the Prologue—a sudden passionate outburst, giving us our first hint of the great lyrical passages to come. The *Strophes* movement also includes among its details an inimitable demonstration by Toscanini of instrumental balance and the art of syncopation. This occurs at the words "quel art" and "rendrait" in the first verse, and "quel roi" and "croi-rait" in the second. I quote the words as providing the easiest means of identifying the passages I mean since the text is included with the records. The Eulenburg miniature score has neither figures, letters nor numbered bars to help with reference, but I recommend it nevertheless because it was this score, though by no means free of literals, that Toscanini consulted in preference to the big Breitkopf & Härtel edition which he found contained several unauthorized alterations of Berlioz's original instructions.

The words I have mentioned above occur in the last bar of page 34 of the Eulenburg score and in the fourth bar of page 35, and they are accompanied by a syncopated passage for two flutes, cor anglais, two clarinets and harp. Toscanini's performance, as I have suggested, is a superb example of perfect instrumental balance.*

The *Scherzetto* for tenor and small chorus of contraltos, tenors and basses which follows shortly after the *Strophes* movement, is a miraculous little episode performed by Toscanini with a breathtaking clarity and lightness of touch. The orchestral accompaniment is one of the composer's most remarkable conceptions—piccolo, flute, violas, violoncellos (divided in two parts and playing pizzicato throughout, except for the last few bars)—and the way Toscanini plays it is yet another demonstration of the astonishing modernity not only of this particular work but of all Berlioz's music. The originality of *Romeo and Juliet* is unmistakable at a first glance of the score; performed with Toscanini's genius for making any work sound as fresh as the day its composer first thought of it, Berlioz's originality is staggering.

PART II

Romeo alone—Sadness—Concert and Ball—Feast at the Capulets

The scene of Romeo alone in his sadness begins Andante melanconico e sostenuto with a phrase for first violins *ppp*. The violins, as so often happens in this score, are then joined by the violas an octave lower. Toscanini brings an intense *melanconia* to the sort of distinctive melodic line Berlioz wrote which Toscanini found infectious enough to sing to from time to time. The long violin tune (Eulenburg pages 57 to 60) is played with all the warmth and *cantabile* phrasing Toscanini could squeeze out of his players and its effect is moving and powerful. At the point where this tune ends on page 60, second violins and violas come in with a *pp* accompaniment of

*See footnote on page 49.

throbbing quaver triplets—the sort of accompaniment which always sounded different with Toscanini because of the care and concentration he lavished on *everything* he saw in a score. It was not just a matter of balancing the dynamics of two parts but of giving them a musical life and significance of their own. Hearing these bars for the first time in this recording, I was reminded how often with Toscanini the simplest, least expected details can make a startling and unforgettable impact. The same sort of thing happens in the case of the pizzicato violoncello accompaniment to the oboe tune in the Larghetto espressivo section which begins a few bars later (page 66). The *pp* sextolet arpeggios could not appear more straightforward on paper, yet one is startled by the way Toscanini makes the actual sound of the pizzicato so much richer and more interesting than one imagined was possible.

The long and brilliant Allegro of the Ball Scene has all the rhythmic fire and dazzling clarity of Toscanini's performance of the *Benvenuto Cellini* overture—the first Berlioz I heard him perform, and an experience I have never forgotten in the 34 years since it happened. This, I remember, was how I thought Berlioz should sound.

Toscanini's performance of the *Grande Fête chez Capulet* scene is a stupendous affair; even those already familiar with it from the recording he made of *Romeo and Juliet* excerpts on LM 1019 (the complete work was broadcast February 9 and 16, 1947; the excerpts recorded on February 17), will find that its effect is even greater when heard where it belongs—in its full dramatic context. It is a performance virtually impossible to describe; one can only listen open-mouthed and marvel at the white heat of Berlioz's musical invention and his orchestral genius, and realize that for the first time so many of the things in the score that looked ineffective on paper can in fact sound wonderful in practice. I was thinking particularly of the remarkable woodwind and horn figures that accompany the strings at the start of the second side of the recording (Eulenburg page 73–78). In Toscanini's performance the passage at last makes—literally—sound sense.

It is not often that Berlioz is helped along with his orchestration, but in the last three bars of the movement, according to page 125 of the Eulenburg score, Toscanini adds brass in support of the woodwind quavers and in doing so certainly improves the flourish of the great *ff* curtain line. Played as Berlioz wrote them, I cannot imagine the woodwinds standing out very strongly and making a maximum effect between the *ff* chords and the rest of the orchestra—unless, of course, the number of players to each part were increased to military band proportions. The addition of the brass at this point may well have been Weingartner's idea, but as I do not know his Breitkopf and Härtel edition of *Romeo and Juliet* I cannot be certain. Whether it is morally correct or not, the physical effect of this modification certainly adds to the general excitement of the music.

PART III*

Love Scene

Calm night—The silent and deserted garden of the Capulets. The young Capulets, as they leave the Feast, pass by singing reminiscences of the ball music.

The Love Scene, in its full context, proves to be even more beautiful than one ever imagined it could be from reading the score. Magic is a word that constantly comes to mind as one listens to this work conducted by Toscanini, and there is magic from beginning to end in this scene. The instrumental sound of the *pppp* opening of the movement, the conception of the off-stage chorus and its orchestral accompaniment, the astonishing simplicity of Berlioz's means of creating the atmosphere and passionate poetry of one of the most beautiful nocturnes in all music—these are things of pure, incomparable magic, and which, like Toscanini's own magical presentation of them, defy all analysis.

PART IV

Queen Mab, or the Dream Fairy

Toscanini's performance of the Queen Mab scherzo was better known than the other excerpts he played from *Romeo and Juliet*, for he performed it more often not only in the United States but also in Europe. When he played it in England in 1937 with the BBC Symphony Orchestra and when his 1951 recording of it was released there, I am sorry to say most of my colleagues classed it as a "show-piece". The 1951 recording of the Scherzo is included in the complete version of *Romeo and Juliet*, which otherwise dates from 1947,

*The RCA brochure includes this in a Part II of its own invention. I have adhered throughout to Berlioz's original divisions as shown in the score.

and I hope my colleagues, when they come to study the work as a whole in Toscanini's performance, will be less patronizing about Queen Mab.

This fantastic Scherzo is one of those typical experiences of Toscanini's genius which, so far from giving up its secret, becomes increasingly astonishing and more difficult to analyse with each hearing. To describe it as "magical" is merely to say that the minimum requirement has been achieved. Berlioz, after Mozart, is the least foolproof of all composers, but some of the magic of the Queen Mab Scherzo will emerge from even the most pedestrian performance. What Toscanini brings to it is not only his unique feeling for the instrumental balance and detail, but his astounding lightness of touch and irresistible rhythm; he reveals the extraordinary newness and modernity of Berlioz's whole way of orchestral thinking with its incredible colouring and its power to create such wonderful, eternally arresting sounds as the sequences for antique cymbals and two harps (Eulenburg pages 218–222).

Like everything else in Toscanini's performance of *Romeo and Juliet*, the Scherzo possesses an inexhaustible ability to surprise the listener with the spontaneity and freshness of its inspiration.

Juliet's Funeral Procession

The constant revelation of Berlioz's genius in this recording by Toscanini never lets up for a moment, or allows us to forget that one is listening to music of unbelievable originality. Juliet's Funeral Procession is a movement of almost unbearable sadness—a fugal march on a fugue subject unlike anything one has ever heard before. The *marche fuguée* is in two parts; at first it is instrumental "with a psalmody on a single note in the voices"; then it is vocal, "with the psalmody in the orchestra". The contrapuntal treatment by the orchestra of the strange, melancholy subject is made typically clear and effective by Toscanini; but it is in the second part, when the voices' reiterated monotone is heard *pp* in the violins and violas, that we hear one of the most astonishing instrumental sounds ever drawn from an orchestra. The quality of this penetrating tolling of the repeated E's over two octaves (first heard on page 239) has a weird, unearthly effect and becomes quite unnerving in the crescendo-diminuendo series of crotchet E's for flutes and violins in octaves which ends with eight bars of *pppp* (page 247). It is an uncanny sound altogether.

Romeo at the Tomb of the Capulets

Invocation—Juliet's awakening.   Delirous joy, despair; last agonies and death of the two lovers.

The Allegro agitato e disperato that begins the scene of Romeo at the Tomb of the Capulets suffers an unexpected moment of ragged playing at the start, but there is no question of the intense agitation and despair of the music. Nor is there anything wrong with the balance and tonal quality of the long brass and woodwind chords and the dramatic tension they create in the pause that precedes the Invocation.

In the Invocation (page 255), Toscanini makes what I can only think of as an instinctive emphasis on the *ppp* two-quaver figure in the violas and violoncellos. He places an accent on the first of the two quavers each time. This is not shown in Berlioz's score, where the only accent marked is on the 3rd, 6th, 9th and 12th quavers of the 12/8 bar in the double bass part alone. Toscanini's instinct was to play this weeping figure as though it was Verdi, where *piangendo* figures like these are always accented in this way.

The long tune of the Invocation itself, played by cor anglais and bassoons in unison with frequent support from one or another of the horns, is a first rate example of how a Berlioz tune should be phrased—or rather, why a Berlioz tune should be phrased in the way he intended and not as some conductors consider he should have phrased it. The unique nature of a Berlioz melody is made wonderfully apparent in Toscanini's faithful adherence to the composer's idiosyncracies of musical inflexion, stress and punctuation which give his tunes their character and peculiar beauty.

What follows the lyrical calm of the Invocation is pure, riveting drama and Toscanini plays it with tremendous force. The *joie délirante* which the lovers enjoy when Juliet awakens is filled with overwhelming and passionate excitement, expressed with all the *fuoco* the composer asks for. This Allegro vivace section also includes some magnificent examples of Berlioz's most characteristic and peculiar writing for the wind section (woodwind, horns, trumpets, cornets), which are played with that clarity and attack only Toscanini could treat them to.

The performance of the final section of the movement, "the last agonies and death of the two lovers" (pages 271–276) is quite terrifying. The realism of this scene has been disapproved of in its time, though on what grounds I cannot imagine; Berlioz achieves all his bloodcurdling effect by purely musical means. The death of the two lovers is painted in colours of utter despair and tragedy; for music that tears the listener's nerves apart there is little in musical drama to compare with the spine-chilling sequence of eleven bars in which unison clarinets play in 4-time against harsh repeated three-in-a-bar chords played by the rest of the wind instruments (page 271), or the searing sound of the abrupt, desperate quaver phrases for violins and violas on pages 272–274, and the unison *con fuoco* descending scale and heartbreaking G-string cadence (bars 5–9, page 276) for violins that leads to the final agonizing *ff* shriek by the whole orchestra. Where some may have found only realism in these bars, Toscanini inevitably found music—and tremendous, gripping drama.

Finale

The Finale starts off full of vigorous movement and a gradual crescendo which Toscanini controls and intensifies magnificently to its dramatic peak at the crowd's cry of "Ciel!" Once into this Finale, there are no more purely orchestral passages; it is a movement for solo voice (Friar Laurence), chorus and orchestra—dramatic music presented in a dramatic manner, with passages of recitative, an aria, and exciting choral episodes.

Friar Laurence's first long solo, in which he reproaches the Montagues and Capulets for their ceaseless feud, has a wonderfully simple accompaniment based on the sort of irresistible rhythm which, once Toscanini had started it off, seems to bowl along effortlessly under its own natural impetus.

The accompaniment of the Air (Larghetto sostenuto) is an endless *cantabile* which Toscanini made one believe was played all in one bow and one breath, its easy flowing tempo emphasised by the most exquisitely timed and pathetic *pochissimo ritenuto* at the top of page 302.

After this beautiful, lyrical interlude the music becomes actively dramatic again, first with a near-ostinato figure for second violins and violoncellos in octaves in a vigorously rhythmic sequence which Toscanini drives along excitingly, and then with a reprise of the fugato which started the symphony, with the voices of the Montagues and Capulets joining in and resuming their quarrelling. Toscanini builds this up relentlessly and with tremendous force before the scene eventually dies down with his moving performance of the beautiful *dolce* and *mezza voce* coda of the warring families finally at peace with each other.

The last section—Friar Laurence's *Serment*, which ends with the Montagues and Capulets vowing to be reconciled—is a noble and splendid finale. Toscanini plays it as instructed, Andante un poco maestoso—that is, at an easy-moving tempo and allowing the music to speak for itself without exaggeration or hint of pomposity. These final pages are regarded by some as "theatrical" (the term used in a derogatory sense, of course). Those who do so obviously think the Verdi Requiem is also "theatrical". What they really mean is that both works are dramatic and therefore not respectable, as choral works should be. Toscanini, who had a genius for noting and digesting composers' instructions, happened to see that Berlioz described his *Romeo and Juliet* as a "dramatic symphony", and he took the composer at his word wholeheartedly and incomparably.

This performance of *Romeo and Juliet* stands out in all my experience of Toscanini as the only masterpiece which I had never heard performed in full until his recording of it. It is an unparalleled introduction to one of the most original and moving pieces of music ever written.

HAYDN
⋞ [1732–1809] ⋟

SYMPHONY No 88 in G
[1786]

NBC Symphony Orchestra
RCA-Italiana LM 20069
1938

This classic performance on 78 rpm is now available in an LP transfer on RCA-Italiana LM 20069 coupled with the Mozart Bassoon Concerto (see page 174). And according to my own experience, it is a record that seems easy enough to come by. I ordered my copy through a shop in Hampstead without any trouble. I will not pretend that the transfer is as good acoustically as the old

78 set which I prefer and still use on broadcasts, if only because the level of volume of the last movement of the LP is so rough and exaggerated that it makes the needle jump about. Nevertheless, it is still recognizable as the same performance I wrote about in my earlier chapter on Haydn and that is what matters (see page 145).

SYMPHONY No 98 in B flat
[1791]

NBC Symphony Orchestra

1945

I am afraid I cannot give a catalogue number to this Haydn symphony which was originally issued in America as M 1025. In 1952, Mr Walter Toscanini tells me, "there was a project to release this symphony coupled with a new re-recording of the Haydn Symphony No 88, because the transfer of this symphony on the album LCT 7 had been a defective one. . . . These two symphonies were scheduled to be released in the Camden Album CAL-601; but RCA-Victor at that time abandoned the publication of all albums on this economical series which was sold in the U.S. for $1.98". Mr Toscanini later sent me a test pressing of the LP transfer of the symphony for which I was most grateful. In the hope, therefore, that this performance will eventually find its way back into the catalogues in some form or other, I have included it here.

Toscanini's performance of No 98, like that of the other two Haydn works which I shall come to later in this chapter, is in accordance, I imagine, with the scores published by Breitkopf and Härtel whose editions of the classics he usually used. This means that what Toscanini plays does not entirely agree with some modern revised editions such as the one made of No 98 by H. C. Robbins Landon from the autograph and original manuscript parts which has now appeared as a Eulenburg miniature score. For the most part the differences are in phrase marks and bowing; the trumpet and timpani parts are also different in the autograph. Corrections have been made in the Eulenburg score by hand—slurs added, and trumpet and timpani parts pasted in to be re-photographed. Not all the old incorrect details have been entirely obliterated by these rather amateurishly executed emendations; but they will be as plain as a pikestaff to anybody listening to Toscanini's performance of the symphony. The difference between what Toscanini's orchestra played and what the Robbins Landon edition suggests they ought to have played is not so enormous in the end. If Toscanini's score marked a scale for strings to be played staccato instead of legato the sound was still in character, and his remarkable feeling for Haydn's style was in no way affected. Only at one point does the difference between editions really matter and that is where neither Toscanini nor any other conductor I have heard has ever suspected that they were not playing what Haydn had written. And supposing they had suspected it, what could they have put in its place? Nothing, of course, because what Haydn in fact wrote was a sheer stroke of genius which couldn't possibly be guessed at. If by any chance someone had guessed at it, second thoughts would inevitably have rejected the idea as being anachronistic.

The point in question is in the slow movement, bar 81, or six bars from the end where the first violin, instead of playing the F as its first note which has been common practice for many years, plays (as shown in Haydn's original manuscript) an entirely unexpected and ravishing E flat, producing the chord known to jazz musicians as "F 7th", or in the harmony books as the tonic chromatic seventh.

It is a pity Toscanini couldn't have used Mr Robbins Landon's edition, but unfortunately it wasn't published before his death. One can only imagine the electrifying effect this sudden chord would have had in a Toscanini performance of the symphony.

In the version which, under the circumstances, he had to use, Toscanini's performance of No 98 is highly stimulating. The unexpectedly solemn unison passages for strings which begin the Adagio introduction to the first movement are superbly dramatic and sombre; they are played with an intensity which contrasts so vividly with the Allegro that follows that one forgets, for a moment, that the opening theme of the Allegro is, in fact, a paraphrase in the major of the tune just heard in the Adagio. The striking change of mood, which Haydn created by this simple device, is beautifully realized by Toscanini whose faultless change of tempo at moments like these was one of the most fascinating features of his Haydn performances.

The Allegro is a robust movement with a dramatic development section which Toscanini played with a characteristic vigour that never threatened the clarity of the counterpoint.

The slow movement—Adagio—was marked *cantabile* by the composer and Toscanini responded as one would expect. This is a beautiful performance and leaves one sorrier than ever that the original Haydn bar I mentioned earlier couldn't have been included. One can do one's own bit of amateur "splicing" at this bar in Toscanini's recording, of course, by singing the missing E flat. It gives a faint idea of the effect of Haydn's little masterstroke.

Haydn wrote two sorts of minuets: fast ones, and not-quite-so-fast ones. The Minuet in this symphony is marked Allegro and has a robust, peasant quality which Toscanini emphasizes with a robust, peasant rhythm. The Trio is taken at the same healthy tempo, but with plenty of time for the charm of phrases like bars 78–80 to register.

The Finale of No 98 is a 6/8 Presto and is full of the exuberant fun and wit that Toscanini so obviously enjoyed in Haydn's finales. This one is exceptionally lovable and includes a surprising interlude for a solo violin with some unexpected harmonic excursions, and a final section where the Presto gives way to a Più moderato in which the movement ends. In addition to the solo passages for violin, the Finale also includes twelve bars of semi-quaver arpeggios for cembalo (right hand only). This sequence occurs on the penultimate page of the score and was written as a final flourish; Haydn played this part himself at the first performance of the symphony. It is not included in Toscanini's performance of the work as it is only the most advanced of modern conductors who have gone back to using the continuo in Haydn's symphonies.

SYMPHONY No 99 in E flat

[1794]

NBC Symphony Orchestra

U.S.A.: Victor LM 6711

1949

My assertion on page 140 of this book that "No 99 was never recorded at all" was true at the time I wrote it and is still true in that the performance listed above was a broadcast that took place in March 1949; the recording we are now concerned with is derived from that performance. In other words, unlike many of the records included in this book it was not the product of a formal gramophone session.

Toscanini's performance of No 99 is another of his typically enjoyable Haydn symphonies, beginning with a dramatic, solemn Adagio which is no less solemn than the introduction to No 98 except that it is in the major this time. The main Vivace assai that follows is played with immense grace but also with vigour, for Toscanini never allowed the rhythm to get flabby just because the music was charming. The vigour is intensified in the development section with a fiery crackling effect which gives powerful point to one of those characteristic dramatic episodes Haydn introduced into even his most light-hearted symphonies.

The second movement, Adagio and *cantabile*, is a beautifully played and masterly display of Toscanini's insistence that *all* the parts in the orchestra should sing, whether they are playing the tune or only helping with the harmony. The warmth and clarity of some of the three- and four-part passages for strings only are exceptionally lovely. This whole Adagio, indeed, is typical of Toscanini's inimitable way of moulding a slow movement into one long, singing phrase apparently taken in a single effortless breath. The pay-off—the last four bars of the movement—is played with an irresistible grace.

The Minuet is one of Haydn's slower movements in this form—Allegretto, that is, instead of the Allegro found in No. 98. Toscanini plays it with great charm and clarity. The Trio, lacking any instructions from the composer that it should be anything else, is taken at the same tempo as the Minuet, but a subtle change of instrumental tone and an added suavity give it a distinctive character of its own. Toscanini's matchless sense of timing comes into play with a magical little touch at the end of the Trio—the faintest hint of a breath pause between the last note of the Trio and the return to the up-beat of the Minuet when it is repeated *Da capo*.

The Finale, Vivace, is sheer delight from start to finish; the beautiful *piano* statement of the theme by the strings, the effervescence and wit of the exquisitely gauged matching dynamics of the dialogue passages for strings and woodwind, the ferocious attack and rhythm of the clear, vigorous counterpoint of the development section, are inimitable features of a superbly exhilarating, typical Toscanini view of a Haydn finale which makes it easy to forgive an unexpected moment of ragged playing by the first violins, in the first of the four slow measures, which suddenly make their appearance at bars 197–200.

The edition of the score used by Toscanini differs in one respect from the Eulenburg edition edited in 1935 by Dr Ernst Praetorius. The cadence that occurs at bar 235 and again at bar 249 of this Finale is given by Praetorius as a crotchet E flat followed by a quaver G and a quaver F. Toscanini plays a crotchet E flat followed by a grace note G and a crotchet F—a form which strikes me as much tidier and which I prefer on account of its greater rhythmic interest.

SYMPHONIE CONCERTANTE in B flat

for Violin, Violoncello, Oboe, Bassoon and Orchestra

[1792]

Mischa Mischakoff (violin)

Frank Miller (violoncello)

Paolo Renzi (oboe)

Leonard Sharrow (bassoon)

NBC Symphony Orchestra

U.S.A.: Victor LM 6711

1948

This is a thoroughly enchanting broadcast performance of a spirited and cheerful work which once more differs in detail from the most recent Eulenburg edition—this time the edition of 1940 by Max Hochkofler. No doubt by modern standards of scholarship the score used by Toscanini would be considered corrupt, but, as before, the differences are effective and undisturbing. In the first movement they mostly affect the solo bassoon whose part is different and more interesting to play at bars 152, 181, 182 and again at bar 262 where the instrument is given a minim G flat in the second half of the bar as a lead-in to its staccato arpeggio run in bar 263.

In the slow movement the only difference I have noted is four solo C's in the second horn part to fill out the last four beats of what would otherwise have been a largely silent 6/8 bar (bar 56).

The last movement includes a number of short pizzicato figures in the accompaniment (bars 116–119, 142–145 and 265–271), an improvement of the solo violoncello part in bars 147 and 148 and a sustained chord for strings under the solo violin's E flat held in bar 282.

Toscanini's performance of this captivating little work (with its Rondo theme neatly filched from the first movement of Mozart's Violin Concerto in D, K. 218) is full of those wonderfully characteristic details which he relished so much in Haydn's music. The slow movement, in particular, is outstanding and includes not only some infectiously warm *cantabile* playing by the strings, but an astonishing opening sequence of that singing pizzicato which Toscanini alone seemed to know how to obtain from an orchestra.

Perhaps the most unexpectedly memorable feature of the Finale is the incisive and dramatic string punctuation of the couple of passages of odd recitative for the solo violin. There are only four of these punctuating chords—two *forte* in the first Adagio and two *piano* in the second, 265 bars later—but their perfect balance and their intensely operatic character take one out of the concert hall straight into the theatre for a couple of unexpectedly evocative and refreshing moments. It is altogether a most entertaining and refreshing performance by Toscanini in a happy and relaxed mood. Above all, it is a shining example of music with that miraculous air of spontaneity which Toscanini achieved by intense rehearsal and the endless, unrelenting pursuit of perfection and the illumination of "what is there" in even the most straightforward and emotionally uncomplicated scores.

MOZART
⚝ [1756–1791] ⚝

THE MARRIAGE OF FIGARO OVERTURE: [1786]
1947

DON GIOVANNI OVERTURE: [1787]
1946

THE MAGIC FLUTE OVERTURE [1791]
1949

NBC Symphony Orchestra

U.S.A.: Victor LM 7026 ("Toscanini Conducts Overtures")

I have included these three overtures because Toscanini's performances of Mozart never cease to intrigue me: when they were good they were unique; when they were bad they were unbelievable. In either case they were always fascinating.

What intrigues me particularly on this occasion is that I have been able to compare Toscanini's performances of these overtures with those by two of the three greatest conductors of Mozart of the past 50 years—namely, Fritz Busch and Bruno Walter (the third, Richard Strauss, made very few records of Mozart and unfortunately I have none of them).

To generations of English orchestral musicians the overture to *Figaro* has been known as "the egg-boiler" "bogey" for its performance being 4 minutes—the time it takes to boil a fresh egg into a palatable state. A first hearing of Toscanini's performance suggests that it is well under par. Not only is the basic tempo uncomfortably fast but he makes an accelerando at the four bars which lead to the recapitulation (bar 139) and whips up the coda (bar 236) into a furious *stringendo e crescendo* which is entirely alien to Mozart's overture.

The hope I expressed on page 163 that Toscanini might one day present us with a classic performance of the *Figaro* overture has proved

vain. The music sparkles but it is with the hard brilliance of diamonds, not burnished gold—the brilliance of Rossini, in other words,
not Mozart. (It was Toscanini's lifelong regret that in spite of his
understanding and love of Rossini, who used so many of the same
notes, Mozart's greatness and peculiar emotional quality somehow
always eluded him.)

Ironically, where in so many of Toscanini's performances it is the
details of the score, the perception of "what is there" that gives them
their unique quality, in his *Figaro* overture it is precisely the details
which contribute most to the unsatisfactory character of the whole.
To take one typical instance, the phrase which Mozart writes

Ex. 196

is played in such a way that the D sharps are *forte* and the E's so
piano as to be almost inaudible. The initial *forte* on the D sharp
should act only as a brief accent; the rest of the bar (including what is
left of the D sharp after the initial attack) is *piano* not *pp*, and is
certainly not a diminuendo. In other words, it should sound

Ex. 197

and not

Ex. 198

The exaggeration of the *fp*, indeed, is typical of the hardness of the
entire performance. There is such a sharp bite to the strings that it
sounds almost as if they were playing *spiccato* all the time, instead of

smoothly *détaché* as they should be. It is the unease of the whole conception, in fact, which creates the illusion of an uncomfortable tempo, and it is an illusion. Toscanini takes no less than 4 minutes 15 seconds to play the *Figaro* overture—well over the egg-boiler bogey (Walter Toscanini's discography gives the timing as 3:55, but nothing I can do will make it less than 4:15—at least, not if it is to be in D major). This means that Toscanini takes 22 seconds longer than Fritz Busch does in his famous Glyndebourne recording of Mozart's opera made in 1934. But Busch's 3:53 (7 seconds under par) somehow sounds completely unhurried; the music bubbles away without effort at 152 beats to the minute, there is no hardness, and the brilliance is the warm brilliance which, as I have already suggested, distinguishes Mozart's rich golden radiance from the sharp adamantine light of Rossini.

The truth is that the most important, deep-rooted difference between the overture to *Figaro* played by Toscanini and played by Busch is that one cannot imagine looking forward with any great excitement to hearing the rest of the opera after Toscanini's overture, whereas Busch's leaves one eagerly impatient to know what happens next. After all that his *Haffner* finale led me to expect, Toscanini's *Figaro* overture is a sad disappointment.

Bruno Walter's performance of the *Figaro* overture, recorded in 1961 when he was 84, has the same ease and elegance as Busch's, although it is 42 seconds slower. The tempo may be attributable to old age, for in his great Charlottenburg days in the 1920's, when I heard him conduct a classic series of *Figaro* performances, Walter's overture was certainly much more lively and more truly Presto. His 1961 recording is nearer Allegro molto, but the typical warmth and, above all, the *sound* that is peculiar to authentic Mozart playing are still unmistakable.

Toscanini's *Don Giovanni* overture suffers from many of the same defects as his *Figaro*. The opening Andante moves comfortably enough, but it is subjected to a number of exaggeratedly dramatic touches—such as hurrying over the *sf-p* phrases in bars 15 and 16 and the groups of three semi-quavers in bars 17 and 19. And in bars 23–26 he breaks his own professed rule that crescendo does not automatically mean accelerando by rushing at the up-and-down scale passages for flutes and violins in a most melodramatic manner. The first result of this, as in the hurried *sf-p* phrases six bars earlier, is to destroy the dramatic tension which Mozart carefully builds up by a steady, relentless four-in-a-bar pattern. The way Toscanini ignores this almost suggests that perhaps he never looked at the finale of the opera to see what the opening Andante was all about.

The tempo of the Molto allegro is no illusion; it is basically too fast (varying from 144 to 152 beats to the minute) and the string tone and phrasing which made the *Figaro* performance such an uncongenial experience have the same effect here. The impression that all scales and passage work are played *spiccato* instead of *détaché* persists and in one recurrent case the bite of the bow on the strings is so fierce that I thought Toscanini had altered Mozart's phrasing altogether. This was at the phrase

Ex. 199

when the last bar sounded as if the slur over the notes E and A had been removed and the five notes were played *staccatissimo*. It was only by playing the record at 16 rpm and hearing the bar played Largo (and an octave lower) that I was able to hear clearly that the two notes were in fact tied in the conventional *scherzoso* bowing manner. Once again, in short, it is the true *sound* of Mozart that eludes Toscanini. In Fritz Busch's 1936 Glyndebourne recording of *Don Giovanni* the overture is another exemplary demonstration that a sense of style and idiom are what count above everything. In the *Figaro* overture Busch's faster tempo was never out of character; in his *Don Giovanni*, after an Andante full of spontaneous dramatic power, his slower tempo for the Molto allegro (about 132 against Toscanini's 144–152) developed its own natural brilliance and excitement without artificial stimulus.

In *The Magic Flute* overture I still find the tone of Toscanini's orchestra too hard and unyielding to be sympathetic. No doubt he had his own very good personal reasons for doing it as he did, but one has only to compare the opening chords of the Toscanini *Magic Flute* with Bruno Walter's 1961 recording to hear how rich and impressively solemn they sound in Walter's performance compared with Toscanini's, where the same passage is arresting but somehow impersonal; in an odd way one is more conscious with Toscanini of how the orchestra is playing the notes than why. The Allegro section is again too fast to be comfortable, but the clarity of the individual parts in the fugue is remarkable even at this speed— about 96 to Bruno Walter's 84. But it is too fast for the charm of the music to make its point, and things which Walter was content to leave unemphasized are brought out sharply by Toscanini. I was thinking particularly of the passage for oboes in thirds which is first heard at bar 185, then again at 187, and repeated twice more in bars 194 and 196. In this 1949 performance of the overture the phrase is so exaggerated and prominent that when it comes to the third and fourth playing of it, the clucking of the oboes is nothing less than irritating.

Toscanini used to say at rehearsals of *The Magic Flute* overture that the fugue subject was music that smiled. It smiles in this recording— after a fashion. But it is a smile that comes from the face; when Toscanini conducted Mozart's opera in 1937 the smile came from the heart. That was the difference and that is why the record he made of the overture with the BBC Symphony Orchestra in 1938 is still, as I wrote on page 158, an admirable synthesis of all that was best in his performance of the opera itself and shows how superbly he brought to life that side of *The Magic Flute* he understood.

SCHUBERT
⤙ [1797–1828] ⤚

SYMPHONY No 9 in C
[1828]

The Philadelphia Orchestra

GREAT BRITAIN: RCA RB 6549

U.S.A.: Victor LD 2663

1941

The posthumous release of this legendary recording, more than twenty years after it was made, has been a matter of great personal relief to me, for it matches very closely the performance I heard Toscanini give in London in 1938 and which I tried to describe in my study of the work in the first half of this book (see page 199). At the time the earlier chapter was written, the only Toscanini recording of the Schubert C major Symphony that had been heard in England was the one made in 1947—by general consent an unsatisfactory interpretation. In 1959, some months after this book had been published, the 1953 recording was issued in England; but while it was an improvement over the 1947 version, in many respects it was still an inadequate example to anyone who wanted to hear how Toscanini had played the symphony at the top of his form.

The outstanding feature of the Philadelphia performance is the Finale, and it is in this movement that the great difference between this and the later recordings lies. In 1941, the Allegro vivace had a fast but regular pulse and Toscanini built his climaxes not by hurrying every time the strings came to their triplets and dotted notes, but by increasing the intensity of tone at the basic tempo of the movement. (In fact, in the 1953 performance Toscanini does not even wait for a climax to build to before the air is full of breathless *stringendo*. He allows the triplets to run away from the tempo as soon as he sees them in bar 38 and hurries unreasonably whenever he comes to the dotted-note passages for strings.)

With the Philadelphia Orchestra the rhythm springs naturally and inevitably from a basic tempo which is always under control. The excitement bubbles out of the music spontaneously instead of being imposed upon it from outside, and one feels that everything is so confident and controlled, so perfectly timed, that like a great tennis player Toscanini always seems to have all the time in the world to make his stroke. This is particularly noticeable in the superbly effective deliberation of the recurrent *ff* phrase of four unison C's (straight from Leporello's terrified "ta, ta, ta, ta!" in the finale of *Don Giovanni*) which are hammered out four times in the coda of the movement.

In terms of the metronome the difference in tempo between this Philadelphia performance of the Finale and that of the 1953 recording is not startling—roughly 104–108 against 112—but it is enough to make the 1941 version more than half a minute longer, and in so doing it gives the music a chance to breathe easily and unhurriedly.

Paradoxically, the other three movements are all faster according to the timing on the Philadelphia recording, and yet the final impression is of an altogether much more relaxed and fluid performance than the 1953 recording. The Trio of the Scherzo, for instance, is noticeably faster in the 1941 version, but the Scherzo as a whole, is nearly a quarter of a minute shorter and has a quality of elegance, together with flashes of *cantabile* lyrical beauty provided by the strings (especially the violoncellos) that the slower 1953 Scherzo does not possess. A great deal of this elegance, of course, can be credited to the strings of the Philadelphia Orchestra, which have a warmth and suppleness reminiscent of the Vienna Philharmonic and which is not lost under the pressure of the vigorous tempo favoured by Toscanini in this superb performance.

This is the Schubert C major Symphony as I remember him playing it.

SHOSTAKOVICH
[BORN 1906]

Many people (I was not among them) were perturbed that Toscanini seemed to be so uninterested in contemporary music. Why didn't he play Berg, Stravinsky, Schoenberg or Bartók? The answer was, of course, that these composers were not his contemporaries. Conductors as a rule seem to perform contemporary music only when they are young. As they approach middle age they rarely study new scores and begin instead to concentrate on the classical repertoire, but keeping in their repertoire those composers whose new works they played when young. Pierre Monteux and Ernest Ansermet are familiar instances of conductors who were famous in their youth for their championship of Stravinsky, for instance, but who, from the age of fifty onwards, began to fill their programmes with Beethoven, Brahms and Schubert. Bruno Walter, so far as I know, never played anything more contemporary when he was young than Mahler and Richard Strauss, and spent the greater part of his life conducting the Vienna classics and Wagner.

Toscanini's contemporaries were Debussy, Richard Strauss, Sibelius, Dukas, Elgar and Puccini. He played their works when they were new and he was still playing them when he was past eighty. His performance of two symphonies by Shostakovich (who was born in 1906, the year Toscanini conducted *Salome* at La Scala for the first time), is therefore an exceptional excursion into the music of our time. What is less clear is why Toscanini preferred to perform them rather than those works by his own contemporaries which for some reason he ignored—like Debussy's *Gigues* and *Rondes de Printemps*, Sibelius' *Tapiola* and Fifth Symphony, and Elgar's Second.

In the case of Shostakovich's First Symphony, which he conducted in 1931, 1937, 1939 and 1944 (at least seven times altogether), the work was obviously played because of its merits. But in the case of the Leningrad Symphony (No 7), I believe Toscanini performed it only for the emotional appeal it had for him at the time he introduced it to American wartime audiences.

SYMPHONY No. 1, Opus 10
[1926]

NBC Symphony Orchestra
U.S.A.: Victor LM 6711
1944

I find, on reflection, that I heard Toscanini conduct this symphony in London in 1937, but as it was followed after intermission by a blazing performance of the Eroica (his first with the BBC Orchestra) it is hardly surprising that I remember virtually nothing about it. For practical purposes, therefore, this recording has been my first opportunity to study Toscanini's approach to a work which, while it is no masterpiece, is a classic of its kind—the first symphony written by a young composer of immense promise. That the promise of this work was not fulfilled by Shostakovich's later music is not the fault of the composer, but of his environment.

This first symphony by Shostakovich is a work whose refreshing and youthful spontaneity Toscanini understood and expressed in an astonishing manner in the performance he conducted only a fortnight before his 77th birthday. In the first movement, in particular, he found an unexpected elegance in the music—episodes like the flute solo (with a richly singing pizzicato accompaniment) at Fig. 13 in the score, and the charming coda to this lyrical section which ends at Fig. 18.

The second movement, the Scherzo, is superbly played with all the clarity, rhythmic drive and precision one would expect, and with a rare discovery of the dramatic undertones of the Meno mosso interlude (Fig. 6 to Fig. 15) which is wonderfully effective.

The performance of the slow movement is distinguished by some warm *cantando* string playing and also by Toscanini's peculiar clarification of passages for the full orchestra which normally sound too thickly scored. Shostakovich's use of alto instead of tenor trombones may account for some of the thickness, especially when they play in the same register as the horns, but Toscanini manages to disentangle them.

The Finale is a vigorous Allegro molto with some tuneful lyrical interludes. Toscanini's electrifyingly rhythmic interpretation of the one is matched by his typically gentle and warmhearted playing of the other. The whole performance is a stimulating experience which I am glad to be able to enjoy again.

There is a textual difference to be noted between Toscanini's recording and the Moscow State Music Publishers' score published in 1962. This occurs in the last movement at Fig. 39 (page 100) where Toscanini completes the timpani phrase with an E flat on the first beat, thus matching the flute and oboe phrase which is obviously meant as an echo of what should be six, not five, drum notes. The absence of the E flat is almost certainly a printing error; the full six-note phrase is correctly shown in the bar before and in the first and second bars after Fig. 36 on the previous page.

SYMPHONY No 7, Opus 60

(Leningrad)

[1942]

NBC Symphony Orchestra

U.S.A.: Victor LM 6711

1942

In his book *Conversations with Toscanini*, B. H. Haggin remarked how "Toscanini's taste could be by-passed by way of his heart". It is a shrewd point and is the only satisfactory explanation of Toscanini's decision to conduct this Leningrad Symphony. It was an emotional decision prompted by Toscanini's passionate hatred of oppression and his belief that, as he confessed to Mr Haggin, "In this symphony I hear suffering of Russian people".

There is certainly nothing to criticize in Toscanini's interpretation of Shostakovich's Seventh Symphony. It is a tremendous performance, packed with drama and great thundering climaxes, with irresistible rhythms and dazzlingly brilliant string and woodwind figures; but there are moments of great lyrical tenderness, too, when Toscanini can be heard joining in with the strings at their most *dolce* and *cantabile*. (It is pleasant to hear the Maestro's familiar voice again; in so many of the later recordings the microphones were placed out of earshot.)

The notorious, dementing crescendo in the first movement, with its reiterated resemblance to "Maxim's" from Lehár's *Merry Widow*, I will admit to having listened to from beginning to end—conscientiously, curiously, and eventually with astonishment at the incredible feat of endurance expected of the listener and achieved by conductor and orchestra. Toscanini's gradual building of the climax is a fantastic demonstration of his ability to draw more and yet more sound from an orchestra which seems to have reached the limit of a man-made *fortissimo* but which can be persuaded, by Toscanini, to produce even greater volumes of sound to make the composer's final *fff* an overwhelming, but still always musical, climax in which the notes can be heard through the noise. The miracle with this particular performance is that the lips of the NBC brass and woodwind players stayed the course without cracking.

It is a pity that this maddening passage should inevitably so exhaust the listener that the many really beautiful sequences in the rest of the work should pass almost unnoticed. Here, at least, the gramophone record can help, and I found that by skipping the "Maxim's" nightmare I could concentrate with a fresh mind on the quieter movements such as the simple and effective lyrical section before the drums start up in the first movement (Fig. 16 to Fig. 19), and the quiet, restful string passage (Fig. 68 to Fig. 70) which precedes the return of the distant side drum that ends the movement.

The second movement, Moderato (poco allegretto), also has long tuneful, charming sequences and a coda which Toscanini handles with an enchanted touch. On the whole, however, I cannot help wishing that all the energy and thought that Toscanini must have lavished on this performance could have been used to better artistic purpose. But if I *have* to listen to the Leningrad Symphony then I'd rather hear Toscanini conduct it than anybody else.

SIBELIUS
≼ [1865–1957] ≽

SYMPHONY No 2 in D, Opus 43
[1902]

POHJOLA'S DAUGHTER
[1906]

NBC Symphony Orchestra
U.S.A.: Victor LM 6711
1940

Sibelius was not a composer one instinctively associated with Toscanini at all—or indeed with any Latin conductor—for his music was so grimly Nordic and individual in its idiom and so plainly lacking in those qualities which one would expect to appeal to a conductor of Toscanini's temperament and reputation. Or so one might have thought. But even my limited experience of Sibelius performed by Toscanini—*En Saga* in London in 1937, and the Second Symphony there the following year—was enough to show how completely wrong this presumption could be.

The Second Symphony, I remember, was full of things which came uniquely to life with Toscanini. What one heard was not necessarily things that had gone unnoticed before (though there was plenty of that, of course), but things which one knew had never sounded as well as one had hoped they would.

The recording now issued which, like *Pohjola's Daughter*, is the broadcast performance of December 7, 1940 reminds me that the performance of the Symphony at the Queen's Hall was every bit as good as I remember it to have been, and that my memory of it has not been coloured by the passing of nearly thirty years.

In the opening bars of the first movement—the gentle throbbing, vamp-till-ready passage for strings—we are aware that the sound of a Sibelius score was unlike anybody else's. The peculiar clarity of the texture and the economy of instrumental means were something Toscanini recognized at once, and which he demonstrated superbly in his performances of Sibelius. He saw, too, that while still clear northern waters might run deep they could also reflect sunlight, and there is a refreshing cheerfulness in the perky little tune played by oboes and clarinets immediately following the opening string passage. This was another tune which, like the second subject of the Schubert C major Finale, Toscanini described at rehearsal as a street tune for whistling.

The whole of this first movement of Sibelius' Second Symphony is full of the composer's characteristic touches which might have been custom-built for Toscanini—the rich singing pizzicato passages, the warm *cantabile* phrases, the great snarling brass crescendos, and the tremendous dynamic and emotional excitement of the typical Sibelius climax-building. It is a score unusually detailed in its markings of both dynamics and variations of tempo, and Toscanini observes them with such care and effect that one realizes that hitherto one had never heard the half of them; other conductors just never seemed able to think quickly enough to get them all in. The coda is particularly charming.

In the second movement, Tempo andante, ma rubato, Toscanini's rare ability to sustain the line of a slow movement in one long effortless breath was heard at its best. It is a movement which combines drama and great lyrical beauty—intense and powerful *stringendo* sequences contrasted with *cantabile* and *espressivo* passages for strings (the string writing is exceptionally effective). These are features which Toscanini played for all they were worth and which stand out in my memory of the London performance, and are confirmed by the recording. Only two details spoil my total enjoyment of the 1940 performance of this movement. The first may well be due to the engineers who balanced the broadcast. The tremendous *fff* for the four horns as they unwind after the first great climax of the movement (eight bars before letter E in the Breitkopf and Härtel score) does not make the impact it should; I know from having heard Toscanini play this symphony that it most certainly did in the studio. It sounds as if the engineers were scared by the sight of the *fff* for the four horns, although they had allowed the big *fffz* for the full brass section immediately before. The next time the passage occurs—four bars before letter K—the horns are a bit more audible. But then this time they are marked only *ff*, so I suppose the engineers thought they could risk it.

The second detail is a more serious blemish, in my opinion. The first trumpet, with its hint of a cornet vibrato in its solo phrases between letters F and G, is not at all to my liking; remembering the pure clear tone of Ernest Hall's trumpet at this point with the BBC Symphony Orchestra under Toscanini, the NBC player's solo sounds altogether out of character. Paradoxically, the flute which echoes each of the trumpet phrases in the same low register sounds much more like the trumpet should.

The third movement, the Scherzo, is marked *Vivacissimo*—an Italian word which Toscanini translated to mean "like lightning". The speed of the string passages with the violins in four parts, the uncanny unanimity of the dynamics, the featherweight pianissimos and sparkling fortes, the crystal clarity of the individual parts scored by Sibelius with such telling economy and certainty of effect, add up to one of the most exhilarating musical experiences ever to come from a Toscanini record. The only real disappointment is the 12/4 Trio section—Lento e suave—which, both times it occurs, is taken just too slowly to allow the simple little oboe tune to breathe naturally and gracefully. At Toscanini's tempo what should be plaintive and charming is rather gloomy and sullen, and not even the splendid unison G-string tone of the strings quite redeems it. This is certainly a passage which sounded better in the London performance, when the interlude was less *lento* and much more *suave*. The unsympathetic nature of this interlude in the recording is forgotten quickly enough when on the first occasion the brass cuts in with its shattering *ff* return to Tempo I°; this is a tremendous moment. But the brief reappearance of the 12/4 tune which leads into the transition to the Finale reminds one once more that Toscanini had made the episode sound much better three years earlier.

The Finale is a little faster than is customary, but then Toscanini takes it Allegro moderato as marked and not *maestoso*, which is how most conductors get bogged down in a movement that can easily become tedious and misfire if the timing and intensity of its climax is not carefully gauged. Toscanini's tempo ensures that nothing misfires and his sense of timing is as miraculous as ever. The great 72-bar *ostinato*—the simple seven-finger exercise figure in D minor which begins *piano* in violas and violoncellos and is worked up to a tremendous dynamic pitch with the help of all the woodwind in unison octaves—has a fascinating inevitability. It builds up inexorably and irresistibly and generates a powerful dramatic vitality which saves the movement from the flabby pompousness it can so easily sink into.

Two points to be noted: first, that Toscanini has added a B flat in the tuba part to the bassoons and basses at letter M—evidently unable to bear the idea that the instrument's A in the bar before should not lead to a B flat like the other instruments. The alteration is not really a success, as the addition of the tuba introduces a disturbingly foreign colour to the sound Sibelius obviously had in mind.

The second point is a detail in the playing of the rising unison semi-quaver scale by violins and violas seven bars after letter B. The crescendo is so powerful it is like a whiplash that takes your breath away. This is something I do not remember ever having heard before; the effect is quite startling and very typical of the outstanding and arresting experience that Toscanini made of this Second Symphony altogether.

Sibelius' tone poem *Pohjola's Daughter* (Pohjola isn't the girl's mother, but means the "North Country") is also known as *Daughter of the North* and must be a piece as characteristic of the composer as anything he ever wrote. Here again Toscanini has everything that one now realizes must have appealed to him in Sibelius—the highly individual orchestral colouring, the fierce dynamic accents and driving ostinatos, the strong rhythms and moments of gentle lyrical warmth and beauty, the sharp contrasts between light and darkness.

Toscanini seems to have performed *Pohjola's Daughter* only once—in the broadcast from which this recording is taken. There were other short pieces by Sibelius he obviously preferred—*En Saga*, *Finlandia* and *The Swan of Tuonela*—but none of them could have been so musically satisfying as this. The mysterious darkness of the opening passage in particular makes one wish more than ever that he could have recorded Sibelius' Fourth Symphony—a work which in fact he played more often than the Second. One can only hope that in time Walter Toscanini will be able to arrange for us an LP transfer of the last performance his father gave of the Fourth Symphony, in a broadcast in April 1940. All Toscanini's NBC broadcasts were recorded by the company's engineers, so it ought really to be no more than a matter of patience.

TCHAIKOVSKY
≼ [1840–1893] ≽

SYMPHONY No 6 in B minor, Opus 74 ("Pathétique")

[1892]

NBC Symphony Orchestra

U.S.A.: Victor LM 1036

1947

I heard Toscanini conduct what I believe were the first two pieces of Tchaikovsky he had ever performed in America. The first was in March 1933, when he played the *Manfred* Symphony; the second was a month later when he played the *Tempest* Overture-Fantasy. It was said at the time that as a result of constant public nagging at him for never playing any Tchaikovsky, Toscanini deliberately chose two unfamiliar, unpopular works to serve his critics right. My own memory of the *Manfred* Symphony is that it was very long and I didn't much like it. Of the *Tempest* overture I remember nothing at this date at all.

So it was that when I came to play Toscanini's record of the Pathétique for the first time, I did so with an innocent ear; I had no idea what to expect. It proved to be one of the most startling of all my listening experiences. Here was a work perhaps even more hackneyed than Beethoven's Fifth. It was certainly more maltreated than the Beethoven had ever been for its very title encouraged conductors to do their worst. It was the ham conductor's show-piece. The fault though was largely Tchaikovsky's. Having unwisely titled the symphony, he then larded his score with expression marks which just ask for trouble; it abounds in sighing *cresc.-dim.* "hair-pin" phrases, in such exaggerated instructions as *pppp-pp-pppp* for horns, clarinets and timpani, and *pppppp* (no less) for the solo bassoon at one point. The strings are asked to play "con lenezza e devozione", an embarrassing enough request. How does one play "with devotion"? As for *lenezza*, this is a word I think Tchaikovsky must have made up, using as its root the poetic adjective *lene*, meaning delicate, soft, gentle. The nearest authentic noun I can find in any dictionary is *lenità*.

The lavish use of extravagant and optimistic dynamic markings like *ppppp* and *pppppp* is another feature of Tchaikovsky's score which has always encouraged the ham conductor to further excesses even though, as is likely, the composer was only following Verdi's principle that to get a genuine *pp* you must write *ppppp* at least.

After making allowances for this sort of familiar exaggeration, Toscanini gave a characteristically literal performance of the Pathétique, removed all the dust and dirt and over-painting of bathos and vulgarity that the work had accumulated over the years and restored an old masterpiece to all its original, brilliant and spontaneous colour.

From the very first moment of the opening Adagio, Tchaikovsky's symphony takes on a new life; the heavy emotional content becomes clear and coherent and so makes its point without slobbering. That Toscanini's is an intensely dramatic conception goes without saying; but as one would expect, it is never for a moment melodramatic in the usual derogatory sense of the word.

Like all his performances, this is full of fascinating detail—the remote melancholy quality of the solo horn's four bars of F sharp in the Adagio, the fire and bite of the violas and violoncellos in the statement of the first subject (Allegro non troppo), the lightness and clarity of the *saltando* figure for the violins first heard at bar 42, and the superb articulation of the brass (the trumpets particularly) on their entries in bars 67–70.

Toscanini's principle of seeing "what is there" was rarely more illuminating than when applied to the lyrical tunes in this Tchaikovsky piece. They are played with all the warmth and beauty they deserve without ever being over-played. Nor do they degenerate into the sentimentality which makes everyday performances of this work so nauseating.

The balance of the accompaniment to the two-octave unison of the second subject played by violins and violas (bars 130–133) is another masterly instance of Toscanini's control of the dynamics of individual inside parts in a score—no mean achievement with Tchaikovsky, whose woodwind writing can so often sound ugly and harsh.

The drama of the development section, with the startlingly literal interpretation of the composer's direction that the string playing should be *feroce*, is an electrifying contrast to the lyrical melancholy that precedes it. The rhythm is tremendous and, in the syncopated passages, demonstrates powerfully that the full effect of syncopation can be made properly only when there is a solid rhythm to syncopate *against*. (In this development section Toscanini seems to have touched up the orchestration a little by adding unison horns to double the bassoon part in bars 185 and 186 and the oboe part in bars 187 and 188. The reinforcement gives extra body to the woodwind writing which is welcome and effective.)

The second movement is marked Allegro con grazia and the *grazia* of the whole episode is breath-taking. The charm of the string playing is such sheer delight that the woodwind cannot match it and one almost resents their intrusion. The use of portamento in the tune after the second-time bar (heard again from bar 112 onwards) is quite ravishing, but controlled with such taste that the effect is never coy or cloying. This movement is an exquisite revelation.

The Scherzo-March is a superb demonstration of the way Toscanini could build up excitement by an irresistible rhythm the effect of which is intensified, not by an increase in speed, but by an increase in the volume and emotional force of what is played in that rhythm. Toscanini's Allegro molto vivace for this movement works out at about 160 beats a minute; I say "about" 160 because no metronome can follow the subtle fluctuations of tempo which supported the conductor's indignant maxim that "man is not a machine".

The scherzo element of this section is an unending joy, presented with a sparkling chamber-music clarity achieved by Toscanini's superhuman attention to detail and the balance of the individual parts that make up the whole. It is a fascinatingly characteristic performance from the moment you first start listening to the movement, and if instinct tells you what Toscanini is going to do, you are still suprised when you hear it happen. This is never more striking than at those points where generations of barnstormers have offered us their colourful view of what they think Tchaikovsky meant. Toscanini makes no change of tempo to suggest that the *fff* tutti statement of the march tune should be *grandioso* or *pomposo*, either at letter Y (bar 229), or again at EE (bar 283). Still less does he think there is any need for the corny exaggerated *stringendo* imposed by others in the passage a few bars after EE—the sequence that starts to build up at about bar 304 towards the *ffff* at bar 312. Toscanini just drives on with increased power without letting up for a moment to create any false effect by artificial means. He lets Tchaikovsky speak for himself, and Tchaikovsky never mentioned a *stringendo* or hinted at *pomposo* or anything like it in his score of this movement. Toscanini saw what was there and he saw what was not there; and one of the things he saw, that nobody else has apparently seen, was that after the words Allegro molto vivace on the first page, there was no other reference to tempo in the entire movement. If ever there was an instance of Toscanini's innocent Emperor's-clothes view of music this is it.

The Finale of the Pathétique is full of instructions from the composer which have undoubtedly contributed a great deal to the general maltreatment of the work. It begins unashamedly Adagio lamentoso, and within a few bars we find the strings playing "con lenezza e devozione", followed by the two trombones (with *cresc.-dim.* "hairpins") playing "con sentimento". Toscanini, with his instinctive sense of proportion, over-emphasizes nothing that is shown in the score and the result is quite beautiful. There is an infinite sadness in the string playing in the first few pages of the Finale (from the beginning to letter D, bar 51, and beyond) and this feeling affects the whole movement so deeply that for the first time in one's life one begins to share Tchaikovsky's self-pity instead of merely feeling rather embarrassed by its vulgarity, as so frequently happens.

The coda (from letter M to the end) is most moving, and is remarkable for the distinct articulation of the divided violoncellos and basses in the lower frequencies which makes the music clearly audible instead of being a vague mush—or, more often, so exaggeratedly *pppp* that it can't be heard at all.

To clean the romantic grime off the classics was one of Toscanini's greatest achievements. To clear the romantic grime off a romantic work like the Pathétique, and to know when to stop the operation before the music is stripped of its character and genuine emotional quality is little short of a miracle.

Toscanini did it.

TABLE OF ORIGINAL AND CURRENT
RECORD NUMBERS

TABLE OF ORIGINAL AND CURRENT RECORD NUMBERS

Composer	Title	Original No (U.S.)	Current No (U.S.)	Original No (G.B.)	Current No (G.B.)	Recorded
Beethoven	Concerto No 4*	LM 2797		RB 6628		1944
Beethoven	Fidelio	LM 6025		ALP 1304/5	VCM-9	1944
Beethoven	Missa Solemnis	LM 6013		ALP 1182/3 RB 16133/4	VCM-9	1953
Beethoven	Symphony No 1	LM 6009	VIC-8000	ALP 1040 RB 16101	VCM-1	1951
Beethoven	Symphony No 2	LM 1723	VIC-8000	ALP 1145 RB 16101	VCM-1	1949/51
Beethoven	Symphony No 3	LM 1042		ALP 1008 RB 16102		1949
Beethoven	Symphony No 3*	LM 2387	VIC-8000		VCM-1†	1953
Beethoven	Symphony No 4	LM 1723	VIC-8000	ALP 1145 RB 16103	VCM-1	1951
Beethoven	Symphony No 5	LM 1757	VIC-8000	ALP 1108 RB 16103	VCM-1	1952

Beethoven	Symphony No 6	LM 1755	VIC-8000	ALP 1129 RB 16104	VCM-2	1952
Beethoven	Symphony No 7*	LCT 1013; CAL-352		DB 2986/90 CDN 1028		1936
Beethoven	Symphony No 7	LM 1756	VIC-8000	ALP 1119 RB 16105	VCM-2	1951
Beethoven	Symphony No 8	LM 1757	VIC-8000	ALP 1108 RB 16106	VCM-2	1952
Beethoven	Symphony No 9	LM 6009	VIC-8000	ALP 1039/40 RB 16106/7	VCM-2	1952
Berlioz	Romeo and Juliet*	LM 7034				1947
Boito	Prologue: Mefistofele	LM 1849		ALP 1363	VCM-6	1954
Brahms	Symphony No 1	LM 1702	VIC-6400	ALP 1012 RB 16097	VCM-3	1951
Brahms	Symphony No 2	LM 1731	VIC-6400	ALP 1013 RB 16098	VCM-3	1952

* The asterisk indicates the performance is discussed in the Supplement, pp. 343–382.
† The dagger indicates first release (and therefore original number) in Great Britain.

Composer	Title	Original No (U.S.)	Current No (U.S.)	Original No (G.B.)	Current No (G.B.)	Recorded
Brahms	Symphony No 3	LM 1836	VIC-6400	ALP 1166 RB 16099	VCM-3	1952
Brahms	Symphony No 4	LM 1713	VIC-6400	ALP 1029 RB 16100	VCM-3	1951
Brahms	Variations on a Theme by Haydn	LM 1725	VIC-6400	ALP 1204 RB 16092	VCM-3	1952
Cherubini	Requiem Mass	LM 2000		ALP 1412	VCM-10	1950
Cherubini	Symphony in D	LM 1745		ALP 1106		1952
Debussy	Ibéria	LM 1833	VIC-1246		VIC-1052†	1950
Debussy	La Mer	LM 1833	VIC-1246	ALP 1070	VIC-1052	1950
Elgar	"Enigma" Variations	LM 1725	VIC/VICS-1344(e)	ALP 1204	VIC-1001	1951
Gluck	Orfeo ed Euridice (Act II)	LM 1850		ALP 1357		1952
Haydn	Symphonie Concertante*	LM 6711				1948
Haydn	Symphony No 88	M 454; LCT 7		DB 3515–7		1938
Haydn	Symphony No 94	LM 1789	VIC-1262	RB 16138	VCM-7	1953

386

Haydn	Symphony No 98*	M 1025				1945
Haydn	Symphony No 99*	LM 6711				1949
Haydn	Symphony No 101	M 57; CAL 375		D 1688/71		1929
Haydn	Symphony No 101	LM 1038	VIC-1262	RB 16138	VCM-7	1946/47
Mendelssohn	Symphony No 4	LM 1851	VIC/VICS-1341(e)	ALP 1267		1954
Mendelssohn	Symphony No 5	LM 1851		ALP 1267		1953
Mozart	Bassoon Concerto	LM 1030				1947
Mozart	Divertimento No 15	LM 2001		ALP 1492	VCM-7	1947
Mozart	Don Giovanni (Overture)*	LM 7026			VCM-7†	1946
Mozart	The Magic Flute (Overture)*	LM 7026			VCM-7†	1949
Mozart	The Marriage of Figaro (Overture)*	LM 7026			VCM-7†	1947
Mozart	Symphony No 35	M 65; CAL 326		D 1782–84		1929
Mozart	Symphony No 35	LM 1038		RB 16137	VCM-7	1946
Mozart	Symphony No 39	LM 2001	VIC/VICS-1330(e)	ALP 1492	VCM-7	1948

Composer	Title	Original No (U.S.)	Current No (U.S.)	Original No (G.B.)	Current No (G.B.)	Recorded
Mozart	Symphony No 40	LM 1789	VIC/VICS-1330(e)	RB 16137	VCM-7	1950
Mozart	Symphony No 41	LM 1030			VCM-7†	1945
Puccini	La Bohème	LM 6006	VIC/VICS-6019(e)	ALP 1081/2		1946
Ravel	Daphnis and Chloë (Suite No. 2)	LVT 1025 LM 7032	VIC-1273	ALP 1070 RB 6666		1949
Rossini	The Barber of Seville	Victor 7255; CAL 336				1929
Rossini	The Barber of Seville	LM 1044; LM 2040	VIC-1274	ALP 1007 RB 16096	VCM-6	1945
Rossini	La Cenerentola	LM 1044 LM 2040	VIC-1248	ALP 1007 RB 16096	VCM-6	1945
Rossini	La gazza ladra	LM 1044 LM 2040	VIC-1274	ALP 1007 RB 16096	VCM-6	1945
Rossini	L'Italiana in Algeri	Victor 14161; M 825		DB 2943		1936
Rossini	L'Italiana in Algeri	LM 7026	VIC-1248		VCM-6†	1950
Rossini	La scala di seta	Victor 15191 M 825		DB 3541	XLP-30079	1938

388

Rossini	Semiramide	M 408; CAL 309		DB 3079/80 CDN 1027		1936
Rossini	Semiramide	LM 2040	VIC-1274	RB 16096	VCM-6	1951
Rossini	Il Signor Bruschino	LM 1044 LM 2040	VIC-1274	ALP 1007 RB 16096	VCM-6	1945
Rossini	William Tell	M 605; LM 14		DA 1695/6		1939
Rossini	William Tell	LM 2040 VCM/VCS 7001(e)	VIC-1274	ALP 1441 RB 16096	VCM-6	1953
Schubert	Symphony No 8	LM 9022	VIC/VICS-1311(e)	BLP 1038 RB 16092		1950
Schubert	Symphony No 9*	LD 2663		RB 6549		1941
Schubert	Symphony No 9	LM 1040		ALP 1120		1947
Shostakovich	Symphony No 1*	LM 6711				1944
Shostakovich	Symphony No 7*	LM 6711				1942
Sibelius	Pohjola's Daughter*	LM 6711				1940
Sibelius	Symphony No 2*	LM 6711				1940
Strauss	Don Juan	LM 1157 LM 7032	VIC-1267	ALP 1173 RB 6606	VIC-1022	1951

Composer	Title	Original No (U.S.)	Current No (U.S.)	Original No (G.B.)	Current No (G.B.)	Recorded
Strauss	Don Quixote	LM 2026		ALP 1493		1953
Strauss	Till Eulenspiegel	LM 1891	VIC-1267	ALP 1404		1952
Strauss	Tod und Verklärung	LM 1891		ALP 1404		1952
Tchaikovsky	Symphony No 6*	LM 1036	VIC-1268			1947
Verdi	Aida	LM 6132	VIC/VICS-6113(e)	RB 16021/2/3		1949/54
Verdi	Un ballo in maschera	LM 6112		ALP 1252/3/4		1954
Verdi	Falstaff	LM 6111		ALP 1229/30/31 RB 16163/4/5		1950
Verdi	La forza del destino (Overture)	11-9010		DB 6314		1945
Verdi	La forza del destino (Overture)	LM 6041	VIC-1248	ALP 1452 RB 16139	VCM-6	1952
Verdi	Inno delle nazioni (Cantata)	LM 6041	VIC/VICS-1331(e)	ALP 1453 RB 16140	VCM-10	1943
Verdi	I Lombardi (Trio)	LM 6041	VIC/VICS-1314(e)	ALP 1452 RB 16139	VCM-6	1943

Verdi	Luisa Miller (Overture and Aria)	LM 6041	VIC/VICS-1314(e)	ALP 1452 RB 16139	VCM-6	1943
Verdi	Messa da Requiem	LM 6018		ALP 1380/1 RB 16131/2	VCM-10	1951
Verdi	Nabucco (chorus)	LM 6041		ALP 1452 RB 16139	VCM-10	1943
Verdi	Otello	LM 6107		ALP 1090/1/2 RB 16093/4/5		1947
Verdi	Otello (Ballet Music)	LM 6041	VIC/VICS-1321(e)	ALP 1453 RB 16140		1948
Verdi	Te Deum	LM 1849	VIC/VICS-1331(e)	ALP 1363	VCM-10	1954
Verdi	Rigoletto (Act IV)	LM 6041	VIC/VICS-1314(e)	ALP 1453 RB 16140	VCM-6	1944
Verdi	La Traviata	LM 6003		ALP 1072/3		1946
Verdi	I Vespri siciliani (Overture)	LM 6041	VIC-1248	ALP 1452 RB 16139	VCM-6	1942
Wagner	Die Götterdämmerung Dawn and Siegfried's Rhine Journey	LM 6020		ALP 1173 RB 16135	VIC-1022	1949

Composer	Title	Original No (U.S.)	Current No (U.S.)	Original No (G.B.)	Current No (G.B.)	Recorded
Wagner	Die Götterdämmerung Immolation Scene	LVT 1004	VIC-1369		VCM-5†	1941
Wagner	Die Götterdämmerung Siegfried's Death and Funeral Music	LM 6020	VIC/VICS-1316(e)	RB 16136	VCM-5	1952
Wagner	Lohengrin Prelude to Act I	LM 6020	VIC-1247	DB 21574 RB 16136	VCM-5	1951
	Prelude to Act III	LM 6020	VIC-1247	RB 16136	VCM-5	1951
Wagner	Die Meistersinger Prelude to Act I	LM 6020	VIC-1247	RB 16136	VCM-5	1946
	Prelude to Act III	LM 6020	VIC-1247	DB 21564 RB 16136	VCM-5	1951
Wagner	Parsifal Prelude and Good Friday Music	LM 6020	VIC-1278	BLP 1033 RB 16135	VCM-5	1949
Wagner	Siegfried Idyll	LM 6020	VIC-1247	RB 16136	VCM-5	1952
Wagner	Siegfried Idyll	LVT 1004		DB 6668-9		1946
Wagner	Tristan und Isolde Prelude and Liebestod	LM 6020	VIC-1278	RB 16135	VCM-5	1952

INDEX

INDEX

A CATALOGUE OF SELECTED DOVER BOOKS
IN ALL FIELDS OF INTEREST

A CATALOGUE OF SELECTED DOVER BOOKS
IN ALL FIELDS OF INTEREST

WHAT IS SCIENCE?, *N. Campbell*
The role of experiment and measurement, the function of mathematics, the nature of scientific laws, the difference between laws and theories, the limitations of science, and many similarly provocative topics are treated clearly and without technicalities by an eminent scientist. "Still an excellent introduction to scientific philosophy," H. Margenau in *Physics Today*. "A first-rate primer ... deserves a wide audience," *Scientific American*. 192pp. 5⅜ x 8.
S43   Paperbound $1.25

THE NATURE OF LIGHT AND COLOUR IN THE OPEN AIR, *M. Minnaert*
Why are shadows sometimes blue, sometimes green, or other colors depending on the light and surroundings? What causes mirages? Why do multiple suns and moons appear in the sky? Professor Minnaert explains these unusual phenomena and hundreds of others in simple, easy-to-understand terms based on optical laws and the properties of light and color. No mathematics is required but artists, scientists, students, and everyone fascinated by these "tricks" of nature will find thousands of useful and amazing pieces of information. Hundreds of observational experiments are suggested which require no special equipment. 200 illustrations; 42 photos. xvi + 362pp. 5⅜ x 8.
T196   Paperbound $2.00

THE STRANGE STORY OF THE QUANTUM, AN ACCOUNT FOR THE GENERAL READER OF THE GROWTH OF IDEAS UNDERLYING OUR PRESENT ATOMIC KNOWLEDGE, *B. Hoffmann*
Presents lucidly and expertly, with barest amount of mathematics, the problems and theories which led to modern quantum physics. Dr. Hoffmann begins with the closing years of the 19th century, when certain trifling discrepancies were noticed, and with illuminating analogies and examples takes you through the brilliant concepts of Planck, Einstein, Pauli, Broglie, Bohr, Schroedinger, Heisenberg, Dirac, Sommerfeld, Feynman, etc. This edition includes a new, long postscript carrying the story through 1958. "Of the books attempting an account of the history and contents of our modern atomic physics which have come to my attention, this is the best," H. Margenau, Yale University, in *American Journal of Physics*. 32 tables and line illustrations. Index. 275pp. 5⅜ x 8.
T518   Paperbound $2.00

GREAT IDEAS OF MODERN MATHEMATICS: THEIR NATURE AND USE, *Jagjit Singh*
Reader with only high school math will understand main mathematical ideas of modern physics, astronomy, genetics, psychology, evolution, etc. better than many who use them as tools, but comprehend little of their basic structure. Author uses his wide knowledge of non-mathematical fields in brilliant exposition of differential equations, matrices, group theory, logic, statistics, problems of mathematical foundations, imaginary numbers, vectors, etc. Original publication. 2 appendixes. 2 indexes. 65 ills. 322pp. 5⅜ x 8.
T587   Paperbound $2.00

THE MUSIC OF THE SPHERES: THE MATERIAL UNIVERSE — FROM ATOM TO QUASAR, SIMPLY EXPLAINED, *Guy Murchie*
Vast compendium of fact, modern concept and theory, observed and calculated data, historical background guides intelligent layman through the material universe. Brilliant exposition of earth's construction, explanations for moon's craters, atmospheric components of Venus and Mars (with data from recent fly-by's), sun spots, sequences of star birth and death, neighboring galaxies, contributions of Galileo, Tycho Brahe, Kepler, etc.; and (Vol. 2) construction of the atom (describing newly discovered sigma and xi subatomic particles), theories of sound, color and light, space and time, including relativity theory, quantum theory, wave theory, probability theory, work of Newton, Maxwell, Faraday, Einstein, de Broglie, etc. "Best presentation yet offered to the intelligent general reader," *Saturday Review.* Revised (1967). Index. 319 illustrations by the author. Total of xx + 644pp. 5⅜ x 8½.
Vol. 1 Paperbound $2.00, Vol. 2 Paperbound $2.00,
The set $4.00

FOUR LECTURES ON RELATIVITY AND SPACE, *Charles Proteus Steinmetz*
Lecture series, given by great mathematician and electrical engineer, generally considered one of the best popular-level expositions of special and general relativity theories and related questions. Steinmetz translates complex mathematical reasoning into language accessible to laymen through analogy, example and comparison. Among topics covered are relativity of motion, location, time; of mass; acceleration; 4-dimensional time-space; geometry of the gravitational field; curvature and bending of space; non-Euclidean geometry. Index. 40 illustrations. x + 142pp. 5⅜ x 8½.   Paperbound $1.35

HOW TO KNOW THE WILD FLOWERS, *Mrs. William Starr Dana*
Classic nature book that has introduced thousands to wonders of American wild flowers. Color-season principle of organization is easy to use, even by those with no botanical training, and the genial, refreshing discussions of history, folklore, uses of over 1,000 native and escape flowers, foliage plants are informative as well as fun to read. Over 170 full-page plates, collected from several editions, may be colored in to make permanent records of finds. Revised to conform with 1950 edition of Gray's Manual of Botany. xlii + 438pp. 5⅜ x 8½.   Paperbound $2.00

MANUAL OF THE TREES OF NORTH AMERICA, *Charles Sprague Sargent*
Still unsurpassed as most comprehensive, reliable study of North American tree characteristics, precise locations and distribution. By dean of American dendrologists. Every tree native to U.S., Canada, Alaska; 185 genera, 717 species, described in detail—leaves, flowers, fruit, winterbuds, bark, wood, growth habits, etc. plus discussion of varieties and local variants, immaturity variations. Over 100 keys, including unusual 11-page analytical key to genera, aid in identification. 783 clear illustrations of flowers, fruit, leaves. An unmatched permanent reference work for all nature lovers. Second enlarged (1926) edition. Synopsis of families. Analytical key to genera. Glossary of technical terms. Index. 783 illustrations, 1 map. Total of 982pp. 5⅜ x 8.
Vol. 1 Paperbound $2.25, Vol. 2 Paperbound $2.25,
The set $4.50

IT'S FUN TO MAKE THINGS FROM SCRAP MATERIALS,
Evelyn Glantz Hershoff
What use are empty spools, tin cans, bottle tops? What can be made from rubber bands, clothes pins, paper clips, and buttons? This book provides simply worded instructions and large diagrams showing you how to make cookie cutters, toy trucks, paper turkeys, Halloween masks, telephone sets, aprons, linoleum block- and spatter prints — in all 399 projects! Many are easy enough for young children to figure out for themselves; some challenging enough to entertain adults; all are remarkably ingenious ways to make things from materials that cost pennies or less! Formerly "Scrap Fun for Everyone." Index. 214 illustrations. 373pp. 5⅜ x 8½. Paperbound $1.50

SYMBOLIC LOGIC and THE GAME OF LOGIC, *Lewis Carroll*
"Symbolic Logic" is not concerned with modern symbolic logic, but is instead a collection of over 380 problems posed with charm and imagination, using the syllogism and a fascinating diagrammatic method of drawing conclusions. In "The Game of Logic" Carroll's whimsical imagination devises a logical game played with 2 diagrams and counters (included) to manipulate hundreds of tricky syllogisms. The final section, "Hit or Miss" is a lagniappe of 101 additional puzzles in the delightful Carroll manner. Until this reprint edition, both of these books were rarities costing up to $15 each. Symbolic Logic: Index. xxxi + 199pp. The Game of Logic: 96pp. 2 vols. bound as one. 5⅜ x 8. Paperbound $2.00

MATHEMATICAL PUZZLES OF SAM LOYD, PART I
selected and edited by M. Gardner
Choice puzzles by the greatest American puzzle creator and innovator. Selected from his famous collection, "Cyclopedia of Puzzles," they retain the unique style and historical flavor of the originals. There are posers based on arithmetic, algebra, probability, game theory, route tracing, topology, counter and sliding block, operations research, geometrical dissection. Includes the famous "14-15" puzzle which was a national craze, and his "Horse of a Different Color" which sold millions of copies. 117 of his most ingenious puzzles in all. 120 line drawings and diagrams. Solutions. Selected references. xx + 167pp. 5⅜ x 8. Paperbound $1.00

STRING FIGURES AND HOW TO MAKE THEM, *Caroline Furness Jayne*
107 string figures plus variations selected from the best primitive and modern examples developed by Navajo, Apache, pygmies of Africa, Eskimo, in Europe, Australia, China, etc. The most readily understandable, easy-to-follow book in English on perennially popular recreation. Crystal-clear exposition; step-by-step diagrams. Everyone from kindergarten children to adults looking for unusual diversion will be endlessly amused. Index. Bibliography. Introduction by A. C. Haddon. 17 full-page plates, 960 illustrations. xxiii + 401pp. 5⅜ x 8½. Paperbound $2.00

PAPER FOLDING FOR BEGINNERS, *W. D. Murray and F. J. Rigney*
A delightful introduction to the varied and entertaining Japanese art of origami (paper folding), with a full, crystal-clear text that anticipates every difficulty; over 275 clearly labeled diagrams of all important stages in creation. You get results at each stage, since complex figures are logically developed from simpler ones. 43 different pieces are explained: sailboats, frogs, roosters, etc. 6 photographic plates. 279 diagrams. 95pp. 5⅝ x 8⅜. Paperbound $1.00

PRINCIPLES OF ART HISTORY,
H. Wölfflin
Analyzing such terms as "baroque," "classic," "neoclassic," "primitive," "picturesque," and 164 different works by artists like Botticelli, van Cleve, Dürer, Hobbema, Holbein, Hals, Rembrandt, Titian, Brueghel, Vermeer, and many others, the author establishes the classifications of art history and style on a firm, concrete basis. This classic of art criticism shows what really occurred between the 14th-century primitives and the sophistication of the 18th century in terms of basic attitudes and philosophies. "A remarkable lesson in the art of seeing," *Sat. Rev. of Literature*. Translated from the 7th German edition. 150 illustrations. 254pp. 6⅛ x 9¼. Paperbound $2.00

PRIMITIVE ART,
Franz Boas
This authoritative and exhaustive work by a great American anthropologist covers the entire gamut of primitive art. Pottery, leatherwork, metal work, stone work, wood, basketry, are treated in detail. Theories of primitive art, historical depth in art history, technical virtuosity, unconscious levels of patterning, symbolism, styles, literature, music, dance, etc. A must book for the interested layman, the anthropologist, artist, handicrafter (hundreds of unusual motifs), and the historian. Over 900 illustrations (50 ceramic vessels, 12 totem poles, etc.). 376pp. 5⅜ x 8. Paperbound $2.25

THE GENTLEMAN AND CABINET MAKER'S DIRECTOR,
Thomas Chippendale
A reprint of the 1762 catalogue of furniture designs that went on to influence generations of English and Colonial and Early Republic American furniture makers. The 200 plates, most of them full-page sized, show Chippendale's designs for French (Louis XV), Gothic, and Chinese-manner chairs, sofas, canopy and dome beds, cornices, chamber organs, cabinets, shaving tables, commodes, picture frames, frets, candle stands, chimney pieces, decorations, etc. The drawings are all elegant and highly detailed; many include construction diagrams and elevations. A supplement of 24 photographs shows surviving pieces of original and Chippendale-style pieces of furniture. Brief biography of Chippendale by N. I. Bienenstock, editor of *Furniture World*. Reproduced from the 1762 edition. 200 plates, plus 19 photographic plates. vi + 249pp. 9⅛ x 12¼. Paperbound $3.50

AMERICAN ANTIQUE FURNITURE: A BOOK FOR AMATEURS,
Edgar G. Miller, Jr.
Standard introduction and practical guide to identification of valuable American antique furniture. 2115 illustrations, mostly photographs taken by the author in 148 private homes, are arranged in chronological order in extensive chapters on chairs, sofas, chests, desks, bedsteads, mirrors, tables, clocks, and other articles. Focus is on furniture accessible to the collector, including simpler pieces and a larger than usual coverage of Empire style. Introductory chapters identify structural elements, characteristics of various styles, how to avoid fakes, etc. "We are frequently asked to name some book on American furniture that will meet the requirements of the novice collector, the beginning dealer, and . . . the general public. . . . We believe Mr. Miller's two volumes more completely satisfy this specification than any other work," *Antiques*. Appendix. Index. Total of vi + 1106pp. 7⅞ x 10¾.
Two volume set, paperbound $7.50

A Short Account of the History of Mathematics,
W. W. Rouse Ball

Last previous edition (1908) hailed by mathematicians and laymen for lucid overview of math as living science, for understandable presentation of individual contributions of great mathematicians. Treats lives, discoveries of every important school and figure from Egypt, Phoenicia to late nineteenth century. Greek schools of Ionia, Cyzicus, Alexandria, Byzantium, Pythagoras; primitive arithmetic; Middle Ages and Renaissance, including European and Asiatic contributions; modern math of Descartes, Pascal, Wallis, Huygens, Newton, Euler, Lambert, Laplace, scores more. More emphasis on historical development, exposition of ideas than other books on subject. Non-technical, readable text can be followed with no more preparation than high-school algebra. Index. 544pp. 5⅜ x 8. Paperbound $2.25

Great Ideas and Theories of Modern Cosmology, *Jagjit Singh*

Companion volume to author's popular "Great Ideas of Modern Mathematics" (Dover, $2.00). The best non-technical survey of post-Einstein attempts to answer perhaps unanswerable questions of origin, age of Universe, possibility of life on other worlds, etc. Fundamental theories of cosmology and cosmogony recounted, explained, evaluated in light of most recent data: Einstein's concepts of relativity, space-time; Milne's a priori world-system; astrophysical theories of Jeans, Eddington; Hoyle's "continuous creation;" contributions of dozens more scientists. A faithful, comprehensive critical summary of complex material presented in an extremely well-written text intended for laymen. Original publication. Index. xii + 276pp. 5⅜ x 8½. Paperbound $2.00

The Restless Universe, *Max Born*

A remarkably lucid account by a Nobel Laureate of recent theories of wave mechanics, behavior of gases, electrons and ions, waves and particles, electronic structure of the atom, nuclear physics, and similar topics. "Much more thorough and deeper than most attempts . . . easy and delightful," *Chemical and Engineering News.* Special feature: 7 animated sequences of 60 figures each showing such phenomena as gas molecules in motion, the scattering of alpha particles, etc. 11 full-page plates of photographs. Total of nearly 600 illustrations. 351pp. 6⅛ x 9¼. Paperbound $2.00

Planets, Stars and Galaxies: Descriptive Astronomy for Beginners,
A. E. Fanning

What causes the progression of the seasons? Phases of the moon? The Aurora Borealis? How much does the sun weigh? What are the chances of life on our sister planets? Absorbing introduction to astronomy, incorporating the latest discoveries and theories: the solar wind, the surface temperature of Venus, the pock-marked face of Mars, quasars, and much more. Places you on the frontiers of one of the most vital sciences of our time. Revised (1966). Introduction by Donald H. Menzel, Harvard University. References. Index. 45 illustrations. 189pp. 5¼ x 8¼. Paperbound $1.50

Great Ideas in Information Theory, Language and Cybernetics,
Jagjit Singh

Non-mathematical, but profound study of information, language, the codes used by men and machines to communicate, the principles of analog and digital computers, work of McCulloch, Pitts, von Neumann, Turing, and Uttley, correspondences between intricate mechanical network of "thinking machines" and more intricate neurophysiological mechanism of human brain. Indexes. 118 figures. 50 tables. ix + 338pp. 5⅜ x 8½. Paperbound $2.00

FABLES OF AESOP,
according to Sir Roger L'Estrange, with 50 drawings by Alexander Calder
Republication of rare 1931 Paris edition (limited to 665 copies) of 200 fables
by Aesop in the 1692 L'Estrange translation. Illustrated with 50 highly
imaginative, witty and occasionally ribald line drawings by the inventor of
"mobiles" and "stabiles." "Fifty wonderfully inventive Alexander Calder
drawings, impertinent as any of the artist's wire sculptures, make a delightful,
modern counterpoint to the thoroughly moral tales," *Saturday Review.* 124pp.
6½ x 9¼.   Paperbound $1.25

DRAWINGS OF REMBRANDT
One of the earliest and best collections of Rembrandt drawings—the Lippmann-
Hofstede de Groot facsimiles (1888)—is here reproduced in entirety. Collection
contains 550 faithfully reproduced drawings in inks, chalks, and silverpoint;
some, hasty sketches recorded on a handy scrap of paper; others, studies for
well-known oil paintings. Edited, with scholarly commentary by Seymour
Slive, Harvard University. "In large matters of appearance, size (9 x 12-inch
page), paper color and weight, uniformity of plate texture, typography and
printing, these two volumes could scarcely be improved," *Arts and Architecture.*
"Altogether commendable . . . among the year's best," *New York Times.*
Editor's introduction, notes. 3 indexes, 2 concordances. Total of lxxix +
552pp. 9⅛ x 12¼.   Two volume set, paperbound $6.00
                                          Two volume set, clothbound $12.50

THE EARLY WORK OF AUBREY BEARDSLEY
Together with *The Later Work*, the standard source for the most important
Beardsley drawings. Edited by John Lane, *Early Work* contains 157 full-page
plates including Burne-Jones style work, the *Morte d'Arthur* series, cover
designs and illustrations from *The Studio* and other magazines, theatre
posters, "Kiss of Judas," "Seigfried," portraits of himself, Emile Zola, and
Verdi, and illustrations for Wilde's play *Salome.* 2 color plates. Introduction
by H. C. Marillier. xii + 175pp. 8⅛ x 11.   Paperbound $2.50
                                                        Clothbound $8.50

THE LATER WORK OF AUBREY BEARDSLEY
Edited by John Lane, collection contains 174 full-page plates including
Savoy and *Yellow Book* illustrations, book plates, "The Wagnerites," "La
Dame aux Camellias," selections from *Lysistrata*, illustrations to *Das Rhein-
gold, Venus and Tannhauser*, and the "Rape of the Lock" series. 2 color
plates. xiv + 174pp. 8⅛ x 11.   Paperbound $2.50
                                                        Clothbound $8.50

Prices subject to change without notice.

Available at your book dealer or write for free catalogue to Dept. Adsci,
Dover Publications, Inc., 180 Varick St., N.Y., N.Y. 10014. Dover publishes more
than 150 books each year on science, elementary and advanced mathematics,
biology, music, art, literary history, social sciences and other areas.